Penguin Books

The New Modern Sociology Readings

Richard Brown is Professor of Sociology at the University of Durham, Past President of the British Sociological Association, and joint author of *The Sociology of Industry*. He was the founding Editor of *Work, Employment and Society*.

Ellis Cashmore is Professor of Sociology at the University of Tampa, Florida. He is author of *Approaching Social Theory, The Logic of Racism* and many other books, especially in the field of race relations.

Peter Halfpenny is Senior Lecturer in Sociology and Director of the Centre for Applied Social Research at the University of Manchester, and author of *Principles of Method*.

Margot Jefferys is Emeritus Professor of Medical Sociology at the University of London and joint author of *Rethinking General Practice*.

Mary McIntosh is Senior Lecturer at the University of Essex and a member of the editorial collective of *Feminist Review*. She is author of *The Organization of Crime* and co-author of *The Anti-social Family*.

Rosemary Mellor is Senior Lecturer in Sociology at the University of Manchester and author of *Urban Sociology in an Urbanized Society*.

Charles Posner is Senior Lecturer in the Sociology of Education at London University's Institute of Education, and specializes on the Mexican educational system.

Wesley Sharrock is Reader in Sociology at the University of Manchester and co-author of *Applied Perspectives in Sociology* and *The Ethnomethodologists*.

Peter Worsley is Professor Emeritus of Sociology at the University of Manchester. He is author of *The Trumpet Shall Sound, The Third World* and *The Three Worlds*, and editor of and contributor to *The New Introducing Sociology*.

The New Modern Sociology Readings

Edited by Peter Worsley

Contributing Editors: Richard Brown, Ellis Cashmore, Peter
Halfpenny, Margot Jefferys, Mary McIntosh, Rosemary
Mellor, Charles Posner, Wesley Sharrock, Peter Worsley

Penguin Books

PENGUIN BOOKS

Published by the Penguin Group
Penguin Books Ltd, 27 Wrights Lane, London W8 5TZ, England
Penguin Books USA Inc., 375 Hudson Street, New York, New York 10014, USA
Penguin Books Australia Ltd, Ringwood, Victoria, Australia
Penguin Books Canada Ltd, 10 Alcorn Avenue, Toronto, Ontario, Canada M4V 3B2
Penguin Books (NZ) Ltd, 182–190 Wairau Road, Auckland 10, New Zealand

Penguin Books Ltd, Registered Offices: Harmondsworth, Middlesex, England

First published 1991
10 9 8 7 6 5 4 3

Printed in England by Clays Ltd, St Ives plc
Filmset in Monotype Lasercomp Ehrhardt

Contents

x   **Contents**

Preface

Most people think of sociologists as people who do surveys, probably because this was the commonest style of research in the early decades of this century, when sociology emerged as a distinct division of the social sciences. It is also still the kind of research that we are most likely to encounter today, for many of us have been approached at one time or another by people doing market surveys and opinion polls.

Survey research usually aims at finding out what is going on in society as a whole or in some sizeable segment of it; it is usually concerned with social structures and social institutions, with large-scale organizations and populations. It therefore relies heavily upon the careful construction of samples of the whole population: having drawn a sample, people are then interviewed – usually following a questionnaire – and the resulting data are then subjected to statistical analysis. Cross-national studies, which look at, say, changes in the family or in industrial organization in more than one society, perhaps even in all 'Western' societies, also tend to be of this kind.

All levels of social organization are also subject to continual change; some of it gradual, some sudden; some only within one sphere of life, some – like the changes that have swept across Eastern Europe – affecting everything. So much research is concerned not just with structures, but with changes of structure – with charting social change and social trends.

The traditional image of the sociologist, then, is that of the survey researcher: the expert who knows more about society than the people he or she is studying. Yet paradoxically sociologists rely upon what their 'informants' tell them for the basic data they collect, whether about patterns of family expenditure or their voting intentions. A problem immediately arises: how do we know that what people tell you is reliable information?

The interview itself, indeed, is by no means as straightforward as some might think. Most people treat 'scare' headlines and the 'evidence' from opinion polls critically. They also do their own sociology on interviewers and on the questions they ask. From clues given in speech, dress, etc., they size them up, and may shape their answers accordingly. They may not wish to offend someone they see as some kind of authority figure, or someone who is simply doing a job for a living; equally, they may not trust the interviewer at all, but see him or her as, say, a social-security snooper. They may regard their financial affairs, their sex lives, their religious affiliation or the party they vote for as purely private matters, which strangers have no right to probe into. Doing sociology, then, is a social activity; it involves both parties in manipulating situations (such as the interview itself) for their own ends. It therefore necessarily also involves ethical issues.

Interviewers have their own categories within which they categorize people: even if they choose them randomly, once they get back into their office, they classify their informants accordingly to some predetermined framework: in market research, into socio-economic classes. Or informants may have been non-randomly selected in the first place as members of a class or some other kind of social group.

Whatever research strategy is adopted, the research process is not simply the collecting of 'facts'. It is the collection of certain kinds of facts that are believed, in the light of some theory about society and social behaviour, to be relevant to understanding the behaviour of certain kinds of people, perhaps even all kinds, or, as in the case of Peggy Reeves Sanday's study of rape (Reading 19), the behaviour of men in general. Nor are the categories used – classes, age-groups, communities – homogeneous: the researcher is concerned with *differences* of behaviour and thought within each of these, with subgroups (manual and non-manual workers *within* the working class, say) and with important differences in beliefs between people who share similar characteristics: the large number of trade unionists, for example, who vote Conservative.

Making sense of these variations calls for models of explanation that can be tested. Any such models have built into them assumptions about human motivation and values – about the springs of action.

And since the behaviour sociologists are primarily concerned with is informed by beliefs, values, ideas, purposes, aims, ends, etc., sociologists are necessarily concerned with ideas, and with the extent to which – and under what conditions – ideas affect the things people do, the choices they make in social life. Some people are even blinded by ideas: people with closed minds and ready-made explanations, for whom 'the facts' simply have to be slotted into pre-existing categories. For some fundamentalist religious believers, for instance, the threat of nuclear extinction or of world-wide ecological disaster is a confirmation of what they already 'know': that we have already entered the Last Days. Less dramatically, for others, the same facts are proof of the intrinsic sinfulness, or folly, of humankind. For some kinds of secular ideologists, every particular instance of social strain, breakdown or difficulty is confirmation, once more, that capitalism is breaking down as a whole and that these problems cannot be solved except by a complete change of the social system.

Ideologists of that kind can be found among sociologists, too. But for most social scientists, it is precisely the theories with which they approach their field of study that have to be questioned and taken as problematic. But collecting the kinds of information that enable us to put our own pet theories to the test is a difficult and often painful operation. Different methods are used to study quite different kinds of events at quite different levels from those which survey researchers are interested in. The groupings they look at can vary in size and permanency from the study of a factory, a pressure group, a school class or a neighbourhood, to a number of families or the habitués of a particular pub. Alternatively, sociologists may study categories of people rather than groups: those who watch a particular TV show, supporters of Manchester United, or consumers of particular kinds of goods.

Sociological research, then, is not just a matter of 'common sense', for what one considers common sense, another considers nonsense. So within sociology itself there are several major kinds of research and, therefore, fierce debate as to the appropriateness of the various rival theoretical approaches. So we begin, in Part One, by looking at some of the more important discussions about the nature of sociology in general, and in Part Two consider the differences, the underlying assumptions, and the choices that have to be made between methods of research that focus on the qualitative and those that rely on statistical procedures. At the end of the book, in Part Twelve, after the reader has become more familiar with the ways in which these various strategies have been used to study very different areas of life, we return once more to take a closer look at the major theoretical schools of sociology.

Other issues arise even when we talk about 'society'. It would, in fact, be impossible to produce a Reader which would equally satisfy people in Lima, Calcutta, Sheffield and Manila, because each of these cities is part of a social order that is imbued with different cultural values, is shaped by a different history, and exhibits great differences of social structure, from the legacy of the first Industrial Revolution in Sheffield's case to the rise of new technologies in new cities inhabited by ex-peasants in the Third World. The pattern of industrialization, and its social consequences, is therefore very different in 'newly industrializing' states and in countries which remain predominantly agrarian. Yet there are commonalities: all of us, not just those who live in these new states, are subject to world-wide economic and political forces. But the forms pioneered by industrial countries in the West are not necessarily repeated or relevant to countries which are seeking today to modernize themselves while avoiding the negative social consequences experienced by the pioneer industrial countries, from the miseries of the poor in Victorian cities to the political repression visited upon the masses in post-revolutionary USSR. Questions about 'development', addressed in Part Three, then, necessitate a vision of sociology which goes beyond the framework of any particular nation-state.

Yet it is natural that people should be primarily concerned with confronting the problems of the society in which they live. This collection therefore concentrates mainly upon studies of British society and other industrialized capitalist societies, notably the USA. There is also a simple technical reason: that the overwhelming bulk of sociological research so far has been produced in these countries.

We have tried, though, always to select pieces (often, inevitably, painfully truncated) that are more than simply descriptive accounts of this or that social problem-area, or simply of interest to people who live in Britain: studies, rather, in which competent research is informed by theorizing in the way C. Wright Mills recommends in the opening Reading, and which help the reader to develop ideas about society that go beyond the immediate piece of reality under discussion.

Even at a time when a recent British Prime Minister has declared that 'there is no such thing as society', and when, in consequence, the discipline of sociology has been treated as undeserving of public support at levels that the more 'practical' disciplines receive, there is still a large and steady demand for sociological knowledge. This comes not only from educational institutions – schools, colleges and universities – but also from the many institutions, from businesses to welfare agencies, that need to know what is happening in society and about the causes of social distress (as well as success) if they are to carry out their own activities effectively.

For the problems which threaten us most are social problems: how to ensure the very survival of the planet; how to avoid nuclear war; how to conserve our finite resources; how to feed the world's hungry; how to distribute wealth within 'rich' countries so that people are not forced to sleep in the street; how to develop and make use of the talents of young people from underprivileged backgrounds. Since they necessarily involve making choices and allocations as between different ends, choices that rest in the final analysis upon social values, these problems cannot be solved simply by technological innovation (which as often generates new problems as it finds solutions to old ones) or simply by producing more.

Indeed, sociology has continued to flourish to such an extent that there exists sociological research on virtually every aspect of social life, from rock music to the design of museums (let alone more unusual topics such as the sociology of sleep or of dwarfs). It has not been possible to include specimens from all these areas of research; we have, however, covered the major frames within which everybody lives their lives, from family, school, the local community and place of work, to gender, class and race, as well as the problems that affect most of us, from crime to illness.

Sociology, then, does not just deal with 'social problems', though the analysis of the miseries of normal everyday life in all too many families is an important area of study. But from a sociological point of view, 'happy families' are *intellectual* problems, equally as worthy of study as 'problem families', for the phenomenon of domestic harmony calls for explanation just as much as the existence of discord. Equally, sociology is not simply an arm of government or of management. It can be used, and has been, to express the perspectives, interpretations of reality and aspirations of the powerless, of the victims as well as the makers and implementers of policy: the unpaid labour of those, usually women, who take care of the chronically ill at home; the schoolchildren who reject not only the curriculum but also the social values teachers try to instil in them; the Blacks who turn their isolation in ghettos into a political resource, or the women who ask why they are denied entry into the better-paid jobs that men monopolize and just how this process of exclusion is managed.

In our final review of the major theoretical schools of sociology, we do not pronounce as to the superiority of one or the other. What we hope to have done is to have presented enough of that variety to enable you to decide for yourself which approach seems most relevant. There is something to be learned from all of them; each has certain strengths that the others lack, and each its weaknesses. This isn't an argument for eclecticism – a bit of this and a bit of that – or for relativism; one approach is as good as another. It is simply a recognition that while Marxism, for instance, has set the terms of the debate about class society for decades, it has failed to carry that analysis down to the level of the small group or face-to-face interaction, which symbolic interactionism has achieved. Now even that latter school is challenged by the rise of ethnomethodology, which sees the activity of doing sociology as no different in kind when the sociologist does it from when any other person does it – so that the sociologist can only make sense of society by following the procedures people use to find their way about in society and to achieve their ends: a rejection, then, of the classical image of the sociologist as someone who knows better than the participants.

We have designed this Reader as an accompaniment to the Penguin textbook *The New Introducing Sociology* (1992), edited by Peter Worsley. Some of the authors contributed to both books, but there are newcomers, too. The following wrote the introductions to each part in this book and also selected the readings used:

This Preface, plus Parts One: Sociology as a Discipline; Three: The Sociology of Development; Nine: Ethnicity and Race; and Ten: Class, are by Peter Worsley;

Part Two: Methodology, Theory and Methods, is by Peter Halfpenny;

Part Four: Sex, Gender and the Family, is by Mary McIntosh;

Part Five: Education, is by Charles Posner;

Part Six: Health, Illness and Medicine, is by Margot Jefferys;
Part Seven: Community and Urban Life, is by Rosemary Mellor;
Part Eight: Work, Industry and Organizations, is by Richard
 Brown;
Part Eleven: Crime and Deviance, is by Ellis Cashmore;
Part Twelve: Theoretical Schools, is by Wesley Sharrock.

Part One
Sociology as a Discipline

C. Wright Mills's classic discussion of the sociological imagination (Reading 1) remains as exciting today as when it was first written. Analysing human behaviour, he shows, is an intellectually demanding business that calls for theoretical rigour, including the readiness to look critically at one's own assumptions and procedures.

Mills's vision is of a sociology that situates the individual within successive levels of society, from membership of face-to-face groups ('close-up scenes') to membership of nation-states and transnational cultural communities. Sociology has to examine both the constraints and pressures exercised by all these kinds of groups upon the thinking and behaviour of the individual and the efforts people make to construct their own identities and make their own choices. Sociology, for Mills has to be a *dialectical* sociology: not treating people as puppets entirely determined by 'social forces', but studying, too, the power those forces do exert. Mills was particularly aware of the power of the modern State and of the capacity of powerful mass media to shape the thinking that guides our actions. Within a sociological perspective, what the individual experiences as 'personal troubles' become 'public issues': 'matters that transcend the local environments of the individual and the range of his inner life'.

To make sense of the welter of happenings in the world around us, people – including sociologists – need appropriate theories and methods. Mills's *The Sociological Imagination* attempts to formulate the principles which should guide inquiry. For him, the actions of human beings in society are different in kind from instinctual animal behaviour, in so far as they are informed by what Weber described as 'orientation to values': i.e. guided by ideas, beliefs and principles – by some kind of ideal – and informed, too, by some kind of purpose (though both the ideal and the purpose may be ones we disapprove of). Such a vision of sociology is necessarily a historical one, for ideals, and institutions too, constantly change, sometimes only very slowly and gradually, at other times with astonishing rapidity. The sociological imagination enables us, then, to 'grasp history and biography and the relations between the two'.

In all these respects, Mills stands in the classic tradition of the nineteenth-century 'Founding Fathers' of sociology – three of whom are represented in this chapter: Karl Marx, Max Weber and Émile Durkheim. Each of them tried to formulate general principles of analysis; each studied major institutions (religion, the economy, legal codes, the machinery of state administration); each was concerned with the overall pattern of human social development and the massive transformations of their times; and each grappled with the problem of how human motivations are shaped by social forces.

Mills was a radical. So deeply entrenched has the image of sociology as a radical discipline become in recent years that it may come as something of a surprise to find Robert Nisbet (Reading 2), a leading student of the history of sociological theory, reminding us (see p. 23 below) that in the early part of the last century sociology began as a 'reaction of traditionalism against analytic reason; of communalism against individualism; and of the non-rational against the purely rational'. He identifies five pairs of themes – community–society; authority–power; status–class; sacred–secular; and alienation–progress – which became the battlegrounds of debate between opposing schools.

Karl Marx (Reading 3), however, was clearly not just a radical, but a revolutionary thinker and a revolutionary practitioner, too. In his own day he had little influence outside microscopic socialist sects. Subsequently, however, he became not only the major source of inspiration for the rapidly growing mass socialist movements that eventually became powerful forces in the modern world, but also a strong intellectual influence, even upon people who were opposed to everything he stood for. He was not given to making general statements about methodology or theory, but we include three short passages which do express his views on the materialist conception of history.

Marx's focus was upon the structures of whole societies and large-scale processes of social evolution. The individual, therefore, is seen very much as a product of these institutions and forces. A similar emphasis is found in the work of Émile Durkheim (Reading 4) (though Durkheim had nothing in common with him politically). Sociology, Durkheim argues, is the study of social facts, and a social fact is characterized by three particular properties: its *externality* (it is something which we do not create ourselves, but find in being, outside our 'skin boundary'); it is *collective* (its power over us derives from the existence of organized social groups); and it is *coercive* (it obliges us to behave in certain ways and not others).

In Durkheim's early writings, the kinds of external constraints he emphasized were those of demography and ecology (the density of population and the ratio between people and resources); later, he came to emphasize cultural, and particularly normative and ideological, constraints, upon behaviour.

But later critics have argued that the whole notion of 'externality' becomes difficult to sustain, since once we accept that human beings *internalize* ideas current in society, they become part of our psyches.

Max Weber, indeed, believed that this insight rendered an approach like that of Durkheim invalid. He directed his fire, however, primarily against Marx (his sociology, it has been said, was a 'debate with the ghost of Marx'). Societies, he insisted, did not think; it was the individuals who made up society that did. Hence it was essential to study the ideas which informed their behaviour. Ideas were no less real than material things like guns; since they affected behaviour, as W. I. Thomas later put it, they were 'real in their consequences'.

Weber's own writing on theory and methodology is unfortunately singularly turgid, so we have used instead a very lucid exposition of Weber's approach to these matters by Frank Parker (Reading 5), a writer who is sympathetic to Weber's ideas, but who also recognizes their shortcomings. He finds, in particular, that the notion of *Verstehen* (understanding), the term Weber used to denote his strategy of examining the 'meaning of the act to the actor', itself generates new problems, for ideas are themselves social products, even if formulated and held by individuals. They also become socially important in some historical situations and not others. Moreover, simply observing that there is a 'correlation' between, say, the growth of Protestantism and the rise of capitalism (see Reading 73 by Weber in Chapter 12) leaves open the question of which causes which – or whether we can speak of 'causes' at all.

Weber did not, as commonly thought, simply ignore the kinds of factors Marx was concerned with, particularly class (though his conception of class was different from that of Marx), or regard them as unimportant. What he did do was to 'accentuate' elements, such as religion, that he thought significant but underemphasized. But these had always to be fitted to other factors: class, power and so forth.

Later theorists such as Berger and Luckmann (Reading 6) and Harold Garfinkel (Reading 77 in Chapter 12) have taken up Weber's emphasis upon understanding, but have abandoned his preoccupation with the study of whole societies and cultures in favour of concentrating upon the face-to-face situations in which individuals acquire ideas, and how these are communicated, sustained or modified in the context of using them in everyday life. To Berger and Luckmann, the 'most important' experience we have of others is in the face-to-face groups within which we lead our daily lives. This, they insist, is the 'paramount reality': in comparison, all other realities are merely 'finite provinces of meaning'.

1   C. Wright Mills

The Sociological Imagination

Excerpt from C. Wright Mills, *The Sociological Imagination*, Oxford University Press, Inc., 1959, pp. 3–11.

Nowadays men often feel that their private lives are a series of traps. They sense that within their everyday worlds, they cannot overcome their troubles, and in this feeling they are often quite correct: what ordinary men are directly aware of and what they try to do are bounded by the private orbits in which they live; their visions and their powers are limited to the close-up scenes of job, family, neighbourhood; in other milieux, they move vicariously and remain spectators. And the more aware they become, however vaguely, of ambitions and of threats which transcend their immediate locales, the more trapped they seem to feel.

Underlying this sense of being trapped are seemingly impersonal changes in the very structure of continent-wide societies. The facts of contemporary history are also facts about the success and the failure of individual men and women. When a society is industrialized, a peasant becomes a worker; a feudal lord is liquidated or becomes a businessman. When classes rise or fall, a man is employed or unemployed; when the rate of investment goes up or down, a man takes new heart or goes broke. When wars happen, an insurance salesman becomes a rocket launcher; a store clerk, a radar man; a wife lives alone; a child grows up without a father. Neither the life of an individual nor the history of a society can be understood without understanding both.

Yet men do not usually define the troubles they endure in terms of historical change and institutional contradiction. The well-being they enjoy they do not usually impute to the big ups and downs of the societies in which they live. Seldom aware of the intricate connection between the patterns of their own lives and the course of world history, ordinary men do not usually know what this connection means for the kinds of men they are becoming and for the kinds of history making in which they might take part. They do not possess the quality of mind essential to grasp the interplay of man and society, of biography and history, of self and world. They cannot cope with their personal troubles in such ways as to control the structural transformations that usually lie behind them.

Surely it is no wonder. In what period have so many men been so totally exposed at so fast a pace to such earthquakes of change? That Americans have not known such catastrophic changes as have the men and women of other societies is due to historical facts that are now quickly becoming 'merely history'. The history that now affects every man is world history. Within this scene and this period, in the course of a single generation, one-sixth of mankind is transformed from all that is feudal and backward into all that is modern, advanced and fearful. Political colonies are freed; new and less visible forms of imperialism installed. Revolutions occur; men feel the intimate grip of new kinds of authority. Totalitarian societies rise and are smashed to bits – or succeed fabulously. After two centuries of ascendancy, capitalism is shown up as only one way to make society into an industrial apparatus. After two centuries of hope, even formal democracy is restricted to a quite small portion of mankind. Everywhere in the underdeveloped world, ancient ways of life are broken up and vague expectations become urgent demands. Everywhere in the over-developed world, the means of authority and of violence becomes total in scope and bureaucratic in form. Humanity itself now lies before us, the super-nation at either pole concentrating its most coordinated and massive efforts upon the preparation of the Third World War.

The very shaping of history now outpaces the ability of men to orient themselves in accordance with cherished values. And which values? Even when they do not panic, men often sense that older ways of feeling and thinking have collapsed and that newer beginnings are ambiguous to the point of moral stasis. Is it any wonder that ordinary men feel they cannot cope with the larger worlds with which they are so suddenly confronted? That they cannot understand the meaning of their epoch for their own lives? That – in defence of selfhood – they become morally insensible, trying to remain altogether private men? Is it any wonder that they come to be possessed by a sense of the trap?

It is not only information that they need — in this Age of Fact, information often dominates their attention and overwhelms their capacities to assimilate it. It is not only the skills of reason that they need — although their struggles to acquire these often exhaust their limited moral energy.

What they need, and what they feel they need, is a quality of mind that will help them to use information and to develop reason in order to achieve lucid summations of what is going on in the world and of what may be happening within themselves. It is this quality, I contend, that journalists and scholars, artists and publics, scientists and editors are coming to expect from what may be called the sociological imagination.

The sociological imagination enables its possessor to understand the larger historical scene in terms of its meaning for the inner life and the external career of a variety of individuals. It enables him to take into account how individuals, in the welter of their daily experience, often become falsely conscious of their social positions. Within that welter the framework of modern society is sought, and within that framework the psychologies of a variety of men and women are formulated. By such means the personal uneasiness of individuals is focused upon explicit troubles and the indifference of publics is transformed into involvement with public issues.

The first fruit of this imagination — and the first lesson of the social science that embodies it — is the idea that the individual can understand his own experience and gauge his own fate only by locating himself within his period, that he can know his own chances in life only by becoming aware of those of all individuals in his circumstances. In many ways it is a terrible lesson; in many ways a magnificent one. We do not know the limits of man's capacities for supreme effort or willing degradation, for agony or glee, for pleasurable brutality or the sweetness of reason. But in our time we have come to know that the limits of 'human nature' are frighteningly broad. We have come to know that every individual lives, from one generation to the next, in some society; that he lives out a biography, and that he lives it out within some historical sequence. By the fact of his living he contributes, however minutely, to the shaping of this society and to the course of its history, even as he is made by society and by its historical push and shove.

The sociological imagination enables us to grasp history and biography and the relations between the two within society. That is its task and its promise. To recognize this task and this promise is the mark of the classic social analyst . . .

No social study that does not come back to the problems of biography, of history and of their intersections within a society has completed its intellectual journey. Whatever the specific problems of the classic social analysts, however limited or however broad the features of social reality they have examined, those who have been imaginatively aware of the promise of their work have consistently asked three sorts of questions:

1. What is the structure of this particular society as a whole? What are its essential components and how are they related to one another? How does it differ from other varieties of social order? Within it, what is the meaning of any particular feature for its continuance and for its change?

2. Where does this society stand in human history? What are the mechanics by which it is changing? What is its place within and its meaning for the development of humanity as a whole? How does any particular feature we are examining affect, and how is it affected by, the historical period in which it moves? And this period – what are its essential features? How does it differ from other periods? What are its characteristic ways of history making?

3. What varieties of men and women now prevail in this society and in this period? And what varieties are coming to prevail? In what ways are they selected and formed, liberated and repressed, made sensitive and blunted? What kinds of 'human nature' are revealed in the conduct and character we observe in this society in this period? And what is the meaning of 'human nature' for each and every feature of the society we are examining?

Whether the point of interest is a great power state or a minor literary mood, a family, a prison, a creed – these are the kinds of questions the best social analysts have asked. They are the intellectual pivots of classic studies of man in society – and they are the questions inevitably raised by any mind possessing the sociological imagination. For that imagination is the capacity to shift from one perspective to another – from the political to the psychological; from examination of a single family to comparative assessment of the national budgets

of the world; from the theological school to the military establishment, from considerations of an oil industry to studies of
contemporary poetry. It is the capacity to range from the most
impersonal and remote transformations to the most intimate features
of the human self – and to see the relations between the two. Back of
its use there is always the urge to know the social and historical
meaning of the individual in the society and in the period in which
he has his quality and his being.

That, in brief, is why it is by means of the sociological imagination
that men now hope to grasp what is going on in the world, and to
understand what is happening in themselves as minute points of the
intersections of biography and history within society. In large part,
contemporary man's self-conscious view of himself as at least an
outsider, if not a permanent stranger, rests upon an absorbed realization of social relativity and of the transformative power of history.
The sociological imagination is the most fruitful of this self-
consciousness. By its use men whose mentalities have swept only a
series of limited orbits often come to feel as if suddenly awakened in
a house with which they had only supposed themselves to be familiar.
Correctly or incorrectly, they often come to feel that they can now
provide themselves with adequate summations, cohesive assessments,
comprehensive orientations. Older decisions that once appeared
sound, now seem to them products of a mind unaccountably dense.
Their capacity for astonishment is made lively again. They acquire a
new way of thinking, they experience a transvaluation of values: in a
word, by their reflection and by their sensibility, they realize the
cultural meaning of the social sciences.

Perhaps the most fruitful distinction with which the sociological
imagination works is between 'the personal troubles of milieu' and
'the public issues of social structure'. This distinction is an essential
tool of the sociological imagination and a feature of all classic work
in social science.

Troubles occur within the character of the individual and within
the range of his immediate relations with others; they have to do
with his self and with those limited areas of social life of which he is
directly and personally aware. Accordingly, the statement and the
resolution of troubles properly lie within the individual as a biographical entity and within the scope of his immediate milieu – the
social setting that is directly open to his personal experience and to

some extent his wilful activity. A trouble is a private matter: values cherished by an individual are felt by him to be threatened.

Issues have to do with matters that transcend these local environments of the individual and the range of his inner life. They have to do with the organization of many such milieux into the institutions of a historical society as a whole, with the ways in which various milieux overlap and interpenetrate to form the larger structure of social and historical life. An issue is a public matter: some value cherished by publics is felt to be threatened. Often there is a debate about what the value really is and about what it is that really threatens it. This debate if often without focus if only because it is the very nature of an issue unlike even widespread trouble, that it cannot very well be defined in terms of the immediate and everyday environments of ordinary men. An issue, in fact, often involves a crisis in institutional arrangements, and often too it involves what Marxists call 'contradictions' or 'antagonisms' . . .

In so far as an economy is so arranged that slumps occur, the problem of unemployment becomes incapable of personal solution. In so far as war is inherent in the nation-state system and in the uneven industrialization of the world, the ordinary individual in his restricted milieu will be powerless – with or without psychiatric aid – to solve the troubles this system or lack of system imposes upon him. In so far as the family as an institution turns women into darling little slaves and men into their chief providers and unweaned dependants, the problem of a satisfactory marriage remains incapable of purely private solution. In so far as the overdeveloped megalopolis and the overdeveloped automobile are built-in features of the over-developed society, the issues of urban living will not be solved by personal ingenuity and private wealth.

What we experience in various and specific milieux, I have noted, is often caused by structural changes. Accordingly, to understand the changes of many personal milieux we are required to look beyond them. And the number and variety of such structural changes increase as the institutions within which we live become more embracing and more intricately connected with one another. To be aware of the idea of social structure and to use it with sensibility is to be capable of tracing such linkages among a great variety of milieux. To be able to do that is to possess the sociological imagination.

2 Robert A. Nisbet

The Unit-Ideas of Sociology

Excerpts from Robert A. Nisbet, *The Sociological Tradition*, Heinemann, 1970, pp. 3–9.

Ideas and Antitheses

The history of thought is commonly dealt with in one of two ways. The first, and oldest, is to begin with the *dramatis personae*, the thinkers themselves, whose writings furnish the bibliographic substance of the history of thought . . .

A second approach directs itself not to the man, but to the system, the school, or the ism. Not the Benthams and the Millses but utilitarianism, not the Hegels and the Bradleys but idealism, not the Marxes and the Proudhons but socialism is here the prime object of attention. This approach is valuable; the history of thought is indubitably a history of systems: as true of sociology as of metaphysics. Presuppositions, ideas and corollaries congeal into systems which often develop the same power over their followers that religions do. Systems can be likened to the psychologist's *Gestalten*; we acquire ideas and facts, not atomistically, but within the *patterns* of thought that form so large a part of our environment. But the pitfalls of this approach are well known. Too often systems are taken as irreducible rather than as the constellations of distinguishable, even separable, assumptions and ideas that they are in fact: all decomposable, all capable of being regrouped into different systems. Systems moreover tend to become lifeless; what excites one generation or century becomes only antiquarian in the next. One need think only of socialism, pragmatism, utilitarianism, and, long before them, nominalism and realism. Yet each of these systems has component elements that are as viable today, though in different ways, as when these systems were being formed. To lose sight of the elements would be unfortunate.

... A third approach ... begins with neither the man nor the system, but the ideas which are the elements of systems ...

What are the criteria by which we select the unit-ideas of an intellectual discipline? Four, at least, are governing. Such ideas must have *generality*: that is, all must be discernible in the works of a considerable number of the towering minds of an age, not be limited to the works of a single individual or coterie. Second, they must have *continuity*: they must be observable in the early as well as late phases of the period, as relevant indeed to present as to past. Third, such ideas must be *distinctive*: they must participate in what it is that makes a discipline significantly different from other disciplines. Ideas like 'individual', 'society', 'order' are useless here – however valuable they may be in more general contexts – for these are elements of *all* the disciplines of social thought. Fourth, they must be ideas in the full sense: that is, more than wraithlike 'influences', more than peripheral aspects of methodology ... An idea is a *perspective*, a framework, a category (in the Kantian sense) within which vision and fact unite, within which insight and observation are brought together. An idea is, in Whitehead's word, a searchlight; it lights up a part of the landscape, leaving other parts in shadow or darkness ...

What are the essential unit-ideas of sociology, those which, above any others, give distinctiveness to sociology in its juxtaposition to the other social sciences? There are, I believe, five: *community*, *authority*, *status*, the *sacred*, and *alienation* ... *Community* includes but goes beyond local community to encompass religion, work, family, and culture; it refers to social bonds characterized by emotional cohesion, depth, continuity, and fullness. *Authority* is the structure or the inner order of an association, whether this be political, religious, or cultural, and is given legitimacy by its roots in social function, tradition, or allegiance. *Status* is the individual's position in the hierarchy of prestige and influence that characterizes every community or association. The *sacred* includes the mores, the non-rational, the religious and ritualistic ways of behaviour that are valued beyond whatever utility they may possess. *Alienation* is a historical perspective within which man is seen as estranged, anomic, and rootless when cut off from the ties of community and moral purpose.

Each of these ideas is commonly linked to a conceptual opposite, to a kind of antithesis, from which it derives much of its continuing meaning in the sociological tradition. Thus, opposed to the idea of community is the idea of society (*Gesellschaft*, in Tönnies' usage) in which reference is to the large-scale, impersonal, contractual ties that were proliferating in the modern age, often, as it seemed, at the expense of community. The conceptual opposite of authority in sociological thought is *power*, which is commonly identified with military or political force or with administrative bureaucracy and which, unlike the authority that arises directly from social function and association, raises the problem of legitimacy. Status has for its conceptual opposite in sociology not the popular idea of equality but the novel and sophisticated idea of *class*, at once more specialized and collective. The opposite of the idea of the sacred is the utilitarian, the profane (in Durkheim's momentous wording), or the *secular*. And, finally, alienation – considered at least as a sociological perspective – is best seen as an inversion of *progress*. From precisely the same assumptions regarding the nature of historical development in modern Europe – industrialization, secularization, equality, popular democracy, and so on – such minds as Tocqueville and Weber drew, not the conclusion of social and moral progress, but the more morbid conclusion of man's alienation from man, from values, and from self; an alienation caused by the very forces that others in the century were hailing as progressive.

Community–society, *authority–power*, *status–class*, *sacred–secular*, *alienation–progress*: these are rich themes in nineteenth-century thought. Considered as linked antitheses, they form the very warp of the sociological tradition. Quite apart from their conceptual significance in sociology, they may be regarded as epitomizations of the conflict between tradition and modernism, between the old order, made moribund by the industrial and democratic revolutions, and the new order, its outlines still unclear and as often the cause of anxiety as of elation or hope.

The Revolt Against Individualism

Obviously, these ideas and antitheses did not arise in the first instance in the nineteenth century. In one form or another they are old. They may be seen in the ancient world: in, for example, Plato's Athens, when Greece, like Europe two thousand years later, was searching for new foundations of order to replace those that had seemingly been destroyed by the ravages of war, revolution and *stasis* ... We see these ideas again, four centuries later, in the works of the Christian philosophers, who were preoccupied, as were so many of their pagan contemporaries, by man's alienation, man's search for the blessed community, for sanctity of authority, and by his proper place in the hierarchical chain of being that culminated in the City of God.

But while these ideas are indeed timeless and universal, they have, like all major ideas of man and society, their periods of ebb as well as flow, of dearth as well as abundance. There are other ages in which these ideas have only small significance, ages when they are placed in the shadow of strikingly different ideas and attitudes regarding man's fate and man's hope. Thus, none of the ideas we are concerned with in this book was especially notable in the Age of Reason that so brilliantly lighted up the seventeenth and eighteenth centuries, reaching its high point in the Enlightenment in France and England.

Then, a different set of words and ideas encompassed moral and political aspiration: ideas like *individual, progress, contract, nature, reason*. The dominant objectives of the whole age, from Bacon's *Novum Organum* to Condorcet's *Sketch of a Historical Picture of the Human Mind*, were those of release: release of the individual from ancient social ties and of the mind from fettering traditions. Towering over the whole period was the universally held belief in the natural individual – in his reason, his innate character, and self-sustaining stability.

The ideas and values of seventeenth- and eighteenth-century individualistic rationalism did not, of course, disappear with the coming of the nineteenth century. Far from it. In critical rationalism, in philosophic liberalism, in classical economics, and in utilitarian politics, the ethos of individualism is continued – together with the vision of a social order founded on rational interest.

But despite a once common and widely expressed point of view among historians of the age, individualism is far from the whole story of nineteenth-century thought ... What is distinctive and intellectually most fertile in nineteenth-century thought is not individualism but the reaction to individualism: a reaction expressed in no way more strikingly than by the ideas that form the central subject of this book.

These ideas – *community, authority, status*, the *sacred*, and *alienation* – taken together constitute a reorientation of European thought quite as momentous, I believe, as that very different, even opposite, reorientation of thought that had marked the waning of the Middle Ages three centuries earlier and the rise of the Age of Reason. Then it had been individualistic rationalism asserting itself against medieval corporatism and authority. Now, in the early nineteenth century, it is the reverse: the reaction of traditionalism against analytic reason; of communalism against individualism; and of the non-rational against the purely rational . . .

We see the historic premise of the innate stability of the individual challenged by a new social psychology that derived personality from the close contexts of society and that made alienation the price of man's release from these contexts. Instead of the Age of Reason's cherished natural order, it is now the institutional order – community, kinship, social class – that forms the point of departure for social philosophers as widely separated in their views as Coleridge, Marx, and Tocqueville. From the eighteenth-century's generally optimistic vision of popular sovereignty we pass to nineteenth-century premonitions of the tyranny that may lie in popular democracy when its institutional and traditional limits are broken through. And, finally, even the idea of progress is given a new statement: one resting not upon release from community and tradition but upon a kind of craving for new forms of moral and social community.

3   Karl Marx

The Materialist Conception of History

Excerpts from the Preface to *A Contribution to the Critique of Political Economy* (first published 1859) and *The German Ideology* (written in 1845–6), in T. B. Bottomore and Maximilien Rubel (eds.), *Karl Marx: Selected Writings in Sociology and Social Philosophy*, Penguin, 1963, pp. 67–9, 79–80 and 93–5.

The general conclusion at which I arrived and which, once reached, continued to serve as the guiding thread in my studies, may be formulated briefly as follows: In the social production which men carry on they enter into definite relations that are indispensable and independent of their will; these relations of production correspond to a definite stage of development of their material powers of production. The totality of these relations of production constitutes the economic structure of society – the real foundation, on which legal and political superstructures arise and to which definite forms of social consciousness correspond. The mode of production of material life determines the general character of the social, political, and spiritual processes of life. It is not the consciousness of men that determines their being, but, on the contrary, their social being determines their consciousness. At a certain stage of their development, the material forces of production in society come in conflict with the existing relations of production, or – what is but a legal expression for the same thing – with the property relations within which they had been at work before. From forms of development of the forces of production these relations turn into their fetters. Then occurs a period of social revolution. With the change of the economic foundation the entire immense superstructure is more or less rapidly transformed. In considering such transformations, the distinction should always be made between the material transformation of the economic conditions of production which can be determined with the precision of natural science, and the legal, political, religious, aesthetic or philosophical – in short, ideological – forms in which men become conscious of this conflict and fight it out. Just as our opinion of an individual is not based on what he thinks of himself, so can we not judge of such a period of transformation by its own consciousness; on the contrary, this consciousness must rather be explained from the contradictions of material life, from the existing conflict between the social forces of production and the relations of production. No social order ever disappears before all the productive forces for which there is room in it have been developed; and new, higher relations of production never appear before the material conditions of their existence have matured in the womb of the old society. Therefore, mankind always sets itself only such problems as it can solve; since, on closer examination, it will always be found that the problem itself arises only when the material conditions necessary for its solution already exist or are at least in the process of formation. In broad outline we can designate the Asiatic, the ancient, the feudal, and the modern bourgeois modes of production as progressive epochs in the economic formation of society. The bourgeois relations of production are the last antagonistic form of the social process of production; not in the sense of individual antagonisms, but of conflict arising from conditions surrounding the life of individuals in society. At the same time the productive forces developing in the womb of bourgeois society create the material conditions for the solution of that antagonism. With this social formation, therefore, the prehistory of human society comes to an end.

(1) In the development of the productive forces a stage is reached where productive forces and means of intercourse are called into being which, under the existing relations, can only work mischief, and which are, therefore, no longer productive, but destructive, forces (machinery and money). Associated with this is the emergence of a class which has to bear all the burdens of society without enjoying its advantages, which is excluded from society and is forced into the most resolute opposition to all other classes; a class which comprises the majority of the members of society and in which there develops a consciousness of the need for a fundamental revolution, the communist consciousness. This consciousness can, of course, also arise in other classes from the observation of the situation of this class.

(2) The conditions under which determinate productive forces can be used are also the conditions for the dominance of a determinate social class, whose social power, derived from its property ownership,

invariably finds its *practical* and ideal expression in a particular form of the State. Consequently, every revolutionary struggle is directed against the class which has so far been dominant.

(3) In all former revolutions the form of activity was always left unaltered and it was only a question of redistributing this activity among different people, of introducing a new division of labour. The communist revolution, however, is directed against the former *mode* of activity, does away with *labour*, and abolishes all class rule along with the classes themselves, because it is effected by the class which no longer counts as a class in society, which is not recognized as a class, and which is the expression of the dissolution of all classes, nationalities, etc., within contemporary society.

(4) For the creation on a mass scale of this communist consciousness, as well as for the success of the cause itself, it is necessary for men themselves to be changed on a large scale, and this change can only occur in a practical movement, in a *revolution*. Revolution is necessary not only because the *ruling* class cannot be overthrown in any other way, but also because only in a revolution can *the class which overthrows it* rid itself of the accumulated rubbish of the past and become capable of reconstructing society . . .

The ideas of the ruling class are, in every age, the ruling ideas: i.e. the class which is the dominant *material* force in society is at the same time its dominant *intellectual* force. The class which has the means of material production at its disposal, has control at the same time over the means of mental production, so that in consequence the ideas of those who lack the means of mental production are, in general, subject to it. The dominant ideas are nothing more than the ideal expression of the dominant material relationships, the dominant material relationships grasped as ideas, and thus of the relationships which make one class the ruling one; they are consequently the ideas of its dominance. The individuals composing the ruling class possess, among other things, consciousness, and therefore think. In so far, therefore, as they rule as a class and determine the whole extent of an epoch, it is self-evident that they do this in their whole range and thus, among other things, rule also as thinkers, as producers of ideas, and regulate the production and distribution of the ideas of their age. Consequently their ideas are the ruling ideas of the age. For instance, in an age and in a country where royal power, aristocracy, and the bourgeoisie are contending for domination and where, therefore, domination is shared, the doctrine of the separation of powers appears as the dominant idea and is enunciated as an 'eternal law'. The division of labour, which we saw earlier as one of the principal forces of history up to the present time, manifests itself also in the ruling class, as the division of mental and material labour, so that within this class one part appears as the thinkers of the class (its active conceptualizing ideologists, who make it their chief source of livelihood to develop and perfect the illusions of the class about itself), while the others have a more passive and receptive attitude to these ideas and illusions, because they are in reality the active members of this class and have less time to make up ideas and illusions about themselves. This cleavage within the ruling class may even develop into a certain opposition and hostility between the two parts, but in the event of a practical collision in which the class itself is endangered, it disappears of its own accord and with it also the illusion that the ruling ideas were not the ideas of the ruling class and had a power distinct from the power of this class. The existence of revolutionary ideas in a particular age presupposes the existence of a revolutionary class . . .

If, in considering the course of history, we detach the ideas of the ruling class from the ruling class itself and attribute to them an independent existence, if we confine ourselves to saying that in a particular age these or those ideas were dominant, without paying attention to the conditions of production and the producers of these ideas, and if we thus ignore the individuals and the world conditions which are the source of the ideas, it is possible to say, for instance, that during the time that the aristocracy was dominant the concepts honour, loyalty, etc., were dominant; during the dominance of the bourgeoisie the concepts freedom, equality, etc. The ruling class itself in general imagines this to be the case. This conception of history which is common to all historians, particularly since the eighteenth century, will necessarily come up against the phenomenon that increasingly abstract ideas hold sway, i.e. ideas which increasingly take on the form of universality. For each new class which puts itself in the place of the one ruling before it, is compelled, simply in order to achieve its aims, to represent its interest as the common interest of all members of society, i.e. employing an ideal formula, to give its ideas the form of universality and to represent them as the only rational and universally valid ones. The class which makes a revolution appears from the beginning not as a class but as the representative of the whole of society, simply because it is opposed to a *class*. It appears as the whole mass of society confronting the single ruling class. It can do this because at the beginning its interest really is more closely connected with the common interest of all other non-ruling classes and has been unable under the constraint of the previously existing conditions to develop as the particular interest of a particular class. Its victory, therefore, also benefits many individuals of the other classes which are not achieving a dominant position, but only in so far as it now puts these individuals in a position to raise themselves into the ruling class. When the French bourgeoisie overthrew the rule of aristocracy it thereby made it possible for many proletarians to raise themselves above the proletariat, but only in so far as they became bourgeois. Every new class, therefore, achieves its domination only on a broader basis than that of the previous ruling class. On the other hand, the opposition of the non-ruling class to the new ruling class later develops all the more sharply and profoundly. These two characteristics entail that the struggle to be waged against this new ruling class has as its object a more decisive and radical negation of the previous conditions of society than could have been accomplished by all previous classes which aspired to rule.

This whole semblance, that the rule of a certain class is only the rule of certain ideas, ends of its own accord naturally, as soon as class domination ceases to be the form of social organization: that is to say, as soon as it is no longer necessary to represent a particular interest as general or the 'general interest' as ruling.

4 Émile Durkheim

What is a Social Fact?

Excerpts from Émile Durkheim, *The Rules of Sociological Method* (ed. George E. G. Catlin), Free Press, Glencoe, Illinois 1950, pp. 1–10, 12–13. (First published 1895.)

Before inquiring into the method suited to the study of social facts, it is important to know which facts are commonly called 'social'. This information is all the more necessary since the designation 'social' is used with little precision. It is currently employed for practically all phenomena generally diffused within society, however small their social interest. But on that basis, there are, as it were, no human events that may not be called social. Each individual drinks, sleeps, eats, reasons; and it is to society's interest that these functions be exercised in an orderly manner. If, then, all these facts are counted as 'social' facts, sociology would have no subject matter exclusively its own, and its domain would be confused with that of biology and psychology.

But in reality there is in every society a certain group of phenomena which may be differentiated from those studied by the other natural sciences. When I fulfil my obligations as brother, husband, or citizen, when I execute my contracts, I perform duties which are defined, externally to myself and my acts, in law and in custom. Even if they conform to my own sentiments and I feel their reality subjectively, such reality is still objective, for I did not create them; I merely inherited them through my education ... The system of signs I use to express my thought, the system of currency I employ to pay my debts, the instruments of credit I utilize in my commercial relations, the practices followed in my profession, etc., function independently of my own use of them. And these statements can be repeated for each member of society. Here, then, are ways of acting, thinking, and feeling that present the noteworthy property of existing outside the individual consciousness.

These types of conduct or thought are not only external to the individual but are, moreover, endowed with coercive power, by virtue of which they impose themselves upon him, independent of his individual will. Of course, when I fully consent and conform to them, this constraint is felt only slightly, if at all, and is therefore unnecessary. But it is, none the less, an intrinsic characteristic of these facts, the proof thereof being that it asserts itself as soon as I attempt to resist it. If I attempt to violate the law, it reacts against me so as to prevent my act before its accomplishment, or to nullify my violation by restoring the damage, if it is accomplished and reparable, or to make me expiate it if it cannot be compensated for otherwise.

In the case of purely moral maxims, the public conscience exercises a check on every act which offends it by means of the surveillance it exercises over the conduct of citizens, and the appropriate penalties at its disposal. In many cases the constraint is less violent, but nevertheless it always exists. If I do not submit to the conventions of society, if in my dress I do not conform to the customs observed in my country and in my class, the ridicule I provoke, the social isolation in which I am kept, produce, although in an attenuated form, the same effects as a punishment in the strict sense of the word. The constraint is none the less efficacious for being indirect. I am not obliged to speak French with my fellow-countrymen nor to use the legal currency, but I cannot possibly do otherwise. If I tried to escape this necessity, my attempt would fail miserably. As an industrialist, I am free to apply the technical methods of former centuries; but by doing so, I should invite certain ruin. Even when I free myself from these rules and violate them successfully, I am always compelled to struggle with them. When finally overcome, they make their constraining power sufficiently felt by the resistance they offer. The enterprises of all innovators, including successful ones, come up against resistance of this kind.

Here, then, is a category of facts with very distinctive characteristics: it consists of ways of acting, thinking, and feeling, external to the individual, and endowed with a power of coercion, by reason of which they control him. These ways of thinking could not be confused with biological phenomena, since they consist of representations and of actions; nor with psychological phenomena, which exist only in the individual consciousness and through it. They constitute, thus, a new variety of phenomena; and it is to them exclusively that the term 'social' ought to be applied. And this term fits them quite well, for it is clear that, since their source is not in the individual, their substratum can be no other than society, either the political society as a whole or some one of the partial groups it includes, such as religious denominations, political, literary, and occupational associations, etc. On the other hand, this term 'social' applies to them exclusively, for it has a distinct meaning only if it designates exclusively the phenomena which are not included in any of the categories of facts that have already been established and classified. These ways of thinking and acting therefore constitute the proper domain of sociology. It is true that, when we define them with this word 'constraint', we risk shocking the zealous partisans of absolute individualism. For those who profess the complete autonomy of the individual, man's dignity is diminished whenever he is made to feel that he is not completely self-determinant. It is generally accepted today, however, that most of our ideas and our tendencies are not developed by ourselves but come to us from without. How can they become a part of us except by imposing themselves upon us? This is the whole meaning of our definition. And it is generally accepted, moreover, that social constraint is not necessarily incompatible with the individual personality . . .

To confirm this definition of the social fact by a characteristic illustration from common experience, one need only observe the manner in which children are brought up. Considering the facts as they are and as they have always been, it becomes immediately evident that all education is a continuous effort to impose on the child ways of seeing, feeling, and acting which he could not have arrived at spontaneously. From the very first hours of his life, we compel him to eat, drink, and sleep at regular hours; we constrain him to cleanliness, calmness, and obedience; later we exert pressure upon him in order that he may learn proper consideration for others, respect for customs and conventions, the need for work, etc. If, in time, this constraint ceases to be felt, it is because it gradually gives rise to habits and to internal tendencies that render constraint unnecessary; but nevertheless it is not abolished, for it is still the source from which these habits are derived. It is true that, according to Spencer, a rational education ought to reject such methods, allowing the child to act in complete liberty; but as this pedagogic theory has never been applied by any known people, it must be accepted only as an expression of personal opinion, not as a fact which can contradict the aforementioned observations. What makes these facts particularly instructive is that the aim of education is, precisely, the socialization of the human being; the process of education, therefore, gives us in a nutshell the historical fashion in which the social being is constituted. This unremitting pressure to which the child is subjected is the very pressure of the social milieu which tends to fashion him in its own image, and of which parents and teachers are merely the representatives and intermediaries . . .

Indeed, certain of these social manners of acting and thinking acquire, by reason of their repetition, a certain rigidity which on its own account crystallizes them, so to speak, and isolates them from the particular events which reflect them. They thus acquire a body, a tangible form, and constitute a reality in their own right, quite distinct from the individual facts which produce it. Collective habits are inherent not only in the successive acts which they determine but, by a privilege of which we find no example in the biological realm, they are given permanent expression in a formula which is repeated from mouth to mouth, transmitted by education, and fixed even in writing. Such is the origin and nature of legal and moral rules, popular aphorisms and proverbs, articles of faith wherein religious or political groups condense their beliefs, standards of taste established by literary schools, etc. None of these can be found entirely reproduced in the applications made of them by individuals, since they can exist even without being actually applied . . .

Such are social phenomena, when disentangled from all foreign matter. As for their individual manifestations, these are indeed, to a certain extent, social, since they partly reproduce a social model. Each of them also depends, and to a large extent, on the organo-psychological constitution of the individual and on the particular circumstances in which he is placed. Thus they are not sociological phenomena in the strict sense of the word. They belong to two realms at once; one could call them sociopsychological. They interest the sociologist without constituting the immediate subject matter of sociology. There exist in the interior of organisms similar phenomena, compound in their nature, which form in their turn the subject matter of the 'hybrid sciences', such as physiological chemistry, for example.

The objection may be raised that a phenomenon is collective only if it is common to all members of society, or at least to most of them

– in other words, if it is truly general. This may be true; but it is general because it is collective (that is, more or less obligatory), and certainly not collective because general. It is a group condition repeated in the individual because imposed on him. It is to be found in each part because it exists in the whole, rather than in the whole because it exists in the parts. This becomes conspicuously evident in those beliefs and practices which are transmitted to us ready-made by previous generations; we receive and adopt them because, being both collective and ancient, they are invested with a particular authority that education has taught us to recognize and respect. It is, of course, true that a vast portion of our social culture is transmitted to us in this way; but even when the social fact is due in part to our direct collaboration, its nature is not different . . .

We thus arrive at the point where we can formulate and delimit in a precise way the domain of sociology. It comprises only a limited group of phenomena. A social fact is to be recognized by the power of external coercion which it exercises or is capable of exercising over individuals, and the presence of this power may be recognized in its turn either by the existence of some specific sanction or by the resistance offered against every individual effort that tends to violate it . . .

A legal regulation is an arrangement no less permanent than a type of architecture, and yet the regulation is a 'physiological' fact. A simple moral maxim is assuredly somewhat more malleable, but it is much more rigid than a simple professional custom or a fashion. There is thus a whole series of degrees without a break in continuity between the facts of the most articulated structure and those free currents of social life which are not yet definitely moulded. The differences between them are, therefore, only differences in the degree of consolidation they present . . . Our definition will then include the whole relevant range of facts if we say: *A social fact is every way of acting, fixed or not, capable of exercising on the individual an external constraint*; or again, *every way of acting which is general throughout a given society, while at the same time existing in its own right independent of its individual manifestations.*

5   Frank Parkin

Weber's Methods and Procedures

Excerpts from Frank Parkin, *Max Weber*, Ellis Horwood, 1982, pp. 18–25, 30–34.

Weber's position is summed up as follows:

for sociological purposes there is no such thing as a collective personality which 'acts'. When reference is made in a sociological context to a state, a nation, a corporation, a family or an army corps, or to similar collectivities, what is meant is . . . only a certain kind of development of actual or possible social actions of individual persons.

Collectivities cannot think, feel, perceive; only people can. To assume otherwise is to impute a spurious reality to what are in effect conceptual abstractions. Furthermore, because it is the task of social science to penetrate the subjective understandings of the individual, to get at the motives for social action, this enterprise is bound to be quite different from that undertaken by the natural sciences. Weber says that we do not 'understand' the behaviour of cells or the movement of the planets. We observe the structure of the cells and the motion of the stars and then try to formulate general laws about structure and motion. We, the observers, impose our own explanations upon these phenomena by the application of our own concepts and categories.

With social behaviour it is all very different. People, unlike molecules or planets, have motives for their actions. Their behaviour is guided by subjective meanings. What is more, social actors have their own ideas and explanations as to why they behave in the way that they do, and these ideas and explanations themselves are an indispensable part of any comprehensive account of their conduct. It is a fairly safe bet that falling apples do not have a concept of gravity . . .

Weber's heavy emphasis on the individual and internal meanings could hardly be in greater contrast to Durkheim's position. For Durkheim, the only unit that really counted for explanatory purposes was the collectivity, and to make individual motives and perceptions the principal object of inquiry would be to forfeit everything of sociological interest . . .

Weber's case for taking the individual's subjective meanings as the starting point of social inquiry is spelled out in the course of his advocacy of the method called *Verstehen*. What is meant by this is the attempt to comprehend social action through a kind of empathetic liaison with the actor on the part of the observer. The strategy is for the investigator to try to identify with the actor and his motives and to view the course of conduct through the actor's eyes rather than his own. Weber did not regard *Verstehen* merely as a way of sounding out a person's own account and evaluation of his conduct by way of interviews and the like. He saw it as a method that could be applied to the understanding of historical events, when there was no one left around to interview. We could seek to show why actors followed a certain path of conduct by reconstructing the situational choices and constraints facing them at the time. We are perfectly capable of putting ourselves in someone else's shoes and imagining how we might have acted in similar circumstances. As Weber puts it 'one need not have been Caesar in order to understand Caesar'. . .

The argument being canvassed by the *Verstehen* approach is that social actors are always faced with choices. Conduct is not governed by inexorable social forces that propel people in one direction or another. Actors decide to take certain courses of action in preference to others, and their decisions are powerfully affected by their perception of opportunities and constraints. It is therefore necessary, in any given case, to get some understanding of how the options were actually weighed up and assessed. This is an approach which is obviously not too congenial to any school of thought that seeks to uncover some hidden purpose or logic to history. Far from unfolding in accordance with a pre-ordained pattern, history becomes virtually open-ended. Almost anything can happen.

Weber distinguishes between two types of *Verstehen*. These are 'direct observational understanding' (*aktuelles Verstehen*) and 'explanatory understanding' (*erklärendes Verstehen*). He gives as an example of direct observational understanding our ability to grasp the fact that someone is angry simply by reading his facial expression.

We experience the same kind of understanding when we observe a woodcutter chopping wood, or a hunter aiming his rifle at an animal. Merely observing these acts is enough to tell us *what* is going on. However, to comprehend *why* it is going on we need to have recourse to explanatory understanding . . .

Weber makes it perfectly plain that the *Verstehen* approach is not to be thought of as the be-all and end-all of social explanation. It has to be supplemented by other techniques of investigation, including the 'scientific' efforts favoured by the positivists . . .

Unlike some of his intellectual heirs, Weber by no means regarded the use of statistical techniques as an exercise in mystification or as a distortion of the subtle realities of social life. Statistical probability was an important check upon the general validity of any proposition. At the same time, caution was called for in attaching explanatory significance to numerical correlations. The fact that two variables showed a consistently high degree of correlation would not in itself suffice to establish a causal connection between them. For causation to be proven it would be necessary to show that the relationship between the variables was intuitively meaningful. If it could be demonstrated that the rise and fall of the pound on the foreign exchange markets exactly paralleled the rise and fall in the divorce rate, we would not be warranted in claiming a causal link between the two events. There is no plausible 'sequence of motivation' that connects actions on the money market with decisions about the fate of marriage . . . All this suggests that *Verstehen* is to be understood not as an alternative to positivism and the scientific method, as it is sometimes said to be, but as a corrective against the too mechanical application of this method.

Be this as it may, Weber's exposition of *Verstehendesoziologie* raises a number of awkward questions that are left for the most part unanswered. In the first place, his distinction between two types of *Verstehen* – direct observational understanding and explanatory understanding – is neither helpful nor altogether plausible. It is difficult to see why the direct observation of an act qualifies as any kind of 'understanding' of it at all. If, for example, we were to come across a group of people sitting in a circle with their eyes shut we would not be in much of a position to understand even *what* they were doing. They could be rehearsing a play, communing with the spirits, or getting quietly stoned. Only when we had garnered further information that would enable us to discover the social purpose of their activity, and relate it to some familiar cultural context, would we be in a position to say that we understood it. Weber regards this as the second type of *Verstehen* – explanatory understanding; this is understanding arrived at by placing the act in question in a wider framework of meaning. But surely this is the only one possible type of understanding. Merely observing an act is no kind of understanding whatsoever. We cannot in fact properly comprehend *what* is going on unless we know *why* it is going on . . .

There are certain other difficulties about *Verstehen* as a method or procedure that Weber now and then alludes to but never really comes to grips with. One such difficulty is that in order to understand the actor's conduct by way of empathy, it is necessary that the observer should be on roughly the same normative and moral wavelength as the actor. If they have widely divergent outlooks or incompatible beliefs the empathetic connection cannot be fully made . . .

It would seem to follow that any procedure based on *Verstehen* would be especially difficult to put into practice if actor and observer were from entirely different cultures. The Western observer of an exotic tribal society would be seriously impeded in his attempts at understanding because of the wide normative gulf between himself and the subjects of his inquiry . . .

The nagging question that haunts all attempts to adopt a *Verstehen* procedure, even where actor and observer do share the same cultural background, is: How can I be sure that I have in fact grasped and understood the subjective state of the actor? How could I know if I had *mis*understood? . . .

There is also something else slightly worrying about Weber's claim that we are unlikely to be able to make sense of activities and beliefs with which we cannot emphathize . . . This is unfortunate in a way, because 'fanatical' commitments of various kinds are generally regarded by sociologists and others as especially intriguing objects of inquiry. If the observer's personal distaste for, or coolness towards, such commitments rendered him unfit to investigate them, the scope of sociology would be considerably reduced. The study of fascism would have to be left to those who sympathized to some extent with the fascist cause; Leninism could only be made sense of by Leninists; and so forth . . .

Weber points out that ideal-types are, of necessity, morally loaded constructs. 'All knowledge of cultural reality . . . is always knowledge from *particular points of view*.'

There can be no such thing as an . . . absolutely 'objective' scientific analysis of culture or . . . of 'social phenomena' independent of special and 'one-sided' viewpoints according to which – expressly or tacitly, consciously or unconsciously – they are selected, analyzed and organized for expository purposes.

Weber drives home the point that social reality cannot be apprehended by letting the facts 'speak for themselves'. Social facts do not exist as things in their own right, waiting to be gathered up like pebbles on a beach. What counts as a social fact is very much determined by the moral spectacles through which we view the world. Weber is scathingly dismissive of those theorists who urge us to evacuate our minds of all presuppositions in order that we might perceive social reality in all its purity . . .

For Weber, on the other hand, since the eradication of all preconceptions was not humanly possible, the social construction of facts was extremely problematic. Because social facts only existed by virtue of the concepts employed to define and organize them, we could in effect bring new facts into being and dispose of others simply by altering our conceptual frame of reference. Entities like social classes, for example, could be abolished at a single conceptual stroke. Now you see them, now you don't . . .

Suppose for example, we wished to construct an ideal type of 'democracy'. One possibility would be to highlight features such as free elections, competing political parties, legal right of opposition, the separation of powers, and the guarantee of civil liberties. Using this as our ideal-type of democracy, we would find that communist or socialist systems diverged considerably from it. Western political systems, by contrast, would show a much closer approximation to it. On that basis, we could conclude that Western capitalist systems were more democratic than socialist systems. However, it would be quite feasible to construct an ideal-type of democracy that gave one-sided emphasis to a different set of criteria. The key features could be regarded as the absence of a property-owning or exploiting class, and the absence of those gross inequalities of wealth that effectively concentrate power in the hands of the few at the expense of the many, notwithstanding the latter's purely formal liberties and rights.

Measured against this conceptual yardstick, Western capitalist states would tend to show greater divergence from the pure type than many socialist states. Socialist states could thus be judged more democratic. Because both constructs are morally slanted, and inevitably so, it is hard to see how either of them could claim explanatory superiority over the other. This is the problem with all ideal-types . . . This being the case, Weber would not seem to be the most likely candidate to champion the cause of 'value-free' social theory. How could sociology ever attain neutrality if its operational tools were saturated with the observer's own values and preconceptions? Given his views on the status of knowledge as an inescapably social and moral construct, it is at first blush puzzling that Weber should have raised such loud and insistent demands for the exclusion of value-judgements from sociological observations . . .

Merely because the investigator refrained from openly ranting or moralizing about his findings would not thereby make them value-free. The working assumptions that guided the research, and the choice of concepts employed, would ensure that the final product had a certain moral colouring. For reasons already alluded to, this might be especially so if ideal-types were used. Weber offers no guidance on how it would be possible to arrive at value-free results with the aid of these constructs.

He would have been on somewhat firmer ground if he had not conflated value-judgements with partisanship. He could have conceded that since all forms of social inquiry entail the use of concepts and constructs that are morally tinted, the research product could not possibly be value-free. At the same time, he could quite reasonably have sustained his case against partisanship in the lecture room and in academic publications. The sociologist cannot, try as he may, avoid making value-judgements in his work. But he *can* avoid spouting his own tedious opinions on this and that. The fact that implicit evaluations cannot be expunged from social enquiry is no warrant for giving a completely free rein to the soap-box brigade.

6   Peter L. Berger and Thomas Luckmann

The Social Construction of Reality

Excerpts from Peter L. Berger and Thomas Luckmann, *The Social Construction of Reality*, Allen Lane The Penguin Press, 1967, pp. 26–7, 35–7, 39, 43, 50, 56–60. First published by Doubleday in 1966.

[In the past] the sociology of knowledge has been concerned with intellectual history, in the sense of the history of ideas. We would stress that this is, indeed, a very important focus of sociological inquiry ... We would argue, however, that the problem of 'ideas', including the special problem of ideology, constitutes only part of the larger problem of the sociology of knowledge, and not a central part at that.

The sociology of knowledge must concern itself with everything that passes for 'knowledge' in society. As soon as one states this, one realizes that the focus on intellectual history is ill-chosen, or rather, is ill-chosen if it becomes the central focus of the sociology of knowledge. Theoretical thought, 'ideas', *Weltanschauungen*, are not *that* important in society. Although every society contains these phenomena, they are part of the sum of what passes for 'knowledge'. Only a very limited group of people in any society engages in theorizing, in the business of 'ideas' and the construction of *Weltanschauungen*. But everyone in society participates in its 'knowledge' in one way or another. Put differently, only a few are concerned with the theoretical interpretation of the world, but everybody lives in a world of some sort. Not only is the focus on theoretical thought unduly restrictive for the sociology of knowledge, it is also unsatisfactory because even this part of socially available 'knowledge' cannot be fully understood if it is not placed in the framework of a more general analysis of the 'knowledge'.

To exaggerate the importance of theoretical thought in society and history is a natural failing of theorizers. It is then all the more necessary to correct this intellectualistic misapprehension. The theoretical formulations of reality, whether they be scientific or philosophical or even mythological, do not exhaust what is 'real' for the members of a society. Since this is so, the sociology of knowledge must first of all concern itself with what people 'know' as 'reality' in their everyday, non- or pre-theoretical lives. In other words, common-sense 'knowledge' rather than 'ideas' must be the central focus for the sociology of knowledge. It is precisely this 'knowledge' that constitutes the fabric of meanings without which no society could exist.

The sociology of knowledge, therefore, must concern itself with the social construction of reality . . .

Different objects present themselves to consciousness as constituents of different spheres of reality. I recognize the fellow men I must deal with in the course of everyday life as pertaining to a reality quite different from the disembodied figures that appear in my dreams. The two sets of objects introduce quite different tensions into my consciousness and I am attentive to them in quite different ways. My consciousness, then, is capable of moving through different spheres of reality. Put differently, I am conscious of the world as consisting of multiple realities. As I move from one reality to another, I experience the transition as a kind of shock. This shock is to be understood as caused by the shift in attentiveness that the transition entails. Waking up from a dream illustrates this shift most simply.

Among the multiple realities there is one that presents itself as the reality *par excellence*. This is the reality of everyday life. Its privileged position entitles it to the designation of paramount reality. The tension of consciousness is highest in everyday life, that is, the latter imposes itself upon consciousness in the most massive, urgent and intense manner. It is impossible to ignore, difficult even to weaken in its imperative presence. Consequently, it forces me to be attentive to it in the fullest way. I experience everyday life in the state of being wide-awake. This wide-awake state of existing in and apprehending the reality of everyday life is taken by me to be normal and self-evident, that is, it constitutes my natural attitude.

I apprehend the reality of everyday life as an ordered reality. Its phenomena are prearranged in patterns that seem to be independent of my apprehension of them and that impose themselves upon the latter. The reality of everyday life appears already objectified, that is, constituted by an order of objects that have been designated *as* objects before my appearance on the scene. The language used in everyday life continuously provides me with the necessary objectifications and posits the order within which these make sense and within which everyday life has meaning for me. I live in a place that is geographically designated; I employ tools, from can-openers to sports cars, which are designated in the technical vocabulary of my society; I live within a web of human relationships, from my chess club to the United States of America, which are also ordered by means of vocabulary. In this manner language marks the coordinates of my life in society and fills that life with meaningful objects.

The reality of everyday life is organized around the 'here' of my body and the 'now' of my present. This 'here and now' is the focus of my attention to the reality of everyday life. What is 'here and now' presented to me in everyday life is the *realissimum* of my consciousness. The reality of everyday life is not, however, exhausted by these immediate presences, but embraces phenomena that are not present 'here and now'. This means that I experience everyday life in terms of differing degrees of closeness and remoteness, both spatially and temporally. Closest to me is the zone of everyday life that is directly accessible to my bodily manipulation. This zone contains the world within my reach, the world in which I act so as to modify its reality, or the world in which I work. In this world of working my consciousness is dominated by the pragmatic motive, that is, my attention to this world is mainly determined by what I am doing, have done or plan to do in it. In this way it is *my* world *par excellence*. I know, of course, that the reality of everyday life contains zones that are not accessible to me in this manner. But either I have no pragmatic interest in these zones or my interest in them is indirect in so far as they may be, potentially, manipulative zones for me. Typically, my interest in the far zones is less intense and certainly less urgent. I am intensely interested in the cluster of objects involved in my daily occupation – say, the world of the garage, if I am a mechanic. I am interested, though less directly, in what goes on in the testing laboratories of the automobile industry in Detroit – I am unlikely ever to be in one of these laboratories, but the work done there will eventually affect my everyday life. I may also be interested in what goes on at Cape Kennedy or in outer space, but this interest is a matter of private, 'leisure-time' choice rather than an urgent necessity of my everyday life . . .

The reality of everyday life further presents itself to me as an intersubjective world, a world that I share with others. This inter-subjectivity sharply differentiates everyday life from other realities of which I am conscious. I am alone in the world of my dreams, but I know that the world of everyday life is as real to others as it is to myself. Indeed, I cannot exist in everyday life without continually interacting and communicating with others. I know that my natural attitude to this world corresponds to the natural attitude of others, that they also comprehend the objectifications by which this world is ordered, that they also organize this world around the 'here and now' of *their* being in it and have projects for working in it. I also know, of course, that the others have a perspective on this common world that is not identical with mine. My 'here' is their 'there'. My 'now' does not fully overlap with theirs. All the same, I know that I live with them in a common world. Most importantly, I know that there is an ongoing correspondence between *my* meanings and *their* meanings in this world, that we share a common sense about its reality. The natural attitude is the attitude of common-sense consciousness precisely because it refers to a world that is common to many men. Common-sense knowledge is the knowledge I share with others in the normal, self-evident routines of everyday life . . .

Compared to the reality of everyday life, other realities appear as finite provinces of meaning, enclaves within the paramount reality marked by circumscribed meanings and modes of experience. The paramount reality envelops them on all sides, as it were, and consciousness always returns to the paramount reality as from an excursion. This is evident from the illustrations already given, as in the reality of dreams or that of theoretical thought. Similar 'commutations' take place between the world of everyday life and the world of play, both the playing of children and, even more sharply, of adults. The theatre provides an excellent illustration of such playing on the part of adults. The transition between realities is marked by the rising and falling of the curtain. As the curtain rises, the spectator is 'transported to another world', with its own meanings and an order that may or may not have much to do with the order of everyday life. As the curtain falls, the spectator 'returns to reality' that is, to the paramount reality of everyday life by comparison with which the reality presented on the stage now appears tenuous and ephemeral, however vivid the presentation may have been a few moments previously. Aesthetic and religious experience is rich in producing transitions of this kind, inasmuch as art and religion are endemic producers of finite provinces of meaning . . .

The most important experience of others taken place in the face-to-face situation, which is the prototypical case of social interaction. All other cases are derivatives of it.

In the face-to-face situation the other is appresented to me in a vivid present shared by both of us. I know that in the same vivid present I am appresented to him. My and his 'here and now' continuously impinge on each other as long as the face-to-face situation continues. As a result, there is a continuous interchange of my expressivity and his. I see him smile, then react to my frown by stopping the smile, then smiling again as I smile, and so on. Every expression of mine is oriented towards him and vice versa, and this continuous reciprocity of expressive acts is simultaneously available to both of us. This means that, in the face-to-face situation, the other's subjectivity is available to me through a maximum of symptoms. To be sure, I may misinterpret some of these symptoms. I may think that the other is smiling while in fact he is smirking. Nevertheless, no other form of social relating can reproduce the plenitude of symptoms of subjectivity present in the face-to-face situation. Only here is the other's subjectivity emphatically 'close'. All other forms of relating to the other are, in varying degrees, 'remote' . . .

A special but crucially important case of objectivation is signification, that is, the human production of signs. A sign may be distinguished from other objectivations by its explicit intention to serve as an index of subjective meanings . . .

Since everyday life is dominated by the pragmatic motive, recipe knowledge, that is, knowledge limited to pragmatic competence in routine performances, occupies a prominent place in the social stock of knowledge. For example, I use the telephone every day for specific pragmatic purposes of my own. I know how to do this. I also know what to do if my telephone fails to function – which does not mean that I know how to repair it, but that I know whom to call on for assistance. Similarly, I have recipe knowledge of the workings of human relationships . . . *Mutatis mutandis*, a large part of the social stock of knowledge consists of recipes for the mastery of routine problems. Typically, I have little interest in going beyond this pragmatically necessary knowledge as long as the problems can indeed be mastered thereby.

The social stock of knowledge differentiates reality by degrees of familiarity. It provides complex and detailed information concerning those sectors of everyday life with which I must frequently deal. It provides much more general and imprecise information on remoter sectors. Thus my knowledge of my own occupation and its world is very rich and specific, while I have only very sketchy knowledge of the occupational worlds of others . . .

One final point should be made here about the social distribution of knowledge. I encounter knowledge in everyday life as socially distributed, that is, as possessed differently by different individuals and types of individuals. I do not share my knowledge equally with all my fellowmen, and there may be some knowledge that I share with no one. I share my professional expertise with colleagues, but not with my family, and I may share with nobody my knowledge of how to cheat at cards. The social distribution of knowledge of certain elements of everyday reality can become highly complex and even confusing to the outsider. I not only do not possess the knowledge supposedly required to cure me of a physical ailment, I may even lack the knowledge of which one of a bewildering variety of medical specialists claims jurisdiction over what ails me. In such cases, I require not only the advice of experts, but the prior advice of experts on experts. The social distribution of knowledge thus begins with the simple fact that I do not know everything known to my fellow men, and vice versa, and culminates in exceedingly complex and esoteric systems of expertise. Knowledge of *how* the socially available stock of knowledge is distributed, at least in outline, is an important element of that same stock of knowledge. In everyday life I know, at least roughly, what I can hide from whom, whom I can turn to for information on what I do not know, and generally which types of individuals may be expected to have which types of knowledge.

Part Two
Methodology, Theory and Methods

The success of sociology can be judged by its capacity to produce empirically grounded explanations of aspects of social life. Other chapters in this book are largely devoted to chronicling some of sociology's successes. This chapter is about the research methods through which such successes are achieved. But before examining the methods themselves, it is important to reflect briefly upon the notion of explanation itself.

If everything that everyone did was entirely random, it would be impossible to explain any aspect of social life. This is because the essence of any explanation is the discovery (or imposition) of non-random patterns, or order, among the occurrences to be explained. The discipline of sociology is only possible because people act and interact in patterned ways. What empirical research in sociology seeks to do is to reveal these patterns.

For the purposes of exposition, sociologists' interests in explanatory patterns can be divided into three, although in practice these three interests are closely interrelated. First there is the question of what *sorts* of patterns sociologists should be looking for. Here, the merits and demerits of rival methodologies or perspectives have to be considered. Second, there is the question of *which* patterns exist. This is where rival theories or explanations are debated. Third, there is the question of *how to locate* the patterns. This is where discussions about appropriate methods and techniques of research take place.

Textbooks on sociological research methods focus primarily on the third question, but it is important that methods are not divorced from methodology and theory, because these provide the context within which methods are practised. They provide the overall agenda for research.

Many different methodologies have found favour with different sociologists, and they are described and named in a bewildering variety of ways by different writers. The question of what type of explanatory patterns the sociologist should seek is important when doing research, and to show this it will suffice to sketch two broad methodologies here, positivism and interpretivism.

Positivists take the view that the explanatory patterns are observable sequences of events. One type of event is seen to co-occur with or is caused by other types of event. Explanations are achieved when these regular co-occurrences are discovered and formulated in general propositions, usually referred to as laws in the positivist literature. For example, the discovery that the amount given to charity is related to being middle-aged and female, and having a high social status and income, can be used to explain why a particular 45-year-old woman barrister makes generous charitable donations. The aim of the positivist is to link up laws into an integrated theory of the area under study.

Interpretivists take the view that the explanatory patterns are shared meanings that make the world understandable to a group of people. The group members' actions and interactions make sense to each other because they are guided by a shared framework of interpretation, a common set of cultural rules. Explanations are achieved when the sociologist becomes familiar with the group's scheme of interpretation. For example, charitable giving within a particular group might be understood as one way its members establish their status in the group, as an alternative to conspicuous consumption.

Being aware of the methodology that informs a piece of research is important because it determines the basis on which rival theories are to be assessed. For example, within the positivist approach, rival theories differ over the factors they identify as co-occurring with (or causing) the event to be explained. Within the interpretivist approach, rival theories differ over the cultural rules they identify as guiding the group members' actions. And as between the positivist and interpretivist approaches, rival methodologists argue over the relative merits of 'explanations' – which depend on identifying laws – and 'understanding' – which depends on identifying actors' shared meanings. Rivalries between theories within perspectives can be settled by further empirical research to establish which patterns do exist and which theories are true. Rivalries between perspectives cannot be resolved by empirical research because they are about the types of pattern or explanation that are appropriate in sociology, which rest upon different assumptions about the nature of sociological knowledge.

An awareness of methodology and theory is important, then, because they identify the objectives of research: for example, to identify or test which factors are related to charitable giving – a positivist theory; or to learn the rules of status attribution in a particular group – an interpretivist theory. These important connections between methodology, theory and research methods are described more fully in Reading 7 by Halfpenny. Reading 8, by Bryman, illustrates how research conducted within different methodologies differs, by comparing two contrasting studies of deviance, one a piece of quantitative research, the other qualitative. As Bryman notes, quantitative and qualitative are sometimes treated as referring to competing *methodologies* and sometimes to alternative (or even complementary) research *techniques*, and writers often vacillate between these two views. This vacillation is another mark of the interrelationship between methodology, theory and method: they bundle together loosely into quantitative and qualitative research traditions in sociology.

Quantitative Research

Two readings outline the quantitative tradition. Abell (Reading 9) provides a succinct statement of the logic of quantitative inquiry (which he calls the model building perspective), beginning with units of study and concepts and working via measurement and variables towards an empirically grounded interrelated set of propositions or theory.

Hellevik (Reading 10) lucidly describes one way that quantitative data can be analysed to move up Abell's hierarchy of sophistication: from variables to propositions, and then to a set of causally related propositions. He starts with the data from a study of Norwegian court decisions which includes information about the variables social status, previous criminal record, and sentence received. He then crosstabulates severe and lenient sentence with high and low social status to produce a two–by–two table. The association between the variables is summarized very simply by calculating the difference between the percentage of high-status people who receive a severe sentence and the percentage of low-status people who receive a severe sentence. By then dividing the crosstabulation table into two, one for people with previous convictions and one for people without, the association between social status and sentence is revealed to differ depending on whether people have a criminal record or not. The attraction of this type of analysis is that it is immediately understandable and it does not involve the sort of complicated mathematical manipulations and statistical formulae that make so many people shy away from quantitative analysis. As Hellevik goes on to show, his tables can be further portrayed as simple causal diagrams that clarify what variables are at work in some social sphere, and how they fit together in explanatory patterns.

Qualitative Research

Two readings outline the qualitative tradition. Spradley (Reading 11) describes the logic of the qualitative tradition, where the goal is an ethnography: a description of the meanings that make up the culture of the people under study. As he emphasizes, this is not a matter only of observation, as in the quantitative tradition, but of inference, because the cultural rules through which people interpret their world are often tacit. As Malinowski stresses in the quotation at the end of the Spradley Reading, people do not formulate them explicitly for themselves or for the ethnographer. This theme is common in discussions of qualitative research. As William Foote Whyte says – reflecting on his participant observation of the 'Norton Street Gang' of Italian-American youths in Boston just before World War Two – the basis of his renowned *Street Corner Society* (1955):

As I spent time with the thirteen men, day after day, I became fascinated by the patterns of their activities and interactions ... I became aware that this informal group had a marked and stable structure of leadership and followership ... Only as a participant [was] I ... able to work out the structure of the group. If my information had been limited to personal interviews, this would not have been possible. When I asked one or another of them who their leader was – as I did from time to time – the answer was always the same: 'We have no leader. We are all equal.' (Whyte, 1984, p. 23).

Qualitative researchers or ethnographers seek to tease out from their data the meanings that guide and make sense of the actions of the people they are studying. Ethnographic research is a process of discovering what is happening in people's own terms. The procedures involved are less codified than those used in quantitative analysis: in effect, no more than a self-conscious and more explicit application of the social skills we all use in everyday life to order and pattern and therefore make understandable the actions of those around us.

In Reading 12, Lofland suggests a sixfold categorization of social affairs – acts, activities, meaning, participation, relationships, setting – as a tool for organizing and presenting ethnographies. But as he stresses, these categories are not immutable, merely a useful way of generating analytic questions with which to address the data. For example, what activities do the people under study see themselves as engaging in here? What phases or cycles do they see their activities passing through? Using these categories, Lofland sketches the analytic core of examples of qualitative research studies, showing how they provide a glimpse of the interpretive frameworks deployed by people to pattern their lives.

The issues covered in this short chapter are only some of the problems involved in doing sociological research. The main theme has been to show how methodologies, theories and methods are linked together in the different sociological research traditions, and to illustrate them briefly by reviewing the overall objectives and the analytic processes in two major traditions of empirical inquiry, the quantitative and qualitative. At least three important areas have had to be omitted. One is *research ethics*: who might be harmed by research, or feel harmed? A second is *statistics*: the tools for summarizing data and calculating precisely the extent to which findings about samples can be generalized to the populations from which they are drawn. The third area is *research techniques*: the varied procedures for collecting data, such as observation, participation, interviews, questionnaires and secondary sources, among others. There are many textbooks available, both elementary and more advanced, in all three of these areas; they should be consulted when doing research or evaluating the research of others.

References

WHYTE, W. F. (1955), *Street Corner Society: The Social Structure of an Italian Slum,* University of Chicago Press.

WHYTE, W. F. (1984), *Learning from the Field: A Guide from Experience,* Sage.

7   Peter Halfpenny

Positivist and Interpretivist Sociology

Extracts from Peter Halfpenny, *Principles of Method*, Longman, York, 1984, pp. 3–8.

Sociology is a pluralistic discipline, made up of a variety of different ideas of what constitutes data, explanation and theory. That is, sociology is characterized by different approaches, which almost have the status of subdisciplines. These different approaches are often described as frames of reference or perspectives or paradigms or orientations, and they are identified and defined differently by different authors. For my purposes here I will describe [two] broad types of approach, without making any claims that this is the only or best way to partition sociology, particularly for purposes other than mine, or that these [two] approaches embrace all varieties of sociology. I select the [two] I do because they are well-established research traditions with sharply contrasting aims in terms of the sociology they attempt to build.

Positivist Sociology

The first approach I call the positivist, although it could also be described as the empiricist or scientific approach. Positivist sociology is founded on the view that observable events in the social world are patterned in regular ways, so that one type of event regularly co-occurs with or is caused by the occurrence of another type of event. Positivist research revolves around discovering these patterned connections and describing them in laws. One way of establishing laws – the inductivist way – is to collect information on several observed variable characteristics of a number of individuals: that is, to measure their values on a number of variables, then to use the multivariate statistical techniques of correlation or regression to identify the existence and form of the co-variation relationships between the variables.

		father's social class	
		Registrar General's classes III, IV & V	Registrar General's classes I & II
pupil's examination result	above average	158	274
	below average	346	86

For example, one might collect information on a school's pupils' fathers' occupations and on the pupils' examination results, and on correlating these (that is, looking to see how their values vary together) discover that there is an identifiable though fairly weak positive relation between these two variables, such that the higher the father's occupational status the better the pupil's examination result tends to be. (A negative relation is one where the higher the value on the first variable the lower the value on the second.) The sort of table that might be constructed from the research data to provide evidence for this tendency statement or law is shown above.

In this joint frequency or contingency table, the independent or predictor variable of father's occupational status and the dependent or predicted variable of child's examination result (both dichotomized here for simplicity) co-vary weakly . . .

In passing, it might be noticed that correlation does not entail causation. The two variables might be correlated because one directly or indirectly causes the other, because the other directly or indirectly causes the one, or because both are directly or indirectly caused by a third variable. (The last case is called spurious or cosymptomatic correlation.) In other words, the evidence in the table above is compatible with all three of the following causal explanations:

(i)   father's occupational status causes child's examination performance

(ii)   child's examination performance causes father's occupational status

(iii) some other variable causes both father's occupational status and child's examination performance.

Although sophisticated statistical manipulation of research data can sometimes reduce the number of causal explanations compatible with the observed correlations, ultimately the choice between them is made in the light of what seems reasonable to the researcher, perhaps in the light of other research, or in terms of the obvious temporal order among the variables. For example, (ii) above might be excluded on the latter count because father's occupational status obviously occurs before child's examination result, and (i) might be preferred to (iii) on the basis of other research in this area.

A different way of establishing laws is to conjecture hypothetical relations between variables and then test these hypothetical laws by searching for evidence that might refute them. This is the hypothetico-deductive method made popular by the philosopher Karl Popper. Using it we might conjecture, for example, that school pupils' examination results would be directly related to the amount of homework they did, and then look to see if there are any good examinees who did very little homework. If there are, our conjecture is falsified and the hypothetical law must be modified or abandoned, whereas if there are not, we can accept the hypothesis, at least until such time as new evidence is found to refute it.

Both methods of establishing laws rely on being able to measure the individuals under study on the variables of interest, that is, on being able to assign unambiguously each individual a single value on each variable. Measurement, then, is an important issue within positivist research, although it does not necessarily involve giving individuals numerical values on the variables . . .

The ultimate aim of the positivist sociologist is to be able to link up a set of laws into an integrated theory about the area under research. For example, the laws relating father's occupation and hours of homework to examination results might be integrated into a theory of educational performance, along with laws about the relations between, say, types of school, parental interest in schoolwork, children's occupational aspirations and their examination results. Positivist theories are often presented in box and arrow diagrams, called causal models, where the boxes contain the variables and the linking arrows represent the relations between the variables that have been induced from the data or conjectured and not falsified by the research. A theory of educational performance might look something like [Figure 1].

A theory is considered successful when sufficient laws have been drawn into it to explain a substantial amount of the variation in the dependent variable, which in this case is examination performance

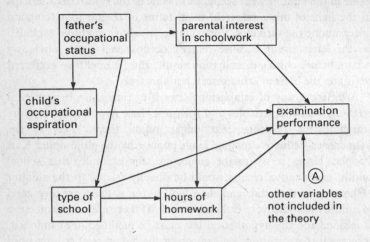

Figure 1

among pupils of the school. In other words, relatively little of the variation in examination performance should remain to be explained by independent variables that are not included in the theory – arrow Ⓐ in the box and arrow diagram above.

In summary, positivists believe that the flux of events in the social world occurs in observable patterns, and they seek to capture those patterns in laws relating variables and theories relating laws. Positivist research revolves around measuring the characteristics of the units under study, that is, describing each characteristic in terms of one of the sets of values that constitute a variable, and establishing whether and how variables co-vary using the techniques of correlation and regression . . .

Interpretivist Sociology

The approach I call the interpretivist might also be called the hermeneutic or phenomenological or interactionist approach. Interpretivist sociology is founded on the view that human beings interpret the world they inhabit, so that the social world is pervaded with meanings in a way that the natural world is not. Although often referred to as subjective meanings, these interpretations are not simply what are in the minds of the people under study. They are not individual, idiosyncratic motives or reasons thought of as the antecedents of actions, but shared meanings that make the social world understandable in the way that it is for a group of people. It is on the basis of these interpretations that social life – actions and interactions – are patterned. Interpretivist research revolves around discovering the shared patterns of meanings – the schemes of interpretation or frameworks of understanding – that constitute the culture of the people under study. This involves grasping the meanings of their actions and interactions in terms that are appropriate within their own culture, and identifying the cultural rules or norms that guide them in patterning their actions, that is, in orienting their actions to the actions of others and interacting competently with the other members of their culture. For example, wanting to understand a group of school pupils described by the staff as anti-school, one would attempt to grasp what their actions mean to them, where they draw the boundaries around their group, and what rules or schemes of interpretation pattern their lives. The pupils' understandings of their group's way of life are likely to be quite different to those of outsiders, such as the school staff who use their own, staff frame of reference to interpret the pupils' actions. An action by a pupil – such as passing round sweets in class – which for her demonstrates the boundaries of her group and her loyalty to it, might be interpreted as insubordination according to the rules of the staff culture.

The rules that make up a framework of understanding or culture are not laws in the positivist sense. They do not determine behaviour but enable us to understand what the actions are. They are normally invisible or taken for granted in everyday social intercourse. It is, moreover, difficult or perhaps impossible to make the rules explicit, especially to an extent that would enable us to predict actions in any detail with certainty. Nevertheless, even though we cannot articulate the rules, we can understand the practicalities of their use sufficiently for us to interact successfully. For example, despite being unable to state explicitly the complete set of rules that guide us in the exchange of polite greetings in our culture, most of us, most of the time, can greet people in a socially appropriate way.

Since understanding cannot be demonstrated by producing an

explicit set of rules or a fully articulated scheme of interpretation, but instead is indicated by the researcher's ability to interact with the people under study with the competence of a native member, then research activity centres around learning to comprehend the people's culture. The positivists' problems of measurement are, in interpretivist research, replaced by problems of interpretation. There are a number of these problems. The first raises the issue of how researchers are to gain practical accomplishment in the alien cultures they wish to study and how they will interpret the native members' conduct correctly. This is obviously more difficult the greater the distance between your own culture and the one you wish to study. Nevertheless, it is possible, though your initial social incompetence might be embarrassing or amusing. The process is analogous to learning a second language the conversational way, or translating between one language and another. You hypothesize that the people you are investigating follow a particular rule to the effect that in a certain context or set of circumstances they say X or do Y. If they don't, or if you do and it is obviously interactionally inappropriate, then you revise your rule, and proceed under the revised rule until it too fails, when further revisions are invoked. So rules are formulated and reformulated, that is, contexts and conduct are described and redescribed, interpreted and reinterpreted, until your interaction with the people proceeds smoothly. Of course, detailing the procedure this way makes it appear more explicit and orderly than it is. In practice it is more immediate, more intuitive and fumbling, just as conversing in a foreign language is until you become a competent speaker in it. Because of this, it is difficult to give an example of the process without it seeming overly mechanical. But risking this, consider researching the so-called anti-school group of pupils, and finding that they enjoy playing football together and play very well. You might hypothesize that a rule of their group culture is that given any opportunity they will play football, and so you would expect them to shine on the field in the games period. But then you observe that they avoid games just as much as they avoid any other lesson. You might then reformulate your hypothetical rule: given any opportunity where their skills reflect well on the group and do not support official school aims, they will play football. Now you understand what football means to them, for it is another way of reinforcing the group's identity as opposed to the official or staff-defined identity of a good pupil . . .

A second problem of interpretation endemic in research in the interpretivist approach concerns cultural relativism. Under an extreme version of cultural relativism that asserted that there were no points of contact between different cultures, there could be no solution to the first problem of interpretation discussed above; it would be impossible to become a competent member of cultures other than our own. Yet both our common humanity and all the evidence from our everyday lives that we do understand people who interpret the world quite differently from us serve to deny such an extreme relativism. But that still leaves a weaker form of cultural relativism, where the problem is one of comparing different cultures. How are we able to say that the understandings of the world that constitute one culture are better or are worse than those that make up some alternative culture? If interpretivist sociology aims to understand cultures in their own terms, how can the meanings of one be compared with the interpretations of another? This problem seems minor when the difference is between calling an action insubordination or a demonstration of group solidarity (although even here the two descriptions will have different consequences for the actor involved). However, the import of the issue becomes greater when the difference is between modern natural science and magic, or one moral code and another. Such differences have enormous practical consequences. Should one treat a sick person by modern scientific medical methods or by magic? Should one punish someone under one moral code (for example, the Official Secrets Act) or reward them under another which interprets that same action differently (for example, by a rule recommending freedom of information)? Despite an enormous amount of argument, this issue of cultural relativism remains unsolved, with some maintaining that there is a supra-cultural standard against which to judge the different interpretations that constitute different cultures and others denying this.

A third problem of interpretation concerns conveying the results of interpretivist research – one's practical accomplishment in a new culture – to an audience. How is it possible to demonstrate to other people who have not had contact with a particular culture, that you have a sufficient comprehension of its rules to be able to interact competently with its native members? (By way of analogy, think of the difficulty of persuading someone who has never heard Italian that you have now mastered that language.) This problem is usually solved by offering detailed descriptions of the activities of the people studied, including verbatim accounts of their talk, and selecting events that serve as key illustrations of their interpretations, especially where these differ from the audience's. It can also help to go chronologically, through, the researcher's gradual process of entering the culture, or describe the people's own changing understandings as they pass along a career path, such as training to be a nurse, which involves their learning a new culture themselves. Done skilfully, these help the audience to follow the researcher or trainees into the new culture.

In summary, interpretivists believe that the flux of social life is patterned on the basis of the interpretations people make of their world, and they seek to understand the patterns in terms of the schemes of interpretation or shared meanings that constitute the culture of the people under investigation. Interpretivist research revolves around learning the cultural rules that make up a scheme of interpretation.

8 A. Bryman

Quantity and Quality in Social Research

Excerpts from A. Bryman, *Quantity and Quality in Social Research*, Unwin Hyman, 1988, pp. 5–10.

What are 'quantitative research' and 'qualitative research'? In some treatments they are viewed as competing views about the ways in which social reality ought to be studied ... essentially divergent clusters of epistemological assumptions ... of what should pass as warrantable knowledge about the social world. For other writers, quantitative and qualitative research are simply denotations of different ways of conducting social investigations and which may be conceived of as being appropriate to different kinds of research question and even as capable of being integrated. When this second view is taken, they are more or less simply different approaches to data collection, so that preferences for one or the other or some hybrid approach are based on technical issues. In this view, the prime consideration is that of dovetailing the appropriate technique to a particular research question. Many writers ... vacillate between these two levels of analysis ...

A Comparison of Two Studies

Two studies which exemplify the contrasting orientations that lie behind the quantitative and qualitative traditions in social research ... are Hirschi's (1969) investigation of delinquency and Adler's (1985) research on drug dealers. These monographs may be taken as reasonably representative of the quantitative and qualitative traditions of social research respectively.

Hirschi's Study of the Causes of Delinquency

Hirschi's examination of delinquency fits squarely with what is usually taken to be a natural science approach to the study of social reality. This predilection is evident in an earlier work, in which he expressed his preference for quantitative research: 'because quantitative data can be analysed statistically, it is possible to examine complicated theoretical problems, such as the relative importance of many causes of delinquency, far more powerfully than with the verbal analysis of qualitative data' (Hirschi and Selvin, 1973, p. xii). In *Causes of Delinquency*, Hirschi (1969) was concerned to test the relative validity of three contrasting theories of the etiology of delinquency; he was particularly interested in how well his own 'social control' theory – which posits that delinquent acts occur when 'an individual's bond to society is weak or broken' (p. 16) – held up to empirical testing. He used a social survey in order to achieve his aims. As 'subjects' he randomly selected a sample of 5,545 school children in an area of California near San Francisco. Great care was taken in the selection of the sample to ensure that it adequately represented the range of schools in the area, as well as the gender and race distribution of the children in the population. The bulk of the data was collected by a self-administered questionnaire which was completed by the students. In addition to questions relating to social background, the questionnaire comprised a great many questions designed to tap the extent to which children were committed or attached to the school, to the family, and to conventional lines of action, in order to test the social control theory which had been formulated. The questionnaire also contained questions designed to gauge the extent of each child's involvement in delinquent activities. Further data were gleaned from other sources, such as information on each child's performance in connection with academic achievement tests from school records.

Hirschi's basic orientation to the research process is clear: one needs to formulate some explicit propositions about the topic to be investigated and design the research in advance specifically in order to answer the research problem. There is a clear concern to be able to demonstrate that the sample is representative of a wider population of school children, though the question of the representativeness of the region in which the research is located is given scant attention. The questionnaire is taken to comprise a battery of questions which 'measure' the main concepts involved (e.g. attachment to society); each question (either on its own or in conjunction with other questions to form an index) is treated as a variable which can be related to other questions/variables in order to estimate relationships among the variables which are relevant to the theories being tested. For example, Hirschi presents a contingency table which shows a clear inverse relationship between an index of 'intimacy of communication between parent and child' (derived from answers to two questions) and the number of self-reported acts of delinquency (p. 91). But Hirschi is rarely content to leave his data analysis simply at the level of estimates of co-variation or correlation among the variables concerned. Much of the time he is concerned to extricate the causal relationships among his variables. Thus, at the end of a chapter on attachments to school, he writes: 'The causal chain runs from academic incompetence to poor school performance to disliking of school to rejection of the school's authority to the commission of delinquent acts' (p. 132). These causal paths are winkled out by multivariate analysis which allows the analyst to sort out the direct and indirect effects by controlling for intervening variables and the like.

In the end, Hirschi finds that none of the three theories of delinquency emerges totally unscathed from the empirical interrogation to which they were submitted. For example, the control theory seems to neglect the role of delinquent friends which his data suggest has considerable importance ...

Adler's Study of Upper-Level Drug Dealers

Adler (1985) and her husband took up residence in California in order to attend graduate school in sociology. They soon made friends with a close neighbour (Dave, a pseudonym), who, it transpired, was a drug dealer. He was not a small 'pusher' of drugs who was trying to provide funds for his own habit, but someone who dealt in vast quantities and who received huge sums of money in exchange, that is an 'upper-level' drug dealer. They ... infiltrate[d] Dave's group of associates in order to carry out a study of such dealers, who are normally highly inaccessible. The nature of Adler's approach to data collection can be gleaned from the following passage:

With my husband as a research partner, I spent six years in the field (from 1974 to 1980) engaged in daily participant observation with members of this dealing and smuggling community. Although I did not deal, myself, I participated in many of their activities, partying with them, attending social gatherings, traveling with them, and watching them plan and execute their business activities ... In addition to observing and conversing casually with these dealers and smugglers, I conducted in-depth, taped interviews, and cross-checked my observations and their accounts against further sources of data whenever possible. After leaving the field, I continued to conduct follow-up interviews during periodic visits to the community until 1983. (Adler, pp. 1–2)

Adler's broad orientation is to focus on the 'subjective understanding of how people live, feel, think, and act' (p. 2) and so 'to understand the world from their perspectives' (p. 11). She sees her work as 'an ethnographic description and analysis of a deviant social scene' (p. 2).

Adler's adoption of a perspective which emphasizes the way in which the people being studied understand and interpret their social reality is one of the most central motifs of the qualitative approach. Through this perspective Adler shows that the views of drug dealing that are often presented in the literature do not fully correspond to the dealers' own perceptions. For example, she argues that the suggestion that drug dealing is simply a form of occupation or business is incongruent with dealers' views; although drug dealing has some of the trappings of occupations in business firms, such as a rational organization, the dealers do not view what they do as just another occupation. Rather, she suggests that they are motivated by a quest for the fun and pleasure which are the products of involvement in the world of upper-level drug dealing. Adler portrays the drug dealers she studied as hedonistic: the copious drugs and their associated pleasures, the ability to afford vast numbers of material possessions, the availability of many sexual partners, considerable freedom and status, and so on, constitute the sources of their motivation. The general orientation of the dealers to the present and their ability to fulfil numerous desires for both experiences and possessions more or less immediately deters many from leaving the world of drug dealing while attracting many newcomers to it.

Adler's monograph is punctuated with many verbatim quotations from interviews and conversations which illustrate many of her points. For example, in characterizing the twin themes of hedonism and abundant money, she quotes a dealer:

'At the height of my dealing I was making at least 10 grand a month profit, even after all my partying. When you have too much money you always have to have something to spend it on. I used to run into the stores every day to find \$50, \$60 shirts to buy because I didn't know what else to do with the money, there was so much.' (Adler, p. 86)

Thus Adler's monograph combines a detailed description of the activities of upper-level drug dealers and an account of their hedonistic life-style and subculture. She sees her subjects as having chosen to enter this deviant world in order to gratify the pleasures they craved and argues that this aspect of entry into certain deviant milieux has received insufficient attention in the literature.

Here then are two highly contrasting studies. They are both about deviance . . . But in style and approach to social research they are very different. Hirschi seeks to test the validity of theories; Adler seems to let her subjects form her focal concerns while retaining an awareness of the literature on deviance and drug use. Hirschi's sample is carefully chosen to reflect the characteristics of the population of school children in the region; Adler's 'sample' is determined by whom she meets and is put into contact with during the course of her field-work. Thus Hirschi's sample is pre-defined at the outset of his research and all of the children received roughly the same amount of attention in that they all fill out the same questionnaire; Adler's sample is constantly shifting and her research entails different degrees of association with each person. Hirschi's research is highly defined at the outset and his questionnaire reflects his concerns; Adler uses a much less standardized approach, relying on observations, conversations, and some informal interviewing. Hirschi's results and analysis are in the form of causal propositions; much of Adler's account is descriptive and is concerned with the dealers' perceptions of their life-style. Hirschi's results reflect the sorts of issue that he thought would be important to the study of delinquency at the outset of the research; Adler's findings reflect what her subjects deem to be important about their lives. The bulk of Hirschi's results is in the form of tables; Adler's results are in the form of quotations and detailed descriptions.

The list of contrasts could go further, but these are some of the chief elements. But what is the status of these two studies, and more particularly of the comparison between them, in terms of the question of whether quantitative and qualitative research reflect different philosophical positions? Perhaps we can fruitfully regard Hirschi's work as reflecting a concern to follow the methods and procedures [claimed by positivists to be those] of the natural sciences, and that his concern with variables, causality, and so on, are symptoms of this predilection; Adler's research could then be viewed as indicative of an approach that ... prefers instead to ground investigations in people's own understandings of social reality, as perspectives like phenomenology are taken to imply ... Alternatively, we may prefer to see these two researchers as being concerned with different facets of deviant activity – Hirschi with causes, Adler with life-style – and as having tailored their methods of data collection and approaches to data analysis accordingly ... This second view suggests that quantitative and qualitative research are different ways of conducting research and that the choice between them should be made in terms of their appropriateness in answering particular research questions. According to the second view, the choice between quantitative and qualitative research is a technical decision.

References

ADLER, P. A. (1985), *Wheeling and Dealing: An Ethnography of an Upper-Level Drug Dealing and Smuggling Community*, Columbia University Press, New York.

HIRSCHI, T. (1969), *Causes of Delinquency*, University of California Press.

HIRSCHI, T. and SELVIN, H. C. (1973), *Principles of Survey Analysis*, Free Press, New York.

9 Peter Abell

The Model Building Perspective

Excerpts from Peter Abell, *Model Building in Sociology*, Schocken, New York, 1971, pp. 1, 4–7.

It is a truism, perhaps barely worth stating, that in our everyday life we attempt to describe and explain the world around us in terms of *concepts*; this is true both of the physical and social worlds. Science also uses concepts – sometimes those we are all familiar with, sometimes not – but science is also characterized by a systematic endeavour to relate these concepts into sets of interrelated propositions; an endeavour which, for the want of a better expression, I will term model building . . .

In this essay, I want to outline some of the logical features of a model building perspective in sociology. I purposely call it a perspective for it is only one among many other markedly different perspectives in the discipline. This particular perspective is, of course, much under-developed in contemporary sociology but the advances we all look for, particularly in theoretical sociology, can surely only come when we recognize that it is not sufficient merely to spin more and more precisely articulated theoretical concepts; rather we must embed our concepts in models which show how they are related, and how the models represent or generate that complicated entity which we all know as social reality . . .

The Hierarchy of Scientific Sophistication

We may start our inquiries with what I term the *hierarchy of scientific sophistication* (Figure 1) which gives us some idea of the complexity of the processes we have to go through in erecting sociological models.

The most fundamental decision that has to be faced at the outset of any sociological investigation is the specification of the *units of analysis* – for example people, social groups, organizations, roles, etc. Perhaps our analysis may involve more than one type of unit; for instance, both organizations and roles or people in the organizations may be involved, in which case our analysis is correspondingly more complex. It is fairly evident that a great deal of sociology is concerned with situations where, as it were, we have to consider differing types of units of analysis. A most common enterprise is to explain a person's or role incumbent's behaviour in terms of his social structural environment, which is perhaps a complex institutional or organizational setting. So we must expect when building models of human behaviour to jump back and forth between different units of analysis . . .

The basic exploratory device of the sociologist is the *concept*; for example, group cohesion, group conflict, rates of suicide, alienation, and so on. Concepts apply to . . . units of analysis – in the broadest sense they are properties of, or relations between, units of analysis. They are thus the basic descriptive categories we employ in our explorations of the social world . . .

The next stage in sophistication is to obtain *measures* of concepts by converting them into *variables*. This is done by assigning a range of *values* to the concepts . . . In Figure 1, then, we can speak of 'degrees' of inter-group conflict, etc. The process whereby values are assigned to concepts is known as measurement and in the social sciences it is often referred to as the *problem* of measurement, because with many concepts one encounters rather acute difficulties in obtaining measures (i.e. variables). Sociological concepts do not very readily lend themselves to measurement, but we may note here that when speaking of measurement in sociology we do not confine ourselves to commonsense ideas about measurement; using real numbers and their properties is only part of the story.

Once our concepts have been measured the next step is to relate them, as variables, in *propositions*. For example, in Figure 1, the proposition is that group cohesion and inter-group conflict are related. The proposition states that increases in one variable *lead to* increases in another, which seems to imply some notion of causality; that is, a causal connection between the variables. Clearly any proposition must contain some sort of connective relating its constituent variables and we . . . have to pay a great deal of attention to their nature and form . . . It may be noted that a proposition contains two concepts or variables and some sort of connective.

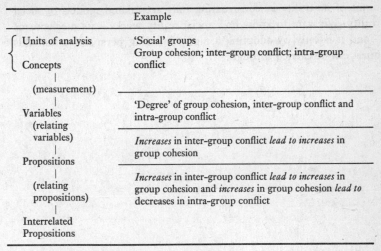

	Example
Units of analysis	'Social' groups
Concepts	Group cohesion; inter-group conflict; intra-group conflict
(measurement)	
Variables (relating variables)	'Degree' of group cohesion, inter-group conflict and intra-group conflict
Propositions	*Increases* in inter-group conflict *lead to increases* in group cohesion
(relating propositions)	*Increases* in inter-group conflict *lead to increases* in group cohesion and *increases* in group cohesion *lead to* decreases in intra-group conflict
Interrelated Propositions	

Figure 1. The Hierarchy of Scientific Sophistication

The next stage in the hierarchy is to try to obtain *interrelated propositions* and, as our example (Figure 1) indicates, one of the most obvious ways of accomplishing this is to consider two propositions with one common variable – 'group cohesion' in this case. This, however, is only one way and very much the simplest. It is really at this point that the idea of a *model* enters. For models of sociological phenomena are nothing more and nothing less than a complex set of interrelated propositions. Many people speak of multivariate propositions, but I prefer to limit the word 'proposition' to the case where only two variables are related and speak of models when more than two variables are involved . . .

It is true to say that, though much contemporary sociological activity is concerned with coining concepts and also converting them into variables with a view to testing isolated propositions, very little indeed goes beyond this. Theories comprising sets of interrelated propositions are . . . relatively rare in sociology, but in terms of the more demanding criterion of scientific activity, it is only when we arrive at this level of analysis that we can really start saying we have anything approaching a theory. Much of what goes for sociological theory is simply a quest for fruitful theoretical and observational concepts . . . But its fruitfulness can ultimately only be settled in terms of its utility in constructing fully articulated models of social reality. We want to know how social reality works – its mechanisms – and it is only by adopting a model building perspective that this quest can be carried through.

10   O. Hellevik

Crosstabulation in Causal Analysis

Excerpts from O. Hellevik, *Introduction to Causal Analysis: Exploring Survey Data by Crosstabulation*, Norwegian University Press, Oslo, 1988, pp. 1–12.

Quantitative Analysis, or What Difference Does a Difference Make?

As individuals we may often find ourselves preoccupied with questions like 'will my university training enhance my chances of getting a well-paid job?', or 'does the fact that I'm a woman affect my political career?' . . .

To answer questions like these a social scientist will systematically collect for a set of individuals information on the properties where they may differ . . .: data showing which values the units have on the relevant variables. A *unit* is the object under study (a person, an organization, a book). A *variable* (for instance, party choice) is a property where the units may take on different characteristics called *values* (Democrat or Republican; Labour, Liberal, or Conservative; or whatever the alternatives are in the country we are considering).

As an illustration of such a research enterprise, we shall use a study of court decisions in a district of Norway [by Aubert] . . . Looking at all defendants in criminal cases for a ten-year period the researchers in each case recorded the occupation and income of the defendant, whether he had previously been convicted, the nature of the offence for which he was tried, and so on.

The information thus collected can be presented as a *data matrix*, where the units (defendants) are listed along the side of the matrix and the variables at the top. In each cell the value that the actual unit has on the variable in question is entered, as shown in Table 1. This (fictitious) data matrix tells us that the first defendant is a white-collar worker with a clean record on trial for embezzlement.

One purpose of compiling such a data matrix is to study the

Table 1. *Data matrix*

	Variables						
Units	Occu-pation	Income	Previous convictions	Offence	Verdict	Sentence	...
Defendant 1	White collar	50,000	None	Embez-zlement	Guilty	Suspended...	
Defendant 2	Out of work	3,000	Three	Larceny	Guilty	6 months' jail	...
Defendant 3	Blue collar	20,000	None	Drunk driving	Not guilty	–	...
.	.	.	.	.	.	.	...
.	.	.	.	.	.	.	...

relationships between the variables, whether a certain value on one variable tends to be combined with specific values on others. Are, for instance, defendants who differ with regard to previous convictions given different sentences by the courts? In a *quantitative analysis* this question is answered by counting how often the various combinations of values on the variables occur in the data matrix. If the matrix is of a moderate size, this may be done with the help of paper and pencil, but usually the information in the data matrix is fed into a computer which takes care of the counting.

The set of units whose value combinations we are counting may consist of all units we are interested in making statements about, the entire *population* of units. Or it may constitute a selection of units from this population, a *sample*. To obtain comparable information about the units their values on the various variables are *measured* in an accurately specified way. As the variables in the data matrix exemplify, the measurement procedures range from the quite primitive to the very elaborate. In some cases measurement implies nothing more than assigning values to the units telling us which are similar and which different with regard to the variable in question (the offence variable). Nothing is said about which is higher or stronger (ranking), or about *how* different (distance). But measurement may also imply locating the units on a measurement scale where distances can be expressed by means of a unit of measurement (the income variable).

For the last kind of variables, which may be called *metric* variables, very sophisticated statistical techniques may be used to analyse what relationships exist between variables in the data matrix. In many fields of social science, however, most variables can only be measured in the more primitive sense of the word. For these *non-metric* variables, the arsenal of statistical techniques has been more restricted. Analysis by means of percentage tables used to be the most common procedure . . .

This [discussion] deals . . . with quantitative analysis of relationships between non-metric variables (also called categorical or attribute variables, or variables with nominal or ordinal levels of measurement). The analysis is carried out on the basis of theoretical assumptions concerning the causal relations between the variables, [and can be] expressed by means of diagrams where the postulated influences are depicted as arrows pointing from cause to effect variable[, as in Tables 3 and 4 below] . . .

[As] a brief example of what is meant by causal analysis by means of crosstabulations . . . we shall take an ordinary percentage table analysis, and then proceed to show how the analysis may be carried further by adopting an explicit causal framework.

Crosstabulations and Differences in Proportions

In Table 2 a selection from the data matrix of the study of Norwegian court decisions is given. The units are the 216 men who were convicted of larceny, and the variables social status (a composite measure based on occupation and income), criminal record (whether they had been previously convicted or not) and the severity of the sentence they received. To save space each single defendant has not been separately listed. Instead the matrix has been contracted by grouping together units with similar value combinations. The number of units in each group is listed to the right of the matrix.

How often is a convicted thief sent to prison? By counting the occurrences of the value 'severe sentence' we find the number to be 139. A more lenient reaction – fine or suspended sentence – occurs in 77 cases (Table 3). These are the *absolute frequencies* for the two values of the sentence variable. By dividing each of the frequencies with their sum, and multiplying by 100, we find their relative share of the total number of units expressed as a *percentage*. If we omit

Table 2. *Data matrix for men convicted of larceny (see Aubert 1964: 138).*

	Variables			Frequency
Units	Social status	Record	Sentence	(No. of units)
Defendant 1 . . . 25	High	Criminal	Severe	25
Defendant 26 . . . 40	High	Criminal	Lenient	15
Defendant 41, 42	High	Clean	Severe	2
Defendant 43 . . . 64	High	Clean	Lenient	22
Defendant 65 . . . 159	Low	Criminal	Severe	95
Defendant 160 . . . 181	Low	Criminal	Lenient	22
Defendant 182 . . . 198	Low	Clean	Severe	17
Defendant 199 . . . 216	Low	Clean	Lenient	18

Social status: composite measure based on occupation and income.
Severe sentence: jail or detention in institution.
Lenient: fine or suspended sentence.

multiplying by 100, we get the corresponding *proportion*. While the absolute figure of 139 in itself conveys little information, the proportion of 0.64 immediately tells us that just below two-thirds of all defendants were sentenced to imprisonment.

A proportion may be interpreted as the *probability* that a unit from our data matrix will have the value in question. If we randomly draw units from the matrix, the probability that a given defendant will have received a severe sentence is defined as the long-run proportion of times that this result occurs. Probabilities vary between 0 and 1, between certainty that a result will *not* occur and certainty that it *will*. If none of the defendants in our data matrix had been severely sentenced, the probability of drawing one with this value would obviously be 0. If all have been severely sentenced, the corresponding probability would be 1.

Usually calculation of univariate distributions is just the first step in an analysis, an introduction to the study of relationships between variables. Suppose that we – as were the researchers who carried out this project – are interested in the relationship between social status and sentence. Does the probability of being given a jail sentence differ between high-status and low-status defendants? To answer this question we count how often the four combinations of values on these two variables occur in the data matrix (Table 4).

Table 4 is a *bivariate crosstabulation*. The values of the variables are listed horizontally or vertically, rendering a matrix where the number of occurrences for each value combination may be entered.

Table 3. *Univariate Frequency Distribution: Severity of Sentence*

Data matrix			Frequencies			Univariate frequency distribution			
Status	Record	Sentence	All	Se	Le				
Hi	Cr	Se	25	25		Sentence	Absolute frequencies	Percentages	Proportions
Hi	Cr	Le	15		15				
Hi	Cl	Se	2	2					
Hi	Cl	Le	22		22				
Lo	Cr	Se	95	95		Severe	139	64	0·64
Lo	Cr	Le	22		22	Lenient	77	36	0·36
Lo	Cl	Se	17	17					
Lo	Cl	Le	18		18	Sum	216	100	1·00
				139	77				

Table 4. *Bivariate Frequency Distribution: Status and Sentence*

Data matrix				Frequencies			
Status	Record	Sentence		Se Hi	Le Hi	Se Lo	Le Lo
Hi	Cr	Se	25	25			
Hi	Cr	Le	15		15		
Hi	Cl	Se	2	2			
Hi	Cl	Le	22		22		
Lo	Cr	Se	95			95	
Lo	Cr	Le	22				22
Lo	Cl	Se	17			17	
Lo	Cl	Le	18				18
				27	37	112	40

Absolute frequencies				Proportions		
	Social status			Social status		
Sentence	High	Low	Sum	High	Low	Differences
Severe	27	112	139	0·42	0·74	−0·32
Lenient	37	40	77	0·58	0·26	0·32
Sum	64	152	216	1·00	1·00	0·00

The two variables have different roles in the analysis. Social status, which is the characteristic used to sort the units into groups we want to compare, is referred to as the *independent variable*. The comparison is made with regard to what kind of sentence the defendants receive, making sentence the *dependent variable*. The task is made easier by using relative frequencies, since differences in the size of the groups mean that the absolute figures cannot be directly compared.

Looking at Table 4 we see that a higher proportion of offenders with low status than with high status are sent to jail. As a measure of the degree of *statistical association* between the two variables, we may calculate the difference between the proportion having a certain value on the dependent variable within each of the two groups defined by the independent variable. The *difference in proportions* in our case is 0·32, showing that the probability of a severe or lenient sentence is clearly different depending on which group we are considering, high-status or low-status defendants.

To be more specific, it is a high social status which means a lower probability of being sent to jail. If we decide to define a severe sentence as the 'high' value on this variable . . . we may say that the relationship between the two variables is a *negative* one. Having a high value on the independent variable goes together with a low probability, comparatively speaking, of having the high value on the dependent variable.

If the value on the independent variable made no difference for the probability of a severe sentence, that is, if the difference in proportions had been zero, we say that there is no statistical association between the variables. The association reaches it maximum when the probability of a severe sentence is 0 in one group and 1 in the other, that is, when the difference in proportions equals 1 (or −1).

Returning to the data matrix we may also be interested in whether a clean or criminal record makes any difference for the chances of a severe sentence. In Table 5 a bivariate analysis similar to the one above is carried out with record as independent and sentence as dependent variable. Defining a criminal record as the high value we find a *positive* association between the two variables of 0·44. The difference in the probability of a severe punishment turns out to be somewhat greater when we compare groups with different records than is the case when we differentiate according to social status.

Some crosstabular analyses do not move beyond studying bivariate relationships. If we suspect, however, that the independent variables may be associated between themselves, a multivariate analysis is in order. We may, for instance, wonder if the difference between high- and low-status defendants with regard to punishment has something

Table 5. *Bivariate Frequency Distribution: Record and Sentence*

Data matrix				Frequencies			
Status	Record	Sentence		Cr Se	Cr Le	Cl Se	Cl Le
Hi	Cr	Se	25	25			
Hi	Cr	Le	15		15		
Hi	Cl	Se	2			2	
Hi	Cl	Le	22				
Lo	Cr	Se	95	95			22
Lo	Cr	Le	22		22		
Lo	Cl	Se	17			17	
Lo	Cl	Le	18				18
				120	37	19	40

Absolute frequencies				Proportions		
	Criminal record			Criminal record		
Sentence	Criminal	Clean	Sum	Criminal	Clean	Differences
Severe	120	19	139	0·76	0·32	0·44
Lenient	37	40	77	0·24	0·68	−0·44
Sum	157	59	216	1·00	1·00	0·00

to do with differences between the two groups when it comes to prior conflicts with the law. If we compare high- and low-status defendants who all have the same value on the record variable, either clean or criminal, perhaps we would find that they are similar with regard to the risk of a severe sentence? To see whether this is actually the case or not we set up a *trivariate table*, with sentence as the dependent variable, and social status and record as independent variables (Table 6).

Comparing the four groups we get by combining values on the two independent variables we find marked differences in the probability of a severe sentence. Worst off are low-status defendants with a criminal past, where the proportion sent to jail is 0·81. At the other extreme we find high-status defendants with a clean record, where the risk of a jail sentence is as low as 0·08. The remaining groups fall somewhere in between these two.

We now turn our attention to the question of what each of the independent variables contributes to the variation between the groups. To assess the association between social status and sentence

Table 6. *Trivariate Frequency Distribution: Status, Record and Sentence*

Data matrix			Frequencies
Status	Record	Sentence	
Hi	Cr	Se	25
Hi	Cr	Le	15
Hi	Cl	Se	2
Hi	Cl	Le	22
Lo	Cr	Se	95
Lo	Cr	Le	22
Lo	Cl	Se	17
Lo	Cl	Le	18

Absolute frequencies				Proportions			
Social status	High		Low		High		Low	
Record	Criminal	Clean	Criminal	Clean	Criminal	Clean	Criminal	Clean
Sentence								
Severe	25	2	95	17	0·63	0·08	0·81	0·49
Lenient	15	22	22	18	0·37	0·92	0·09	0·51
Sum	40	24	117	35	1·00	1·00	1·00	1·00

we this time must calculate *two* differences in proportions, between high- and low-status defendants who have a clean record, and likewise for defendants with a criminal record. Record here functions as a *control variable*, whose value is kept *constant* each time we calculate the association between status and sentence.

Among defendants with a clean record, we find that a high status decreases the probability of a jail sentence with 0·41 compared with low status, while the corresponding figure is 0·18 among defendants with a criminal record. These figures represent the *partial associations* between status and sentence, controlling for criminal record. The term partial is used because each coefficient applies to a part of the total data matrix, namely, those units with a specific value on the control variable.

Table 7, which is a simplified version of Table 6, just giving the proportions for one of the values on the dependent variable, shows the partial associations between each of the independent variables and the dependent variable.

Table 7. *Proportion Receiving a Severe Sentence, Depending on Social Status and Criminal Record*

Criminal record	Social status High	Low	Difference (partial associations for social status)
Criminal	0·63	0·81	−0·18
Clean	0·08	0·49	−0·41
Difference (partial associations for criminal record)	0·55	0·32	

Table 7 tells us that the size of the partial associations between an independent variable and sentence is different according to which value we keep constant on the control variable. This is called *statistical interaction* between the independent variables. In other cases the degree of association turns out to be the same regardless of which value the units have on the control variable. It may be weaker, stronger, or similar to what we found in the bivariate table before introducing the control variable. Comparing Table 7 with Tables 4 and 5 we see that for both independent variables one partial association is stronger and the other weaker than the bivariate association with the dependent variable . . .

Causal Analysis by Means of Contingency Tables

When we are trying to make sense of what is going on around us, the notions of cause and effect are important tools. Regularities observed in the flow of events are interpreted as a result of a prior event influencing a latter. Also for social scientists working on a research problem, such ideas usually play a prominent role, even if they are not always explicitly stated. In what is called a causal . . . analysis, however, the assumptions concerning how the variables influence each other are accurately specified by means of a *causal model* [or] *causal diagrams*, where the variables are represented by boxes and the influences by arrows pointing from the causal to the effect variable. If we assume that whether a defendant has a clean or criminal record will affect what kind of sentence he is given by the court, we will draw the causal diagram shown in Figure 1:

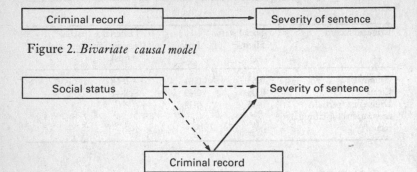

Figure 2. *Bivariate causal model*

Figure 3. *Trivariate causal model*

What about the causal relationship between the third variable, social status, and the two others? One of the ideas underlying the study of Norwegian court decisions was that the social status of a defendant might be of consequence for the sentence he was given by the court. In Figure 2 this assumption is represented by an arrow linking status with sentence, broken to symbolize a *negative* influence (high status is supposed to decrease the risk of a severe – that is, 'high' – sentence). The broken arrow linking status with record symbolizes that high status is assumed to reduce the probability of getting repeatedly into conflict with the law . . .

A causal model like the one in Figure 2, of course, constitutes a drastic simplification compared to the social phenomena it portrays. Just a few aspects of a complex process have been singled out for attention . . . However, for the moment just take it for granted that our model is a reasonable representation of the central aspects of the real-world phenomena we are studying.

In the model social status is a *causal variable* and sentence an *effect variable*. Record serves in both capacities, it is a causal variable in relation to sentence, and an effect variable in relation to social status. Its position in the model may be described as *intervening* between the two other variables.

What, then, are the implications of the causal assumptions put forward in our model? With regard to social status, the model says that when a defendant faces the court, his chances of getting away with a lenient sentence will depend *directly* upon whether he has a high or a low status. In addition, his social status has an *indirect effect* on the sentence through his record. Both effects are negative, that is, reducing the probability of a jail sentence for high-status defendants compared with low-status defendants. With regard to the indirect effect, the lower risk of recidivism works to the advantage of high-status defendants, since a criminal record means increased chances of a severe sentence.

Turning to the relation between record and sentence our model postulates that in addition to the direct effect there will exist some amount of statistical association which is a result of both variables having a common cause, the *prior variable* status. A disproportionately large number of the recidivists according to our model will come from the low-status category of defendants. Since low status in itself is supposed to increase the risk of a jail sentence, the difference in social composition between defendants with a clean record and defendants with a criminal past will necessarily contribute to the difference in the probability of a severe sentence between the two groups. A part of the statistical association between record and sentence is thus created by the status variable, instead of being a causal effect of record on sentence. Such *non-causal association* is often referred to as *spurious effect*, it may look like a causal effect without in fact being so.

The above discussion shows how the model provides us with a tentative answer to the question of why we find statistical association between the variables. Provided the assumptions of the model are adequate . . . the association between social status and sentence is explained as a result of status influencing sentence, directly and indirectly through the intervening variable record. The association between record and sentence is interpreted as partly a result of a direct effect of record on sentence, and partly as spurious effect which is created by the prior variable status . . .

Reference

AUBERT, V. (1964), *Likhet og Rett: Essays om Forbrytelse og Straff*, Pax, Oslo.

11 J. P. Spradley

Ethnography and Culture

Excerpts from J. P. Spradley (1979), *The Ethnographic Interview*, Holt, Rinehart and Wilson, New York, 1979, pp. 3–9.

Ethnography is the work of describing a culture. The essential core of this activity aims to understand another way of life from the native point of view. The goal of ethnography, as Malinowski put it, is 'to grasp the native's point of view, his relation to life, to realize *his* vision of *his* world' . . . Field work, then, involves the disciplined study of what the world is like to people who have learned to see, hear, speak, think, and act in ways that are different. Rather than *studying people*, ethnography means *learning from people*. Consider the following illustration.

Elizabeth Marshall, a young American, had travelled for miles across the Kalahari Desert . . . And then [she met] a young woman who appeared to be in her early twenties . . .

'Presently she smiled, pressed her hand to her chest, and said: "Tsetchwe." It was her name.

'"Elizabeth," I said, pointing to myself.

'"Nisabe," she answered, pronouncing after me and inclining her head graciously. She looked me over carefully without really staring, which to Bushmen is rude. Then, having surely suspected that I was a woman, she put her hand on my breast gravely, and, finding that I was, she gravely touched her own breast. Many Bushmen do this; to them all Europeans look alike.

'"Tsau si" (woman), she said.

'Then after a moment's pause, Tsetchwe began to teach me a few words; the names of a few objects around us, grass, rock, bean shell, so that we could have a conversation later. As she talked she took a handful of the beans out of her kaross, broke them open, and began to eat them' . . .

'Tsetchwe began to teach me . . .' This is the essence of ethnography. Instead of collecting 'data' about people, the ethnographer seeks to learn from people, to be taught by them.

'Tsetchwe began to teach me . . .' In order to discover the hidden principles of another way of life, the researcher must become a *student*. Tsetchwe, and those like her in every society, become *teachers*. Instead of studying the 'climate', the 'flora', and the 'fauna' which make up the Bushmen's environment, Elizabeth Marshall tried to discover how the Bushmen define and evaluate drought and rainstorm, *gemsbok* and giraffe, *torabe* root and *tsama* melon. She did not attempt to describe Bushmen social life in terms of what we know as 'marriage' or 'family'; instead she sought to discover how Bushmen identified relatives and the cultural meaning of their kinship relationships. Discovering the *insider's* view is a different species of knowledge from one that rests primarily on the *outsider's* view. Even when the outsider is a trained social scientist.

Imagine that Tsetchwe, curious to know our way of life, travelled to Cushing, Wisconsin, a small farm town with a population of about 100 people. What would this young woman, so well schooled in the rich heritage of Bushmen society, have to do in order to understand the culture of these Wisconsin townsfolk? How would Tsetchwe discover the patterns that made up their lives? How would she avoid imposing Bushmen ideas, categories, and values on everything she saw?

First, and perhaps most difficult, Tsetchwe would have to set aside her belief in *naïve realism*. This almost universal belief holds that all people define the *real* world of objects, events, and living creatures in pretty much the same way. Human languages may differ from one society to the next, but behind the strange words and sentences, all people are talking about the same things. The naïve realist assumes that *love*, *rain*, *marriage*, *worship*, *trees*, *death*, *food*, and hundreds of other things have essentially the same meaning to all human beings. Although there are few of us who would admit to such ethnocentrism, the assumption may unconsciously influence our research.

Ethnography starts with a conscious attitude of almost complete ignorance. 'I don't know how the people of Cushing, Wisconsin, understand their world. That remains to be discovered.'

Like Elizabeth Marshall, Tsetchwe would have to begin by learning the language spoken in Cushing. Observations alone would not be sufficient. She could walk up and down the one or two streets in this farm community and record what she saw, but only when she asked questions and learned what the natives saw would she grasp their perspective. Observing the co-op creamery, where each morning local farmers bring their cans of fresh milk, the post office filled with letters and advertising circulars about farm implements, the two bars which attract a jovial crowd on Saturday nights, the row of white houses that line the main street, or the Lutheran church around the corner, would not, in themselves, reveal much. Tsetchwe would have to learn the *meanings* of these buildings and the *meanings* of all the social occasions that took place in them. She would have to listen to townsfolk and farmers, depending on them to explain these things to her.

The essential core of ethnography is this concern with the meaning of actions and events to the people we seek to understand. Some of these meanings are directly expressed in language; many are taken for granted and communicated only indirectly through word and action. But in every society people make constant use of these complex meaning systems to organize their behaviour, to understand themselves and others, and to make sense out of the world in which they live. These systems of meaning constitute their culture; ethnography always implies a theory of culture.

Culture

... Culture, as used in this book, refers to *the acquired knowledge that people use to interpret experience and generate social behaviour.* The following example will help to clarify this definition. One afternoon in 1973, I came across the following news item in the *Minneapolis Tribune:*

CROWD MISTAKES RESCUE ATTEMPT, ATTACKS POLICE

Nov. 23, 1973. Hartford, Connecticut. Three policemen giving a heart massage and oxygen to a heart attack victim Friday were attacked by a crowd of 75 to 100 persons who apparently did not realize what the policemen were doing.

Other policemen fended off the crowd of mostly Spanish speaking residents until an ambulance arrived. Police said they tried to explain to the crowd what they were doing, but the crowd apparently thought they were beating the woman.

Despite the policemen's efforts the victim, Evangelica Echevarria, 59, died.

Here we see people using their culture. Members of two different groups observed the same event but their *interpretations* were drastically different. The crowd used their culture to (a) interpret the behaviour of the policemen as cruel, and (b) to act on the woman's behalf to put a stop to what they saw as brutality. They had acquired the cultural principles for acting and interpreting things in this way through a particular, shared experience.

The policemen, on the other hand, used their culture (a) to interpret the woman's condition as heart failure and their own behaviour as a life-saving effort, and (b) to give cardiac massage and oxygen to the woman. Furthermore, they interpreted the actions of the crowd in a manner entirely different from how the crowd saw their own behaviour. These two groups of people each had elaborate cultural rules for interpreting their experience and for acting in emergency situations. The conflict arose, at least in part, because these cultural rules were so different.

By restricting the definition of culture to shared knowledge, we do not eliminate an interest in behaviour, customs, objects, or emotions. We have merely shifted the emphasis from these phenomena to their *meaning*. The ethnographer observes behaviour, but goes beyond it to inquire about the meaning of that behaviour. The ethnographer sees artifacts and natural objects but goes beyond them to discover what meanings people assign to these objects. The ethnographer observes and records emotional states, but goes beyond them to discover the meaning of fear, anxiety, anger, and other feelings . . .

Making Cultural Inferences

. . . People everywhere learn their culture by observing other people, listening to them, and then *making inferences*. The ethnographer employs this same process of going beyond what is seen and heard to *infer* what people know. It involves reasoning from evidence (what we perceive) or from premises (what we assume). Children acquire their culture by watching adults and making inferences about the cultural rules for behaviour; with the acquisition of language, the learning accelerates. Elizabeth Marshall could infer that '*tsau si*' meant 'woman' because Tsetchwe said it immediately after touching her own breast. Whenever we are in a new situation we have to make such inferences about what people know . . .

In doing field work, ethnographers make cultural inferences from three sources: (1) from what people say; (2) from the way people act; and (3) from the artefacts people use. At first, each cultural inference is only a hypothesis about what people know. These hypotheses must be tested over and over again until the ethnographer becomes relatively certain that people share a particular system of cultural meanings. None of the sources for making inferences – behaviour, speech, artefacts – are foolproof, but together they can lead to an adequate cultural description. And we can evaluate the adequacy of the description [, as Frake puts it,] 'by the ability of a stranger to the culture (who may be the ethnographer) to use the ethnography's statements as instructions for appropriately anticipating the scenes of the society' . . .

Sometimes cultural knowledge is communicated by language in such a direct manner that we can make inferences with great ease. Instructions to children such as 'wash your hands before dinner' and 'don't go swimming after you eat or you'll get cramps' represent expressions of such *explicit cultural knowledge*. In [a] study of sky divers, Reed learned from informants that the jumps he observed actually involved three different kinds: *fun jumps*, *single work* (to perfect three forms of falling), and *relative work* (jumping in groups in preparation for competition). Informants could easily talk about this cultural knowledge. It is important to point out that studying explicit culture through the way people talk does not eliminate the need for making inferences. It only makes the task less difficult.

However, a large part of any culture consists of *tacit knowledge*. We all know things that we cannot talk about or express in direct ways. The ethnographer must then make inferences about what people know by listening carefully to what they say, by observing their behaviour, and by studying artefacts and their use. With reference to discovering this tacit cultural knowledge, Malinowski wrote:

. . . we cannot expect to obtain a definite, precise and abstract statement from a philosopher, belonging to the community itself. The native takes his fundamental assumptions for granted, and if he reasons or inquires into matters of belief, it would be always in regard to details and concrete applications. Any attempts on the part of the ethnographer to induce his informant to formulate such a general statement would have to be in the form of leading questions of the worst type because in these leading questions he would have to introduce words and concepts essentially foreign to the native. Once the informant grasped their meaning, his outlook would be warped by our own ideas having been poured into it. Thus, the ethnographer must draw the generalizations for himself, must formulate the abstract statement without the direct help of a native informant ... (Malinowski, 1950, p. 396)

References

MALINOWSKI, B. (1950), *Argonauts of the Western Pacific*, Dutton, New York.
THOMAS, E. M. (1958), *The Harmless People*, Random House, New York.

12   John Lofland

The Basic Categories of Qualitative Analysis

Excerpts from J. Lofland (1971), *Analysing Social Settings: A Guide to Qualitative Observation and Analysis*, Wadsworth, Belmont, California, pp. 4, 6–7, 14–17, 24, 28, 31–2, 34–5, 41, 45–6, 54.

The [ethnographer's] commitment to get close, to be factual, descriptive, and quotive, constitutes a significant commitment to represent the participants *in their own terms* ... One faithfully depicts what goes on in their lives and what life is like for them, in such a way that one's audience is at least partially able to project themselves into the point of view of the people depicted ...

A major methodological consequence of these commitments is that the qualitative study of people *in situ* is a *process of discovery*. It is of necessity a process of learning what is happening. Since a major part of what is happening is provided by people in their own terms, one must find out about those terms rather than impose upon them a preconceived or outsider's scheme of what they are about. It is the observer's task to find out what is fundamental or central to the people or world under observation ...

Let us next ask in what sense analysis is necessary to [qualitative] sociological studies ... A first step is to recognize that any participants under study are themselves analytic. They order and pattern their views and their activities. While their world may seem random and chaotic to an outsider, it is safe to bet it is not that way to insiders ... In order to capture the participants 'in their own terms' one must learn their analytic ordering of the world, their categories for rendering explicable and coherent the flux of raw reality. That, indeed, is the first principle of qualitative analysis. Since it is the job of the analyst to dwell upon their analytic order (while the participants are living it more than analysing it), it becomes possible for him to provide a more articulate and clearer portrayal of that order than the participants are likely to work up. *The qualitative analyst seeks to provide an explicit rendering of the structure, order, and patterns found among a set of participants.*

Having come this far, a final step to full [qualitative] sociological analysis may be suggested, although not insisted upon. The elements of the analytic order discovered among the participants may themselves be sociologically categorized. Since, happily, sociological discourse in particular is an elaborated version of everyday discourse, little discontinuity may be necessary. That is, one can begin to work with such sociological and participant categories as 'recruitment', 'socialization', 'social control', 'hierarchy', 'career', and 'deviance', among a host of other ordering ideas . . .

Abstracting, conceptualizing, and ordering – the activities of the social scientist – are activities we carry on anyway. Through them we understand the world better. Through a detailed rendering of the reality of other peoples' worlds, we understand other people better. Through the concerted effort *self-consciously and explicitly* to carry on *simultaneously* detailed description and careful analysis, we can hope to have even better understanding . . .

In what follows [I] present . . . examples of accomplished qualitative analyses. In order to emphasize analytic structure, the examples are stripped down to the basic categories that constitute their analytic thrust. It is hoped that through contemplating what others have done with qualitative materials, the novice observer-analyst can better figure out how to use his own.

Six Units

In thinking about presenting the examples in an orderly fashion, it seemed best to arrange them along a continuum from the most *microscopic* social phenomenon to the most *macroscopic*. While the materials in fact shade one into another, in order to be more precise, I have chopped the continuum into six categories. Ranging from microscopic to macroscopic, these are as follows:

1. *Acts*. Action in a situation that is temporally brief, consuming only a few seconds, minutes, or hours.
2. *Activities*. Action in a setting of more major duration – days, weeks, months – constituting significant elements of persons' involvements.
3. *Meanings*. The verbal productions of participants that define and direct action.

4. *Participation*. Persons' holistic involvement in, or adaptation to a situation or setting under study.
5. *Relationships*. Interrelationships among several persons considered simultaneously.
6. *Settings*. The entire setting under study conceived as the unit of analysis . . .

We can now ask: What are the characteristics of acts, activities, meanings, participation, relationships, and settings, the forms they assume, the variations they display? Let me emphasize, however, that there is nothing magic or immutable in this set of six terms. It is merely a device, useful, I hope, in making an orderly and therefore more understandable presentation of many years of accomplished qualitative analysis in sociology . . . [There is not space to illustrate them all here.]

1. Acts

There is a large . . . range of acts that are more or less recognized by the participants but remain without explicit naming. These are likely to be instantly recognizable to the participants but simply 'something I never thought much about'. In a study of cab drivers Fred Davis noted that these urban types could be seen to engage in certain acts calculated to ensure themselves what they considered to be a proper tip. Watching for incidents of such acts, he reports that their tactical gambits include:

1. Fumbling in the making of change.
2. Giving the passenger a hard-luck story.
3. Making fictitious charges for service.
4. Providing a concerted show of fast, fancy driving.
5. Displaying extraordinary courtesy (Davis, 1959) . . .

3. Meanings

The term 'meaning' is intended to single out participants' verbal productions as a significant unit of comprehension in itself . . .

What is here called the level of meanings has otherwise been called 'culture', 'values', 'norms', 'understandings', 'social reality', 'definitions of the situation', 'typifications', 'ideology', 'beliefs', 'world view', 'perspective', 'stereotypes', and the like. Such terms have in common a focus upon a humanly constructed set of symbolic objects, consciously singled out as important aspects of reality. Meanings tend to be transbehavioural in the sense that they define [and] justify . . . behaviour and are not simply a description of it. Meanings *interpret* behaviour among participants in a social world (even though they may also describe it) . . .

Analyses of meanings often centre on the question of how members define for themselves a given problematic topic . . . Thus in observing a religious group that strongly believed they were destined to make thousands of new converts and who worked hard to achieve that goal I found them failing time after time. They themselves perceived this failure as well. How, then, did they define this chronic gap between aim and actuality? Members of the group seemed to possess three basic definitions or explanations of the disparity:

First, the American group was an offshoot of [a] Korean founding body, which had gone for years without success before beginning to make large numbers of converts. They would remind themselves that they were perhaps only following 'the Korean pattern'.

Second, they would apply their general 'principle of restitution' which held that God and Satan alternated in their influence. Current failure was due to Satan's dominant influence, which would later be counterbalanced by God's good influence on prospects in the making of converts.

Third, members believed that God would deliberately withhold his help from them in order to see how well they could do on their own. Current failure was testing their strength (Lofland, J., 1966) . . .

4. Participation

[As with the other six categories] we need again to draw a distinction between the observer's attempts to discern participation patterns already identified and employed by the natives of the setting, and those that he constructs out of the existing but unarticulated patterns of participation found in the setting . . .

Member-Identified Types. Member-identified or folk types vary along dimensions of the degree of centrality and the degree of longevity in a social setting. Although perhaps important to members, some participation patterns are short-term, situational, and *relatively* peripheral to a given organized system. In observing the clinical activities of medical students, Becker, Geer, Hughes, and Strauss found these students using the term 'crock' to 'refer to patients who disappoint them by failing to have pathological findings' (Becker et al., 1961:328). This student-identified pattern of patient participation then provided clues as to what constituted, in the students' minds, more 'proper' patterns of patient participation. The fleeting and short-term context of taxicab use is reported to produce 'an extensive typology of cab-users' in the minds of taxicab drivers. The main such patterns, as learned by Fred Davis, include:

1. The Sport.
2. The Blowhard.
3. The Businessman.
4. The Lady Shopper.
5. The Live Ones (Davis, 1959).

The primary dimensions used by cab drivers in identifying these types are the probability of a tip and the likely size of the tip . . .

Observer-Articulated or Constructed Types. Patterns of participation vary in the degree to which participants have themselves articulated and designated variance in participation. At one remove from instances such as those just recounted are participant-designated patterns for which the analyst assumes the task of articulation of uncrystallized participation identifications. At the farthest remove from participant-articulated designations, the analyst assumes the task of *constructing* patterns that appear to exist but remain unconceived in the phenomenology of the participants. It is this latter task of observer construction that is the most hazardous and most subject to the legitimate charge of imposing a world of meaning on the participants that better reflects the observer's world than the world under study. When the observer constructs participation patterns he is more likely to impute participation than to discern it. None the less, it still seems worthwhile to attempt construction . . . The best and most stringent test of observer constructions is their recognizability to the participants themselves. When participants themselves say 'Yes, that is there, I had simply never noticed it before,' the observer can be reasonably confident that he has tapped into extant patterns of participation.

Attempts to articulate or construct may themselves be distinguished in terms of the duration and scope of the pattern of participation. At the temporally brief and situationally specific end of these variables, Lyn Lofland, in observing waiting behaviour in public places, noted that 'waiters' tended to vary in the degree to which their behaviour was restricted or self-protective. Along this dimension of self-protectiveness, people waiting in public places tended to fall into five main 'management styles'.

1. *The Sweet Young Thing.* [Generally a female] once having taken a position, usually a seated one, she rarely leaves it. Her posture is straight; potentially suggestive or revealing 'slouching' is not dared.
2. *The Nester.* Having once established a position, such persons busy themselves with arranging and rearranging their props, much in the manner of a bird building a nest.
3. *The Investigator.* Having first reached a position, the investigator surveys his surroundings with some care. Then . . . he leaves his position to begin a minute investigation of every inanimate object in sight.
4. *The Seasoned Urbanite* . . . is easy and relaxed . . . within the confines of legitimate setting use and proper public behaviour.
5. *The Maverick* . . . is . . . a non-style . . . Its users are those who either do not know how, are not able, or do not care to protect themselves in public settings . . . There are three types . . . [of] mavericks: *children*, or those with insufficiently developed selves; the *constantly stigmatized*, or those with spoiled selves; and *eccentrics*, or those with irresponsible selves (Lofland, 1972) . . .

5. Relationships

We move now to a unit that by its nature transcends individuals. We turn to relationships . . .

One of the more complex and insightful analyses of relationships has been performed by Edwin Lemert on interactional processes leading up to a person's being labelled and hospitalized as a 'paranoid'. Lemert's account of relationships that promote the growth of a paranoid 'delusion' is of the following character.

1. The person who is conducively oriented to participate in subsequent stages already displays one or another kind of interpersonal

difficulty with his work associates, in particular a tendency to disregard primary group loyalties, to violate confidences, and to presume on privileges not accorded him.

2. His associates tend for a time to perceive the person as a variant normal, but one or more events precipitate a reorganization of the associates' views, seeing him now as 'unreliable', 'untrustworthy', 'dangerous', or someone with whom others 'do not wish to be involved'.

3. Associates begin to engage in patronizing, evasive, and spurious interaction with the person, to avoid him, and to exclude him from interaction.

4. The person perceives the associates' tendencies to patronize, avoid, and exclude him from interaction, strengthening his initial tendencies to disregard confidences, etc. (1 above) and promoting his demands to know what is happening.

5. The associates deal with the increasing difficulties posed by the person by strengthening their own patronizing, avoidance, and exclusion (2 above). They begin, moreover, to *conspire* among themselves in developing means to deal with the person.

6. The person senses this conspiracy, but it, and all other difficulties, tend to be denied by the associates. The person's situation becomes increasingly one of declining flow of information to him, a widening discrepancy between expressed ideas and affect among his associates, and increasing ambiguity for the person as to the nature of situations and his associates.

7. These three phases (4, 5, and 6 above) *concatenate*. The person and the associates mutually respond to the difficulties posed by the other, in a process that spirals and feeds upon itself, a process that is *mutually* constructed.

8. Finally, if all the associates' efforts to discharge or transfer the person fail, sick leave, psychiatric treatment, or, in the extreme case, mental hospital commitment may be accomplished (summarized and quoted from Lemert, 1962) . . .

What have been outlined above are . . . *elements* with which to sort and classify observations and to build some *other kind* of analytic scheme for one's observational materials. These are building blocks that can be utilized in designing one's own building and/or in portraying the building that has been constructed in or by some social setting. The creative and organizing capacities of the observer-analyst remain a fundamental necessity. None the less, his creative task is presumably facilitated by a familiarity with the kinds of construction materials at his disposal.

References

BECKER, H. S., GEER, B., HUGHES, E., and STRAUSS, A. (1961), *Boys in White: Student Culture in Medical School*, University of Chicago Press.

DAVIS, Fred (1959), 'The Cabdriver and his Fare: Facets of a Fleeting Relationship', *American Journal of Sociology*, 65:158–65.

LEMERT, Edwin M. (1962), 'Paranoia and the Dynamics of Exclusion', *Sociometry*, 25:2–20.

LOFLAND, John (1966), *Doomsday Cult: A Study of Conversion, Proselytization, and Maintenance of Faith*, Prentice-Hall, Englewood Cliffs, New Jersey.

LOFLAND, Lyn H. (1972), 'Self-Management in Public Settings: Part II', *Urban Life and Culture*, Vol. 1, pp. 217–31.

Part Three
The Sociology of Development

Sociology is not just about Western society. The majority of humankind live outside the 'West', in the 'Third World'. They are experiencing, today, many of the changes that transformed societies in Europe, within living memory, from predominantly agrarian societies to industrial ones (and, some would now say, into '*post*-industrial' ones). To explain those changes – which made Great Britain and then the United States into the world's leading power, and which have now led to the emergence of Japan as the world's newest economic superpower, we need a theory of development: a theory which seeks to explain social change in human history and, in particular, why and how it was that the pioneer industrial countries were able not only to innovate so successfully but to impose their rule on the entire globe during the epoch of high imperialism. Development theory, too, needs to explain why it is that many ex-colonial countries have not followed these Western models of economic development.

The direct political control the Western powers established in their empires did make possible the often forcible transformation of the entire globe: agriculture was reorganized to produce cash-crops for a world market, both on peasant plots and on new giant plantations; mines and oil-wells were developed to supply the needs of the industrial countries; self-sufficient producers were turned into consumers of Western manufactured goods.

But the ending of Western political control after the Second World War rarely resulted in the replication of Western political forms, in particular parliamentary ones. More often, there were various forms of populism and, later, one-party and military regimes. A few countries, including the most populous nation on earth, China, opted for communism.

Most underdeveloped countries, however, believed that the best hope for economic success lay in following one or other model of *capitalist* development, an optimism shared by proponents of 'modernization theory', the most influential statement of which was W. W. Rostow's *The Stages of Economic Growth*, written in 1960 (Reading 13). International agencies still cleave to the notion that if the relevant 'factors' of growth (industrial know-how, capital, the 'Protestant Ethic' – which were crucial to industrialization in the West) could be exported to the underdeveloped countries, via 'aid' programmes, then a similar pattern of growth would ensue.

Yet governments and planners in the newly independent countries became increasingly disillusioned at the rate of development of their countries. It was only after they had won political independence that they began to realize how limited their power was and that, however much they increased output, the real power lay not just with the states that had been their colonial masters, but also with the large economic institutions within those states: the banks, the world commodity exchanges where their primary products such as foodstuffs and minerals were bought and sold, and which they were quite unable to control; and with the multinational corporations to whom any one country was only part of a much wider global operation.

Frustrated planners and politicians in developing countries now began to criticize those theories that had assumed that evolution was *bound* to take place. They were not necessarily radical, though they were nationalistic in the sense of wanting to promote their countries' economic growth. But they were increasingly persuaded by theories that argued that development could never take place under capitalism and would only be possible when they escaped from the 'neo-colonial' economic control exercised by those who dominated the world market.

Latin America, in particular, had experienced a century and a half of political independence followed by the development of an economy that depended on the export of its agricultural products, such as Argentinian meat, to Europe and North America, which in turn led to the political domination of that continent firstly by Great Britain and later by the USA.

So a new school of 'dependency' theorists grew up. Reading 14 is an extract from the writings of André Gunder Frank, who influenced a whole generation. His formulation of the problem – in the title of one of his books – as one of *Underdevelopment or Revolution?* convinced many that the only way forward lay through some national variant of the armed revolutions that had so recently won the day in China, Cuba, and Vietnam.

His theory, however, met with increasing criticism, even from many who shared his general political views. Immanuel Wallerstein's later model of the world system, backed by impressive historical research, recognized that it was too crude simply to divide the world into 'core' (developed) states and 'peripheral' ones: there were also '*semi*-peripheral countries, which were, in fact, developing, often rapidly: notably the 'newly industrializing' states such as Brazil and Mexico, and the 'four little tigers' of East Asia: Hong Kong, Taiwan, South Korea and Singapore. Meanwhile, the revolutionary regimes had run into serious economic problems.

Although Wallerstein has written a great deal, it is difficult to find a short passage which expresses his general views succinctly. We have therefore used instead Reading 15, by Peter Worsley, which makes a résumé of Wallerstein's model, and then proceeds to criticize it. But the interested reader should read Wallerstein's own writings on *The Modern World-System*.

Turning from theory to practical development programmes, it would, of course, be impossible to discuss the enormous variety of development strategies adopted in every part of the globe, So we have focused on two major 'revolutions', not armed communist or nationalist revolutions, but modern capitalist technological revolutions on an enormous scale: Byres, Crow and Ho's study of the Green Revolution in India (Reading 17) and Henderson's study of the microchip revolution, with particular reference to Hong Kong (Reading 18), both of which show that in those countries rapid development has taken place, with social costs as well as benefits. Whether these countries can be taken as models which can be imitated anywhere, or whether large parts of the globe will stay underdeveloped, is left for the reader to judge, as is the possibility that Western forms of development will prove inappropriate and inimitable in a world where material resources are finite and where the environment on which the whole of human civilization depends is being increasingly threatened.

13   W. W. Rostow

The Stages of Economic Growth

Excerpts from W. W. Rostow, *The Stages of Economic Growth: a non-Communist Manifesto*, Cambridge University Press, 1960, pp. 4–11.

It is possible to identify all societies, in their economic dimensions, as lying within one of five categories: the traditional society, the preconditions for take-off, the take-off, the drive to maturity, and the age of high mass-consumption.

The traditional society

First, the traditional society. A traditional society is one whose structure is developed within limited production functions, based on pre-Newtonian science and technology, and on pre-Newtonian attitudes towards the physical world . . .

The conception of the traditional society is, however, in no sense static; and it would not exclude increases in output. Acreage could be expanded; some *ad hoc* technical innovations, often highly productive innovations, could be introduced in trade, industry and agriculture; productivity could rise with, for example, the improvement of irrigation works or the discovery and diffusion of a new crop. But the central fact about the traditional society was that a ceiling existed on the level of attainable output per head. This ceiling resulted from the fact that the potentialities which flow from modern science and technology were either not available or not regularly and systematically applied.

Both in the longer past and in recent times the story of traditional societies was thus a story of endless change. The area and volume of trade within them and between them fluctuated, for example, with the degree of political and social turbulence, the efficiency of central rule, the upkeep of the roads. Population – and, within limits, the level of life – rose and fell not only with the sequence of the harvests, but with the incidence of war and of plague. Varying degrees of manufacture developed; but, as in agriculture, the level of productivity was limited by the inaccessibility of modern science, its applications, and its frame of mind.

Generally speaking, these societies, because of the limitation of productivity, had to devote a very high proportion of their resources to agriculture; and flowing from the agricultural system there was an hierarchical social structure, with relatively narrow scope – but some scope – for vertical mobility. Family and clan connections played a large role in social organization. The value system of these societies was generally geared to what might be called a long-run fatalism; that is, the assumption that the range of possibilities open to one's grandchildren would be just about what it had been for one's grandparents. But this long-run fatalism by no means excluded the short-run option that, within a considerable range, it was possible and legitimate for the individual to strive to improve his lot, within his lifetime . . .

Although central political rule – in one form or another – often existed in traditional societies, transcending the relatively self-sufficient regions, the centre of gravity of political power generally lay in the regions, in the hands of those who owned or controlled the land. The landowner maintained fluctuating but usually profound influence over such central political power as existed, backed by its entourage of civil servants and soldiers, imbued with attitudes and controlled by interests transcending the regions.

In terms of history then, with the phrase 'traditional society' we are grouping the whole pre-Newtonian world: the dynasties in China; the civilization of the Middle East and the Mediterranean; the world of medieval Europe. And to them we add the post-Newtonian societies which, for a time, remained untouched or unmoved by man's new capability for regularly manipulating his environment to his economic advantage . . .

The Preconditions for Take-Off

The preconditions for take-off were initially developed, in a clearly marked way, in Western Europe of the late seventeenth and early eighteenth centuries as the insights of modern science began to be translated into new production functions in both agriculture and industry, in a setting given dynamism by the lateral expansion of world markets and the international competition for them. But all that lies behind the break-up of the Middle Ages is relevant to the creation of the preconditions for take-off in Western Europe. Among the Western European states, Britain, favoured by geography, natural resources, trading possibilities, social and political structure, was the first to develop fully the preconditions for take-off.

The more general case in modern history, however, saw the stage of preconditions arise not endogenously but from some external intrusion by more advanced societies. These invasions – literal or figurative – shocked the traditional society and began or hastened its undoing; but they also set in motion ideas and sentiments which initiated the process by which a modern alternative to the traditional society was constructed out of the old culture.

The idea spreads not merely that economic progress is possible, but that economic progress is a necessary condition for some other purpose, judged to be good: be it national dignity, private profit, the general welfare, or a better life for the children. Education, for some at least, broadens and changes to suit the needs of modern economic activity. New types of enterprising men come forward – in the private economy, in government, or both – willing to mobilize savings and to take risks in pursuit of profit or modernization. Banks and other institutions for mobilizing capital appear. Investment increases, notably in transport, communications, and in raw materials in which other nations may have an economic interest. The scope of commerce, internal and external, widens. And, here and there, modern manufacturing enterprise appears, using the new methods. But all this activity proceeds at a limited pace within an economy and a society still mainly characterized by traditional low-productivity methods, by the old social structure and values, and by the regionally based political institutions that developed in conjunction with them . . .

Politically, the building of an effective centralized national state – on the basis of coalitions touched with a new nationalism, in opposition to the traditional landed regional interests, the colonial power, or both, was a decisive aspect of the preconditions period; and it was, almost universally, a necessary condition for take-off . . .

The Take-Off

We come now to the great watershed in the life of modern societies: the third stage in this sequence, the take-off. The take-off is the interval when the old blocks and resistances to steady growth are finally overcome. The forces making for economic progress, which yielded limited bursts and enclaves of modern activity, expand and come to dominate the society. Growth becomes its normal condition. Compound interest becomes built, as it were, into its habits and institutional structure . . .

During the take-off new industries expand rapidly, yielding profits a large proportion of which are reinvested in new plant; and these new industries, in turn, stimulate, through their rapidly expanding requirement for factory workers, the services to support them, and for other manufactured goods, a further expansion in urban areas and in other modern industrial plants. The whole process of expansion in the modern sector yields an increase of income in the hands of those who not only save at high rates but place their savings at the disposal of those engaged in modern sector activities. The new class of entrepreneurs expands; and it directs the enlarging flows of investment in the private sector. The economy exploits hitherto unused natural resources and methods of production.

New techniques spread in agriculture as well as industry, as agriculture is commercialized, and increasing numbers of farmers are prepared to accept the new methods and the deep changes they bring to ways of life. The revolutionary changes in agricultural productivity are an essential condition for successful take-off; for modernization of a society increases radically its bill for agricultural products. In a decade or two both the basic structure of the economy and the social and political structure of the society are transformed in such a way that a steady rate of growth can be, thereafter, regularly sustained . . .

The Drive to Maturity

After take-off there follows a long interval of sustained if fluctuating progress, as the now regularly growing economy drives to extend modern technology over the whole front of its economic activity. Some 10–20 per cent of the national income is steadily invested, permitting output regularly to outstrip the increase in population. The make-up of the economy changes unceasingly as technique improves, new industries accelerate, older industries level off. The economy finds its place in the international economy: goods formerly imported are produced at home; new import requirements develop, and new export commodities to match them. The society makes such terms as it will with the requirements of modern efficient production, balancing off the new against the older values and institutions, or revising the latter in such ways as to support rather than to retard the growth process.

Some sixty years after take-off begins (say, forty years after the end of take-off) what may be called maturity is generally attained. The economy, focused during the take-off around a relatively narrow complex of industry and technology, has extended its range into more refined and technologically often more complex processes; for example, there may be a shift in focus from the coal, iron, and heavy engineering industries of the railway phase to machine-tools, chemicals, and electrical equipment. This, for example, was the transition through which Germany, Britain, France, and the United States had passed by the end of the nineteenth century or shortly thereafter . . .

Formally, we can define maturity as the stage in which an economy demonstrates the capacity to move beyond the original industries which powered its take-off and to absorb and to apply efficiently over a very wide range of its resources − if not the whole range − the most advanced fruits of (then) modern technology . . .

The Age of High Mass-Consumption

We come now to the age of high mass-consumption, where, in time, the leading sectors shift towards durable consumers' goods and services . . .

As societies achieved maturity in the twentieth century two things happened: real income per head rose to a point where a large number of persons gained a command over consumption which transcended basic food, shelter, and clothing; and the structure of the working force changed in ways which increased not only the proportion of urban to total population, but also the proportion of the population working in offices or in skilled factory jobs − aware of and anxious to acquire the consumption fruits of a mature economy.

In addition to these economic changes, the society ceased to accept the further extension of modern technology as an overriding objective. It is in this post-maturity stage, for example, that, through the political process, Western societies have chosen to allocate increased resources to social welfare and security. The emergence of the welfare state is one manifestation of a society's moving beyond technical maturity; but it is also at this stage that resources tend increasingly to be directed to the production of consumers' durables and to the diffusion of services on a mass basis, if consumers' sovereignty reigns. The sewing-machine, the bicycle, and then the various electric-powered household gadgets were gradually diffused. Historically, however, the decisive element has been the cheap mass automobile with its quite revolutionary effects – social as well as economic – on the life and expectations of society.

For the United States, the turning point was, perhaps, Henry Ford's moving assembly line of 1913–14; but it was in the 1920s, and again in the post-war decade, 1946–56, that this stage of growth was pressed to, virtually, its logical conclusion. In the 1950s Western Europe and Japan appear to have fully entered this phase, accounting substantially for a momentum in their economies quite unexpected in the immediate post-war years. The Soviet Union is technically ready for this stage, and, by every sign, its citizens hunger for it; but Communist leaders face difficult political and social problems of adjustment if this stage is launched.

14 André Gunder Frank

Development and Underdevelopment

Extracts from André Gunder Frank, *Latin America: Underdevelopment or Revolution?*, Monthly Review Press, 1969, pp. 19–27.

Stages of Growth

Rostow's stages and thesis are incorrect primarily because they do not correspond at all to the past or present reality of the underdeveloped countries whose development they are supposed to guide. It is explicit in Rostow ... that underdevelopment is the original stage of what are supposedly traditional societies – that there were no stages prior to the present stage of underdevelopment. It is further explicit in Rostow that the now developed societies were once underdeveloped. But all this is quite contrary to fact. This entire approach to economic development and cultural change attributes a history to the developed countries but denies all history to the underdeveloped ones. The countries that are today underdeveloped evidently have had a history no less than have the developed ones. None of them, for example India, is today the way it was centuries or even decades ago. Moreover, reference to even any schoolboy world history confirms that the history of the now underdeveloped countries has been most intimately related to the history of the now developed ones for at least several centuries.

Indeed, the economic and political expansion of Europe since the fifteenth century has come to incorporate the now underdeveloped countries into a single stream of world history, which has given rise simultaneously to the present development of some countries and the present underdevelopment of others. However ... Rostow and others have examined the developed countries as if they had developed in isolation from this stream of world history. It stands to reason that any serious attempt to construct theory and policy for the development of the now underdeveloped countries has to be based on the examination of the experience of the underdeveloped countries themselves – that is, on the study of their history and of the world historical process which has made these countries underdeveloped . . .

It is impossible, without closing one's eyes, to find in the world today any country or society which has the characteristics of Rostow's first, the traditional, stage. This is not surprising since the construction of Rostow's stages takes account neither of the history of the now underdeveloped countries, nor of their crucial relations with the now developed ones over several centuries past. Rostow's approach obliterates the fact that through these relations, the now developed countries have totally destroyed the pre-existing fabric of these societies (be it 'traditional' or not). This was most notably the case in India, which was de-industrialized; Africa, where the slave trade transformed society long before colonialism did so again; and Latin America, where the high civilizations of the Incas and the Aztecs were wiped out altogether. The relationship between the mercantilist and capitalist metropolis and these colonies succeeded in supplanting the pre-existing – or, in the case of the *tabula rasa* situations of Argentina, Brazil, the West Indies and elsewhere, in implanting – the social, political, and economic structure they now have: that is, the structure of underdevelopment.

This long relationship between the now underdeveloped and now developed countries within the same historical process did not affect only the export enclave in the underdeveloped countries, as the almost universally accepted and just as empirically and theoretically erroneous 'dual' society or economy thesis has it. On the contrary, this historical relationship transformed the entire social fabric of the peoples whose countries are now underdeveloped, just as in the developed countries . . . Rostow's . . . second stage . . . is even more conspicuous by its absence. Characteristic of Rostow's second stage is the penetration of underdeveloped countries by influences created abroad – mostly in the developed countries – and diffused to the underdeveloped ones, where they destroy traditionalism and simultaneously create the preconditions that will lead to the subsequent take-off in the third stage . . .

[Even if] the now underdeveloped Asian, African, and Latin American parts of the world . . . were traditional in the Rostowian sense before their contact with Europe – a dubious thesis, considering the high civilizations and technological development that had been achieved on all three continents – [they] certainly have been and still are affected by conditions in, and penetrated by influences emanating from, the now developed metropolis . . .

The nearly two thirds of the world's population living in these countries [today] feel and know that these metropolitan-imposed second stage conditions, far from furthering their economic development as Rostow and other metropolitan pundits claim, not only hinder their economic development, but even increase their underdevelopment. The reason for all this is that the reality of underdevelopment, which Rostow's first and second stages obscure and even deny, is that the incorporation of these lands and peoples into the expanding mercantilist and then capitalist world system first initiated their underdevelopment; that, furthermore, their continued participation in this same system still maintains and even aggravates that underdevelopment . . .

Today, more than half of both the area and the population of Latin America – especially Argentina, Uruguay, Brazil, and all of the West Indies – occupies regions which, at the time of their incorporation into the European-centred mercantile system, were either entirely unpopulated or were repopulated after the rapid extermination of the pre-contact population. None of these countries ever experienced Rostow's first stage: the mercantile metropolis did not conquer and settle these regions to institute Rostow's traditionalism, but to exploit them through the establishment of exclusively commercial mines, sugar plantations and cattle ranches. If anything, these regions and peoples entered world history by stepping right into Rostow's second stage. But after more than four centuries, Rostowian second-stage conditions and contact have not led to the third-stage take-off in these regions, much less to the fourth or fifth stage of development. Today these previously unpopulated regions are just as underdeveloped as are the previously populated ones which were similarly incorporated into the world-embracing capitalist system. Indeed, contrary to Rostow's conception of the second stage – and, as we will see below, contrary to most of the diffusionist thesis – the more intimate the past contact of these regions with the metropolis, the more underdeveloped they are today. Among the many examples are the ex-sugar exporting regions of the Caribbean and the Brazilian North-east and the ex-mining export regions of Minas

Gerais in the centre of Brazil, of Bolivia and Peru in the Andean Highlands and of the famous Zacatecas and Guanajuato mining regions in the centre of Mexico.

Abundant historical evidence from the underdeveloped countries shows that Rostow's first two stages are fictional. Contemporary evidence from them shows that his last two stages are Utopian ...

In the unfortunate reality of the underdeveloped countries it is precisely the structure of their underdevelopment ... and their structural relations with the developed countries ... that have for so long prevented the realization of the last two stages. By Rostow's count, we are then left only with the third stage and by my count with the second crucial flaw in Rostow's entire argument.

Rostow would have us believe that in his third stage, the take-off, he has theoretically synthesized the dynamic qualitative change between the structure of underdevelopment and that of development. However, his theory is not dynamic and he does not isolate structural characteristics or change. Least of all, does he incorporate the real structure of underdevelopment and development into his theory. On the contrary, he fails to consider it altogether. Like most, but not all, stage theories of history, Rostow's is an exercise in comparative statics. While he identifies stages of development, he does not say anything about how to get from one to the other. This is no less the case for the third stage than it is for the four others. The unreality of Rostow's dynamic should not surprise us: for as we have seen even his statics are entirely unreal; his stages correspond to no reality in the underdeveloped countries at all. How, then, could his development from one stage to another correspond to the underdeveloped world's reality?

... Rostow ... places the major burden for development in the third stage on the mere rate of investment and growth. The conclusive evidence of the theoretical inadequacy of Rostow's stages for understanding and eliminating the structure of underdevelopment goes far beyond that, of course. In completely ignoring the history of the underdeveloped countries, Rostow necessarily completely ignores the structure of their underdevelopment. The changes in institutions and investment he posits as the take-off out of underdevelopment do not begin to affect the real structure of underdevelopment. The proof is that countries such as Argentina, which Rostow claims to be taking off into development, are becoming ever more structurally underdeveloped and that, indeed, no underdeveloped country has ever managed to take off out of its underdevelopment by following Rostow's stages . . .

Rostow bases so much of his policy for the underdeveloped countries on his picture of the developed ones. Rostow is particularly explicit in claiming that England was the first country to industrialize and that it did so by domestically mobilizing its own resources after having experienced certain internal structural changes. Others among the now developed countries, he says, also developed on their own except in so far as the prior development of England and others helped to create the preconditions for their take-off. Again, Rostow is wrong on both empirical and theoretical grounds. That England and other countries did not develop by relying only on their own efforts has been exhaustively proven . . .

[Many writers from the eighteenth century onwards] . . . have demonstrated the crucial role played by the underdeveloped countries in financing the capitalization of the now developed ones. If the now underdeveloped countries were really to follow the stages of growth of the now developed ones, they would have to find still other peoples to exploit into underdevelopment, as the now developed countries did before them.

This misrepresentation of reality by Rostow must, of course, lead to (or does it follow from?) a theoretical error of the first magnitude [: the view of] the characteristics of development and underdevelopment as *sui generis* to the country concerned. When they proceed to the study of any structure at all . . . they confine themselves to examining only parts of the domestic structure of the country concerned. In none of these modes is there an examination of the actual structure of development and underdevelopment – of the structure of the historical system which gave rise to and includes them both . . .

[The] reality of the underdeveloped countries . . . is the product of the very same historical process and systemic structure as is the development of the now developed countries: the world-embracing system within which the now underdeveloped countries have lived their history for centuries; it is the structure of this system which constitutes the historical cause and still contemporary determinant of underdevelopment. This structure is ubiquitous; it extends from the most developed part of the most developed country to the most underdeveloped part of the most underdeveloped country . . .

On all grounds then, empirical, theoretical, and policy, the first approach to economic development and cultural change must be rejected as inadequate.

15   Peter Worsley
World-System Theory

Excerpts from Peter Worsley, 'One World or Three? A Critique of the World-System Theory of Immanuel Wallerstein', in J. Saville and R. Miliband (eds.), *Socialist Register 1980*, Merlin Press, 1980, pp. 300–302, 304–6, 309–13.

System-theorists say [that] we must abandon the view that the world is composed of so many nation-states, each with 'separate parallel histories', for 'societies' are merely 'parts of a whole reflecting that whole' and it is this whole – 'one capitalist economic system with different sectors performing different functions' – that must therefore be taken as the basic logical and historical-sociological framework within which the 'society' can then be located. 'A state', [Wallerstein] rightly observes, 'no more has a mode of production than does a firm. The concept "mode of production" describes an *economy*, the boundaries of which are . . . an empirical question.' In the case of the capitalist mode of production, its boundaries are world-wide. 'To understand the internal class-contradiction and political struggles of a particular state, we must first situate it in the world-economy.' And that economy is 'a single capitalist world-economy, which had emerged historically since the sixteenth century and which still exists today'.

The parts within this whole, then, are determined by an international division of labour which allots 'tasks' as between the industrialized 'core' countries and those on the periphery: an international division of labour which is not just a functional division, but also a relationship of exploitation.

The core countries are those which began by successfully developing 'a complex variety of economic activities – mass-market industries . . ., international and local commerce in the hands of an indigenous bourgeoisie, and relatively advanced forms of agriculture . . . with a high component of yeoman-owned land'. The peripheral countries became monocultural economies, specializing in cash crops produced by coerced labour; and the semi-peripheral countries were those that went downhill, *de*industrializing and losing their former core status. In these latter, the forms of labour are typically intermediate between 'the freedom of the lease system and the coercion of slavery and serfdom . . ., for the most part, sharecropping'.

Now pluralists equally accept that the three or more worlds they identify are not economically, politically or culturally sealed off from each other, but form part of an over-arching world-order. But this world-order is not a capitalist world-order. Within it, there is a capitalist *sector*, which is still the most powerful sector. Within that capitalist sector, there are two distinct sub-sectors: the developed, industrial countries and the dependent, agrarian ones. But the world is no longer a capitalist world, whatever may have been the case in the past. Rather, the capitalist 'world', like the other 'worlds', has *another* major system-alternative and rival, communism. Hence the system as a whole is *neither capitalist nor communist*, but a system of oppositions based on two major polarities: developed v. underdeveloped, and capitalist v. communist . . .

For world-system theory, there is only *one* world, divided into three components (completely different from the three 'worlds' discussed above): the core, peripheral, and semi-peripheral countries. Communist societies, though they have special characteristics of their own which set them off from capitalist countries, are not a set of countries *different in kind* from capitalist ones. Hence the communist 'world', in this model, is decomposed, and its component countries also treated variously as core, peripheral, or semi-peripheral . . .

For Wallerstein, Russia possesses a productive system in which 'private ownership is irrelevant', a negative formulation which he amplifies elsewhere more positively: the communist state is merely a 'collective capitalist firm so long as it remains a participant in the market of the capitalist world-economy'. Since there can only be *one* world-system at global level, and since existentially that system is a capitalist one, 'there are today no socialist systems in the world-economy', and the USSR is merely a 'core power in a *capitalist* world-economy'.

This treatment of what to me is *the* central division in the world derives from a methodological assumption that capitalism is a system in which 'production is for exchange, that is . . . determined by its profitability on a market'. In my view, this mistakenly locates the defining properties of capitalism in exchange and not in the relations that govern the way commodities are produced: in trade rather than in production. A 'capitalist' system for Wallerstein is merely one in which the producer receives less than he produces. All then, are 'objectively proletarian', even peasants: 'Africans working on the land in the rural areas should be thought of as "peasants" who are members of the "working class", that is who sell their labour-power even when they are technically self-employed cash-crop farmers.'

Slaves, too, are 'proletarians' ... 'Proletarian', in this sense, simply means any exploited producer. Wallerstein distinguishes eight varieties of proletarians, only one of which meets the classical model, and instances the wage-worker, the 'petty producer' (or 'middle peasant'), the tenant farmer, the share cropper, the peon and the slave ... at the level of implications for social action, it is a picture of a world *so* determined by capitalism, and particularly by those who control the core capitalist states, that it leads logically to fatalism and resignation, for it becomes difficult to see how any part of such a tightly knit system can possibly break away. Indeed, movements which purport to do so, or already to have done so, are, we are told, either deluding themselves or those who believe in them, or both ...

For it is a model which emphasizes the capacity of the ruling classes to manipulate the system, and others in it, as they wish, whilst underplaying resistance to their domination. 'The system', at times, is ... endowed with ... logic, power and even quasi-personality ... But systems do not take decisions. Ruling classes do. They try to run the system in their own interests. In this, overall, they succeed — by definition, otherwise they wouldn't continue to rule. But those they rule also try to maximize their interests. Such models therefore underestimate agency, especially resistance to domination. In the colonial context, they also underestimate the role of the 'collaborators' — those who possess or develop *local* political power and who use it actively to assist the colonizers, firstly, in establishing colonial institutions and then in participating in their operation as junior partners.

Of course, primary resistance did not prevent the onward sweep of capitalism and its final consolidation. In the dialectic of opposition between rulers and ruled, the rulers of the core countries had their way. But the triumph was long in the making, and the hegemony of capitalism has been a very uneven process along the way, in different zones, at different times, and with differing degrees of penetration and success.

The spread of capitalism is also discontinuous, not linear. The operations of mercantile traders; the establishment of colonies with predominantly non-capitalist production-systems; then of capitalist relations; the final integration of the world under capitalism; and the replacement of colonial political institutions by independent states constitute its main phases . . .

The process that led up to this final consolidation certainly did begin in the sixteenth century. But it was not unambiguously a capitalist process, firstly, because the early leading countries were themselves feudal societies; secondly, because what they implanted was based upon pre-capitalist, unfree labour. Hence accounts of colonialism which present it as the story of 'capitalism', without qualification, are profoundly unhistorical. Not only do they underplay the non-capitalist dimensions; they also underplay the quite distinctive kinds of capitalism and the phases of its development.

The model is also a one-way model in that it discounts the consequences for colonialism of the profound differences in the nature of the *pre*-capitalist societies and cultures the colonizers encountered. The social space that became the colonial world was inhabited by many different kinds of society, each possessing a variety of institutions and cultural codes which can only residually be labelled 'pre-capitalist', since this merely tells us, negatively, what they were *not*, not what they were. In fact, there were many different *kinds* of society, which differed from each other and not only from capitalism: acephalous bands and bureaucratic empires, to name but two extremes, and the differences of cultural logic, of social structure, of sheer scale of organization were to impose themselves on colonial institutions, too, since those responsible for constructing colonial political institutions had to come to terms with them . . .

The legacy of the pre-colonial heritage tends to get neglected if we concentrate on only one side of the colonial question: the undoubted success of capitalism in imposing its cultural logic upon what it was to turn into the 'periphery' and upon the people it was to turn into 'natives'. So does the resistance offered to invasion and continued after defeat. Even if in the encounter between colonizers and colonized, the power of the colonizers was superior, their victims never ceased to try and maximize their own interests.

But as various writers have shown e.g. Ranger for Africa, resistance was not the only form of reaction to conquest. There were also those who went along with the conquerors from the beginning – the allies of Cortés and Pizarro, for instance . . .

But reaction to conquest also included despair, resignation, fatalism and defeatism. Further, there were many individuals and groups who collaborated with the new authorities and who manipulated new institutions to their own advantage in ways both left-wing and liberal writers do not approve of: the *comprador*, the collaborating chief, the feudal lord, even the enterprising peasant who became a capitalist farmer, and so on. The colonized, then, whether they resisted or collaborated, were not simply inert objects pushed around by some impersonal 'logic of the system', or, more concretely, by government and settler.

It is also important not to over-emphasize the continuity of capitalist expansion. It was in fact discontinuous politically, involving successive reorganizations of political relations between centre and periphery of which the most important, politically, were the initial establishment of direct colonies and their subsequent emergence as new, independent, nation-states. The crucial economic transition was the shift from trade with the centre in goods produced along non-capitalist lines to production based on wage labour. In the core countries themselves, the crucial watersheds were the industrial revolutions which occurred at different times at different rates in different countries, when the feudal agrarian pre-eminence of landowning classes was replaced by the new bourgeoisies. The process was not simply one of political transformation *following* economic differentiation, and the consequent struggle between old and new classes for supremacy. Rather, the development of the economy depended upon the *prior* conquest of political power, which then afforded opportunity for economic entrepreneurs to innovate and expand.

But in the colonies, no such economic transformation occurred. And it was the political power of the metropolis that doomed their economies thenceforth to underdevelopment in the interests of London and Madrid. Even with the establishment of political independence, they remained obdurately economically dependent states, restricted to the role of suppliers of primary commodities to the metropoli and, except where the needs of the core countries called for capitalist innovation (plantations, mines, etc.), non-capitalist in their production systems. Pre-capitalist patterns of obligation to render dues in kind or in labour continued right up to our own times in the Andes, for instance, and outright slavery persisted in Brazil until 90 years ago (not to mention the southern states of the USA) . . .

Production along capitalist lines, in response to metropolitan industrialization, and particularly in sectors devoted to exports, became widespread even in the colonial period, in some parts, as mines and plantations were developed ultimately on the basis of wage labour and not forced labour, and as wage labour was increasingly used to produce cash crops for the world-market and handicrafts for the internal market. But the stranglehold exercised by the world-system was not absolute. Some colonies did make the breakthrough not only to political independence, but also to a thoroughly capitalistic economy, notably the 'first new nation'. It *was* therefore possible for some to escape from dependence . . .

The metropolitan stranglehold normally, however, proved decisive. And it led to a special kind of capitalist production: a *colonial* mode, in which State power was deployed initially to induce the production of commodities wanted by Europe. That State power might later be wielded by local landowners and merchants, rather than by agents of Madrid or London, but production still depended upon the direct coercion of labour to produce, in forms ranging from slavery to serfdom, from debt-peonage to indentured labour. Even manufacturing, as in the *obrajes*, depended upon compulsory obligations to deliver, backed by extremes in violence. The State too, intervened in the form of taxes . . .

These differences in modes of controlling labour are fully recognized in Wallerstein's schema. That labour was normally coerced in the periphery is central to his model. The differences between slavery, serfdom, wage labour or indentured labour, however, are all forms, for him, of *capitalist* labour relations, dictated by the different *technical* needs of different products, e.g. different kinds of crops. *Per contra*, I am arguing that capitalist relations of production based on wage labour – which requires the dispossession ('freeing') of the producer from the means of production – are a late development, and that slavery, serfdom and unfree, coerced labour in general are not modes of capitalist *production* at all. The beginnings of the implantation of those relations could not occur until the centre itself had been transformed along capitalist lines. Only then did the parcelling-out of the world get completed; only then did the capitalist organization of production get under way, though only a very little of this was in manufacturing. In this process, it was inevitably the leading industrial countries which also became the leading colonial powers. That general process of capitalist expansion is therefore highly uneven and occurs chronologically at quite different times in quite different parts of the world, due to a double determination: the nature of the colonizing core country, and the nature of the zone being colonized: not as something 'allotted' by some reified functionalist 'logic' of a system.

16   Bill Warren

Imperialism: Pioneer of Capitalism

Excerpts from Bill Warren, *Imperialism: Pioneer of Capitalism*, Verso Books, 1980, pp. 170–73, 175–85, 190–91, 200, 211–12, 215–16, 223, 231–2, 236–8, 241–2, 244, 252.

All the normal indicators of 'dependence' point to *increasingly* non-subordinate economic relations between poor and rich countries as regards trade diversification ... The distribution of world economic power is becoming less concentrated and more dispersed, and the countries of Asia, Africa, and Latin America are playing ever more independent roles, both economically and politically.

Political independence must be counted among the major achievements of the countries of the Third World ...

By whatever standard it may be judged, the view that economic relations between rich and poor countries have changed only marginally since independence must be rejected ... The ex-colonies have, for example, significantly diversified their market outlets and sources of supply in a remarkably short time ...; [and] have diversified their exports into manufactured goods, which by 1970 accounted for more than 25 per cent of the value of their exports. They have exercised mounting control over foreign-owned or -controlled economic activity within their borders, including rather widespread nationalization, especially but not exclusively of resource-based foreign-owned enterprises. Among the more positive effects of this control have been improved division of rent (gross profits, interest charges, royalties, and licence fees) especially from resource-based industries, by taxation and other means; an already substantial and steadily rising training of indigenous personnel; a constant increase in the local content of non-labour (as well as labour) inputs, which is rapidly reducing 'enclave' features of foreign-owned or -controlled manufacturing enterprises, a process that has gone quite far in Latin America; the spread of shareholding and investment in manufacturing enterprises in countries previously inexperienced in these ac tivities; the expansion of exports of manufactures; and the transfer of modern technology . . .

The lack of any significant trend towards a reduction in profit shares of expatriate manufacturing enterprise is the result of a rational desire to obtain the benefits of advanced technology and organization. It reflects the fact that the governments of less developed countries (LDCs) are realistic enough not to take seriously the ridiculous notion that because the outflow of profits and dividends exceeds the original investment, the host country has lost . . .

Private foreign investment in the LDCs is economically beneficial irrespective of measures of government control . . . To the extent that political independence is real, private foreign investment must normally be regarded not as a cause of dependence but rather as a means of fortification and diversification of the economies of the host countries. It thereby reduces 'dependence', in the long run . . .

In practice . . . the recurrent payments problems of many countries can be shown to be due to specific (incorrect) policies rather than inherent tendencies . . . , [policies] in some respects harmful both to the interests of the advanced countries and to themselves – particularly [those] whose effect was to reduce potential production and/ or raise the relative prices of some primary products for various countries. The neglect of agricultural production for export was in many cases partly the result of the mistaken belief that there had been a secular trend towards a downward movement in the terms of trade for primary relative to manufactured products. The rapid global development of manufactured exports by the Third World (albeit relatively highly concentrated in a few countries), together with the bias against such efforts until recently, strongly suggest an unrealized potential that has been stunted by policy . . .

Nor can the dependency thesis be sustained by reference to an alleged new type of dependence based on the technological superiority of the West or on a new international division of labour enabling the Western multinationals to exploit the cheap labour of the LDCs for assembly industries or the manufacture of components . . .

Dependence on Western technology flows logically from a perfectly sensible desire to make use of that technology, and the amazing achievements of some of the LDCs in the twentieth century would have been inconceivable without this technological transfer . . . It is by no means clear that the purchase of technology should necessarily imply economic, military, or political dependence ... for as Japan has shown, initial acquisition of foreign technology, however costly, can lead eventually (without undue subordination) to great economic power, itself the basis for substantial independent technological innovation ...

Significant diversification of the economic structure has been occurring in the Third World, and growth rates of output during the past twenty-five years have been higher for heavy than for light industries in developing countries.

The concept of dependence has always been imprecise; such significance as it has relates almost entirely to *political* control of one society by another. Since national economies are becoming increasingly *interdependent*, the meaning of dependence is ever more elusive, not to say mystical. Every multinational with a branch or subsidiary in an underdeveloped country is dependent on the continued goodwill (economic reasoning being an element of goodwill) of that country to ensure that its investment pays off, or possibly to ensure that it establishes an early stake in a potentially large and rapidly expanding market ... [The more] trade or investment dependent they are, the more prosperous they tend to be. The cross-sectional relationship between trade dependence and per capita income in the Third World is positive; the wealthier countries are those most dependent on foreign investment ... But ... the concept of dependence is totally misleading in present world circumstances, because it is one-sided, unidirectional, and static in its approach to international economic relationships ... The idea of 'neo-colonialism' – that the formal political independence of almost all the former colonies has not significantly modified the previous domination and exploitation of the great majority of humanity in Asia, Africa, and Latin America by the advanced capitalist world – is highly misleading and affords an assessment of post-war world capitalism that omits most new developments ... Bourgeois nationalism is a fundamental ideological condition for the creation of modern nation-states out of states previously characterized by feudal particularism, religious and communal division, and all varieties of patriarchal backwardness.

But the fact that the theory of neo-colonialism ... [denies] the importance of political independence in stimulating indigenous capitalism in the Third World. But any serious examination of the underdeveloped countries since independence demonstrates that these countries have made important gains in a context in which nationalism has forced the pace of economic development.

[Employment]

In terms of the standard measure of economic progress, GNP per capita, the post-war record of the Third World has been reasonably, perhaps even outstandingly, successful as compared *either* with their pre-war performance *or* with whatever past period of growth in the developed market economies (DMEs) may be taken as relevant for comparison. *Any argument that the post-war economic growth of the LDCs has been a relative or absolute failure must therefore rest on other grounds . . .*

The widespread belief that the rapid economic progress in the Third World since the Second World War has generally been associated with worsening aggregate inequality is not borne out by the [admittedly scanty and unreliable] time-series data or by the more plentiful cross-section data . . .

In sum, such increasing income inequalities as are manifest in the Third World – and the evidence does not support the view that they dominate over trends towards greater equality – cannot be assumed to be detrimental to the poorest sections of the community, except in a strictly arithmetical sense (i.e. the top 5 per cent have gained 'at the expense of' the bottom 40 per cent), since there are strong grounds for arguing that these inequalities are as much a cause as a consequence of economic growth and therefore of an eventual absolute improvement in the living standards of the majority . . .

The misleading impression has often been given that unemployment rates in the LDCs are extremely high and even rising, especially in urban areas. This picture is usually based on employment-exchange statistics. The only worthwhile evidence, however . . . derived from census or sample survey data . . . actually shows that open unemployment in the urban areas of the LDCs is considerably less than has generally been supposed . . .

It is difficult to establish long-term trends for the poor countries as a whole on the basis of hard data . . . but the limited evidence available lends no support to the view that unemployment rates have been rising; it rather suggests the contrary . . . [Nor can it be] assumed automatically that the activities of the urban informal sector are primarily of a time-filling, redistributive (e.g. beggars and thieves), or duplicatory (e.g. hawkers) character . . . [Rather,] a wide variety of essential goods and services are provided at relatively low cost to a substantial proportion of the population by the informal sector . . .

What is called underemployment in the Third World, at least in the urban areas, is the result of a shift from less to more remunerative occupations, at least for the bulk of rural-urban migrants. The principal basis for characterizing them as 'underemployed' is that they fall below some arbitrary dividing line demarcating the superior productivity or earnings of the rest of the urban labour force, even if the incomes of the 'underemployed' have actually improved over time.

The concept of marginalization . . . [which] arose with a valid descriptive function (referring to shanty towns on the outskirts of Third World cities) . . . is a way of referring to the anarchic, chaotic, unplanned, sometimes brutal, but nevertheless vigorous fashion in which urbanization expands the market, stimulates commercialization of the whole of society (especially the agricultural sector), and thereby increases the division of labour and thus the *integration* of society, as Adam Smith noted long ago. The real process is just the opposite of that implied by the word; it is one of increasing *integration*. The shanty towns, unlike slums, are not the result of deterioration, but represent improvements over rural conditions . . .

[Welfare]

Changes in various basic individual indicators of welfare in recent years are also consistent with the view that there has been considerable progress in material welfare for the populations as a whole and not simply for the privileged few. Calorie intake as a percentage of requirements in developing market economies, for example, rose from 93 per cent in 1961 to 97 per cent in 1969–71, following a much steeper improvement during the previous period, 1948–52 to 1957–8.

Truly remarkable advances have also been achieved in education, especially primary but also secondary . . . Equally spectacular results are evident in the field of health, the two most significant indicators – infant mortality and life expectation at birth – showing marked improvements. Data on changes in housing conditions ... [in] the majority of developing countries show substantial improvements ... even though there has been deterioration for some of the 'low income' countries ...

[Agriculture and Industry]

Agriculture has failed not only in responding adequately to the needs of the rest of the economy, but also relative to its technical-economic potential ... But a gradual social revolution in agriculture has been under way ... This social revolution consists of the displacement and/or transformation of subsistence and semi-commercial, small-scale family farming by capitalist farming, plus rising social differentiation within capitalist farming, which tends to concentrate advantages on the richer farmers [but has also resulted in a] very rapid increase in the proportion of the agricultural output that is marketed; swift development of a market for hired labour unconstrained by non-economic ties and obligations; substantial expansion of domestic markets for agricultural means of production, both land and produced means of production; rising social differentiation among rural producers.

A number of more immediate and prosaic factors also suggest that the prospect for agriculture is not unfavourable. Relative failure in this domain is not inevitable, but is largely the result of mistaken policy, lack of suitable incentives, and allocation of insufficient resources to agriculture. These policy errors are now being rectified ...

Despite assertions and predictions to the contrary, the underdeveloped world as a whole has made considerable progress in industrialization during the post-war period ... For the LDCs as a whole, manufacturing accounted for 14.5 per cent of gross domestic product in 1950–4; the figure rose to 17.9 per cent in 1960 and 20.4 per cent in 1973. In the developed capitalist countries manufacturing contributed 28.4 per cent to GDP in 1973. *The difference is therefore becoming rather small* ...

Thus, contrary to widespread populist-liberal opinion, the Third World has not been marked by stagnation, relative or absolute, in the post-war period. On the contrary, significant progress in material welfare and the development of the productive forces has been made, in an acceleration of pre-war trends.

17   T. J. Byres, Ben Crow and Mae Wan Ho

The Green Revolution

Extracts from T. J. Byres and Ben Crow, with Mae Wan Ho, *The Green Revolution*, Open University Press, 1983, pp. 18–20, 22, 24, 26–38, 40–42, 47.

Agrarian Structure in the Early 1950s

In 1947, at the apex of India's agrarian structure stood a *landlord class*, which leased out land to a peasantry and extracted from that peasantry a surplus in the form of rent. Within this class there were two broad groups . . .: a class of large, usually absentee landlords, who tended to hold land in more than one village . . . and one of smaller, normally resident proprietors, who typically held land in one village . . . It was in the interests of both groups to keep rents as high as possible.

Some landlords [were also] moneylenders, [and] drew from the peasant interest as well as rent, often using the usurious relationship to keep the peasant in *debt bondage* . . .

Rich peasants were likely to be part-owners and part-tenants, although some might actually lease out land . . .; they might sometimes be moneylenders . . . The *middle-peasant* stratum was also made up of part-owners/part-tenants, owning a larger part of the land they worked than poor peasants and a smaller part than rich peasants . . .

Some *poor peasants* rented land, and were tenants to a far greater degree than other peasants. They were particularly likely to be *sharecroppers*, paying a proportion of their harvest to a landlord for the use of the land . . .; they were forced to obtain cash for various pressing purposes (rent, debt repayment, land revenue) or to buy necessities such as cloth, salt or kerosene . . . An important characteristic of poor peasants was the degree to which they had to supply their labour to others, in order to survive . . . Throughout India the highest yields were achieved on their 'dwarf' holdings, by dint of very intensive application of labour to the land . . .

In 1951, fifteen per cent of all agricultural families were [*landless labourers*] without land. They . . . might be paid in kind or in money, sometimes a fixed wage and sometimes on a share basis; debt bondage was common. Among labourers it is important to distinguish [between] permanent or attached labourers, those who were hired for a year or longer, and casual labourers, those who were hired for a single crop season, for a single operation (like ploughing, transplanting, weeding, or harvesting), or on a daily basis . . .

Professional moneylenders were not the only source of credit. They were certainly, however, far and away the most common, around 80 per cent of all rural credit in India in the 1950s being supplied by them.

Access to institutional credit (cooperative credit, government loans), which carried low rates of interest, was limited to rich peasants and landlords . . . A sharecropper, for example, would be excluded because he lacked collateral (that is, titles to land or other assets), as would a poor peasant who had some collateral because it was insufficient. Such classes were also in a weak position in relation to traders. Traders would frequently buy the standing crop in advance of harvest, from poor peasants desperately in need of cash, at prices far below those which held at harvest time, selling some of it back later to the very same peasant (who then needed to eat it) at a higher price . . .

By the mid 1960s [the] major change was a diminution . . . of the power of landlords, and a significant increase in the economic and political strength of rich peasants. These shifts were hastened by land reform . . ., an ambitious programme, couched in terms of social justice, and designed to secure . . . an agrarian structure that would have at its centre *individual peasant farming*, composed of peasants with broadly equivalent land holdings . . . It did not bring about any semblance of cooperative farming among poor peasants . . ., but the largest landlords . . . experienced, through land reform, a blow from which they could never fully recover . . . The medium to smaller landlords, who were often resident and sometimes cultivating, received no such blow. Their survival was assured, but on a rather different basis to their former condition . . .

By far the greatest beneficiaries of these changes, and of land reform, were the rich peasants. They were stabilized as independent proprietors, and were on the way to becoming, in many areas of

India, the new dominant class in the emerging agrarian structure . . .
Poor peasants, landless labourers, and most village artisans and craftsmen gained very little . . .

The New Technology

. . . In the early 1950s . . . the land itself was cultivated in holdings
that were fragmented, with a consequent overall loss of efficiency.
Methods of production were backward. *Instruments of production* were
primitive . . .; less than 15 per cent of the total arable area was
irrigated in 1950 . . .

Significant efforts were made by the state with regard to *irrigation*,
through investment in major and minor irrigation works . . . yet
between 1950 and 1965, the percentage of the total arable area which
was irrigated had risen only from 14.6 to 16.9 . . .

Land consolidation . . . had been part of the land reform programme.
But it was successful in only one state, the Punjab . . .; there was some
activity with respect to the production of *improved seeds* . . . and *plant
protection*, [and] some spread of improved practices in *rice* cultivation.

Fertilizers received some attention, with new fertilizer manufacturing plants set up in the first three Five Year Plans. Yet of all Indian
industries chemical fertilizers had by far the most abysmal production
record . . . There was some spread of mechanization . . . but only on
a relatively small scale . . .

By the mid 1960s, indeed, Indian agriculture appeared to have
entered a crisis of alarming proportions; its rate of growth was
insufficient to sustain a significant rate of industrial growth or to
lead to any rise in *per capita* food availability. Until then it had
managed to grow to an annual compound rate of just under 3 per
cent . . . It was a rate that meant that India had still to import large
quantities of foodgrains and to seek food aid from the USA . . .

More than half of the 3 per cent had, up to the early 1960s, come
from *extension of the cultivated acreage* (and less than half, therefore,
from rising yields per unit of land) . . . Indian agriculture continued
to be a precarious 'gamble on the rains'. The monsoons failed in
1965–6 and 1966–7 and . . . output fell drastically, to 72.3 million
tonnes and 74.2 million tonnes respectively, levels not experienced
since the bad year of 1957–8. The results were devastating: . . . the
first famine since Independence – in 1967 . . .

In December 1965, [however, the Minister of Food] assured the
. . . lower house of parliament that 'his Ministry had finally found "a
formula [and] a program" which would take India to self-sufficiency
in foodgrains by 1971' . . . The 'formula and program' were the
'Green Revolution strategy' . . .

Indian agricultural production in the mid 1960s, as it had been in
1947, was dominated by foodgrains, with 75 per cent of the total
cropped area under foodgrains in 1964–5. A 'Green Revolution' in
India had to be a *foodgrain* revolution . . . By far the most important
foodgrain was *rice*: . . . in other words, an 'agricultural revolution' in
India must not simply be a foodgrain revolution. It must primarily
be a *rice* revolution . . . Wheat and rice are the so-called 'superior'
or 'fine' foodgrains, to which the poor have little recourse. They are
the staples of the rich and better off . . . The poor depend heavily
upon the 'inferior' or 'coarse' cereals (maize and millets) and pulses
(like chickpeas and lentils) . . .

By now the Indian planners had set themselves a target of 5 per
cent per annum as necessary if India were to get her industry
growing at a respectable rate (industrial advance being, for several
reasons, dependent upon a growing agriculture in a country like
India) and begin to make any inroads into her massive problems of
poverty, hunger and unemployment . . . What was being asked [was]
a shift from zero growth to a sustained 5 per cent per annum. This is
a rate of agricultural advance never achieved before in India's history,
and achieved by very few countries in world economic history . . .
[As Frankel has noted,]

the new strategy, advanced by the Food and Agriculture Ministry, stood in
striking contrast to the basic assumptions of past policies. Whereas the older
approach had relied mainly on more intensive utilization of traditional inputs,
for example, reclamation of cultivable wasteland, and the more efficient
application of underemployed labour, the Ministry now urged the utmost
importance of applying 'scientific techniques and knowledge of agricultural
production at all stages' . . .

The *application of modern inputs* became the spearhead of the effort
to secure substantial output increase from the mid 1960s onwards
. . . [based on] *biochemical* innovations and *mechanical* innovations.
The former comprise the new high-yielding seeds, chemical fertilizers, pesticides, and the regulated flow of irrigation water. The

latter consist of tractors, threshers, seed-drills, mechanical pumps for irrigation, mechanical reapers, combine harvesters . . . The biochemical inputs [were] portrayed, therefore, as being ideal for wide diffusion of benefits among all classes of cultivator. [But] the application of the biochemical inputs alone, by allowing multiple cropping in shorter growing periods, sets up pressures towards mechanization . . . [These] entail a *sizeable increase in working capital requirements*, by comparison with traditional inputs. They have to be *bought*, and . . . poor peasants (and, indeed, middle peasants) do not have the means to buy them . . .

The seeds . . . could not operate on their own . . . 'Biochemical' inputs are to a certain extent *complementary*: that is, one of them will not significantly increase yields in the absence of any one of the others. So . . . they were seen as a *package* of inputs . . .

Only 17 per cent of India's arable acreage was irrigated in the mid 1960s . . . At the outset, then, at least 80 per cent of India's arable acreage was excluded from the Green Revolution . . . While government agencies and their officers were earmarked to play a role, *private* agents, not at all within effective government control, were very important from the outset, both as seed growers and as seed distributors . . . The government pledged itself, secondly, to take the necessary steps to promote the use of fertilizers . . . Again, one must stress the importance of *private* interests. The government might take action at all of the levels noted, but the fertilizer market was dominated by private traders . . .

There was to be some further government investment in *major* irrigation works, but government activity was to 'concentrate on consolidation of irrigation schemes already completed, through construction of field channels etc.' . . . with stress laid upon a significant extension of *tubewells* . . . As we have seen [this] package . . . was beyond the means of many Indian peasants without a concomitant extension or rural credit, at 'reasonable' rates of interest . . . The 'new technology' meant far greater dependence upon the *market* for inputs. Inputs now had to be bought . . . Long-term credit would come through the banks for major investments, such as a tubewell or a tractor. Short- and medium-term loans – for expenditure with a more immediate return, such as on seed, fertilizer, pesticide or weedkillers – would be exclusively in cash, and would be repayable in cash; shorter-term loans would be made partly in cash and partly in kind (say in seed or fertilizer) . . .

Much of this programme was in the hands of a variety of government officials ... At the lowest level of all, that of the *village*, government implementation finds its essential functionary: the Village Level Worker (VLW). The VLW is a kind of multi-purpose government agent, responsible for, perhaps, ten villages in a block. It is the VLW who has day-to-day and face-to-face contact with the peasants ...

There was early success with the new *wheat* seeds ... Progress in rice has been considerably less spectacular ... A 'rice revolution' in India remains to be achieved. Thus *regional inequality* has been worsened not only by unequal endowment with irrigation, but also by an uneven development of suitable seed strains ... [But] 'coarse cereals' [too] are predominantly rain-fed crops grown in drought-prone areas – areas which the Green Revolution has passed by ... [and] the Green Revolution has increased the rate of decline of pulse production ... On this evidence, the 'new strategy' has, if anything worsened the lot of India's poor. I will have more to say about the poor below.

With fertilizers ... supply has ... been a problem. Moreover, India's capacity to *import* fertilizers was severely strained when fertilizer prices doubled within a short space of time, in the wake of the 1973 oil crisis ... India continues to have to import all of its potassium fertilizers and 36 per cent and 30 per cent respectively of nitrate and phosphate fertilizers. Indeed, these figures are misleading. India, surely, could use *more* imported fertilizer. If it could afford to buy from abroad all that might be productively utilized, the imported proportions would be far bigger ... We recall that [in the mid 1960s] only 17 per cent of India's arable land was irrigated, and that its regional spread was most uneven ... But [by 1976] 75 per cent of India's cultivated area [was] still excluded. Not only that, but the regional concentration of irrigation has worsened ... The *mechanical* inputs ... have been the monopoly of the dominant classes and they have spread because their use has proved highly profitable ... The use of tractors has also ... been given powerful encouragement by the arrival of the biochemical inputs. The adoption of these latter heightens considerably the time-bound nature of agricultural operations. It does so by shortening the maturing period, making two or more crops possible in a year, and, consequently, making it crucial that harvesting be completed quickly ...; labour might not be available at these periods in sufficient quantity at precisely the right time [but] tractors can cope with the land preparation constraint, and are a way of avoiding 'problems for labour management, discipline and supervision' . . .

Credit

Credit has been advanced in increasing quantities through government sources . . . The land mortgage banks and the cooperative banks have, also, expanded apace . . . But it is significant that *still* the dominating influence in the provision of rural credit, even in Green Revolution areas, is the village moneylender, who continues to lend at exorbitant rates of interest (sometimes as much as 300 per cent per annum) . . .

These are the various inefficiencies and inadequacies which have limited the spread and reduced the effectiveness of the 'new strategy'. They have not, however, rendered the 'new strategy' completely ineffective. Far from it . . . There has [also] been consistent intervention to *keep agricultural prices high*. It is to be stressed, however, that this had been the result less of an independent desire on the part of government to so act than of the organized pressure of the increasingly powerful rich peasant lobby . . . The 'losers' include agricultural labourers, if their wages rise less rapidly than food prices; and poor peasants, who may have to sell at a relatively low price at harvest . . . only to buy back later in the season, at a greatly increased price.

Results of the New Strategy

. . . After the disasters of the mid 1960s, growth in agriculture appears to have returned to a trend compound rate of around 3 per cent per annum. To have returned to the former trend growth rate after the apparent prospect, in the mid 1960s, of something not far from zero is, indeed, an achievement. But there has been no question of reaching the 5 per cent per annum which the Indian planners have believed to be necessary . . . That area expansion should still constitute 20 per cent or more of growth, when its *future* scope must remain doubtful, is disquieting . . . *Rice* has . . ., in fact, slowed off somewhat (3.4 per cent per annum to 2.2 per cent) [and] the 'coarser' grains have been most disappointing in their performance . . . These are figures which augur ill for India's poor . . .

The effect upon unemployment is, obviously, of central importance . . . On the whole, the result was an increase in employment opportunities in Green Revolution areas. We should not, however, exaggerate this. Certainly, there has been a rise in *wage employment*, but that has been offset by a decline in *self-employment* . . . As mechanization spreads and intensifies . . . it is certain that labour will be displaced. This would not matter if such labour could be absorbed in industry. Indeed, it would represent an ultimate increase in material welfare. In India, there is no prospect of that happening in the foreseeable future. Industrial advance has been and will be of the kind (essentially capital-intensive: heavy on capital, light on jobs) . . .

As we have seen, by the mid 1960s a *rich peasant stratum* was well established, in certain areas particularly, as a powerful class . . . Rich peasants tended to adopt both the biochemical and the mechanical inputs. [They] (and landlords) had greatly superior resource endowment . . . They had far greater access to information about the new inputs and their likely performance as a result of class ties, this time with block officials who disseminated information, control of village social clubs (which would exclude poor peasants), greater literacy, greater likelihood of ownership of a radio, and deliberate restriction of knowledge. [They] could [also] afford to purchase the new inputs . . . The 'new technology' has hastened the process of differentiation . . . It has served to consolidate the rich peasantry as a powerful, dominant class: the rich peasantry has become stronger economically and has taken on more of the characteristics of a class of capitalist farmers.

What we must now ask is whether the 'new technology', as part of the foregoing process, contributes to *rural proletarianization* (that is, the creation of a class which survives and reproduces itself simply by selling its labour power) and whether we can discern a tendency towards *depeasantization* (the separation of peasants from land and the means of production) . . . In north-west India . . . many poor peasants, finding that their small piece of land has become inadequate to provide the household's subsistence, have started to lease it out to rich peasants . . . The poor peasantry are, increasingly, being pushed out of *self-employment* into *wage labour* . . .

If we examine further the nature of the emerging rural proletariat, we find that, in north-west India at least, some of its features are such as to blunt any concerted class action.

The first is a change in the structure of the labour force: away from a preponderance of *casual* labour (employed on a daily or occasional basis) and towards *permanent* labour (employed for a season, year or longer). This is a shift associated with growing mechanization.

Secondly, permanent or attached labour ... is now paid mainly in cash (rather than in kind), at a predetermined fixed money rate (rather than as a proportion of the crop) and according to a *contract* the length of whose term is increasing ... Such contracts have been conceived precisely with the aim of countering any possible bargaining power that the labour might attempt to acquire ...

As far as *casual labour* is concerned, the 'new technology' has stimulated an increase in the use of *migrant labour* ... There has been some suggestion that the 'new technology' will bring about an overall decline in female employment in agriculture ... For northwest India ... the 'new technology' has led to the *withdrawal* from direct participation in agriculture – from outdoor agricultural life – of the women of those rich peasant households which have adopted the 'new technology' and partaken of the Green Revolution gains ...

At the other end of the spectrum, we may say that with respect to poor peasant households and those of landless labourers there is no question of withdrawal of women from labour. Those women of such households who have to sell their labour may be displaced by mechanization, as their menfolk may be ... Women are, however, *casual labourers*, often in large number, but only for limited periods of the year, and doing the most poorly paid and often the most exacting tasks ... It is the women of subordinate classes, however, who actually suffer most. Their situation *vis-à-vis* that of men is captured by the wife of an agricultural labourer in the Punjab ...:

It is much better to be a man. A man can be ritually pure and clean. A woman ... well, you know what I mean, she menstruates every month and can never be as pure as a man. And then you have to clean the babies when they shit, collect cowdung and all that kind of work, you know.

... The rich peasants have emerged as masters of the Indian countryside.

18 Jeffrey Henderson

The New International Division of Labour

Extracts from Jeffrey Henderson, *The Globalization of High Technology Production: Society, Space and Semiconductors in the Restructuring of the Modern World*, Routledge, 1989, pp. 3–5, 16–18, 20–21, 36–8, 42–3, 45, 49–51, 53–5, 58–61, 73, 75, 80, 87, 94, 106–11, 114–16, 154–5, 164–5.

The varied products which constitute the basis of [microelectronic] 'revolution' . . . have one thing in common. They have the same technological core . . .: the semiconductor in the form of the transistor or diode, but particularly the integrated circuit ('silicon chip') . . . Without semiconductors, industrial societies would be unworkable, and social life within them, almost unthinkable . . . Semiconductors are now accorded a strategic role for national economies similar to that of steel fifty years ago . . .

Four elements . . . distinguish electronics industries from those manufacturing processes . . .:

(1) Electronics industries utilize a distinctive raw material: know-ledge . . .

(2) A fundamental task of electronic products is to process informa-tion . . .

(3) Electronics production . . . has generated social and technical divisions of labour . . . quite unlike those of most other manufac-turing industries . . .: relatively large numbers of engineers and technicians . . . very large . . . numbers of unskilled workers, [and] very few skilled manual workers . . .

(4) Electronics production . . . is organized in terms of a combina-tion of *technically disarticulated* labour processes . . .; particular labour processes can be dispersed to selected locations within the home country or overseas . . .

[By the 1970s,] the 'self-expansion' of industrial capital could no longer be achieved solely within the national boundaries of the core economies of the USA and Western Europe . . . A vast increase in foreign direct manufacturing investment [took place not only] in the core economies themselves . . . [but also] in certain 'third world' or 'peripheral' societies. The latter process has helped to create what are currently amongst the world's most productive economies, the so-called 'newly industrializing countries' . . .

Manufacturing activity . . . has come to be increasingly organized and coordinated at a global level, largely by transnational corporations . . .

The migration of industrial capital from the core to the periphery of the world system . . . has resulted in the development . . . of industrial enclaves composed of 'world-market factories', which manufacture commodities . . . primarily for export . . . [despite theories which] rule out the possibilities of 'national' capitalist development within the world system . . . [A more adequate theory] would allow for the material and social transformations which have constituted (and which their populations *feel* as though they have constituted) genuine development in such semiperipheral units as Hong Kong and Singapore . . . [and particularly the] development of production facilities by *particular* industrial branches or firms in *particular* territorial units . . .

The initial development of Silicon Valley, [in California] from the late 1950s to the early 1970s, [involved an] extraordinary rate of horizontal disaggregation of the semiconductor industry . . . Vertical disaggregation was also proceeding apace . . .: a marked breakdown of production activities into many specialized units . . . The result of this process was not only a mushrooming of producers in Santa Clara County, but also the development of an industrial system based on small-batch production . . .

All component labour processes were effectively confined to the United States in the early period of development when markets were limited and specialized, when they were monopolized by US producers and when the military constituted the principal end-user. With the rise of more standardized commercial markets (at first overwhelmingly associated with demands for transistors for the booming radio industry), and the emergence of intense Japanese competition, the conditions for the internationalization of particular labour processes were brought to fruition . . .

US semiconductor companies, confronted by stiff Japanese competition in discrete (especially transistor) markets, internationalized their most labour intensive production process (assembly) as a cost-lowering strategy . . . American electronics-systems corporations . . . have only rarely set up semiconductor plants (assembly *or* wafer fabrication) outside of the United States . . . In East Asia the most important *initial* determinant, was . . . the presence of enormous pools of cheap and underemployed labour. But . . . Hong Kong had a number of additional special advantages . . .: (a) political stability, (b) an open financial system with no limits on the repatriation of profits . . . (c) excellent telecommunications and air transport facilities . . . [and] (d) a workforce that was habituated to the kinds of labour processes characteristic of semiconductor assembly . . . Furthermore, the existence of a flourishing informal sector in Hong Kong, together with state subsidies, helped to keep industrial wages down . . . Hong Kong was [also] able to supply the small but crucial demand for qualified engineers and technicians . . . [Yet] there was an exclusive concentration not only of organizational control functions in the USA . . . but also of the labour processes requiring the most advanced scientific and technological skills (R & D) . . .; only the most labour-intensive assembly processes had been implanted in the region . . . The wafers were fabricated in the United States, air-freighted to East Asia, assembled into discretes or integrated circuits and air-freighted back to the United States for final testing . . . By the mid-1980s . . . certain changes seem to have taken place: the 'gang of four', but especially Hong Kong and Singapore, have become the recipients of investment in final testing facilities . . .; circuit-design centres have also been set up in Hong Kong and Singapore by a number of US companies . . .; a number of companies have established their Asian regional headquarters there . . .; [and] in 1987 National Semiconductor became the first US company . . . to establish a wafer fabrication plant in the developing world when it began fabrication at its plant in Penang, Malaysia . . .

During the 1970s and 1980s, manual labour costs . . . increased substantially relative to those in the units at the periphery of the regional division of labour. Thus much of the new investment in labour-intensive assembly work . . . has shifted to these persistently low-wage countries . . .

Whereas previously each plant, or national operation within the region, would assemble its quota of semiconductors and ship them directly to the United States for testing and distribution to domestic and world-wide markets, the emergence of the regional division of labour ... has altered both product flows and the spatial chain of command. What increasingly tends to happen is that although fabricated wafers are shipped from the United States or Europe directly to assembly plants in, say, Malaysia or the Philippines, once assembled, they are routed to the respective company's testing centres in Hong Kong and Singapore, and from there directly to US, European or Asian customers ...

Hong Kong and Singapore ... have developed extensive housing, educational and welfare programmes. Indeed their spectacular economic growth and rising living standards would have been inconceivable without such state intervention ...

Repression, [indeed], is not the only route to political stability, nor is it the most successful in the long run. 'Legitimation expenditure' on such things as public housing programmes coupled with representative democratic forms are often more reliable routes to political stability ...

The numbers employed as technicians and engineers tends to be directly related to the capital intensity of the labour process. In Motorola's Hong Kong plant ... only about 300 of the 750 workforce are manual production workers. The majority of the rest are technicians and engineers ...

By the late 1950s, competition from US and domestic producers, and rising wages in Japan, resulted in Sony's partial internationalization of radio assembly. They developed a joint-venture operation in South Korea [and began] to assemble radios in Hong Kong ... By 1960, [local] companies had begun to produce their own radios even more cheaply than the Japanese ... Hong Kong's continuing development as an industrial society ... is narrowly based on two sectors, clothing and textiles ... and electronics: two-thirds of the territory's domestic exports. [But] the contribution of the clothing and textile sector declined [between] 1961 and 1987, [while] the contribution of electronics has grown dramatically ... from 2.5 to nearly 23 per cent of exports ... The rapid proliferation of factories during the 1970s and 1980s, ... coincided with a significant reduction in average size [and] a proliferation of the subcontract assembly of particular parts of the products to small (often no more than 10 workers), family-run firms ... The electronics workforce in Hong Kong is [also] over-whelmingly female ... US and Japanese business interests in the electronics industry . . . provided 97.2 per cent of foreign direct investment and 91.1 of foreign sector jobs in the industry . . . The United States was, and remains, the dominant market for Hong Kong's electronics products with an average annual share of 44.4 per cent (1976–87), the principal EEC markets (UK, West Germany, France and The Netherlands) are also particularly important.

While the Hong Kong Government has not intervened directly in the capital market or in funding R & D, . . . it has intervened directly in the labour market and indirectly in both the capital and labour markets . . . [in] the form of very low corporate and personal taxation (both currently standing at 16 per cent maximum) . . . By far the largest source of non-taxation revenues has been sale of leases on Government-owned land, and in Hong Kong, the Government owns over 95 per cent of *all* land. Its subsidies to private capital, by means of low taxation, and then, in large measure, a result of the fact that perhaps unique amongst capitalist societies, land in Hong Kong is nationalized . . . Since 1954, [it] has developed the second largest public housing system in the world . . . [while Singapore houses] about 45 per cent of the total population, and over 80 per cent of the territory's working class . . . In addition, the Government organizes what is in effect a cartel to control the prices of basic foodstuffs such as rice and vegetables . . . The Chinese Government from the beginning (1949) has been involved in subsidizing the wages of Hong Kong workers . . . by supplying the bulk of the territory's food requirements (rice, poultry, meat, vegetables) at . . . prices significantly below those on the open market . . . The combined efforts of the Hong Kong and Chinese Governments subsidize the household expenditure of Hong Kong's working-class population to the tune of 50.2 per cent! [The] Hong Kong trade union movement . . . has not . . . mobilized its members around the standard (for Western trade unions) issues of wages and working conditions. Neither has it adopted a militant stance to the workplace problems of its membership. Indeed, . . . labour militancy gauged in terms of strike activity . . . has declined substantially in recent years . . . labour legislation has operated, additionally, to discourage workplace solidarity and mobilization . . . In Hong Kong, . . . an overwhelming majority of the workforce are women . . . [whose] principal life interests . . . lie not within the experience of labour, but rather are heavily determined by familial obligations . . .

[Although] Hong Kong, along with the other members of the 'gang of four', were successively 'priced-out' of the cheap labour market . . . US producers, in large part, remained in Hong Kong, but on the basis of a technologically upgraded operation. A major reason for the retention of restructured production units . . . was that by the mid to late 1970s, the Hong Kong education system could provide qualified engineers and technicians . . . Electronics engineering and technical labour can be provided there, not only reliably, but also far more cheaply than it can, in (for instance) the USA and Scotland. Thus in 1981, annual wages for electronics engineers in Hong Kong were 60 per cent lower than they were for their equivalents in the United States, *three years earlier*, in 1978 . . . Once a production complex begins to develop . . . there may well be compelling economic, social and technical reasons for continuing to invest and upgrade production there, rather than at other, potentially competitive, locations . . .

It is no longer possible, then, to understand local economic, and social change in a global context by means of the core-periphery categories . . . We are confronted with a changing international division of labour which is becoming less organized on the basis of cores, peripheries and semiperipheries . . . It still makes considerable sense to speak in terms of processes of 'dependent development' controlled from 'cores' and 'world cities' . . . But . . . this increasing flexibility in the world system, unfortunately does not mean that we can now look forward to the 'end of the Third World' . . . Those territorial units which for whatever reason are unable to offer foreign electronics corporations anything but cheap, unskilled labour . . . [are] unlikely to be even touched by the new mode of industrialization, never mind become recipients of some of its benefits. It is for this, among other reasons, that we must resist the temptation to assume that the gang of four, for instance, with their rising living standards, based . . . in part on semiconductor and other forms of electronics production, constitute a viable mode for development elsewhere across the globe. The Third World remains very much with us . . .

Part Four
Sex, Gender and the Family

The concerns of sociologists are commonly the concerns of the societies they live in, so it is not surprising to find that there has been an explosion of work on sex, gender and the family in the period since the re-emergence of Western feminism in the early 1970s. The first writers who were widely read – Simone de Beauvoir, Kate Millett and Germaine Greer – came from arts backgrounds and emphasized the way in which culture, and literature in particular, is male-centred and presents women as 'other', as sexual objects and as repositories of every characteristic that men wish to suppress and conquer. In the following decades, sociologists, and many feminist theorists, have pursued these insights more theoretically and made them the basis for much solid research and scholarship. In particular, sociologists have developed a distinction between 'sex' and 'gender'. Sex refers to biological differences, gender to the elaborate differences and distinctions that are built on top of biology by culture and by the division of labour between men and women in the family and throughout society. Some sociologists have taken up Kate Millett's concept of 'patriarchy' to characterize societies in which men dominate women and to draw attention to the dimension of power in gender divisions.

As well as these theoretical developments, the concerns of feminism have been reflected in a variety of ways throughout sociology. One has been quite simply a flowering of women's studies – studies of women's lives and women's social worlds, which the previous male-centred sociology had tended to ignore or trivialize. Such occupations as housewife and secretary had not been worthy of study before; and part-time work, home-work, or the return to employment after a period spent at home might never have existed. Some of these studies of women were concerned to document the ways in which women are oppressed: the unfair division of labour in the household, discrimination against women in employment, sexual harassment, rape and other violence against women. At the same time, there have begun to be studies of men *as men*, in which their masculinity, their role as breadwinner, their reliance upon having a housewife, their ways of retaining power are all brought to the foreground instead of being taken for granted. No longer are men the norm and women peculiar; both are equally peculiar once we start to question gender divisions.

Every field of sociology needs to be rethought to take account of gender divisions. Interestingly, some fields have proved more amenable than others. The study of the family has been completely colonized by gender. 'Gender roles' in the family had long been subject to research, but now there can be few family studies in which gender does not play a central part. Conversely, it is clear that the family is the primary locus for the construction of gender. Most of what we understand by masculinity and femininity, most of the ideology of gender and much of the division of labour between men and women is associated with the institution of the family. That is why they are in one section in this book and why half the items in this section are about aspects of the family. But, as Cynthia Cockburn argues, there are also other spheres in which men exercise power, to oppress women, to exclude them or to disadvantage them. The sphere of employment is one that is very much structured by gender, and Cockburn argues that distinct aspects of gender are constituted here. Reading 52, by Veronica Beechey, on 'Explaining Women's Employment' (in Part Eight below), shows how taking women into account has raised problems for theories of the labour market and how taking the family into account has revealed unnoticed aspects of *men's* participation in the labour force as well as women's.

In the study of social class there have been major debates within mainstream and Marxist sociological theory about the place of women in the class structure. Do women, who themselves are likely to be housewives for at least part of their lives, have their own class position or do they share the class position of their husband? Is the unit of stratification 'the family' or the individual? Is the fact that women have been left out of class analysis a reflection of male bias or a realistic recognition that they tend to be dependent on their husbands?

The study of social policy is another field that has been transformed by gender considerations. For it has become apparent that much social policy is premised upon the assumption that a particular family form predominates; the welfare state steps in where this family fails. So provision for income support assumes that if a child or young person has a parent, or an adult has a spouse, who can provide, they should turn to them first and not claim state benefit. And the provision of welfare services is such that most of the care of children, the disabled, the mentally ill and the elderly is done by women in the family, as an extension of their responsibility for housework. Reading 38, by Margaret Stacey (in Part Six below), shows how women come to contribute so much to the nation's health care.

The first excerpt in this Part, Reading 19, by Peggy Reeves Sanday, challenges assumptions commonly made about differences between women and men. The social fact of rape is commonly taken to be caused by the innate nature of men's sexuality. If even sexuality varies from one society to another, then how many other 'male' and 'female' characteristics are really social rather than biological? The second excerpt, Reading 20, by Felicity Edholm, uses the same method of cross-cultural contrasts to show that our current ideas of the family are far from universal and that bonds such as those between husband and wife, parent and child, are also social rather than purely natural. Peter Laslett, author of the third item, Reading 21(a), is a social historian who has made an important contribution to understanding changes in the English family, disproving the idea that during the Industrial Revolution a nuclear family household of two parents and their dependent children replaced an older extended family household which had included more generations or a wider span of kin. Here, in a salutary corrective to sociologists' tendency to overgeneralize, he gives a summary of family history that emphasizes variety rather than stereotyped family forms. To illustrate this, we have also included a brief account of the family forms of other British ethnic groups by David Eversley and Lucy Bonnerjea (Reading 21(b)), taken from the same book.

In the next item, Reading 22, Janet Finch is critical of another myth about family change, the idea of a golden age in which family responsibilities were stronger than they are today. A sense of family obligation, to offer economic aid, practical help and personal care, is both compelling and subtle. There is a tendency for childcare and support for the elderly to be regarded as women's business in families, while money is men's business. But this is not due solely to cultural norms; it is also because women are less likely to have access to financial resources, more likely to be involved in caring for their own children and more likely to have a part-time job, or one they can give up without great sacrifice. This Reading can usefully be read in conjunction with Reading 38, by Margaret Stacey, in Part Six below. Reading 23, by Anthony Heath, on 'The Social Mobility of Women', is also concerned with the interface between the family and the wider world. It shows how, given that a woman's life chances are determined to some extent by her husband's position, women have an additional means of upward and downward social mobility – marriage – but one which apparently does little overall to compensate for the fact that their chances of upward occupational mobility are lower than men's.

Finally, Reading 24, which we have called 'Jobs for the Boys', comes from Cynthia Cockburn's study of technological change in the printing industry (later published as a book: *Brothers: Male Dominance and Technological Change*, Pluto Press, 1983). Women's disadvantage in the labour market has been well documented. Work is highly segregated into 'men's jobs and 'women's jobs' and women tend to be lower down the ladder and in lower-paid and less secure employment. The excerpt by Veronica Beechey (Reading 52 in Part Eight below) outlines the problems of explaining these patterns. Cynthia Cockburn takes up a particular issue: how it is that these inequalities persist despite major technological changes. She argues that women's disadvantage is not just a product of their particular position in the family but that men have combined at work to exclude women from the best jobs and define them as incompetent. The defence of their craft, their pay and their conditions of service, on the part of male trade unionists, and their struggles to ensure that new technology does not deskill them, are not only class struggles but also struggles for a privileged male monopoly.

19   Peggy Reeves Sanday

The Social Context of Rape

Excerpts from Peggy Reeves Sanday, 'The Social Context of Rape', *New Society*, Vol. 61, No. 1037, 1982, pp. 540–42.

[The] attribution of violence to males, and victimization to females, [is] a common theme in western social commentary on the nature of human nature. Most of its popularizers present what amounts to a socio-biological view of human behaviour which traces war, violence, and now rape, back to the violent landscape of our primitive ancestors, where, early on, the male tendency in these directions became genetically programmed in the fight for survival of the fittest . . .

I want to depart here from the familiar assumption that male nature is programmed for rape, and to demonstrate . . . that human sexual behaviour, though based on a biological need, 'is rather sociological and cultural force than mere bodily relation of two individuals' . . .

As an anthropologist, I shall look principally at rape in tribal society. The incidence of rape, in fact, varies between different societies. How do 'rape-free' and 'rape-prone' tribes differ?

I define a 'rape-prone' society as one in which the incidence of rape is high, rape is a ceremonial act, or rape is an act by which men punish or threaten women. On a standard anthropological cross-cultural sample of 95 tribes world-wide, 17 tribes could be categorized as definitely rape-prone. Forty-five were rape-free. In 33, rape occurs but with no information on frequency or typicality.

Writing in 1959, Robert LeVine gave one example of a rape-prone society, the Gusii tribe of south-western Kenya . . . Based on court records for 1955 and 1956, LeVine estimated the annual rate of rape at 47.2 per 100,000 population. But he thought that this figure grossly underestimated the Gusii rape rate. During the same period, the annual recorded rape rate in urban areas of the United States was 13.85 per 100,000 (13.1 for rural areas). Thus, the rate of Gusii rape is extraordinarily high.

Normal heterosexual intercourse between Gusii males and females is conceived as an act in which a man overcomes the resistance of a woman and causes her pain. When a bride is unable to walk after her wedding night, the groom is considered by his friends 'a real man'. He is able to boast of his exploits, particularly if he has been able to make her cry.

Older women contribute to the groom's desire to hurt his new wife. These women insult the groom, saying:

'You are not strong, you can't do anything to our daughter. When you slept with her you didn't do it like a man. You have a small penis which can do nothing. You should grab our daughter and she should be hurt and scream – then you're a man' . . .

LeVine . . . distinguishes between three types of rape: rape resulting from seduction; premeditated sexual assault; and abduction.

Given the hostile nature of Gusii sexuality, seduction classifies as rape when a Gusii female chooses to bring the act to the attention of the public. Premarital sex is forbidden, but this does not stop Gusii boys from trying to entice girls to intercourse. The standard pose of the Gusii girl is reluctance, which means that it is difficult for the boy to interpret her attitude as being either willing or unwilling. The boy may discover the girl's unwillingness only after he has forced himself on her.

Fear of discovery may turn a willing girl into one who cries rape. If a couple engaging in intercourse out of doors are discovered, the girl may decide to save her reputation by crying out that she was being raped. Rape may also occur in cases when a girl has encouraged a young man to present her with gifts, but then denies him sexual intercourse.

In some cases one or more boys may attack a single girl in premeditated sexual assault – the second type of rape. The boys may beat the girl badly and tear her clothing. Sometimes the girl is dragged off to the hut of one of them and forced into coitus. After being held for a couple of days the girl is freed.

The third type of rape occurs in the context of wife abduction. When a Gusii man is unable to present the bridewealth necessary for a normal marriage and cannot persuade a girl to elope, he may abduct a girl from a different clan. The man's friends will be enlisted to carry out the abduction. The young men are frequently rough with the girl, beating her and tearing her clothes. When she arrives at the home of the would-be lover, he attempts to persuade her to remain with him until bridewealth can be raised. Her refusal is ignored, and the wedding-night sexual contest is performed with the clansmen helping in overcoming resistance . . .

In [some cultures,] it is fairly frequent to find the threat of rape used to keep women from the men's houses or from viewing male sacred objects . . . .

The Mundurucu believe there was a time when women ruled, and sex roles were reversed, with the exception that women could not hunt. During that time, it is said, women were the sexual aggressors and men were sexually submissive and did women's work. Women controlled the 'sacred trumpets' (the symbols of power) and the men's houses. The trumpets contained the spirits of the ancestors who demanded ritual offering of meat. As women did not hunt and could not make these offerings, men were able to take the trumpets from them, thereby establishing male dominance.

The trumpets now are secured in special chambers within the men's houses. No woman can see them under penalty of gang rape. Such a threat is necessary because men believe that women will attempt to seize from the men the power they once had. Gang rape is also the means by which men punish sexually 'wanton' women . . .

In rape-free societies, women are treated with considerable respect. Prestige is attached to female reproductive and productive roles. Interpersonal violence is minimized. People's attitude to the natural environment is one of reverence, rather than exploitation. Turnbull's *The People of the Forest* gives a profile of [the Mbuti pygmies,] a rape-free society. Violence between the sexes, or between anybody, is almost absent among the net-hunting Mbuti pygmies when they are in their forest. The Mbuti attitude toward the forest reflects their attitude towards one another. The forest is addressed as 'father', 'mother', 'lover' and 'friend'.

The Mbuti say that the forest is everything – the provider of food, shelter, warmth, clothing and affection. Each person and animal is endowed with some spiritual power which 'derives from a single source whose physical manifestation is the forest itself'.

The ease of the Mbuti relationship to their environment is reflected in the relationship between the sexes. There is little division of labour by sex. The hunt is often a joint effort. A man is not ashamed to pick mushrooms and nuts if he finds them, or to wash and clean a baby. In general, leadership is minimal and there is no attempt to control, or to dominate, either the geographical or human environment.

Decision-making is by common consent. Men and women have equal say, because hunting and gathering are both important to the economy. The forest is the only recognized authority of last resort. In decision-making, diversity of opinion may be expressed; but pro-longed disagreement is considered to be 'noise', and offensive to the forest. If husband and wife disagree, the whole camp may act to mute their antagonism, lest the disagreement become too disruptive to the social unit.

The outstanding feature of [rape-free] societies is the ceremonial importance of women and the respect accorded the contribution women make to social continuity, a respect which places men and women in relatively balanced power spheres.

In the West African kingdom of Ashanti, for example, it is believed that only women can contribute to future generations. Ashanti women say:

'I am the mother of the man . . . I alone can transmit the blood to a king . . . If my sex die in the clan, then that very clan becomes extinct, for be there one, or one thousand male members left, not one can transmit the blood, and the life of the clan becomes measured on this earth by the span of a man's life.'

In Ashanti religion, priestesses participate with priests at all major rituals. The Ashanti creation story emphasizes the complementarity and inseparability of male and female. The main female deity, the Earth Goddess, is believed to be the receptacle of past and future generations as well as the source of food and water. Only one incident of rape is reported by the main ethnographer of the Ashanti, R. S. Rattray. The man involved in the case was condemned to death . . .

Interpersonal violence is uncommon in rape-free societies. It is not that men are necessarily prone to rape. Rather, where inter-personal violence is a way of life, violence frequently achieves sexual expression . . .

This is not only true in East Africa. In his study of rape in Philadelphia, M. Amir placed the rapist squarely within the subcul-ture of violence. Rape statistics in Philadelphia showed that in 43 per cent of the cases examined, rapists operated in pairs or groups. The rapists tended to be in the 15–19 age bracket, the majority were not married, and 90 per cent belonged to the lower socio-economic class and lived in inner city neighbourhoods were there was also a high degree of crime against the person. In all, 71 per cent of the rapes were planned . . .

It is important to understand that violence is socially and not biologically programmed. Rape is not an integral part of male nature, but the means by which men, already programmed for violence, express their sexual selves. Men who are conditioned to respect the female virtues of growth and the sacredness of life, do not violate women. In tribal societies where nature is held sacred, rape occurs only rarely.

The incidence of rape in our own society will be reduced to the extent that boys grow to respect women and the qualities so often associated with femaleness in other societies – nurturance, growth and nature . . .

20 Felicity Edholm

The Unnatural Family

Excerpts from Felicity Edholm, 'The Unnatural Family', in Elizabeth Whitelegg et al. (eds.), *The Changing Experience of Women*, Martin Robertson, Open University, 1982, pp. 166–77.

It was, and still is, widely argued that some form of the family, and, in some cases, of the nuclear family, was universal, and was found in all societies ... Groups very similar to those which we identify as the family do [indeed] exist in the majority of societies known to anthropologists. Furthermore, anthropologists have tended to assume that an adequate explanatory definition of any given social or cultural trait can be extended to similar traits in other cultures ... When anthropologists talk about the family, it is primarily in terms of kinship. At its simplest, kinship refers to the ties which exist between individuals who are seen as related, through birth (descent) and through mating (marriage). It is thus primarily concerned with the ways in which mating is socially organized and regulated, the ways in which parentage is assigned, attributed and recognized, descent is traced, relatives are classified, rights are transferred across generations and groups are formed ... Kinship is above all concerned with relationships which are socially constructed; relatives are not born but made.

When we look at the societies studied by anthropologists and at the variation in kinship systems, it is clear that the range of social options is enormous, that the constraints on human behaviour do not produce uniformity, and that those assumptions we make about what is 'natural' in respect of fundamental human kinship relations, are profoundly challenged by the evidence from widely different societies ...

Conception

Notions of blood ties, of biological connection, which to us seem relatively unequivocal, are [in fact] highly variable. Some societies of which we have anthropological record recognize only the role of the father or of the mother in conception and procreation. The other sex is given some significance, but is not seen, for example, as providing blood . . . as having any biological connection. Only one parent is a 'relation', the other parent is not. In the Trobriand Islands, for example, it is believed that intercourse is not the cause of conception, semen is not seen as essential for conception. Conception results from the entry of a spirit child into the womb; the male role is to 'open the passage' to the womb, through intercourse, and it is the repeated intercourse of the same partner which 'moulds' the child. A child's blood comes from its mother's side and from her siblings, her mother and mother's brother, not from the father. A child will not be related by blood to its father, but will look like its father since he has through intercourse created its form . . .

The Lakker of Burma on the other hand consider that the mother is only a container in which the child grows; she has no blood connection with her children, and children of the same mother and different fathers are not considered to be related to each other . . .

Incest

Incest is another area of human relations which is widely discussed in terms of some kind of innate, instinctive abhorrence for sexual relations with 'close kin' and is often attributed to a subconscious realization of the genetic danger of in-breeding. It is not [, however,] uniformly accepted that in-breeding is inevitably disadvantageous.

Incest taboos, defined as prohibitions on sexual relations between individuals socially classified as kin, as relations, are nearly universal. But the prohibition does not inevitably apply to the individuals whom we would identify as primary kin. The most dramatic exceptions to incest are found in certain royal dynasties (Egypt, Hawaii) where in-breeding (brother-sister) was enforced in order to keep the purity of the royal line, as well as in Ptolemaic and Roman Egypt where apparently father-daughter and brother-sister sexual relations were relatively common. In most other known societies, sexual relations between those socially recognized as 'biologically' related are taboo. The Trobrianders, for example, do not consider the children of one father and different mothers to be related and sexual relations between those children are thus entirely legitimate, whereas sexual relations with women who have the same mother, or whose mothers are siblings, is taboo. The Lakker of Burma do not consider that the children of the same mother have any kinship links. 'Incest' does not apply to these non-kin and sexual relations are permitted. In other societies in which, for example, the category of mother or sister is extended to include all males or females of the same generation who are descended through one parent from a common grandfather, or great-grandfather, it is frequently this whole group which is sexually unavailable. It is the social definitions of significant kinship relations that are important in defining incest rather than any concept of natural biological imperatives militating against sexual intercourse within a 'natural family unit'.

Parent/Child Relations: Adoption

It is nearly universally accepted in all anthropological texts on the family . . . that 'the mother-child tie is inevitable and given', that 'the irreducible and elementary social grouping is surely the mother and her children'. This is seen as determined by the imperatives of infantile dependence and the need for breast-milk, and . . . other psychological needs on the part both of the mother and of the child. It is in this context instructive to consider the implications of the widespread practice of adoption. In many societies, children do not live with their 'real' parents, but often stay with their mothers until some time after they have been weaned, when, as they say in N. Ghana, they have 'gained sense' (at about six). However, throughout Melanesia and Polynesia, children are adopted just after weaning or, in some instances, well before – a phenomenon which is considered as absolutely acceptable. In some instances, babies are adopted and breast-fed by their adopted mother . . .

In Tahiti, young women often have one or two children before they are considered, or consider themselves to be, ready for an approved and stable relationship. It is considered perfectly acceptable for the children of this young woman to be given to her parents or other close kin for adoption, while she is freed to continue what is seen as the 'business of adolescence'. The girl can decide what her relationship to the children will be, but there is no sense in which she is forced into 'motherhood' because of having had a baby; 'motherhood' in such a situation can be seen as a status reached by women at a particular stage of development, as involving a psychological and social readiness, not something inevitably attached to the physical bearing of children . . . In Tahiti, it is considered an ultimate shame for adopted children to leave the house of their adopted parents, since the relationship between those who have lived together and who have grown 'familiar' ('matau') with each other (the essential ingredient for all good relations) is seen as inevitably far closer than that between biological 'natural' parents . . .

Marriage

It has been claimed that some form of marriage is found in all human societies. The definitions of marriage, however, again give some indication of the kind of complexity that is involved in the attempt to provide universals. One famous definition by Goodenough (1970) defines marriage [as]

. . . a transaction and resulting contract in which a person (male or female, corporate or individual, in person or by proxy) establishes a continuing claim to the right of sexual access to a woman . . .

Other definitions stress above all the significance of marriage in determining parentage – in allocating children to different groups. The definitions have to be understood in relation to the kinds of social arrangements which are entirely inconsistent within our notions of marriage.

The Nayar of Northern India provide one of the most problematic cases of 'marriage'. The basic social group among the Nayar is the Taravad, a unit composed of men and women descended through the female line from a common ancestress. Thus it is brothers and sisters, mothers and children who cohabit. A child becomes a member of the mother's Taravad, not the father's. Nayar girls were involved, before they reached puberty, in a formal ritual with a man from an equivalent caste to her own, and then was able to take as many lovers as she wished; the 'husband' – the man who had been involved in the ritual – only had a very minimal ritual attachment to his 'wife', although he too could be one of her lovers . . . Husbands and fathers, in such a context, are entirely peripheral to the domestic life of their wives and children – and never cohabit.

Among the Nuer of the Nile Basin, one of the most common forms of marriages are what have been called 'ghost' marriages (the anthropologist Evans-Pritchard who worked among the Nuer estimates that nearly 50 per cent of all marriages correspond to this form). Ghost marriage refers to the situation in which a man dies unmarried or with no children of his own. If this happens, a close kinsman (related to him through his father's line) will marry a wife 'to his name' and children born of this union will be seen as the dead man's children. A man who has been involved in marrying in this way and bearing children for another man will, when he dies and if he has not contracted a second marriage in his own name – only possible if his wife dies – have to become in his turn a proxy father and a subsequent ghost marriage will be contracted. If a married man dies, his widow then should ideally be married by a brother or close male kin of the dead man and again, children born of this union will be considered to be those of the dead man, not of the living husband.

The Nuer also have another contractual form of 'marriage' in which an old and important, usually barren, woman may marry a younger woman . . . Marriages of this kind indicate the importance among the Nuer both of becoming a parent, or rather a male parent, in order to become an ancestor – for only 'fathers' with offspring are remembered and have status as ancestors – and also of the inheritance of property. Nuer marriages also demonstrate that the marriage indicates a contract between the group of related 'men' who are seen in some sense as equivalents and a woman married to one of them.

These two widely differing examples illustrate one of the other critical elements in the relations defined by marriage: the difference between the 'legally' recognized father or mother and the person who was involved in conception, or birth. In both the cases cited above, the person we would see as the father, he who had impregnated the woman, is not given any social recognition at all. It is the person, not necessarily male, who is given the social position of father who is recognized through the ritual of 'marriage'. The two males are distinguished in anthropological literature thus: the biological father is the *genitor*, the biological mother the *genetrix*, the 'socially' recognized father the *pater*, the socially recognized mother the *mater* . . .

Paternity is of crucial importance in societies in which status, positions and property are transmitted through the male line. The notion of the group, related through the male line, can in some societies have such force that sexual relations between a woman and any male from the same group as that into which she was born (and such a group can include a considerable number of individuals, all the descendants of a common great-grandfather, for example) are regarded as incestuous. We can see with the example of the Nayar (although the Nayar do constitute an exceptional case) that paternity has far less social significance if all important social attributes are gained through inheritance down the female line. (It is important to recognize that such a system of inheritance does not imply that men are marginalized in such an inheritance system, but that it is brothers rather than husbands who are the significant social males.) . . .

Household and Residence

. . . There are three basic forms of residence as isolated by anthropologists: virilocal, where a married couple and their children live with the kin of the husband; matrilocal, where the couple live with the kin of the wife; and neolocal where the couple live independently of either group of kin. This scheme is however further complicated by the fact that in many societies in which descent is traced through the female line (matrilineal societies), the children might initially live with the mother and father with the father's kin, and then later move to live with their mother's kin; in other words, with their mother's brothers, those from whom they will inherit property, status or position. Often in such societies (such as the Trobriand Islanders) daughters never live with their mother's kin – they stay with their father's until they marry and then move to their husband's kin . . . households as units of parents and their children are not a necessary or permanent social arrangement . . . In most matrilineal societies men will circulate and often a man will split his available time and space between kin and conjugal roles. In some societies of this kind, men will live alternately in two places, or will frequently visit two different units, or move at different stages from one to another . . . Children similarly will shift residence in many societies

... Households then can often be extremely fluid units, with shifting membership.

In most of the known societies of the world, monogamy is the exception rather than the rule. Some anthropologists claim that over 90 per cent of the world's cultures involve plural polygamous marriages ... In some polygynous societies, almost invariably those in which descent is traced through the male line, households consist of a series of relatively self-contained living quarters, in which a man and his wives, each with her own children, live, one wife in a relatively autonomous domestic unit. In others, domestic arrangements are dominated by a group of brothers, with their wives and their offspring.

The domestic existence of each smaller unit within such a group is determined by the existence of the larger group and is ultimately dependent on the authority of those males who are in control of the unit as a whole.

In such situations it is again difficult to arrive at a useful definition of such a unit if we are concerned to consider households purely as kinship entities. Is such a mother and children unit an entity, or is it a sub-household within a much larger household? ...

While in a sense each wife who has a separate hut and her children constitute a separate domestic unit, the larger compound group – a patrilineal extended family augmented by outsiders – is the central domestic unit of everyday life and of collective economic enterprise ...

Kinship ties ... thus ... constitute the relation of production. The compound, for example, is essentially a means of reuniting and controlling necessary labour, both productive and reproductive ... The form of the household must therefore be analysed in terms of the economic structure of the society as a whole and cannot simply be seen as a unit containing the 'family', essentially defining sets of affective relations ... In New Guinea, very different domestic arrangements exist and these cannot be analysed in terms of the same economic determinants: ... domestic organization constructs very considerable separation between men and women. Special men's houses provide the focal point for all male life (often including sleeping and eating) and there are often stringent taboos on women having access to such houses and, in general, on contact between males and females.

Conclusion

The family, particularly the nuclear family [, then,] is not, as has so often been claimed, some kind of 'natural' instinctive and 'sacred' unit . . . [Hence] the whole notion of the 'natural' must, in terms of human relations, be challenged, and the 'unnatural' – in these terms the social construction of relationships – must be fully recognized.

21(a) Peter Laslett

The Changing Family in Britain

Excerpts from Peter Laslett, 'Foreword' to R. N. Rapoport, M. P. Fogarty and R. Rapoport (eds.), *Families in Britain*, Routledge & Kegan Paul, 1982, pp. xi–xiv.

Families in Britain in the 1980s find themselves in the wake of the following far-reaching changes in the structure of society. The first is a century-long fall in fertility. This has reduced the number of the average mother's offspring to something below the two and a little more which is required for replacement. It has also brought about a truly formidable rise in the proportion of the elderly and aged, making the British population one of the oldest which has ever existed.

The second is the ending of a necessary interconnection between regular and habitual sexual pleasure and sexual fulfilment on the one hand, and the responsibilities of procreation on the other hand. This consequence of highly efficient contraception and its spread throughout the whole population has altered our sexual comportment and the bond between spouses, altered them irreversibly.

The third is the introduction into our society of a substantial number of people not born into 'British' families, though a high proportion were born in Britain. Many or most of them have been brought up in family systems which are different, some of them very different indeed, from the Christian, predominantly Protestant, monogamous, nuclear model. This had prevailed almost universally in our country until the 1950s and for an unknown number of generations before that, perhaps for as far back as our knowledge is ever likely to go.

In the present winter of 1982 it is tempting to add a fourth fundamental change. Such is the final cessation of that rapid rise in the national wealth which is associated with successful industrialization. This began in Britain 250 years ago and, after notable vicissitudes in the 1920s and 1930s, proceeded during the 1950s and

1960s, during what may now seem to be its final stages, at a particularly rapid pace. By national wealth I intend to convey not only its total sum, but the amount available to each and every family group and individual.

It may turn out to be wrong, of course, to suppose that any of these processes is now at an end. It could be that the means of subsistence and of self-enhancement available to Britons will begin to go up again later in this decade. The resources available for redistribution by the State would then increase as well, and it is known that social transfers are easier to institute under such circumstances, likely to diminish when they are absent. Birth rates could certainly pick up again in Britain, as they did in the 1950s, if not very dramatically. Immigration might possibly be resumed. Divorce could conceivably begin to fall in its incidence, after the steep and continuous rise of the last twenty years or so. It is even just imaginable that the secular growth of leisure, and expenditure on leisure, will be interrupted.

It seems to me, nevertheless, that under all possible circumstances it will be the effects on [the British family] of the profound and irreversible social changes I have listed which will have to be taken into account . . .

It has immediately to be added that 'The British Family' is *not* the phrase to use, but a phrase consciously to abandon. For there is now no single British family, but a rich variety of forms, states, traditions, norms and usages, a plurality which it is [important] to underline. And this in a country which, as far as we can yet tell, has had until quite recently and over many centuries, a greater homogeneity by region and a greater continuity over time than any other national society, in all matters to do with kinship and family life. Nevertheless, the historical sociologist feels bound to add that not all the circumstances pointed to as novelties, sometimes as alarming novelties, [often] . . . are in fact without precedent, or indeed without earlier solutions, in British familial history as it is now becoming known . . .

The stereotype of family group consisting of father, mother and at least two residing children, young children, is entirely misleading in contemporary Britain. A majority of our households now consist in solitaries, people living with persons not their relatives, couples (married or unmarried) without accompanying offspring, or single-parent households. To these have to be added the even less 'familially' disposed individuals maintained in institutions, a small but woefully expensive minority. When Britain was still a pre-industrial society, however, something like 30 to 35 per cent of all groups were constituted in the same way, and among the solitaries and the few in institutions, a high proportion were the old and very old, just as is the case in the 1980s.

[Observers often comment on] the great and growing number of illegitimate children in Britain and [on] the very widespread flouting of the 'Christian' marriage rule which forbade sexual relationship outside marriage. Yet it has recently been estimated that between 20 and 40 per cent of all first conceptions have always taken place before marriage in England, that the 'Christian' marriage rules were never obeyed with anything like universality and that traditional, even respectable sexual conduct was never quite what the morally minded have supposed.

This is especially true of that class of personally upright, socially responsible late Victorians who founded our tradition of social inquiry. They would, no doubt, have been surprised to learn that during the early years of Victoria's reign, regarded by them as it is by us as the apogee of familial correctness and solidity, the illegitimacy level was higher than it had been for at least 300 years, indeed the highest ever recorded until the late twentieth century, and that this was *not* due to industrialization or urbanization . . .

That the longer term, and the wider horizon, are gradually establishing themselves in studies of this kind is quite evident [if we look at] parallel positions and policies of other nations in Western Europe, and in high industrial societies everywhere. We should never forget as we read about ourselves as we are now, that the German population, east and western, has an age structure which is even more top-heavy that the British; that Scandinavians have developed a sexual and procreative behaviour far less 'Christian' than our own; that all economically and technically advanced countries are under pressure to receive additions from economically and technically less advanced countries, with actual and potential familial consequences similar to those which we experience. The singularity of our own position in the 1980s is in the extent of recent immigration from cultures and areas so very dissimilar from traditional Britain, and in the severity of the check to the expected growth of economic resources.

The student of social structure over time can only be uneasy after having committed himself to so abbreviated an historical analysis. Of course, the huge rise in divorce, and the increases in illegitimacy and in single-headed households cannot be accounted for by the simple citation of the separation of sex from procreation. Of course movements in opinion and conviction have to be taken into account, other than the virtual disappearance of religious beliefs and practices. The most important is perhaps the movement for women's liberation . . .

21(b) David Eversley and Lucy Bonnerjea

The Family among Ethnic Minorities

Excerpts from David Eversley and Lucy Bonnerjea, 'Social Change and Indicators of Diversity', in R. N. Rapoport, M. P. Fogarty and R. Rapoport (eds.), *Families in Britain*, Routledge & Kegan Paul, 1982, pp. 83–4.

Britain is a multiracial society: there are about three million immigrants and immigrant-descended people, about half of whom are white, from Europe, Ireland and the Old Commonwealth, while the other half are from the New Commonwealth countries of Asia, Africa and the West Indies. It has already been pointed out that ethnic minorities are concentrated: there are few in the North, in East Anglia and the south east, outside London, and south west. Greater London, Birmingham and Bradford have relatively high concentrations. In 1977 in Greater London 4 per cent of the population was of West Indian origin and 4 per cent of Asian origin; in Birmingham 5 per cent West Indian, 6 per cent Asian; in Bradford 0.6 per cent West Indian, 8 per cent Asian.

It is inaccurate to refer to Punjabis, Tamils, Pakistanis and Bangladeshis simply as Asians, since they do not identify with the global terms and their cultural differences are as great as their similarities; nevertheless ... the term Asian is used to refer to these generalized characteristics ...

Most of the early Asian arrivals were male workers; women migrated later, and only as dependants of men. By the late 1960s, Indians tended to have balanced sex ratios, were enjoying family life, spending money on consumer goods and developing a community with shops and cinemas, while Pakistani men still out-numbered Pakistani women three to one and often lived in all-male, overcrowded hostels. By 1971 there was greater balance amongst the Pakistani population. In the field of employment, Asians are most likely to be in manual jobs, and overtime work has become a feature of immigrant life. Great prestige is attached to white-collar jobs, and these are sought, through education, for many Asian sons.

Partly due to the relative spatial segregation, and partly due to strong adherence to traditional cultural values, a relatively distinct 'Asian' family type exists. For most Asians marriage continues to be an alliance between families, as much as a union of a man and a woman. It involves both families' reputations and statuses; active involvement in the choice of children's marriage partners is the norm and divorce is rare.

Asian children, like those of other ethnic minorities, tend to be brought up in two cultures: the culture of their parents and the culture of the host community. This usually involves different languages, different food and different values ... Many Asian families take social behaviour for granted, and what is right and wrong behaviour is not a subject for discussion. Parents may project their ambitions on to their children – fostering anxiety and competitiveness amongst male Asian teenagers about their educational success and/or their employment opportunities. Girls used to be seen as economic liabilities; this has now changed, although they still may be discouraged from further education and jobs which involve contact with the opposite sex. Women, and particularly mothers, are seen as the guardians of values and traditions of the community.

It is important to stress that there is variation within the Asian family 'type'; for example, Sikhs pride themselves in their freer attitudes to the position of women in society than Moslem tradition does. Nevertheless, Asian families do come close to portraying the 'traditional family' patterns, with extended kinships, multi-generation and family solidarity.

One aspect of Asian family life which has been of some concern amongst the host population has been the high birth rates of women. This led to considerable anxiety expressed in the media and to projections based on faulty methodology. At least one confusion was due to the substitution of the birth rate (the number of births per 1,000 Asians) for fertility (the number of births per 1,000 Asian women between the ages and 15 and 45). The birth rate was high, and is still relatively high, because a very high proportion of Asian women were, and still are, in the most fertile age groups. There is evidence of the fertility of those in the main child-bearing groups declining, and the proportion within the fertile age groups is falling.

The second main ethnic type to be discussed is the West Indian one. Again, it is important to remember that the West Indies consist of several different islands, and the West Indian family type is merely a model. West Indians come from a society with a different family structure. Marriage is an event which follows after having achieved a certain standard of living and having made a home; it is not a binding contract taken regardless of a family's circumstances. [As] Fitzherbert argues, 'Today, it is still more important as a statement of economic achievement and class affiliation, than as a context for a sexual relationship, a shared home, or raising children.'

In practice this means many women have their first child at home, enter into a more or less stable union and marry when economic stability is achieved. This is shown in the large number of West Indian births (48 per cent) which are illegitimate, occurring before a marriage ceremony, but not necessarily without a stable partner. The family size of West Indians is relatively small and the proportion of births to West Indian women has fallen considerably.

The absence of a strong patriarchal tradition has certain implications: for example, responsible stepfatherhood and declining role segregation. The main difference from other family types, and it is an important difference, is the social context: the economic system combined with racial discrimination confines many West Indians to low status and poorly paid jobs, and to above-average periods of unemployment. It is these constraints which contribute to the West Indian pattern, and it is hardly surprising that the mother's role is the strongest in the West Indian family system. However ... the 'matrifocal' type of family (characteristic of Caribbean as well as English settings) is only one variant of the West Indian family, albeit a distinctive one.

22 Janet Finch

The Family and the State

Excerpts from Janet Finch, *Family Obligations and Social Change*, Polity Press, 1989, pp. 7–11, 237–43.

The Role of the State in Defining Family Obligations

It has been a long-running theme in British social policy that families, especially working-class families, regrettably do not always fulfil their natural obligations towards each other, and that therefore the state has to step in to ensure that people do not abandon their responsibilities ... The views propounded by the Royal Commission [of 1909] ran something like this: support between parents and children is a duty which rests on natural feelings, which are acknowledged in all human societies; England is the only country in Europe where these duties are neglected by some; such deficiencies have to be made good by public authorities, who both make alternative provisions and also punish people who do not acknowledge their duties ... public support was given only as a last resort; assistance was at a minimal level; costs of support were reclaimed from relatives if at all possible ...

The political consensus about the desirability of 'supporting the family' in order to enable it properly to 'care for its members' ... clearly makes an assumption about the 'naturalness' of family obligations and the desirability of the state's reinforcing them. However, in comparison with Victorian debates about the same issues, references to matters of morality are somewhat muted for the most part. It is really only in the writings of the radical right on family responsibilities where one finds echoes of the same approach: family units based on ties between spouses and parents and children are the natural order of things; state policies must support and reinforce the 'normal family' rather than deviant versions (such as single-parent households, gay or unmarried couples); family members will support each other as a matter of course except where the state has taken these responsibilities away from them . . .

State policies about family responsibilities . . . are concerned with drawing the boundaries between the state and the family and defining the proper role of each. Part of that process entails making a moral and political statement about who can make claims upon whom . . .

The state family boundary . . . is not absolute. It shifts over time, and it also changes between different circumstances, so that we ought properly to speak of boundaries in the plural . . . In times of economic stringency there is a tendency for the state to redraw the boundaries so that more responsibility is placed upon the family. There is also a very important question about whether people's right to make claims either upon the state or upon their relatives should vary according to both need and resources. Do people who are less well-off have particular rights to make claims upon those who have more resources? Does this principle apply to claims made upon one's family, or upon the state, or to both? . . .

Drawing the boundaries between family and state responsibility is a process which is politically contentious and where there are a number of competing principles. The dominant view appears to be that for most purposes claims on the family are treated as prior, with claims upon the state only coming into play when these are exhausted . . . Both in welfare policies and in the enforcement of the law, there has always been a considerable reluctance to make provision from state resources for people who 'ought' to be relying on support from their relatives, especially where that support is underpinned by a legal obligation.

However, running counter to this idea of the state providing only residual support, and having had a considerable impact upon social policy in the twentieth century, is the different principle of citizenship rights . . . Its emphasis is upon the individual, not the family, as the unit of support. Individual citizens have the right to adequate resources for survival, and the claims which they make to secure these are upon the community as a whole, not upon their own families. The state acts as the mechanism through which such claims are made, by collecting taxes then redistributing resources. The concept of citizenship was embodied most obviously in the changes associated with the establishing of a welfare state in the early part of the twentieth century, and after the Second World War . . .

Another area where the state/family boundary is contested is in relation to gender . . . 'Supporting the family' in effect means that a particular type of household, and set of personal relationships, are being encouraged. In this type of household and kin group, women provide the unpaid labour which secures the reproduction of the population and the care of the sick and elderly . . .

Third, even the most cursory attempt to understand where and how the boundaries between the state and the family are drawn demonstrates a deep ambivalence about the family and its relationship to the state. This is not surprising, given the competing principles just outlined . . . The mixed messages are: the autonomy of the family must not be interfered with, but as an institution it needs to be protected; the family is the 'natural' unit of support, but the state must ensure that people fulfil their obligations in practice . . .

It is regarded as of utmost importance that the independence of the family should be protected, and that it is proper for the state to secure this end, but paradoxically, excessive interference by the state can undermine the whole enterprise . . . It produces social policies which sometimes appear quite contradictory in practice. This confusion is exacerbated when the emphasis upon different principles shifts over time . . .

The family is the place where we care for each other, where we practise consideration for each other. Caring families are the basis of a society that cares.

This much-quoted statement . . . by James Callaghan when he was Labour Prime Minister . . . represents a succinct statement of the politics of the family in recent years . . .

Does the concept of 'caring families', of the idea that 'caring' is distinctively associated with family life, make any sense as a description of how most people in Britain live in the later part of the twentieth century? Does it represent a model of family life which most people would regard as right and proper, an ideal to which they ought to aspire? When governments try to encourage this model, are they simply supporting what the majority of people do in any case? . . .

The evidence . . . suggests that assistance from relatives still is of considerable importance to many people – in some respects more so than is often imagined, for example the use of kin networks to help in finding jobs. The lives of some people (most of them women) are dominated by the assistance which they give to a relative, especially people who are the main carer for someone who is handicapped and infirm. Yet at the same time kin support in many ways is unpredictable. By this, I mean that we cannot predict simply from knowing that someone has a sister, or a father, or five grandchildren, what assistance if any is passing between them now, or has ever done. Nor is it easy to predict what will happen when a particular set of circumstances arises where a person needs some help – financial difficulties caused by unemployment, a car accident in which they sustained broken bones, the grief of a bereavement, or whatever. They may well get assistance from relatives, but we cannot be sure precisely what they can expect, or from whom. It all depends on their particular circumstances ... For the most part people do not regard a loan of money, or the offer of temporary accommodation, or anything else, as given automatically by reflex action on the part of relatives. Rather, the appropriateness of offering a particular type of assistance is something to be weighed up and judged in particular circumstances, and to be negotiated between the parties concerned.

... I do not mean to imply that it is completely random. We can detect some patterns in who gives what to whom, but often those patterns are not visible unless we know a good deal about the individuals concerned. The most visible elements concern gender, ethnicity, generation and economic position ... but we can predict, for example, that older generations give support to younger more than the other way round; that people of Asian descent living in Britain are more likely than white British people to be giving help to their in-laws; that giving financial assistance is more common in better-off families than in poorer ones; that most women are involved more extensively than most men in exchanges of assistance between relatives. I am not suggesting that any of these patterns is a fixed and immutable part of family life: we can see how they derive at least in part from social and economic circumstances. Women are more involved than men because they need to be: the division of labour in our society accords them a range of domestic and caring responsibilities for which they need the support of others ...

There are also relatively predictable variations within the kin network itself: assistance, especially significant assistance, is more likely to pass between certain kin than others. I have spoken of inner and outer circles, and corresponding variations in support ... For the white majority, one's own parents and children normally fall in the inner circle, and people as distant as aunts or cousins normally do not, but there are considerable variations between kin groups in precisely who gets defined in, and this itself can change over time. Further, many individuals will be members of more than one 'inner circle' ... I cannot afford to do too much decorating for my husband's sister, because my own sister will notice and feel hurt unless I do the same for her; on the other hand, having to be fair to both is rather a good excuse when my sister-in-law asks me once too often ...

The principle of reciprocity ... is the key to understanding how patterns of support build up over time. An expectation that assistance should flow in two directions, and that no one should end up in a position where they are receiving more than they are giving, is at the heart of many of the negotiations which take place about support in families. This does not necessarily mean direct and immediate 'paying back': the reciprocal gift may come much later, and perhaps be given to another person. The important thing is that each person's balance sheets should be kept even. The only partial exception to this is parents' gifts (of various kinds) to their children, where it seems quite common for parents to continue to be net givers of gifts throughout their lifetimes without any real pressure on children to pay back an equivalent amount ...

Support between kin ... does not operate to the kind of fixed rules ... The idea, promoted by various governments, that the family should be the first port of call for people who need some assistance, does not align with what happens in practice ... Most people see their kin as a 'last resort' rather than a first. Kin support is reliable in this sense only: you know that you can fall back on your relatives – especially your close kin – if all else fails. Even then you cannot assume that assistance will be given automatically ... For most people the desirable situation is never to have to use that safety-net except for relatively minor assistance which can be repaid easily.

The Sense of Obligation

The other dimension to family support is what I have called throughout the 'sense of obligation' ... the 'ought' dimension ... the belief that people *should* be prepared to assist their relatives, even if this does not always happen in practice. For many people this sense of obligation is the key defining characteristic of family ties, especially between close kin. You feel 'duty bound' to help your family, and this gives kin support an inescapable quality ... However, that morality does not ... tell me I should be prepared to look after my father when he is ill, but that I need not make the same offer for my uncle, or that I could ask my brother for a loan of £200 but not £2,000 ...

People negotiate their relationships with one another and work out what to do in particular circumstances. Such negotiations are conducted between real people, not simply between human beings who occupy the social positions 'daughter' 'grandfather' 'brother' and so on ... That is why the commitments which I develop towards my mother will have their own distinctive character: she is *my* mother, not simply *a* mother ... Kin relationships are especially suited to this (although not exclusively so), because membership of the kin group into which you were born is automatic and irrevocable: you do not join and there is a sense in which you cannot leave ... This makes them especially suited to developing relationships, in which people become committed to assist each other. I would place considerable emphasis upon the 'become'. Commitments to assist one's kin develop and change over time; they get reaffirmed through reciprocal assistance ...

People in the present are not necessarily any more or less willing to support their relatives than in the past; but the circumstances under which they have to work out these commitments themselves have changed and created new problems to be solved. External conditions of this kind ... affect the nature of the choices which present themselves. For example (to stay with the question of the care of elderly people), a decision about whether you should take an elderly father to live with you looks very different if you are an only child, than it would have done under the demographic conditions of earlier generations, when you could expect to have several siblings. It looks different again if economic circumstances have worked in your favour, so that you can afford to pay a professional nurse to look after him, by comparison with someone for whom the choice about co-residence also entails using their own labour to provide nursing care.

Into this complex equation we also have to insert the action of governments who, through the law and through their policies, modify the external circumstances under which commitments to relatives are negotiated ... There have been several times during the last two centuries when governments have tightened the screws, to try to ensure that people relied on their families rather than on the state for financial assistance: the creation of the New Poor Law in 1834; the tightening of Poor Law regulations in the late nineteenth century; the creation of the household means test for unemployed people in the 1930s ... [Yet] if anything it has been the state's assuming some responsibility for individuals – such as the granting of old age pensions – which has freed people to develop closer and more supportive relationships with their kin. It seems that it is not in the power of governments straightforwardly to manipulate what we do for our relatives, let alone what we believe to be proper.

Anthony Heath

The Social Mobility of Women

Excerpts from Anthony Heath, *Social Mobility*, Fontana, 1981, pp. 114–23.

Occupational Mobility: Inequalities between Men and Women

If we restrict ourselves to marital mobility ... we find slightly greater movement for women than for men, or, to put it more strictly, a man's class position is likely to be more similar to his father's than to his father-in-law's. There is both more downward and more upward mobility through marriage for women than there is through the labour market for men. In this sense a woman's 'class fate' is more loosely linked to her social origins than is a man's.

Marital mobility [however,] is ... a somewhat sexist concept. But occupational mobility may fall into the opposite trap. The occupations of many married women are part-time; they affect, for many people quite crucially, their overall standard of living but will not be the major component of family income. And if, as many sociologists argue, we should take the family as the unit of stratification, the relationship between a married woman's own occupation and her position in the class structure will be in many cases a loose one. Again, however, I would argue that the relation between a woman's social origins and her occupational position is of interest in its own right, and we shall present such evidence as is available on it.

Despite the general omission of women from mobility surveys, there is fortunately one recent source which we can utilize. This is the General Household Survey conducted for the government by the Office of Population Censuses and Surveys. It is mainly used to obtain information required by government departments, but the 1972 and 1975 surveys also obtained the basic biographical informa-

Table 1. *Women's occupational mobility: outflow*

Father's class	Respondent's class (%)								
	I	II	III	IV	V	VI	VII	Total	N
I & II	8·4	24·1	52·7	0·4	0·0	2·9	11·6	100·1	490
III	4·4	21·8	54·8	0·8	0·0	2·4	15·7	99·9	248
IV	2·6	16·2	47·2	0·4	0·8	5·1	27·7	100·0	235
V	2·3	10·9	55·8	0·8	0·8	1·6	27·9	100·1	129
VI	1·6	11·2	49·6	0·2	1·6	6·4	29·3	99·9	1101
VII	1·2	10·3	47·4	0·0	1·5	5·2	34·3	99·9	842
%	2·9	14·3	50·0	0·3	1·1	4·9	26·6	100·1	(3045)

Source: GHS, 1975; a special tabulation prepared by George Psacharopoulos.
Sample: women aged 25–64 in 1975 who reported income.

tion required for mobility studies from representative national samples including both men and women. Unfortunately, the data on father's occupations are not coded in the same way as in the earlier studies we have used, and so in addition to the Hall-Jones classification and Goldthorpe's schema, used respectively by Glass and the Oxford Social Mobility Group, we must now get used to a third one based on the socio-economic groups distinguished by the OPCS. I have grouped these into seven classes . . .

Table 1 crosstabulates the current (i.e. 1975) occupation of employed women by their fathers' occupations. It includes both married and single women, both full-time and part-time workers. To compare women's occupational mobility with men's the corresponding table was calculated for the male respondents in the General Household Survey.

Table 1 [shows that the] occupational distribution of women is very different from that of men: it is a 'bimodal' one with women heavily concentrated in lower white-collar work and semi- or unskilled manual work and grossly under-represented both in higher-grade professional and managerial and in skilled manual work. Not surprisingly, then, women from Class I and II origins tend to be downwardly mobile in large numbers, and there is nothing like the tendency for daughters to follow in their fathers' footsteps that there was for the sons from Class I. There appears to be gross inequality of opportunity between men and women here. Among both there is a surplus of upward over downward mobility, but the surplus is much smaller for the women, 27 as against 32 per cent moving up and 26 as against 19 per cent moving down.

Our first view of the material, then, suggests that women have considerably poorer mobility chances than men – if we take their own occupational achievements rather than their husbands' as the yardstick. They are more likely to be downwardly mobile and less likely to be upwardly mobile than men from the same class origins. And this, of course, is due to their enormous concentration in 'women's work' – their employment as secretaries, shop assistants, clerks, telephone operators, waitresses, cooks and hairdressers.

This pessimistic conclusion about women's chances, however, is particularly sensitive to the assumptions we make about what counts as 'upward' and 'downward' mobility. Many women from working-class homes cross the manual/non-manual line to enter 'white-blouse' jobs, and we could do a good cosmetic job on the ugly face of sexual inequality by counting Class III as 'higher' than Class VI and thus generating a large number of apparently upwardly mobile women.

This raises the conceptual questions about occupational classification . . . If we are interested in questions of class formation and class action, as Westergaard and Goldthorpe are, then movement across the manual/non-manual borderline becomes of considerable potential interest and makes it vital to differentiate Classes III and VI. What are the political and social consequences, we have to ask, of increasing numbers of wives and daughters of manual workers getting a foot inside the world of non-manual work? But if we are interested in questions of equality of opportunity to obtain rewarding jobs, the relevant distinctions are rather different. It is by no means obvious that junior white-collar jobs are 'better' than skilled manual ones in terms of their general desirability. They command considerably less pay (as we have already seen), and while it is one of the clichés of contemporary British sociology that white-collar workers make up for this with their improved working conditions, fringe benefits, promotion prospects and job security, no one has quantified these properly even for men and it is highly doubtful whether these advantages apply to anything like the same extent to women. Nor should one ignore the not negligible attractions of skilled manual work: its attractiveness to the 'educationally unsuccessful sons of high-status fathers' and [the] considerable respect and status within the working-class community [enjoyed by] the skilled manual worker. We have no study comparing the 'general desirability' of these junior white-collar 'women's jobs' with those of 'men's jobs' such as skilled manual work, but it is a reasonable guess that they rank lower. The results of Goldthorpe and Hope's inquiry on the social grading of occupations may be relevant here, although not conclusive as it was intended to cover men's jobs only. Judgements were obtained from a national sample of respondents about the social grading of a number of selected occupations, and Goldthorpe and Hope interpret the results as indicating the general desirability of the various jobs. They found that fitters and tool-makers ranked markedly higher than clerical workers and cashiers; setters and sheetmetal workers ranked higher than cooks and hairdressers; machine-tool operators and assemblers ranked higher than shop assistants. One suspects that the differences would be magnified if the respondents had been asked to consider female shop assistants, for example, rather than male.

We should not, then, overturn our initial conclusion that women have inferior chances of occupational mobility than men. The 'losses' experienced by the daughters of high-status fathers are not balanced by 'gains' accruing to those from low-status origins. The concentration of women in lower white-collar work of 'intermediate' status works to the disadvantage not benefit of women as a whole. To think otherwise would be a kind of middle-class 'ethnocentrism' which saw white-collar jobs as intrinsically superior to manual ones and which failed to recognize that women's exclusion from skilled manual work, from those jobs which command the greatest pay, power and respect within the working-class community, constitutes yet another disability attached to their sex.

There is, however, a second and more cogent objection to our analysis. If we are considering women's mobility chances or *opportunities* rather than their *experiences*, is it fair to include the jobs, often part-time, of married women? It could be argued that women have the opportunity in a formal sense to obtain good full-time jobs but opt instead for low-level part-time work, marriage and a family. The point is another important conceptual one. Mobility data do not tell us about opportunities for advancement but about the actual *use* made of such opportunities as exist. To talk of an opportunity is to assume that people could refuse to make use of it if they wished; it implies a voluntaristic approach to social action. And so we cannot reject out of hand the objection that the opportunities are there for the women who wish to use them. True, we might want to argue that women have been socialized into stereotyped role-expectations and are thus not free to choose a career rather than a family, but then the language of opportunities becomes inappropriate. We are adopting a deterministic rather than a voluntaristic model.

It is not important in the present context which side we come down on. The reader is free to reinterpret and translate the evidence into his own preferred language of choice or determinism. I do not wish to get embroiled in semantic and philosophical questions about the meaning of free-will and determinism. However, if, for the sake of argument, we grant the point made by the voluntaristic critic, there is a simple empirical test which we should make: we should look at the mobility of single women, at those women who have made (or had forced upon them) a different choice, opting for career rather than family and marriage.

The number of single men and women in the 1975 General Household Survey is too small for us to present a detailed mobility table on the lines of Table 1. Instead we shall report the social origins and present occupations of the single people, together with some summary statistics. Table 2 gives the occupational distributions.

Table 2 sheds a very different shade of light on the inequalities between men and women. There is, to be sure, the expected concentration of women in lower white-collar work and their exclusion from skilled manual labour, but they also do much better than the men in gaining access to Class II and in avoiding Class VII. Overall (using our usual definition of upward and downward) 37 per cent of the single women but only 27 per cent of the single men were upwardly mobile; and 17 per cent of the single women as against 25 per cent of the men were downwardly mobile. The picture we now see is the mirror image of the earlier one. True, the upwardly mobile women tended to enter a small range of 'women's' jobs – school-teaching, nursing and social work – all of which are included in Class II (both in the present classification and in Goldthorpe's). I do not therefore deny that there is still considerable sexual segregation (and probably discrimination) even within higher levels of non-manual work which may be of great importance both socially and individually. But if we concentrate simply on questions of *vertical* mobility, it would seem to be the case that the 'helping professions' provide a definite channel of upward mobility for career-orientated women (if such we can take the single to be). Nor do I deny that

Table 2. Single men and women: origins and destinations

	Father's class		Respondent's class	
	Men	Women	Men	Women
I	17·5	23·5	10·2	13·1
II			12·1	24·9
III	9·8	12·2	16·5	40·3
IV	6·7	4·1	1·0	0·0
V	4·8	5·4	4·1	1·4
VI	34·6	27·6	28·6	4·5
VII	26·7	27·1	27·6	15·8
Total	100·1	99·9	100·1	100·0
N	315	221	315	221

Source: GHS, 1975; a special tabulation prepared by George Psacharopoulos.
Sample: single men and women aged 25–64 in 1975 who reported income.

women are still under-represented at the very highest levels, both of the helping professions and of white-collar work generally. The most that the present data suggest is that single women have been able to make use of such opportunities as are available to them to obtain jobs of generally higher social standing than their male equivalents.

We now have two radically different accounts. The first, based on the comparison of employed women with employed men, suggests that the former have markedly inferior opportunities for occupational mobility; the second, based on the comparison of single women and single men suggests that the former have rather better chances. Is it then fair to conclude after all that the employment opportunities facing women are as good as those for men (at least in terms of their general desirability) but that only this tiny minority of career-orientated women choose to make full use of them?

The question may seem simple but, as so often, the answer is not. Even if we accept the evidence at face value, there is still a crucial complication which arises if we take the notion of opportunity seriously. There may be occupational opportunities for a few women, but if everyone chose to take them up the opportunities would vanish. We all have the same formal opportunity to walk down, say, the High Street, but if we all choose to do so at once, the street becomes jammed and no one can get through. Similarly, the current supply of 'women's work' may give excellent opportunities to the few women who want continuous full-time careers at the moment, but if the great majority of married women were to opt out of domestic labour and seek paid employment instead, the demand for jobs would far outrun the supply and the opportunities facing women would be much reduced. The problem does not apply to men, since the great majority are already in full-time employment or actively seeking it. And the problem would not apply specifically to women if there were not the barriers which effectively exclude women from skilled manual or managerial jobs in industry. Sexual discrimination in the labour market may only reveal itself clearly if more women sought work, but the very existence of such discrimination may itself deter more women from seeking work.

There is a second problem, too. In comparing single men and women's occupational mobility we assume that the two groups have the same qualifications and aptitudes, in other words that we are comparing like with like. But is this a fair assumption? For most men the choice of work or marriage does not present itself as a dilemma; the two are complementary not antagonistic. But for most women it is a dilemma. The typical role-expectations confronting a wife and mother reduce her ability to pursue a career effectively. She cannot usually maximize her contributions in one role without sacrificing those in the other. This suggests that the woman who actually does opt for a career by staying single may have a greater commitment to work than the single man who has not had to make the same sacrifices. This might be reflected in the single woman's seeking and obtaining higher educational qualifications than the single man ... The single women, therefore, may well differ markedly from the married women in their greater occupational ambitions; but there is no reason to expect that the single men differ likewise from their married counterparts.

All we have really managed to do, therefore, is to set upper and lower bounds to our estimates of male/female differences in mobility chances. The decidedly poor chances of employed women taken as a whole mark the lower bound; the moderately good chances of the single women represent the upper bound. The truth lies somewhere in between ...

24 Cynthia Cockburn

Jobs for the Boys

Excerpts from 'The Material of Male Power', *Feminist Review*, No. 9, October 1981, pp. 44–6, 48–9, 51–2, 55.

The Hand Compositor: Appropriation of Technique

Letterpress printing comprises two distinct technological processes, composing and printing. Before the mechanization of typesetting in the last decade of the nineteenth century compositors set the type by hand, organizing metal pieces in a 'stick', and proceeded to assemble it into a unified printing surface, the 'forme', ready for the printer to position on the press, coat with ink and impress upon paper.

The hand compositor, then, had to be literate, to be able to read type upside down and back to front, with a sharp eye for detail. He had to possess manual dexterity and have an easy familiarity with the position of letters in the 'case'. He had to calculate with the printers' 'point' system of measurement. Furthermore he had to have a sense of design and spacing to enable him to create a graphic whole of the printed page, which he secured through the manipulation of the assembled type, illustrative blocks and lead spacing pieces. The whole he then locked up in a forme weighing 50lbs or more. This he would lift and move to the proofing press or bring back to the stone for the distribution of used type. He thus required a degree of strength and stamina, a strong wrist, and, for standing long hours at the case, a sturdy spine and good legs.

The compositor used his craft to secure for himself a well-paid living, with sometimes greater and sometimes less success depending on conditions of trade. Through their trade societies (later unions) compositors energetically sought to limit the right of access to the composing process and its equipment to members of the society in a given town or region, blacking 'unfair houses' that employed non-society men . . .

They sought to control the numbers entering the trade and so to elevate their wage-bargaining position by a system of formal apprenticeship. They tried to limit the number of apprentices through an agreed ratio of boys to journeymen and to keep the period of apprenticeship as long as possible. The introduction of unapprenticed lads, ... was always a source of fear to compositors. Comps' jobs were kept within the class fraction by the custom of limiting openings wherever possible to members of existing printer families ...

How did women enter this story? The answer is, with difficulty. Women and children were drawn into industrial production in many industries in the first half of the nineteenth century but in printing their entry was almost entirely limited to the bookbinding and other low-paid finishing operations held to require no skill. Girls were not considered suitable for apprenticeship. Physical and moral factors (girls were not strong enough, lead was harmful to pregnancy, the social environment might be corrupting) were deployed ideologically in such a way that few girls would see themselves as suitable candidates for apprenticeship. A second line of defence against an influx of women was of course the same socio-political controls used to keep large numbers of boys of the unskilled working class from flooding the trade.

Women who, in spite of these barriers, obtained work as non-society compositors were bitterly resisted and their product 'blacked' by the society men, i.e. work typeset by women could not be printed ... The composing room was, and in most cases still is, an all-male preserve with a sense of camaraderie, pin-ups on the wall and a pleasure taken in the manly licence to use 'bad' (i.e. woman-objectifying) language.

Electronic Composition: The Disruption of Class and Gender Patterns

In the half-century between 1910 and 1960 the printing industry saw relatively little technical change. Then, in the 1960s two big new possibilities opened up for capital in the printing industry ... The first was web offset printing ... the second letter assembly on film or photographic paper by the techniques of computer-aided photocomposition ...

In the latest electronic composing technology ... the computer itself holds instructions that enable it to generate characters, in an almost limitless range of typefaces and sizes and at enormously rapid speeds, on the face of a cathode ray tube. The inputting operation is performed with a keyboard associated with a video display unit on which the operator can assist computer decisions and 'massage' the copy into a desired order before committing it to the computer memory. The matter is transmitted direct from computer to photosetter and may now be produced in complete sections as large as a full newspaper page, making paste-up unnecessary.

The process is clearly seen by capital as a means of smashing the costly craft control of the compositor. The system is greatly more productive and requires less manpower. It would require less still if operated in the manner for which it is designed, i.e. avoiding two keyboarding processes by having typists, journalists, editors and authors key matter direct on to the computer disc for editing on screen and thence to direct output.

The work is much lighter, more sedentary. The abilities called upon are less esoteric, more generally available in the working population outside print. Inputting requires little more than good typing ability on the QWERTY board, something possessed by many more women than men. The implications for compositors of this twist in their craft history are dramatic. Combined with a recession it is causing unemployment in the trade, something unknown since the thirties. The individual tasks in the overall process have become trivialized and the men feel the danger of increased sub-division, routinization and substitution of unskilled workers.

The union response has not been to reject the new technology. Instead it has fought an energetic battle to retain the right to the new equipment as it did to the old. It resists 'direct input' by outsiders, asserts exclusive right to the photosetting keystroke (if necessary to a redundant second typing), to paste-up and the control of the photosetters, and where possible the computers. It is demanding increased pay and reduced hours in exchange for agreement to operate the new technology. And it is insisting (in principle at least) that all composing personnel get the chance to retrain for all aspects of the *whole* photocomposing job . . . an uphill struggle for reintegration of the now transformed craft.

Skill and Its Uses

An extensive literature has demonstrated the effect of craft organization on the structure of the working class. [As Hobsbawm has remarked,] 'The artisan creed with regard to the labourers is that the latter are an inferior class and that they should be made to know and be kept in their place'. The loss of demands on manual skill brought about by electronic photocomposition does not necessarily mean the job has become more 'mental'. On the contrary, present-day compositors feel their new work could be done by relatively unskilled workers. Many members feel they have lost status and some resent the strategic necessity to seek amalgamation of the National Graphical Association (NGA) with the unions representing the less skilled.

Our account shows, however, that the purposeful differentiation between skilled and unskilled workers was also a step in the construction of *gender*. This is a more recent conception. Heidi Hartmann has suggested that 'the roots of women's present social status' lie in job segregation by sex and demonstrates the role of men and their unions in maintaining women's inferiority in the labour market by deployment of skill. The fact that females in the closed-shop NGA (which embodies a large proportion of the better paid workers in the printing industry) until recently amounted to no more than 2 per cent of its membership is directly connected with the fact that women's average earnings have always been lower relative to men's in printing than in manufacturing occupations as a whole. Through the mechanisms of craft definition women have been constructed as relatively lacking in competence, and relatively low in earning power. Women's work came to be seen as inferior. Now that the new composing process resembles 'women's work' stereotypes it is felt as emasculating. The skill crisis is a crisis of both gender and class for comps.

Anne Phillips and Barbara Taylor propose that skill is a direct correlate of sexual power. 'Skill has increasingly been defined against women . . . Far from being an objective economic fact, skill is often an ideological category imposed on certain types of work by virtue of the sex and power of the workers who perform it.'

It is important to recognize this ideological factor. It has become increasingly important in printing with the advance of technology. The compositor sitting at a keyboard setting type is represented as

doing skilled work. A girl typist at a desk typing a letter is not –
though the practical difference today is slight. None the less, the
formulation here again, posing the ideological as foil to the economic,
leads to an under-emphasis on the material realities (albeit socially
acquired) of physical power and with them the tangible factors in
skill which it is my purpose to reassert . . .

The tangible factors in skill may be overstated for purposes of self-
defence and are variably deployed in socio-political struggle. Thus,
against the unskilled male, defined as corporally superior to the
skilled, hot metal comps have defended their craft in terms of (a) its
intellectual and (b) its dexterity requirements. Against women, with
their supposed superior dexterity, the skilled men on the contrary
used to invoke (a) the heavy bodily demands of the work and (b) the
intellectual standards it was supposed to require. (Among comps
today it is sometimes done to keep a list of the 'howlers', they detect
in the typescripts coming to them from the 'illiterate' typists
upstairs.) . . .

Control of Technology

Capitalists as capitalists and men as men both take initiatives over
technology. The capitalist class designs new technology, in the sense
that it commissions and finances machinery and sets it to work to
reduce the capitalist's dependency on certain categories of labour, to
divide, disorganize and cheapen labour . . .

There are many mechanized production processes in which women
are employed. But there is a sense in which women who operate
machinery, from the nineteenth-century cotton spindles to the
modern typewriter, are only 'lent' it by men, as men are only 'lent' it
by capital. Working-class men are threatened by the machines with
which capital seeks to replace them. But as and when the machines
prevail it is men's hands that control them. Comps now have twice
adopted new technology, albeit with bad grace, on the strict condition
that it remain under their own control. They necessarily engage in a
class gamble (how many jobs will be lost? Will wages fall?) but their
sexual standing is not jeopardized . . .

Do we then assume that male supremacy is on the wane in the
workplace? I think not. The gap between women's earnings and
men's in printing has widened in the last few years. What we are

seeing in the struggle over the electronic office and printing technology is a series of transformations within gender relations and their articulation with class relations. The class relations are those of capitalism. The gender relations are those of a wider, more pervasive and more long-lived male dominance system than patriarchy. They are those of a sex-gender system in which men dominate women inside and outside family relations, inside and outside economic production, by means which are both material and ideological, exercising their authority through both individual and organizational development. It is more nearly andrarchy than patriarchy.

Part Five
Education

The sociology of education is concerned with the totality of social constraints on learning, socialization and social positioning; with the ways in which values are transmitted and internalized through systems of social apprenticeship; and with the ways in which we acquire the basic frameworks within which we interpret the world. Though the sociology of education is concerned with formal education, notably schooling and subsequent educational experience, it is therefore also concerned with the family and with a child's peer groups, since these condition not only success or failure within formal education, but life-chances themselves.

Like industrial sociology, the sociology of education is one of the more obvious practical applications of sociology. The empirical research carried out by sociologists of education, however, has to be based upon general sociological theory, and in turn has contributed both to the refinement of research procedures and to general theory.

Émile Durkheim and other French sociologists, as well as pioneer sociologists in this country and the USA, helped shaped an agenda for the sociology of education which is still relevant today, including the ways in which values are inculcated and reproduced and the role that the transmission and reproduction of knowledge plays in reproducing society as a whole, as well as the more specific question of how changes in educational institutions and practices can bring about changes in the social division of labour.

The growth of mass education during the late nineteenth century led to the development of two approaches that have dominated the field ever since: the 'institutional' approach, developed by Max Weber, concerned with studying the growth, expansion and replacement of institutions, focusing upon individuals and groups, and the 'structural' approach of Durkheim and the French *Année Sociologique* school, which concentrated on the role that belief systems play in both social reproduction – the process through which the hierarchy of social values is inculcated and absorbed – and social change.

Durkheim and his fellow-researchers soon came to the conclusion that the division of labour created by industrialization was not the only important source of social cooperation. Nor did it provide a material base for a more developed, cooperatively organized society in the future. As social anthropologists, Durkheim and his collaborator, Marcel Mauss, started from the premise that societies were held together by 'invisible messages': social control depended upon the absorption of the dominant social values by the individual, during his or her 'social apprenticeship'. There was thus a 'logical conformity' between the transmission of social values and social order.

This process did imply, however, that different messages could be sent. The educational system could therefore help to create a new and, hopefully, superior moral and social order. To Durkheim, national systems of education offered the possibility of bringing into being a more cooperative social division of labour in place of a division of social labour shaped purely by industrialization.

In Reading 25, an extract from Durkheim's lectures on moral education, he shows how one of the primary tasks of the school, in societies with an advanced division of labour, is to separate children from the immediacy of family values, and to inculcate instead those of a supposedly superior moral order: that of the child's eventual social position within the polity. The values presently being communicated in schools, however, were not, in Durkheim's view, necessarily the right ones. He was thus concerned with moral issues. If the division of labour could succeed, by itself, in creating a cooperative – or, as Durkheim called it, a truly collective – society, based on shared values, there would be no problem. But the division of labour brought about by the Industrial Revolution had merely substituted one form of inequality for another. What Durkheim sought was a kind of 'moral education' that could break the pattern of submission to aberrant rules and norms and perhaps create another one. Thus for Durkheim and Mauss, both influenced strongly by Kant, the school was not just an object of study but a key to social change.

In his later works, Durkheim was concerned with the transmission and reception of knowledge, dividing his research between the development of educational systems and practices in Europe and the study of quite different kinds of society. This latter avenue of inquiry, indeed, led them to establish modern French anthropology. They were also beginning to interest themselves in certain aspects of Freud's ideas. But all of this was cut short by the First World War. Their pioneering work in the sociology of education was to be taken up later in the United States by Willard Waller and, much later, in Britain, after the failure of massive educational reform to bring about social change. A similar, more radical attempt to use education to bring about social change crystallized in the thinking of Paulo Freire in Brazil in the 1960s.

We cannot deal with all aspects of the sociology of education in a few brief extracts. Here we concentrate, therefore, on two issues: the transmission and reception of knowledge through systems of social apprenticeship, and the effects of this in the subsequent allocation of young people to positions in adult society.

The influence of the classic Durkheimian themes can be seen in virtually all the subsequent work done by modern sociologists of education. In this country, the research from which Reading 26, by Halsey, Heath and Ridge, is drawn, is the latest contribution to a series of researches that began with a project directed by David Glass – in the tradition of 'political arithmetic' and oriented to policy formation and planning – which examined the changes in class structure in Britain brought about by the Second World War. The educationalists in this team focused upon the changes which resulted from the 1944 Education Act. With Jean Floud and F. M. Martin, Halsey later undertook a pioneering study of *Social Class and Educational Opportunity*, and in the 1970s a more elaborate and sophisticated study, *Origins and Destinations*, of the links between education and social mobility. In Reading 26, taken from this study, Halsey and his colleagues find social class to be still the main factor in educational achievement in general, and the main constraint upon working-class educational achievement – and therefore of their chances of upwards social mobility – in particular. But they also note that there has been significant upwards social mobility through the educational system, and defend the view that the school can make a difference in educational achievement, at least at the secondary level. They also point out that in order to understand the impediments facing working-class children and the way these affect their life-chances, we need a deeper understanding of the kinds of educational experiences they undergo, particularly its more invisible aspects and the socialization they have already experienced before they even start their schooling. We need to look at families as well as schools.

Basil Bernstein's research (Reading 27), strongly influenced by Durkheim, has been very influential and wide-ranging. His theory of linguistic 'codes', and later of 'framing' and 'classification', broke new ground. These codes, and the basic interpretive frameworks underlying them, he argued, were rooted in differences in the language practices of dominant and dominated social groups, and reflect the hierarchy of values within society and the general social division of labour. Skill in using the linguistic codes, which are used in formal teaching as in other formal situations of public life, is socially learned, and not just in the school. Hence the ability to use them reflects differences in socialization rather than differences in innate competence. He also points to other connections between the organization of education and the organization of society generally, which take him beyond the theory of linguistic codes. Starting from Durkheim's classic distinction between mechanical and organic types of society, Bernstein goes on to develop a distinction between 'closed' and 'open' schools, to examine boundary relations within schools: from classroom organization to the way in which knowledge gets parcelled up into recognized 'subjects': and concludes by pointing to the relationship between the ways in which school life is ordered – including teaching and learning – with the way the order of society generally is maintained.

William Tyler (Reading 28) combines Bernstein's work on the way school life is structured and experienced with more traditional organization theory and applies this to an examination of how the school functions as an institution. The visible characteristics of the formal organization of the school – pedagogic systems and practices – he argues, are not the most important aspect of school life. Far more important are the deeper structures that communicate messages concerned with social control.

Pierre Bourdieu and Jean-Claude Passeron (Reading 29) argue, in somewhat different language, that education systems in contemporary Europe play a double role: the exclusion of children from working-class backgrounds, and the provision of a mechanism for the reproduction of the 'cultural capital' of those sections of the middle classes whose sole stock-in-trade is their manipulatory knowledge. Working-class knowledge, ways of seeing, and systems of logic are systematically excluded through the use of what they term 'pedagogic violence'. Conversely, the education system, and the ideologies on which it is based, provide the means through which the cultural capital of the socially privileged middle classes is reproduced. The message is a deeply pessimistic one, because they see no way in which change can occur, since, 'in matters of culture absolute dispossession excludes awareness of being dispossessed'. Such a view stands in contradistinction to Bernstein, who suggests that the excluded or dominated voice can, under certain conditions, find a fertile space and time for its enfranchisement: a theme which is more strongly emphasized in the more optimistic works of writers like Paulo Freire.

The texts that we have used so far are widely regarded as seminal or classical texts in the field of the sociology of education. It may come as something of a surprise, therefore, that our last text (Reading 30) should come from a relatively young researcher, Diego Gambetta, and was written only very recently. The reason for this is that Gambetta's work is based upon 'rational choice' theory, and is an attempt to revive certain ideas about intentionality which summarize a variety of earlier criticisms of the view that social class and constraints are all-important, as well as challenging those who continue to take social class as the central issue in the sociology of education. In *Were They Pushed or Did They Jump?*, Gambetta argues forcefully, in the light of research undertaken among working-class children in northern Italy, that intentionality can override social background.

Gambetta should be heeded: we do need to pay more attention to transmission and receptivity. The centre of *reception* – whether Bernstein's concept of 'code' is used as a basic interpretive framework or Bourdieu's concept of 'habitus' as a filter of experience – should be looked at more critically than sociologists wedded to a structural deterministic position have done. However, Gambetta's revival of the concept of intentionality ignores the work of Maurice Merleau-Ponty, who combined both class background and intentionality; it also has to answer the larger question as to whether intentionality itself is not a reflection of social position and social positioning.

These texts, focused upon one major problem-area first marked out by Durkheim — how societies transmit invisible messages of social control, how these are absorbed, and the role they play in social reproduction — necessarily exclude important texts concerned with issues such as the analysis of educational policy, as well as a large range of topics other than those concerned with social class. The extracts we have used all point to a central paradox: that educational institutions and practices cannot be changed without a significant change in the social division of labour, but that the social division of labour cannot be changed without a change in systems of social apprenticeship. The paradox is felt particularly poignantly in the daily experience of educationalists and teachers in Third World countries. Emphasis upon the 'moral' side of Durkheim's work, largely absent in European writing, has survived and now flourishes in Latin America, notably in the participatory research work of Freire and others. Because of this close relationship between theory and practice, particularly in the field of adult education — in societies where access to school is anything but universal for children and where new solutions are being looked for — the research going on in Latin America is particularly exciting. Newer work in Europe is increasingly concerned, too, with other forms of social differentiation and consequent inequality: with gender, race, ethnic differences and their relationship to social class. These two currents of contemporary research will undoubtedly revolutionize our understanding of education and its relationship to society and, in a few years' time, will figure prominently in collections like this one.

25   Émile Durkheim

The General Influence of the School Environment

Excerpts from Émile Durkheim, *L'education morale*, Alcan, Paris, 1925.
(Translated by Charles Posner.)

In order to understand the crucial role that the school environment
can and must play in moral education we must initially look at what
children face when they first enter the school. Until then they have
experienced only two kinds of groups.

The first is the family, where the feeling of solidarity stems from
blood relationships, from the moral affinities which are derived from
these bonds and strengthened by the constant and instant contact of
their associated consciousnesses and by a mutual interpenetration of
their lives. The second are the intimate groups of freely chosen
friends and companions which exist outside the ambit of the family.

However, the wider society exhibits neither of these two characteristics. The ties bonding citizens of the same country together
depend neither on kinship nor personal proclivities. Hence we find
that there is a great distance between the moral state of children
upon leaving their families and the one towards which they must
strive. The road cannot be travelled in one go. Intermediary stages
are required. The school environment is the best possible staging
post. On the one hand, because the school neither originates in
blood relationships nor in free choice but in casual yet inescapable
association amongst individuals of approximately the same age and
social group it provides more extensive associations than either the
family or the child's intimate groups of friends can provide. In
this way it is similar to a social polity. On the other hand, it is
limited enough to permit the crystallization of personal relations.
In this way the school is similar to the family and the groups of
friends. The experience of a shared existence within the classroom

constitutes a natural introduction to those higher feelings which we wish to develop in the child.

Hence it is more natural to use the school to achieve these aims since it is precisely groups of young persons, more or less similar to those which make up the social system of the school, which have [made possible] the formation of societies larger than the family. Examining populations of birds and mammals, Espinas has demonstrated that they could not have developed if, at a certain moment in their lives, the young had not separated to form new societies which no longer had domestic characteristics. Indeed, wherever the family holds on to its members it is easily self-sufficient. Consequently, each individual family tends to isolate itself from others with the aim of achieving a higher level of self-sufficiency, and under these conditions it is impossible for a wider or different type of society to be formed. The social appears only where the new generation has been raised to free itself from the familial setting in order to develop a new kind of collective existence. Similarly, if primitive human societies are not limited from the outset to the household, if they include in their simplest form a group of families, this is to a great extent because, due to these circumstances, the moral education of children is not undertaken separately and directly by each parent but collectively by the clan's elders for each generation. The elders would assemble young people of the same age group and initiate them as a group into the religious beliefs, rites and traditions – in a word, into everything which comprises the intellectual and moral heritage of the group. Due to the gathering of the young into special groups determined by age and not by degree of blood relationships, exogamous societies developed and perpetuated themselves. The school exhibits the characteristics of these groups by recruiting its pupils according to the same principle. The bringing together of young neophytes who are directed and instructed by their elders, as can be observed in primitive societies, can be seen as actual societies of scholars and therefore can already be considered to be the first expression of the school.

For our country the role played by the school is both necessary and of great importance. Aside from the school there is no social institution which lies between the family and the State. All such groups which occupied the territory between domestic society and political society and which required the participation of all their members have been totally suppressed or barely survive. Today the province and the guild are only memories; parish life is impoverished and occupies no more than a secondary place in our consciousness. The causes are well known. In order to achieve the political and moral unity of our country, the monarchy fought against all forms of local particularism with the aim of more easily and completely fusing the collective personality of France. In this regard, the Revolution continued and completed the monarchy's work. Moreover, the spirit which animated the revolutionaries displayed a kind of superstitious terror of all intermediate groupings to such an extent that until recent times our laws have been quite openly hostile towards societies of this kind.

Such a state of affairs leads to an exceptionally serious crisis, because if we are to provide a firmly based morality citizens must feel an interest in the life of the collectivity, since only under these conditions can citizens be bonded to the aims of the collectivity. However, one cannot automatically acquire these propensities. Above all, only by means of constant practise can one acquire sufficient strength to mould behaviour. If one's experience of the social is to be sufficiently pleasurable so that one cannot do without it, one must have developed the habit of acting and thinking in common with others. One must learn to appreciate social bonds which asocial beings experience as heavy chains. Through experience one must learn how cold and colourless the pleasures of solitude are in comparison. Such a temperament and mental constitution can only be formed through repeated practise and by means of continual encouragment. If one is only asked to act like a social being from time to time one can find but little pleasure in an existence to which one can but only adapt oneself imperfectly.

It follows that the nature of political life is such that we can only take part in it intermittently. The State is distant from our everyday concerns: we are not directly involved in its activities. Among events which affect the State, only the most important have repercussions that reach us.

If with the exception of the family there is no collective life in which we participate, if in all the forms of human activity (scientific, artistic, professional, etc.) — in other words, in all that constitutes the essence of our lives — we are used to acting on our own, our social temperament has only rare opportunities to strengthen and develop itself. Consequently, we are inevitably inclined to a more or less gloomy isolation, at least in regard to our extra-familial life. In effect, one of the most salient characteristics of our national temperament is the weakness of the spirit of association. We have a marked inclination towards a fierce individualism, which makes the social obligations which are the hallmark of any society appear to be intolerable, and prevent us from experiencing its pleasures.

We seem to think that we can neither join nor take part in any society without boxing ourselves in and diminishing our individual stature. Hence, we participate with distaste and as infrequently as possible. Nothing is more instructive in this respect than a comparison between the life of the German and French students. In Germany, everything revolves around the group: singing, outings, playing, philosophizing, studying the sciences or literature. In France, on the other hand, until very recently, the rule was that of isolation; and if a tendency towards social activities is beginning to revive, it is far from being very deep. This is true of adults as well as young people. The only kind of social relations for which we show any inclination are those sufficiently external so that our commitment is no more than superficial. That is why *salon* life has taken on such importance and has developed to such a great extent in this country. The *salon* is a way of satisfying to some extent – or rather a way to satisfy superficially – that need of sociability, which, in spite of everything, still survives in us. Need we demonstrate how illusory that satisfaction is, since that form of life in common is only a game without any connection to the serious aspects of life?

No matter how necessary it may be to remedy this situation, there can be no question of reviving groupings from the past nor of allotting to them their former activities; they disappeared because they were no longer in tune with the new conditions of collective life. What we must do is to try to create new groupings which are in harmony with the present social order and the principles upon which it is based. However, the only way this can be achieved is by reviving a spirit of association. Such groupings cannot be created by force. In order for them to be firmly rooted it is imperative that they be demanded by public opinion, that people feel them to be necessary and wish to form such groupings themselves. Thus we seem to be caught in a vicious circle, because these societies and associations cannot be reborn without awakening the spirit of association, that is, the sense of the group; and, as we have seen, this sense can only be acquired through practise in the context of already existing associations. We can only reinvigorate collective life, reviving it from its torpor by appreciating it; but we cannot learn to appreciate it unless we live it, and in order to do so it must exist. Precisely at this juncture the role played by the school can be considerable because it is the means, perhaps the only means, to break out of the vicious circle.

In effect, the school is a real and existing group, totally distinct from the family, of which the child is both a natural and necessary part. Unlike the family it does not exist especially to allow feelings of the heart and emotional expressions to develop. All the forms of intellectual activity exist in an embryonic form in the school. Consequently, the school provides us with the means to introduce the child to collective activities different from those the child experiences within the family. We can inculcate habits which, once acquired, will survive beyond the school years and demand the satisfaction that is their due. Hence this constitutes a unique, decisive and irreplaceable phase in life at which we can empower children, a phase when the gaps in our social organization have not yet been able to change their nature profoundly and awaken in them feelings which make them somewhat rebellious to collective life. Here we find a virgin territory in which we can sow seeds that, once taken root, will develop by themselves. Of course, I am not saying that educators on their own can overcome all obstacles and that institutions requiring the action of legislators are not necessary. But such action can only be successful if it is rooted in public opinion and if it is demanded as a result of deeply felt needs. Thus although we can only dispense with the school with the greatest of difficulty in order to instil a sense of the social in the child, and although we find here a natural function from which the school must never be separated, today, because of the critical situation in which we find ourselves, the services the school can provide are of incomparable importance.

26   A. H. Halsey, A. F. Heath and J. M. Ridge

Origins and Destinations

Excerpts from A. H. Halsey, A. F. Heath and J. M. Ridge, *Origins and Destinations: Family, Class and Education in Modern Britain*, Clarendon Press, Oxford, 1980, pp. 198–205.

Cultural Capital and Educability

Our fundamental theoretical concern has been with the question of whether education can change the class character of childhood. A strong strand in liberal traditions of political and social thought assert that it can . . .

On the Left writers such as Bourdieu have argued that the educational system serves merely to reproduce the distribution of cultural capital. Those who can receive what the school has to give are those who already are endowed with the requisite cultural attributes – with the appropriate cultural capital. A parallel argument comes from the Right. Bantock argues that many working-class children are 'for cultural reasons likely to be inhibited from gaining the best of what is offered them even if they were to be offered "chances" in these terms; and this because they have already been formed by historical sociocultural forces which make the segment of "high" culture for them pretty meaningless.' Their political differences do not prevent them from arriving at the same hypothesis: the culture of the working class . . . will inhibit them from taking advantage of what the school has to offer.

To test this hypothesis we looked first at the proportion of 'first-generation' grammar- and technical-school boys. In our sample as a whole, the great majority of those who attended selective secondary schools came from homes where both parents had been to non-selective schools. Eighty per cent of boys at the technical schools and two thirds of those at grammar schools came from homes with no tradition of formal academic schooling. Even at the apex of the educational system, 88 per cent of the boys at university came from families in which neither parent was a graduate, and 41 per cent from homes in which neither parent had been to selective schools. The state system of education, therefore, gave 'superior' education to vast numbers of boys from 'uneducated' homes. It is the dissemination rather than the reproduction of cultural capital that is more apparent here. And even within the private sector there has been a large minority of boys from these less educated backgrounds. Only the independent HMC schools could really be said to maintain a 'cycle of privilege' in which cultural capital is reproduced among those from educated homes.

In other words the educational system has undoubtedly offered chances of securing cultural capital to large numbers of boys to whom the ethos of the grammar and technical schools was new. But did 'historical socio-cultural forces' mean that these chances were largely spurious, that there was *formal* but not *effective* opportunity for these first-generation grammar-school boys? The answer is an unequivocal No. As we have noted, two thirds of our respondents at grammar school were 'first generation', and two thirds of these went on to secure some kind of academic credential. Moreover, their chances of success were very little different from those of second-generation grammar-school boys. The kind of education which the parents had received was of little value as a predictor of success or failure in the grammar schools.

We used path analysis ... to explore the determinants of educational attainment, incorporating two measures of family background which we labelled 'material circumstances' and 'family climate' respectively ...

The results are clear. Cultural capital influences selection for secondary school, but thereafter its importance is minimal. The effect of 'family climate' on the respondent's school-leaving age or examination success is wholly indirect, being mediated by type of secondary school and, to a lesser extent, by IQ. Among boys who attended the *same* type of secondary school 'family climate' does not discriminate between the academic successes and failures. IQ is slightly better as a discriminator, and 'material circumstances' better still, although we should note that none of these variables, not even 'material circumstances', is a particularly powerful discriminator among boys within a given type of school.

At all events, it would seem to be class, not culture or IQ, which is the more important source of, for example, early leaving from grammar school. Our evidence holds no comfort for those who would believe that class differences in educational attainment reflect a fair distribution of opportunities to those with the intellectual ability or cultural capacity to profit therefrom . . .

Our evidence suggests that 'the pool of ability' – the number of children with the capacity to obtain O-Levels, A-Levels, or university degrees – was larger than is usually supposed . . . Given that by the 1970s the number of boys obtaining at least one A-Level was actually somewhat larger than the number staying on until eighteen, we may reasonably conclude, assuming current conceptions of educability, that *at least* 7000 boys each year could have obtained A-Level passes but were not in fact remaining at school long enough to do so. Further back in time, of course, the wastage was much greater. In the early sixties it was running at an annual rate of around 30,000 and in the early fifties it would have been well over 40,000.

These figures bring out clearly the enormous strides that have been made since the Second War in the provision of sixth-form education, but this past progress cannot be a source of current complacency. We have shown that the chances of becoming an undergraduate have declined for boys with A-Levels. Two thirds of them went on to university in the fifties, but only half of them did so in the sixties. The expansion of the universities failed to keep pace with the expansion of the sixth forms – a reminder of one of the recurrent features of the British educational system – inequity between generations caused by educational inflexibility. Able children unfortunate enough to have been born in years of baby boom were at a serious disadvantage in the competition for university places compared with their siblings born a few years earlier or later.

At university level, then, there is a double wastage. There are the children who could have obtained A-Levels, but failed to stay at school long enough. And there are the children who obtained A-Levels but failed to find a university place because of the unresponsiveness of our system to changes in the demand for education . . . Much of this was a wastage of working-class talent . . . [By contrast,] 38 per cent of the service class were already staying on until the age of 18 in our youngest cohort, and this was the same figure as our predicted saturation level. Assuming that these were the cleverest 38 per cent of the service class, then boys with measured IQ at least as low as 113 were staying on until 18 and obtaining A-Levels. Our IQ assumptions entail that 14 per cent of working-class boys had measured IQ scores above 113, but only 6 per cent in fact stayed on until 18. It follows that the proportion of working-class boys reaching A-Level, and *pari passu* securing places at university, could comfortably be doubled without any necessary lowering of standards. At the time that our youngest cohort was of university age, the working class was obtaining less than half the number of places which, by service-class standards, it was entitled to.

Equality of Opportunity

Equality of opportunity is a phrase with many different meanings. A minimal definition of it can be described as formal equality of opportunity with the implication that no legal barrier exists to prevent a child from entering any form of education in the way that Jews were once kept out of Oxford and Cambridge, or black Africans are excluded from white South African universities. In this minimal sense formal equality of opportunity existed in the British schools throughout our period. The real debate, at least in the years before 1944, turned on strengthening the definition to take account of inequalities of circumstances, and especially financial ones. It was these, whether in the form of school fees or earnings foregone where boys stayed on beyond the statutory leaving age, that were in dispute: and the 1944 Act brought the final elimination of fee paying in state selective secondary schools. If, therefore, we define equality of opportunity in a second way to include the elimination of financial barriers then the reduction of these through the expansion of free places before 1944 and their total abolition after 1944 was clear progress towards equality of opportunity . . .

It is also important and relevant to this second definition of equality of opportunity to notice the financial implications of a developing non-financial selective system. As we have seen, the 1944 Act continued the growth of selective secondary schooling and, particularly in the 1960s, there was expansion of higher education on a selective basis. The costs of the different forms of education have been such that success in the selective process did not diminish but, if anything, widened the distance between those who got most and those who got least out of the public purse towards the cost of their schooling.

Given, then, that the selective stakes became, if anything, higher it is all the more crucial to note the actual distribution between social classes of educational costs, educational experience and examination results. In consequence, the third definition of equality of opportunity on which we have concentrated is one which compares the relative chances of access to schools and qualifications which were, *substantively* as distinct from *formally*, open to the children of different social classes. In effect, taking the word 'equality' to have its normal meaning in common speech, the definition now shifts from equality of opportunity to equality of outcome.

This third meaning of equality of opportunity in the sense of equality of access to superior forms of education yields a much less comforting picture. At the secondary-school stage access has been more unequal at the higher levels of the academic hierarchy as we have defined it. Class differentials are most extreme in the case of the independent HMC schools; a boy from the service class had nearly forty times the chance of his working-class peer of entering one of these schools. In the case of the Direct Grant schools his chance was twelve times as good, and in that of the grammar schools it was three times as good. Only in the technical schools has there been equality of class chances, and even this apparently more equitable distribution of opportunity has had much more to do with their lower standing in the academic pecking order than with the fairness of their methods of selection; relatively few boys from the service class went to the technical schools simply because so many had already gone to notionally superior secondary schools.

In general, then, class chances of access vary according to position in the academic hierarchy . . . Class differentials in access are necessarily reflected in school differences of class composition. Only the technical schools contained anything resembling a representative cross-section of the population, while the HMC schools remained socially the most exclusive. About 90 per cent of those at the private schools came from the service and intermediate classes. In contrast, over one third of boys in the state grammar schools came from the working class. Admittedly, the grammar schools may have served more to assimilate these working-class boys into middle-class life and culture than to break down class boundaries, but the social experience they offered must undoubtedly have been significantly different from that of the private sector . . .

This picture of unequal access to the superior secondary schools has remained depressingly constant over time. For the selective secondary schools as a group, chances of access rose at all levels of the class structure in the middle of our period, leading to some slight narrowing of class differentials, but they then fell back again to levels very like those of a generation earlier. Thus the likelihood of a working-class boy receiving a selective education in the mid fifties and sixties was very little different from that of his parents' generation thirty years earlier ... Grammar-school chances steadily improved for all three social classes among the first three cohorts [in our sample], followed by small and uneven retrogression in the final cohort. As a result, class differentials narrowed appreciably; in the first cohort the service-class boy's chance was over four times that of his working-class contemporary, but in the final cohort it was little more than twice as high. But what was given to the grammar schools was taken away from the technical schools ... Small increases at the beginning of our period were followed by long and steady decline, and what the working class gained through the expansion of the grammar schools, they largely lost through the decline of the technical schools. Over the period as a whole 100 working-class families sent an extra eight boys to grammar schools, but eight fewer to technical schools.

So much, then, for patterns of entry to the secondary schools. But what of exit? The short answer is that class differentials widen at each rung up the educational ladder. The boy from the working class was much more likely than his service-class contemporary to drop out of school as soon as the minimum leaving age was reached, was less likely to continue his school career into the sixth form, and less likely to enter a university or some other form of education after school ...

On the other hand, despite the continuing class differences, survival rates also show a tendency to converge. The secondary effects of stratification, as Boudon termed them, although reasserting themselves on each higher rung of the educational ladder, do so with less and less vigour. For the school population as a whole, the biggest difference is at the minimum school-leaving age; over three quarters of our working-class respondents dropped out at this stage whereas about three quarters of those from the service class stayed on. But at the gate of the university the gap narrowed appreciably. Of those who had survived long enough in the educational system to secure at least one A-Level or Higher School Certificate, 63 per cent from the service class went on to university, while the working-class percentage was not so greatly lower at 53 per cent. *For those who survive*, inequalities of opportunity are much reduced, although not entirely eliminated. They are, however, a small and select band. Less than one in forty of our working-class respondents acquired Higher School Certificate or an A-Level pass compared with one in four from the service class. The convergence of the survival rates, therefore, occurs too late in the school career to be relevant to more than a tiny handful of working-class children. Inequalities of opportunity have already done their damage at earlier stages of the school career.

However, patterns of exit from the secondary schools offer a slightly more encouraging trend than patterns of entry. Sustained expansion replaces the inverted U. The picture is at its most encouraging if we focus on the percentage staying on until 16 or later. In the earliest cohort a boy from the service class had nearly six times the chance of his working-class contemporary of being found in school at the age of 16: in the final cohort his chance was less than three times as high. But even this optimism must be tempered by the finding that while the *rate of increase* was greater for the working class, their *absolute* gains were less. Thus for every 100 working-class boys there were an extra twenty-two staying on until 16 or later by the end of our period; but for every 100 service-class boys there were an extra twenty-six staying on. In this sense, then, the difference between the classes had actually widened until, in 1974, the raising of the school-leaving age brought statutory equalization.

The proportion of 18 year olds staying on at school again shows steady expansion with larger absolute gains going to the service class. An extra twenty-two service-class boys for every 100 stayed on till 18, but for the working class the increment was a meagre three per 100. In consequence, relative chances as well as the absolute differences widened.

In summary, school inequalities of opportunity have been remarkably stable over the forty years which our study covers. Throughout, the service class has had roughly three times the chance of the working class of getting some kind of selective secondary schooling. Only at 16 has there been any significant reduction in relative class chances, but even here the absolute gains have been greater for the service class. If the 'hereditary curse upon English education is its organization upon lines of social class', that would seem to be as true in the 1960s as it was in 1931 when Tawney wrote.

27 Basil Bernstein

Open Schools – Open Society?

From Basil Bernstein, 'Open Schools – Open Society', in Basil Bernstein, *Class, Codes and Control, Vol. 3: Towards a Theory of Educational Transmission*, Routledge & Kegan Paul, 1975, pp. 67–75.

There has been much talk among sociologists concerned with education about the possibilities of analysing the school as a complex organization. The approach to current changes in the structure of the contemporary school system, which I attempt in this article, was initially set out by Durkheim over seventy years ago in his book *The Division of Labour*. I shall interpret the changes in terms of a shift of emphasis in the principles of social integration – from 'mechanical' to 'organic' solidarity. Such changes in social integration within schools are linked to fundamental changes in the character of the British educational system: a change from education in depth to education in breadth. I shall raise throughout this article the question of the relationship between the belief and moral order of the school, its social organization and its forms of social integration.

The concepts, mechanical and organic solidarity, can be used to indicate the emphasis within a society of one form of social integration rather than another. Organic solidarity is emphasized wherever individuals relate to each other through a complex interdependence of specialized social functions. Therefore organic solidarity presupposes a society whose social integration arises out of *differences* between individuals. These differences between individuals find their expression becomes crystallized into *achieved* roles. Mechanical solidarity is emphasized wherever individuals share a common system of belief and common sentiments which produce a detailed regulation of conduct. If social roles are achieved under organic solidarity, they are *assigned* or 'ascribed' under mechanical solidarity.

Wherever we have mechanical solidarity, according to Durkheim, punishment is necessary in order to revivify shared values and sentiments; i.e. punishment takes on a symbolic value over and beyond its specific utilitarian function. The belief system is made palpable in the symbolization of punishment. Durkheim took what he called repressive (criminal) law as an index of mechanical solidarity.

Under conditions of organic solidarity, the concern is less to punish but more to reconcile conflicting claims. Social control, in conditions of organic solidarity, is concerned with the relationships between *individuals* which have in some way been damaged. Durkheim took what he called restitutive law (civil) as his index of organic solidarity. Here the system of social control becomes restitutive or reparative in function. Whereas under mechanical solidarity, individuals confront one another indirectly, their confrontation being mediated by the belief system – under organic solidarity, in situations of social control, the belief system recedes into the background and the individuals confront one another directly.

Mechanical solidarity, according to Durkheim, arises in what he called a segmental society. He meant by this a type of society which could lose much of its personnel without damage to its continuity. Organic solidarity would correspond to the differentiated society, with diverse specialization of social roles; consequently the loss of a particular group of specialists might seriously impair the society. One can infer that segmental societies would make clear distinctions between inside and outside; whereas in differentiated societies the boundaries, as all symbolic boundaries, between inside and outside would become blurred.

Durkheim argued that a secondary cause of the division of labour arose out of the growing indeterminacy of the collective conscience (the value system). He said that sentiments would be aroused only by the infringement of highly general values, rather than by the minutiae of social actions. This, he said, would give rise to wider choice and so would facilitate individualism.

Organic solidarity refers to social integration at the level of individualized, specialized, interdependent social roles whereas mechanical solidarity refers to social integration at the level of shared beliefs. Under mechanical solidarity, there would be little tension between private beliefs and role obligations. In organic solidarity, the tensions between private belief and role obligations could be severe. This tension might be felt particularly by those individuals in socializing roles – for example, parents, teachers, probation officers, psychiatrists.

This is the shift of emphasis in the principles of social integration in schools – from mechanical to organic solidarity – that I shall be talking about. I am not concerned whether all the relationships I refer to are factually present in all schools. Clearly, some schools will have shifted not at all, others more; the shift may be more pronounced in the education of special groups of pupils or within different subjects. I am interested only in the general movement which at the moment may exist at the ideological rather than the substantive level. However, the list of shifts in emphasis may form a measure or scale of the change in the principles of social integration.

Consider, first, the forms of social control. In secondary schools there has been a move away from the transmission of common values through a ritual order and control based upon position or status, to more personalized forms of control where teachers and taught confront each other as individuals. The forms of social control appeal less to shared values, group loyalties and involvements; they are based rather upon the recognition of differences between individuals. And with this there has been a weakening of the symbolic significance and ritualization of punishment.

Look now at the division of labour of the school staff. Irrespective of the pupil/teacher ratios, the staff is now much larger. The division of labour is more complex from the point of view of the range of subjects taught. Within the main subjects, the hierarchy of responsibility has become more differentiated. The teacher's role itself has fragmented to form a series of specialized roles (vocational, counselling, housemaster, social worker and so on). Still within the broad category of the division of labour consider – very briefly, for the moment – the organization of pupils. The pupils' position in the new schools in 'principle' is less likely to be fixed in terms of sex, age or IQ, for ideally their position, within limits, is achieved in terms of their individual qualities.

Thus we find (a) a movement towards a more complex division of labour among the staff and a greater differentiation of the teacher's role; and (b) at the same time, the pupils' relationships with other pupils in principle arise from their expression of their educational differences. This is good evidence of a shift towards organic solidarity.

Let us turn, next, to shifts in emphasis in the curriculum, pedagogy, the organization of teaching groups and teaching and pupil roles. Here we are at the heart of the instrumental order of the school: the transmission of skills and sensitivities.

Take the organization of teaching groups first. Here we can begin to see a shift from a situation where the teaching group is a fixed structural unit of the school's organization (the form or class), to secondary schools where the teaching group is a flexible or variable unit of the social organization. The teaching group can consist of one, five, twenty, forty or even 100 pupils and this number can vary from subject to subject. At the same time there has been an increase in the number of different teaching groups a pupil of a given age is in. The form or class tends to be weakened as a basis for relation and organization.

One can raise the level of abstraction and point out that space and time in the new schools − relative to the old − have (again within limits) ceased to have fixed references. Social spaces can be used for a variety of purposes and filled in a number of different ways. This potential is built into the very architecture.

Now for the changes in pedagogy. There is a shift − from a pedagogy which, for the majority of secondary school pupils, was concerned with the learning of standard operations tied to specific contexts − to a pedagogy which emphasizes the exploration of principles. From schools which emphasized the teacher as a solution-giver to schools which emphasize the teacher as a problem-poser or creator. Such a change in pedagogy (itself perhaps a response to changed concepts of skill in industry) alters the authority relationships between teacher and taught, and possibly changes the nature of the authority inherent in the subject. The pedagogy now emphasizes the *means* whereby knowledge is created and principles established, in a context of self-discovery by the pupils. The act of learning itself celebrates choice.

But what about the curriculum? I mean by curriculum the principles governing the selection of, and relation between, subjects. We are witnessing a shift in emphasis away from schools where the subject is a clear-cut definable unit of the curriculum, to schools where the unit of the curriculum is not so much a subject as an *idea* − say, topic-centred inter-disciplinary inquiry. Such a shift is already under way at the university level.

Now, when the basis of the curriculum is an idea which is *supra* subject, and which governs the relationship between subjects, a number of consequences may follow. The subject is no longer dominant, but subordinate to the idea which governs a particular form of integration. If the subject is no longer dominant, then this could affect the position of teacher as specialist. His reference point may no longer be his subject or discipline. His allegiance, his social point of gravity, may tend to switch from his commitment to his subject to the bearing his subject has upon the *idea* which is relating him to other teachers.

In the older schools, integration between subjects, when it existed, was determined by the public examination system, and this is one of the brakes on the shift I am describing. In the new schools, integration at the level of idea involves a new principle of social integration of staff: that of organic solidarity. This shift in the basis of the curriculum from subject to idea may point towards a fundamental change in the character of British education: a change from education in depth to education in breadth.

As a corollary of this, we are moving from secondary schools where the teaching roles were insulated from each other, where the teacher had an assigned area of authority and autonomy, to secondary schools where the teaching role is less autonomous and where it is a shared or cooperative role. There has been a shift from a teaching role which is, so to speak, 'given' (in the sense that one steps into assigned duties), to a role which has to be *achieved* in relation with other teachers. It is a role which is no longer made but *has to be made*. The teacher is no longer isolated from other teachers, as where the principle of integration is the relation of his subject to a public examination. The teacher is now in a complementary relation with other teachers at the level of his day-by-day teaching.

Under these conditions of cooperative, shared teaching roles, the loss of a teacher can be most damaging to the staff because of the interdependence of roles. Here we can begin to see the essence of organic solidarity as it affects the crucial role of teacher. The act of teaching itself expresses the organic articulation between subjects, teachers and taught. The form of social integration, in the central area of the school's function, is organic rather than mechanical.

How is the role of pupil affected? I said that, under mechanical solidarity, social roles were likely to be fixed and ascribed, aspirations would be limited, and individuals would relate to each other through common beliefs and shared sentiments. These beliefs and sentiments would regulate the details of social action. In the older secondary schools, individual choice was severely curtailed, aspirations were controlled through careful streaming, and streaming itself produced homogeneous groups according to an imputed similarity in ability. The learning process emphasized the teacher as solution-giver rather than problem-poser. The role of pupil was circumscribed and well defined.

Now there has been a move towards giving the pupil greater choice. Aspirations are likely to be raised in the new schools, partly because of changes in their social organization. The learning process creates greater autonomy for the pupil. The teaching group may be either a heterogeneous unit (unstreamed class) or a series of different homogeneous units (sets) or even both. The pupil's role is less clearly defined. Of equal significance, his role conception evolves out of a series of diverse contexts and relationships. The enacting of the role of pupil reveals less his similarity to others, but rather his difference from others.

I suggested earlier that, where the form of social integration was mechanical, the community would tend to become sealed off, self-enclosed, and its boundary relationship would be sharply defined. Inside and outside would be clearly differentiated. These notions can apply to changes both within the school and to its relation to the outside.

Schools' boundary relations, both within and without, are now more open. This can be seen at many levels. First of all, the very architecture of the new schools points up their openness compared with the old schools. The inside of the institution has become visible. Of more significance, the boundary relation between the home and school has changed, and parents (their beliefs and socializing styles) are incorporated within the school in a way unheard of in the older schools. The range and number of non-school adults who visit the school and talk to the pupils have increased. The barrier between the informal teenage subcultures and the culture of the school has weakened: often the non-school age group subculture becomes a content of a syllabus. The outside penetrates the new schools in other fundamental ways. The careful editing, specially for schools, of books, papers, films, is being replaced by a diverse representation of the outside both within the library and through films shown to the pupils.

Within the school, as we have seen, the insulation between forms and between teaching roles has weakened, and authority relationships are less formal. The diminishing of a one-to-one relation between a given activity, a given space and a given time – i.e. flexibility – must reduce the symbolic significance of particular spaces and particular times. The controls over flow in the new schools carry a different symbolic significance from the controls over flow in the old schools.

Let me summarize at a more general level the significance of these shifts of emphasis. There has been a shift from secondary schools whose symbolic orders point up or celebrate the idea of purity of categories – whether these categories be values, subjects in a curriculum, teaching groups or teachers – to secondary schools whose symbolic orders point up or celebrate the idea of mixture or diversity of categories. (These concepts have been developed by Mary Douglas in her book *Purity and Danger*.) For example:

(1) The mixing of categories at the level of values. Changes in the boundary relationships between the inside and the outside of the school lead to a value system which is more ambiguous and more open to the influence of diverse values from outside.

(2) The mixing of categories at the level of curriculum. The move away from a curriculum where subjects are insulated and autonomous, to a curriculum which involves the subordination of subjects and their integration.

(3) The mixing of categories at the level of the teaching group. Heterogeneous rather than homogeneous teaching groups and differentiated sets of pupils rather than fixed forms or classes.

The secondary schools celebrate diversity, not purity. This may be symptomatic of basic changes in the culture of our society, particularly changes in the principles of social control. Until recently the British educational system epitomized the concept of purity of categories. At the apex of the system sat the lonely, specialized figure of the arts Ph.D., a dodo in terms of our current needs.

There was also the separation of the arts and the sciences, and within each the careful insulation between the 'pure' and the 'applied'. (Contrast all this with the United States.)

The concept of knowledge was one that partook of the 'sacred': its organization and dissemination was intimately related to the principles of social control. Knowledge (on this view) is dangerous, it cannot be exchanged like money, it must be confined to special well-chosen persons and even divorced from practical concerns. The forms of knowledge must always be bounded and well insulated from each other; there must be no sparking across the forms with unpredictable outcomes. Specialization makes knowledge safe and protects the vital principles of social order. Preferably knowledge should be transmitted in a context where the teacher has maximum control or surveillance, as in hierarchical school relationships or the university tutorial relation. Knowledge and the principles of social order are made safe if knowledge is subdivided, well insulated and transmitted by authorities who themselves view their own knowledge or disciplines with the jealous eye of a threatened priesthood. (This applies much more to the arts than to the sciences.)

Education in breadth, with its implications of mixture of categories, arouses in educational guardians an abhorrence and disgust like the sentiments aroused by incest. This is understandable because education in breadth arouses fears of the dissolution of the principles of social order. Education in depth, the palpable expression of purity of categories, creates monolithic authority systems serving élitist functions; education in breadth weakens authority systems or renders them pluralistic, and it is apparently consensual in function. One origin of the purity and mixing of categories may be in the general social principles regulating the mixing of diverse groups in society. But monolithic societies are unlikely to develop education in breadth, in school systems with pronounced principles of organic solidarity. Such forms of social integration are inadequate to transmit collective beliefs and values.

It might now be helpful to drop the terms mechanical and organic solidarity and refer instead to 'closed' and 'open' schools.

Individuals, be they teachers or taught, may be able (under certain conditions) to make their own roles in a way never experienced before in the public sector of secondary education. But staff and students are likely to experience a sense of loss of structure and, with this, problems of boundary, continuity, order and ambivalence are likely to arise. This problem of the relationship between the transmission of belief and social organization is likely to be acute in large-scale 'open' church schools. It may be that the open school with its organic modes of social integration, its personalized forms of social control, the indeterminacy of its belief and moral order (except at the level of very general values) will strengthen the adherence of the pupils to their age group as a major source of belief, relation and identity. Thus, is it possible that, as the open school moves further towards organic solidarity as its major principle of social integration, so the pupils move further towards the 'closed' society of the age group? Are the educational dropouts of the fifties to be replaced by the moral dropouts of [today]?

None of this should be taken in the spirit that yesterday there was order; today there is only flux. Neither should it be taken as a long sigh over the weakening of authority and its social basis. Rather we should be eager to explore changes in the forms of social integration in order to re-examine the basis for social control. This, as Durkheim pointed out decades ago, is a central concern of a sociology of education.

References

BERNSTEIN, B., ELVIN H. L. and PETERS R. S. (1966), 'Ritual in education', *Philosophical Transactions of the Royal Society of London*, Series B, 251, No. 772.

DOUGLAS, M. (1966), *Purity and Danger*, Routledge & Kegan Paul.

DURKHEIM, E. (1947), *The Division of Labour in Society*, Free Press, Chicago.

DURKHEIM, E. (1961), *Moral Education*, Free Press, Chicago.

28 William Tyler

School Organization

Excerpts from William Tyler, *School Organization: a Sociological Perspective*, Croom Helm, 1983, pp. 222–8.

What is distinctive about schools as organizations? The answer seems to be that the visible marks of school organization – bells, timetables, chalk, corridors, registers, examinations, uniforms, assemblies, noise, hierarchy and staff meetings – are its least important and enduring institutional features. Nor should we confuse school organization with a certain historically bound arrangement of teaching and learning such as the age-graded curriculum ... The defining features of school organization are not to be found in its concrete practices, nor yet in a particular bureaucratic form ...

The definition of the school [as] 'a localized administrative entity concerned with the face-to-face instruction of the young' ... produces two poles ... The first of these were the tensions between the formal structure and the face-to-face situations of teaching and learning. How tightly does the one control and regulate the other? To what extent does the formal structure depend on the ability of teachers and pupils to 'cope' in everyday classroom encounters? How much is the formal system really a response to the problems of order and control at the classroom level? This basic tension between formal structure and classroom interaction can be thought of as the 'horizontal' axis of school organization. The second, the 'vertical' axis of organization, is less obvious, found in the tensions between the 'surface' phenomena of empirically observed behaviour (whether these are in the administrative or in the classroom spheres) and the 'deeper' kinds of relations between people, events and things. Can appearances of autonomy and 'looseness' in school organization often be misleading? Is a visibly 'loose' organization to some extent like an unstructured conversation, informal on the surface but underneath governed by linguistic and meta-linguistic rules . . .?

The study of school organization has suffered from the imposition of the so-called 'factory' model . . . The application of such a model has not led to many important insights into the nature of schools as organizations. Nowhere is this seen more than in the 'top-down' attempts at innovation in the 1960s and 1970s where it was assumed that a change in the technical core would automatically follow the redeployment of teachers and the re-design of classroom space. Not only did these approaches have a patchy and often negative impact, the studies which followed up on these (notably in the open-plan team-taught primary shcool) showed just how fragile and indeterminate are the causal relations between the technical operations of the modern school and its administrative apparatus.

The theoretical effect of the decline of the 'factory' model was to focus attention on the institutional arrangements which underpin both the autonomy of the classroom teacher and the formal classifications of competence which are managed by educational administrators. This led in turn to an assessment of the school organization as a sophisticated and highly efficient institution which allows highly skilled and experienced practitioners to operate in a loosely coupled structure under the umbrella of a legitimizing set of myths and symbols. The technical core of the school, in contrast to that of a factory, cannot be easily 'de-skilled', since it depends on the specialization of the person rather than of the task. It therefore relies heavily on the external links which allow it to innovate, develop and perform within a complex institutional environment. However, as its outputs become less and less specialized and the criteria of competence become more diffuse, schools become vulnerable to attempts to restore the visible controls of the factory and the office, as teachers are perceived to be acting beyond a narrowly defined brief. Recent administrative and legislative initiatives in the advanced industrial countries to render schools more 'accountable' have therefore been associated with two reactions in the sociology of the school. On the one hand, there has been the search for the 'instructionally effective school' which by its ethos or its organizational structure may be seen to 'deliver the goods' expected by parents and employers. On the other, there has been a resurgence of interest in the school's cultural (as distinct from formal organizational) properties through the study of the collective symbols of legitimacy and identity.

These organizational types of questions, however, bear only a remote relation to the 'interaction order' of the school, in effect its daily activities of teaching and learning. Here the study of 'face-to-face' encounters with others who are physically 'co-present' imposes an entirely different perspective on the study of the school. Here school structure becomes a framework of interaction which is produced and reproduced through the coping and survival strategies of the pupils and teachers . . .

The interactionist approach . . . shares an important feature with the school effectiveness literature, in that it is concerned largely with empirical phenomena. The limitations on both of these approaches become obvious if, for example, one is trying to explain the changing patterns of deviance in schools, or to pin the interpretations of pupils in a cross-cultural classroom against a wider canvas . . .

Structuralist approaches appear to be particularly valuable in linking the various components of organization met in the literature – administrative structure, discipline regime, institutional environment, architecture and ideologies of surveillance and control – since they make connections among these 'deeper' patterns of structure and meaning . . . In the case of the school, it is suggested that a combination of the perspectives of Bernstein and Foucault may identify these discursive axes, the first as the visibility/invisibility of control (Bernstein) and the second as the political construction of the pupil, whether as a bodily object, as in the disciplinary regimes of the past, or as a subject, as in the therapeutic and confessional technologies (Foucault). This two-dimensional framework underpinned types of school or educational organization. While the monitorial school, characterized by extremes of disciplinary power and visible control, is encompassed by a 'factory' model, there emerge from the framework other possible combinations of organization/environment, administrative/technical links which could go far beyond the organizational forms which we now identify as schools.

Are we any closer then to identifying the organizational properties of the 'school' in the ordinary sense of this word? . . . Irrespective of how we may isolate patterns of formal organization whose explicit function is public instruction, we will still need first to consider the communicative and discursive principles by which these are constituted. Not all educational organizations are necessarily producers of educational discourse, nor can all organizations outside the formal sphere of public schooling (or its recognized private counterpart) be denied the title of 'school' for purely formal reasons. The autonomy of the discursive field . . . is often of no less interest than the organizational forms through which these are expressed and realized. By linking the communicative and the organizational spheres of rational action, sociologists may be able to explore the specific form of the instructional apparatus and at the same time provide important bridges between the 'macro' sociologies of social reproduction and the 'micro' sociology of the classroom. The above analysis suggests a need to develop institutional mechanisms which may protect or buffer the discursive core of schooling (both in its technical and its administrative aspects) from those discourses which are not directly concerned with teaching and learning. This need should be supported by a recognition by all educational professionals of the radical transformation that is now taking place of the discursive conditions of public schooling away from disciplinary and visible modes of power and control.

29 Pierre Bourdieu and Jean-Claude Passeron

Social Reproduction through Education

Excerpts from Pierre Bourdieu and Jean-Claude Passeron, *Reproduction in Education, Society and Culture*, Sage, 1971, pp. 179–83, 196–7, 199–201, 210.

The Particular Functions of the General Interest

Never before has the question of the 'aims' of education been so completely identified with discussion of the contribution education makes to national growth. Even the preoccupations apparently most foreign to this logic, such as the ostentatious concern to 'democratize educational and cultural opportunity' increasingly draw on the language of economic rationality, taking the form, for example, of denunciation of the 'wastage' of talent. But are economic 'rationalization' and 'democratization' so automatically linked as well-intentioned technocrats like to think? . . .

The technocratic thinking which, reviving the philosophy of history of social evolutionism in its simplest form, claims to extract from reality itself a unilinear, one-dimensional model of the phases of historical change, obtains without much effort the yardstick of a universal comparison which enables it to hierarchize the different societies or educational systems univocally, according to their degree of development or 'rationality' . . . Consequently, whether one confines oneself to indicators as abstract as illiteracy rate, enrolment rate and teacher–pupil ratio, or takes into account more specific indicators of the efficiency of the educational system or of the degree to which it makes use of the intellectual resources potentially available, such as the role of technical education, the proportion of student intake successfully graduating, or the differential representation of the sexes or social classes in the different levels of education, it is necessary to reinstate these relations within the systems of relations on which they depend, in order to avoid comparing the incomparable or, more subtly, failing to compare the really comparable.

More profoundly, all these indicators rest on an implicit definition of the 'productivity' of the educational system which, in referring exclusively to its *formal, external* rationality, reduces the system of its functions to one of them, itself subjected to a reductive abstraction . . . An indicator as univocal in appearance as the number of certificate holders at each level in each speciality cannot be interpreted within the formal logic of a system of juridical equivalences: the economic and social profitability of a given diploma is a function of its scarcity on the economic and symbolic markets, i.e. the value which the sanctions of the different markets confer on the different diplomas and different categories of diplomas. Thus, in a country with a high rate of illiteracy, the mere fact of literacy or, *a fortiori*, possession of an elementary diploma, is sufficient to ensure a decisive advantage in occupational competition.

Similarly, because traditional societies generally exclude women from schooling, because the use of all intellectual capacities is demanded by the development of the economy, and because the entry of women into male occupations is one of the main social changes accompanying industrialization, one might be tempted to see the rate of feminization of secondary and higher education as an indicator of the degree of 'rationalization' and 'democratization' of the educational system. In reality, the Italian and French examples suggest that one must not be misled by a very high rate of feminization and that the educational careers girls are offered by the richest nations are often simply a more expensive and more luxurious variant of traditional upbringing or, to put it another way, a reinterpretation of the most modern studies for women in terms of the traditional model of the division of labour between the sexes, as is attested by female students' whole attitude towards their studies and, still more visibly, by the choice of discipline or the rate of vocational use of their diplomas, which are both a cause and an effect of their attitude. Conversely, even low rates of feminization may express a clear-cut break with the traditional definition of female upbringing in a Muslim country whose whole tradition tended to exclude women from higher education completely. More precisely, the overall rate of feminization has a different significance depending on the social recruitment of the female students and the distribution of the rates of feminization of the various faculties and disciplines. Thus, in France, the fact that the chances of university entrance are virtually the same for boys and girls does not imply the disappearance of the traditional model of the division of labour and the ideology of the distribution of 'gifts' between the sexes: girls are still consigned more often than boys to certain types of studies (arts subjects in the main), the more so the lower their social origin. Even indicators as unequivocal at first sight as the proportion of women graduates making vocational use of their academic qualification are subject to the system effect: to measure adequately the social profitability of the diploma held by a woman, one must at least take into account the fact that the 'value' of an occupation (such as, in France, that of primary or secondary school teacher) steadily diminishes as it is feminized.

Another example: the apparently most unimpeachable indicator of an educational system's efficiency, the 'wastage' rate (defined by the number of students in a given intake who fail to complete the course successfully) remains meaningless until it is seen as the effect of a specific combination of the social selection and technical selection that an educational system always carries out inseparably. The 'waste product' is in this case as much a transformed product as is the finished product; consider the system of dispositions towards the educational institution, his occupation and his whole existence which characterizes the 'failure', as well as the technical and above all social profits accruing – unequally, depending on the society and the class – from the fact of having had some higher education, albeit intermittent or interrupted. What is the value of a comparison between the wastage rates of British (14 per cent), American or French universities, if one fails to consider, in addition to the degree of selection before entry which distinguishes Britain from France or the US, the diversity of the procedures the different systems use to carry out selection and to cause its effects to be internalized, ranging from the categorical exclusion operated by French-style examination, especially the State competition, to the painless elimination ('cooling out') made possible in the US by the hierarchy of university establishments? . . .

Because pedagogic work (whether performed by the School, a Church or a Party) has the effect of producing individuals durably and systematically modified by a prolonged and systematic transformative action tending to endow them with the same durable, transposable training (habitus), i.e. with common schemes of thought, perception, appreciation and action; because the serial production of identically programmed individuals demands and historically gives rise to the production of programming agents themselves identically programmed and of standardized conserving and transmitting instruments; because the length of time necessary for the advent of a systematic transformation of the transformative action is at least equal to the time required for serial production of transformed reproducers, i.e. agents capable of exerting a transformative action reproductive of the training they themselves have received; because, above all, the educational institution is the only one in full possession, by virtue of its essential function, of the power to select and train, by an action exerted throughout the period of apprenticeship, those to whom it entrusts the task of perpetuating it and is therefore in the best position, by definition, to impose the norms of its self-perpetuation, if only by using its power to reinterpret external demands; and finally because teachers constitute the most finished products of the system of production which it is, *inter alia*, their task to reproduce – it is understandable that, as Durkheim noted, educational institutions have a relatively autonomous history and that the tempo of the transformation of academic institutions and culture is particularly slow. The fact remains that if one fails to relate the relative autonomy of the educational system and its history to the social conditions of the performance of its essential function, one is condemned . . . to put forward a circular explanation of the relative autonomy of the system in terms of the relative autonomy of its history and vice versa.

The generic characteristics every educational system owes to its essential function of inculcation and to its relative autonomy cannot be fully explained without taking into account the objective conditions which, at a given moment, enable an educational system to achieve a determinate degree and particular type of autonomy. It is therefore necessary to construct the system of relations between the educational system and the other sub-systems, specifying those relations by reference to the structure of class relations, in order to perceive that the relative autonomy of the educational system is always the counterpart of a dependence hidden to a greater or lesser extent by the practices and ideology authorized by that autonomy. To put it another way, to a given degree and type of autonomy, i.e. to a determinate form of correspondence between the essential function and the external functions, there always correspond a determinate type and degree of dependence on the other systems, i.e. in the last analysis, on the structure of class relations . . .

It is precisely its relative autonomy that enables the traditional educational system to make a specific contribution towards reproducing the structure of class relations, since it need only obey its own rules in order to obey, additionally, the external imperatives defining its function of legitimating the established order, that is, to fulfil simultaneously its social function of reproducing the class relations, by ensuring the hereditary transmission of cultural capital, and its ideological function of concealing that social function by accrediting the illusion of its absolute autonomy. Thus, the full definition of the relative autonomy of the educational system with respect to the interests of the dominant classes must always take into account the specific services this relative autonomy performs for the perpetuation of the class relations: it is precisely its peculiar ability to autonomize its functioning and secure recognition of its legitimacy by accrediting the representation of its neutrality that gives the educational system its peculiar ability to mask the contribution it makes towards reproducing the class distribution of cultural capital, the concealment of this service being not the least of the services its relative autonomy enables it to perform for the conservation of the established order. The educational system succeeds so perfectly in fulfilling its ideological function of legitimating the established order only because this masterpiece of social mechanics succeeds in hiding, as if by the interlocking of false-bottomed boxes, the relations which, in a class society, unite the function of inculcation, i.e. the work of intellectual and moral integration, with the function of conserving the structure of class relations characteristic of that society . . .

Thus, the educational system, with the ideologies and effects which its relative autonomy engenders, is for bourgeois society in its present phase what other forms of legitimation of the social order and of hereditary transmission of privileges were for social formations differing both in the specific form of the relations and antagonisms between the classes and in the nature of the privilege transmitted: does it not contribute towards persuading each social subject to stay in the place which falls to him *by nature*, to know his place and hold to it, *ta heatou prattein*, as Plato put it? Unable to invoke the right of blood – which his class historically denied the aristocracy – nor the rights of

Nature – a weapon once used against the distinctions of nobility but liable to backfire against bourgeois 'distinction' – nor the ascetic virtues which enabled the first-generation entrepreneurs to justify their success by their merit, the inheritor of bourgeois privileges must today appeal to the academic certification which attests at once his gifts and his merits. The unnatural idea of culture by birth presupposes and produces blindness to the functions of the educational institution which ensures the profitability of cultural capital and legitimates its transmission by dissimulating the fact that it performs this function. Thus, in a society in which the obtaining of social privileges depends more and more closely on possession of academic credentials, the School does not only have the function of ensuring discreet succession to a bourgeois estate which can no longer be transmitted directly and openly. This privileged instrument of the bourgeois sociodicy which confers on the privileged the supreme privilege of not seeing themselves as privileged manages the more easily to convince the disinherited that they owe their scholastic and social destiny to their lack of gifts or merits, because in matters of culture absolute dispossession excludes awareness of being dispossessed.

30   Diego Gambetta

Were They Pushed or Did They Jump?

Excerpts from Diego Gambetta, *Were They Pushed or Did They Jump?*, Cambridge University Press, 1987, pp. 169–72, 175–7, 186–7.

Educational institutions shape the set of feasible options for everyone, irrespective of their social background. They establish length of compulsory education, types of high school, selective procedures and so on. Subjects distribute themselves among options which are on offer, and it would not make sense to ask why they did not choose a course of education that does not exist ... The power to alter the feasible set does not lie with any one individual alone. It is exclusively in this broad and special sense that institutions 'explain' individual acts. To the extent to which the institutional set-up is of universal significance within a society (i.e. it applies to everyone indiscriminately), differences in individuals' educational behaviour *within* that society cannot be explained by the presence of institutions of a given form.

There is none the less one way in which institutions operate in a discriminating fashion, but rather than directly acting as constraints they do so by not lifting constraints which exist independently, for instance, by not providing economic aid or by indirectly increasing the costs of education through a particular selection system. Neither the Italian nor the British educational institutions provide economic support for poorer students at the crucial point at which they leave compulsory education ...

More important than institutional constraints seem to be the economic constraints, which are indeed unequally distributed within most societies. These constraints play a crucial part in explaining educational decisions, particularly at the beginning of high school: the tighter they are the lower the probability both that education will be continued and, if continued, that it will be in the longer and more demanding types of high school. In this respect education can be seen as a consumption commodity subject to budget constraints ...

There are relevant differences between the way in which working-class and middle-class families react to variations in income when deciding about their children's education: the lower the income the lower the probability that a working-class child will go to high school; if he or she does go to high school income is less relevant in determining which type of high school is chosen. By contrast, middle-class children are more likely to continue to high school even when income is low, but here the economic pressure is then felt on the choice of the type of high school: the lower the income the shorter or the less demanding the type of high school selected. This inter-class difference . . . cannot be adequately accounted for by the structuralist model with which we have started. It means that the effect of economic constraints of similar entity is also *filtered* by other mechanisms which are related to the class of origin and, possibly, to class-specific preferences. Before we come to the model that can make sense of this difference in the responsiveness of the social classes to income variations, we still have to take a few steps.

Cultural constraints − or the amount of 'cultural capital' children find at their disposal in the family − appear as generally less important than economic constraints, and, particularly for the working class, the latter seem to have a binding effect which overrides that of the former. Working-class children do not seem to be able to reach that point in which cultural constraints could make themselves directly felt. Only the most deprived section of the working class . . . does seem to run into cultural difficulties. While in fact working-class migrant families send their children to high school as much as any other working-class family, they meet a less fortunate educational fate during the course of high school.

More generally, cultural constraints operate strongly mainly upon the ambitious and culturally ill-equipped section of the middle class whose children seem to share a fate which, *mutatis mutandis*, is analogous to that of the migrants' children in the working class. This part of the middle class seems to act on the basis of a lexicographic preference for having its children sent to high school, a preference that, if not accompanied by an adequate amount of 'cultural capital', leads them to a high risk of failure and of abandoning high school before completion. In this case cultural constraints really seem to act as a barrier which is encountered without foresight. They explain why children of poorly educated middle-class families are pushed out of school. They do not explain, however, the reasons why the middle class seems to be so light-heartedly prone to expose its children to failure – especially if compared with the extreme *caution* shown by the working class, whose children, if they go to high school at all, are comparatively more likely to make it through to the end. Once again the structuralist model can explain educational behaviour only up to a point.

Let us now take a further step and introduce a second model, which, unlike the previous one, essentially refers to intentional rather than causal processes. In deciding about their education subjects take into account *the expected probability of success of a given course of action relative to the other available options.* Here we are in the realm of the 'economic approach to human action', which, as we have already pointed out, constitutes a particular version of the rational approach to action. In this model the assumption is that – once the effects of constraints on opportunities are taken into account – what really discriminates between available alternatives is a standard preference for 'the more the better', where the more refers essentially to material benefits. It does not necessarily deny the explanatory value of constraints, whose role it can easily incorporate, but it stresses that – beyond constraints – what explains differences in individual choices are the differences in the structure of the expected rewards that can fulfil that basic preference. This model too exhibits considerable explanatory power . . .

It is possible to hold the view that all our preferences are causally shaped. Thus, action would intentionally follow from our preferences, but in turn these would be causally shaped and constrained by the outside world we live in. It is also plausible to believe that we may sometimes be aware of the causal influences on our preferences and able to interact with them, to the point of exercising some control over the relevant processes. However, it would be an impossible task – as well as a useless one from the point of view of a social scientist – to try to map the potentially infinite set of causes to which we are randomly exposed or to which we may intentionally expose ourselves. The only preferences whose explanation is crucial for the social sciences are those which are shaped according to some social pattern. But preferences which are generated at random with respect to relevant social conditions have to be taken as given, and action must be accounted for exclusively as the intentional product of these preferences.

This leads us to introduce a third explanatory model: *educational choices result from how subjects plan their future lives*, irrespective of whether these are primarily based on economic preferences and irrespective of relevant social conditions that could shape preferences behind the subjects' backs ... Preferences whose origin cannot be traced to social class of origin or to other unevenly distributed social attributes play a part in explaining educational choices. The most basic condition for planning one's life, i.e. the length of the time perspective within which a subject projects him or herself into the future, was shown as having a dramatic effect on the probability of going to university. Similarly, the degree of one's ambitions relative to one's career has very much the same consequences. In essence, what one *wants* to do does count ... A middle-class pupil with a preference for an interesting job is significantly more likely to go to university than those other middle-class pupils who do not have such a preference, whereas for a working-class pupil, going to university is associated with that preference only when it is held to be unrenounceable. Similarly, a preference for higher earnings is associated with a higher probability of going to university only when it is entertained by working-class subjects, for middle-class subjects probably enjoy more opportunities of satisfying that preference without necessarily gaining higher educational credentials.

Here, the explanation of educational decisions comes full circle and the third model, higher-order purposeful behaviour, brings us back to the model we started with – i.e. constraints as the key variable. The question is now whether the models we have sequentially reviewed can be merged in one single explanatory apparatus. Given that each of them separately can make theoretical sense of different empirical findings and that all together can account for a large part of the empirical findings, this question is indeed central ...

Life-plans and preferences can be seen as including a basic set of elements such as the length of the time perspective on the basis of which subjects project themselves into the future and expectations concerning the intensity and quality of their working career as well as their cultural and economic ambitions. A useful way of representing educational and other preferences within a population is to imagine that they are distributed along a bell-shaped continuous line: at one extreme we have those who entertain life-plans which strongly exclude education, verging on a lexicographic preference for other options; at the other extreme there are those whose life-plans contemplate education 'at all costs'. Most subjects will tend to be distributed somewhere between these extremes and we can expect the distribution to be skewed towards the latter extreme. In other words, we can expect that more people would have a general interest in education, but they would initially tend to be somehow uncertain about whether or not to pursue that interest and up to what level of education. In other words, fewer people would tend to seek education taking little or no account of other circumstances.

We are ... in a position to amend the overall model elaborated above and sum up our theoretical conclusions: subjects tend to evaluate rationally the various elements for making educational decisions, which include economic constraints, personal academic ability and expected labour market benefits. This process of evaluation takes place on the basis of their personal preferences and life-plans, which are partly the result of personal characteristics subject to socially random influences. Preferences and life-plans, though, are in turn 'distorted' by specific class biases which act as weights that subjects sub-intentionally apply to the elements of their rational evaluation. The formation of these class-specific preferences may be due to a variety of processes, such as a tendency to extremizing behaviour, a cautious 'view of the world' related to difficult past experiences, or normative effects of reference groups. Furthermore, *within* each class – particularly the working class – there are shifts of the distribution which depend on the amount of parents' education ...

The impression of complexity may, by this stage, appear less worrying than initially feared, and we can conclude by returning to our original question. So, *were they pushed or did they jump?* If anything, they jumped. They jumped as much as they could and as much as they perceived it was worth jumping. The trouble, though, is that not all children can jump to the same extent and the number of pushes they receive in several directions, shaping their opportunities as well as preferences, varies tremendously in society. What does not seem to vary is that the pushes are likely to push in the wrong direction:

wrong in general because of the strong degree of social inequality involved. But wrong in particular too, because several of those who are pushed upwards risk failures later on and are often in no position to make good use of the education they receive, other than for satisfying tenacious family pride; and because some of the others, those who are pushed downwards and do not simultaneously enjoy the relaxing gift of self-deception, are left wondering whether they could not have made a better job of it had they been given a better chance.

Part Six
Health, Illness and Medicine

The sociology of health and illness is one of the fastest growing branches of sociology and rightly so. All of us, even the healthiest, may fall ill at some time, and we are all affected, too, by the illness of those near and dear to us. Our illness experience is certainly not all in the stars or in our genes – predetermined before we start life – although what we inherit from our parents does play a part. What principally matters, however, is our life experiences, and these, as sociologists see it, are socially determined.

We are right, therefore, to ask ourselves – especially when someone's life is threatened – why it is that some people, and not others, fall ill. Is it something to do with age or with working and living conditions? Or social pressures: the demands of running a home and raising a family, strains in marriage or in dealing with kinsfolk, or simply in meeting the expectations of other people? Can certain kinds of situations – typically encountered in families, at work, at leisure – induce illness or health in individuals, because of the way they are organized and give or withhold power and self-determination to their participants?

Sociologists ask themselves these and other comparable questions and investigate them systematically. They do so by converting questions of this kind into propositions which can be tested against what is actually known about patterns of illness and methods of responding to it or of trying to maintain health.

They go further. They try to discover why the beliefs which people hold about the causes of health and illness, and what to do to maintain the one and avoid or cope with the other, are often so different, not merely across the world but even in one country. They also try to establish why it is that those we call doctors in this country come to have the power and authority they appear to have over their patients, over the latter's relatives and all the others who care for patients in the health services. And they ask why medicine, in the contemporary world, appears to be crucially involved in aspects of our individual and collective behaviour that previous generations would have regarded as the province of the priest, the judge or the gaoler.

In doing so, sociologists find that they have to go back in history to see the origins of particular ideas and the circumstances in which they acquired salience. This work is not just esoteric, of interest only to historians. It is important for illustrating the way in which, today, certain groups of healers establish and maintain their authority over other healers with alternative theories and practices, and how they maintain their authority over patients. Such knowledge makes it much easier to understand the nature of the issues which face every country in deciding what kind of health services will be provided, how they will be organized and how paid for.

Modern 'Western' medicine has its roots in ancient Greece, but it was profoundly influenced by the nineteenth-century revolution in natural science, which led it into experimentation – not all of it very scientific – and to the transformation of hospitals from hospices for the dying to laboratories for the active treatment of the sick. None the less, the reasons for the drastic reductions of the past 150 years in the killer infections which took their toll of babies, children and young adults (including pregnant and nursing mothers) are primarily the improvement in the physical environment – drains, water supplies, food hygiene and housing – better nutrition and better preventive immunization procedures. Advances in medical and surgical procedures only began to make an impact on the broad health picture in the second half of the twentieth century.

The effect of all these developments has been to change the pattern of health and illness in our society. Many of those who earlier would have died in infancy or childhood now survive into middle and old age; many face chronic illnesses to which modern medicine has, as yet, found no answer. Moreover, because it concentrated so exclusively on the physical aspects of illness, using drugs or surgery to treat them, many medical practitioners, including some of the most distinguished who served as role models for younger doctors, all but ignored the fact that disease affected the whole person – that is, his or her sense of fulfilment and self-esteem as well as livelihood – and that person's social network.

As a result, we have all become aware that Western medicine is only one kind of medicine and that there are a variety of others, some of very ancient origin, some very new, which have offered hope, comfort and even 'cure' to people who have used them. Some orthodox medical practitioners have regarded the 'alternative' healers as charlatans and competitors; others have taken seriously their patients' claims to have been treated effectively by unorthodox practitioners and have begun to study their ideas and call these ideas 'complementary' medicine, in order to emphasize that they are not competitive with their own.

Sociologists have also detected a change in the willingness of considerable sections of the people to submit passively to 'doctors' orders'. The claims of most professional groups – including doctors – to superior wisdom that entitles them to unquestioned obedience are now challenged daily in doctors' surgeries up and down the country. As a result, governments, while still dependent on the smooth operation of the health service to maintain their image as caring authorities, are increasingly willing to challenge the claim of 'clinical autonomy', which it used to cede unquestioningly to the medical profession.

There is now a rich body of sociological literature on the organized health services and on the people who work in them, from hospital specialists and general practitioners to ward orderlies and home helps. Each category of worker plays a different part within a complex division of labour. Its members are socialized through their specialized training into a set of interlinked subcultures, each with its own combination of beliefs, rules, etiquette, hierarchies, conventions, myths and prejudices.

Hospitals are singularly large and powerful organizations within modern health-care systems. In important respects, they exhibit many of the attributes of other kinds of work-based organization: business organizations, universities, even prisons. But there are some unique features which arise because they are 'processing' people and are concerned with life and death matters. Doctors play an important role in the hospital, but it is no longer one of undisputed authority. Managers without medical training now have greater legal authority to control resources. And most of the work in hospital, much of it routine and humdrum, but much very responsible and crucial too, including most of the caring, is actually performed by nurses and by people in paramedical occupations, backed up by domestic workers and catering staff. Each group naturally seeks to extend its power to influence the way in which the hospital operates. Recent sociological work emphasizes the dynamic relationships of power and authority which, although subject to certain overall structural constraints, can lead to variations between any two hospital units.

Doctors and other health-service employees are not the only providers of health care: families, kin, friends and neighbours or the local chemist are often the people we turn to first when we experience painful or disturbing symptoms. The decision to go to the doctor often comes much later. So the story of health-seeking and health-providing has to be followed through stage by stage. In one classic discussion, Talcott Parsons described how falling ill involves being assigned a new role in society: that of being sick, the 'sick role'. Others have argued that the process involved is akin to that of a career in any other role, with its timetables, schedules and so forth.

The selections in this Part reflect these major themes. In each case they have been extracted from a long chapter or paper in a journal and provide only the bare bones of a theory or research finding. It is strongly recommended that students and other interested readers who are stimulated by the readings go to their libraries to examine the original publication.

First, René Dubos (Reading 31) outlines the basic assumptions of Western medicine, particularly the Hippocratic tradition, the philosophical influence upon medicine of the Cartesian body–mind 'dualism', and the conception of the body as a machine. Ray Fitzpatrick (Reading 32) invites us to look at the medical ideas and practices of some of the very different cultures studied by anthropologists and at the folk beliefs within different Western cultures which deviate from the ideas of official medicine (though doctors, being members of those cultures, may also be influenced by some of these ideas).

Graham Scambler (Reading 33) deals with those illnesses which may not necessarily involve physical pain, but at the least, like deafness, are felt to be embarrassing and, at worst, like leprosy, are seen as dangerous threats to the social order. Ostracism, avoidance and other forms of painful and damaging social stigma are normal consequences of these illnesses.

R. G. Wilkinson (Reading 34) discusses recent evidence concerning the persistence of marked differences in the mortality and morbidity of people of different social classes. He suggests that these differences are very real and cannot be attributed, as some investigators have suggested, to a biased choice of evidence or to variations in the definitions used to denote a person's social class.

In a classic paper, Julian Tudor Hart (Reading 35), who some time ago formulated what he called the 'Inverse Care Law', shows that the resources of society were not used to relieve the sufferings of those most exposed to disease. He argued that the availability of good medical care varied *inversely* with the need of the population served.

Irving Zola (Reading 36) then discusses the tendency in modern industrial society towards the 'medicalization of everything', from sewage systems to diet and marital relations, a development which he sees as potentially dangerous for society. He concludes, ruefully, that 'living is injurious to health'.

Morgan, Calnan and Manning (Reading 37) take us into the hospital, reviewing the major kinds of theory that have been used to analyse the workings of those large institutions. Finally, Margaret Stacey (Reading 38) reminds us that health workers of many kinds (many of them, especially women, ill-paid or unpaid) contribute significantly to the curing and welfare of patients, and that patients play the major part in the management of their own illnesses and should be regarded as health workers – not just consumers of health services.

René Dubos

Biomedical Philosophies

Extracts from René Dubos, *Man, Medicine and Environment*, Penguin,
1970, pp. 75–7, 81–5, 87–91, 94.

The Human Past and Modern Medicine

Just as the long-domesticated dog still retains the fundamental characteristics of the wolf, so modern man retains many biological characteristics of his remote ancestors. Without question, the same set of
genes that controlled the life of man when he was a Palaeolithic
hunter or a Neolithic farmer still determine his physiological needs
and drives, his potentialities and limitations, his essential psychic
and behavioural characteristics, and his responses to environmental
stimuli. This evolutionary heritage combines with the experiences of
his immediate past to determine his medical history and influence
the medical problems he will face.

In order to analyse the effects of environmental factors on health
and on disease, it is therefore necessary to keep in mind that man's
life always involves a complex interplay between the conditions of
the present and the attributes he has retained from his evolutionary
and experiential past . . .

The Gods of Medicine

Like animals, primitive man had health instincts to help him overcome or minimize the effects of accidents or disease. In addition to
these instincts, he must early have recognized some direct and
obvious cause-and-effect relationships between certain empirical practices and the improvement of wounds or the alleviation of symptoms.
Also, many forces he regarded as mysterious because they were
indirect or outside the range of his conscious apprehension affected
the health of primitive man. Magic thus early became an essential

component of his attitude toward the causation and control of disease.

Medicine therefore had a dual nature from its very beginning. It included the empirical knowledge of effective procedures and belief in magical influences ... Throughout history, and whatever the level of civilization, the structure of medicine has been determined not only by the state of science but also by the prevailing attitudes towards disease. These in turn are influenced by religious and philosophical beliefs. This is just as true of the most evolved urban and industrialized societies as it is of the most primitive populations. Like his Stone Age ancestors, modern man lives by myths ...

The Hippocratic Tradition

In all the countries of Western civilization, physicians recite the Hippocratic Oath, or a modification of it, either when they graduate from medical school or during the ceremonies of initiation into learned medical societies. This gesture implies allegiance to the high ethical principles inherited by the medical profession from its distant past. It constitutes also a tacit acknowledgement of the profound influence of Hippocratic doctrines on the development of Western medicine ...

Hippocratic philosophy contends that medicine is not an appendage to religion; it can and should be practised as a true scientific discipline. Commonplace as this attitude appears today, it developed slowly and has yet to be adopted universally ... According to the Hippocratic doctrines, this scientific approach leads to the following conclusions:

1. The well-being of man is influenced by all environmental factors: the quality of the air, water and food; the winds and the topography of the land; and the general living habits. Understanding the effects of environmental forces on man is thus the fundamental basis of the physician's art.
2. Health is the expression of harmony among the environment, the ways of life, and the various components of man's nature. For the Greco-Roman physicians, four humours determined man's nature: the relationship between blood, phlegm, yellow bile and black bile controlled all human activities.

3. Whatever happens in the mind influences the body and the body has a like influence on the mind. Mind and body cannot be considered independently of each other. Health means therefore a healthy mind in a healthy body. It can be achieved only by governing all activities of life in accordance with natural laws so as to create an equilibrium between the forces of the organism and those of the environment.

4. Whenever the equilibrium is disturbed, rational therapeutic procedures should be used to restore it by correcting the ill effects of natural forces; these procedures should include the use of regimens, drugs and surgical techniques.

5. The practice of medicine implies an attitude of reverence for the human condition and must be based on a strict code of ethics ... Much of modern medicine consists in the unfolding and elaboration of [these] Hippocratic concepts ...

The Body Machine

René Descartes and his followers introduced the most far-reaching scientific simplification of the study of man in health and in disease. Descartes predicated the assumption that man consists of two separate entities, body and mind, linked during life but profoundly different in kind. He claimed that since the mind is a direct expression of God its nature cannot be understood by science. In contrast, he taught that the body is a machine whose structure and operations fall within the province of human knowledge. Many scientists, philosophers and theologians question the validity of the body–mind dualism concept, but no one doubts that Descartes' philosophy has exerted an immense influence on the evolution of biological sciences in general, particularly in medicine.

Whatever its philosophical limitations, the concept of body–mind dualism has proven operationally useful; it has helped scientists to delineate more precisely the scope of their investigations. Instead of attempting the hopeless task of understanding man as a whole, scientists have felt free to deal *seriatim* with the various aspects of man's nature.

Descartes' philosophy led scientists to neglect questions pertaining to the nature of the mind and the soul and encouraged them to focus their efforts on the much simpler, more concrete, problems of body structure and operation. They could apply knowledge of physics and chemistry, derived from the study of inanimate matter, to the problems of the body without fear of debasing the more lofty manifestations of man's nature, those of his soul. The self-imposed limitations and the intellectual freedom that biologists derived from Cartesian dualism gave them a general tendency to study man as a non-thinking, non-feeling entity . . .

Though Descartes' philosophy of body–mind dualism provided a favourable environment for the emergence of the modern biomedical sciences, the validity of the philosophy itself is open to question. Many medical scientists believe that Cartesian dualism, useful as it has been, is leading medicine into a blind alley precisely because it is philosophically unsound. They contend that the processes of the 'mind' are not different in principle from those of the 'body' but are merely less understood because of their complexity. Presently, great efforts are being made to apply the methods of the natural sciences to the problems of the mind . . .

The Whole Man

Even the most casual observer can see from daily life that the condition of the body affects mental processes, and that, reciprocally, our state of mind affects most organic processes. In practice, problems of the mind have been the specialized province of experts who tend to remain aloof from the problems of the body. These experts have been subdivided into several groups hardly in communication with each other. Depending upon their scientific philosophy, the different schools of psychologists and psychiatrists have looked at the mind, each from a different point of view. All have been affected by the social and religious doctrines prevailing in their communities.

Frequently in the ancient world mentally deranged people were assumed to be in contact with supernatural forces and were believed to be endowed with superior, extraordinary powers. Insanity was often revered as a gift for prophecy. Later, the belief developed that insanity was caused by demonic possession and could be cured only by exorcizing the devil and other demons from the demented person. As time went on, insane people came to be regarded not as true human beings but as sinful and subhuman creatures; in consequence, they were removed from normal society and held in chains like savage beasts. Surprising as it may seem to us, this attitude prevailed in the most civilized countries of Europe during the eighteenth century and it persisted until the early part of the nineteenth century . . .

Social and scientific attitudes concerning mental diseases began to change one hundred and fifty years ago when humanitarianism and respect for the individual emerged as dominant social philosophies . . . Ivan Pavlov's celebrated experiments at the beginning of the twentieth century on conditioned reflexes constituted the earliest systematic investigations of biological mechanisms involved in mental processes . . . Sigmund Freud, the other towering historical figure in the study of the mind, also was originally concerned with the interrelationships between mental and organic processes. His first investigations dealt with the physiological effects of drugs on certain mental states. As a result of observations on hypnotic states and the development of the psychoanalytic method, Freud, and more so his followers, abandoned these early physiological preoccupations. Freud himself did not forget the physiological origin of his studies; late in life he expressed his conviction that the 'complexes' he had described in purely psychiatric terms would one day be traced to faulty organic processes. The psychoanalytic schools, however, have evolved almost independent of the physiological sciences and of other fields of biomedical knowledge . . .

Clinical and epidemiological studies show that the inextricably interrelated body, mind and environment must be considered together in any medical situation whether it involves a single patient or a whole community. In a long, roundabout way, scientific medicine is thus returning to the unitarian concept of disease intuitively perceived by the Hippocratic physicians two and a half thousand years ago. Whatever the complaints of the patient and the signs or symptoms he manifests, whatever the medical problems of the community, disease cannot be understood or successfully controlled without considering man in his total environment.

32   Ray Fitzpatrick

Lay Concepts of Illness

Extracts from Ray Fitzpatrick, 'Lay Concepts of Illness', in Ray Fitzpatrick, John Hinton, Stanton Newman, Graham Scambler and James Thompson (eds.), *The Experience of Illness*, Tavistock, 1984, pp. 12, 15–25.

The Anthropological Investigation of Beliefs

Illness is one realm of life in which anthropology has vividly demonstrated cultural variation between societies, often documenting beliefs that appear on the surface to be most bizarre and irrational. One of the best-known examples of strange beliefs held in relation to illness is the widespread explanation of illness in terms of witchcraft . . .

Several important lessons emerge from anthropological investigations of such exotic belief systems. They demonstrate the survival of forms of explanation of illness that differ completely from interpretations found in Western science. More importantly such beliefs can be seen to form a coherent pattern of ideas in terms of which illness is explained. Ideas, which on the surface seem bizarre, can be seen to make sense when considered more carefully . . .

The Content of Western Lay Beliefs

In recent years investigators have begun to consider the form and content of beliefs about illness of modern western communities. The most striking result of such studies is the variety and importance of ideas about the causes of illness . . . Chrisman (1977) provides a framework from a review of cross-cultural evidence of folk ideas about illness in which he identifies different modes of thought about the causes of illness. He calls such modes of thought 'logics' and identifies four basic kinds:

1. A logic of degeneration in which illness follows the running down of the body.

2. A mechanical logic in which illness is the outcome of blockages or damage to bodily structures.

3. A logic of balance in which illness follows from disruption of harmony between parts or between the individual and the environment.

4. A logic of invasion which includes germ theory and other material intrusions responsible for illness.

These logics may be viewed as dominant themes or metaphors which permeate beliefs about illness and vary in importance from one culture to another. Thus the logic of balance is fundamental to traditional Latin American beliefs about the implication of 'hot' and 'cold' factors in illness and is also important in classical Indian ideas of the balance between 'humours' determining health . . .

In modern Britain the logic of invasion is an important mode of thinking about illness and must partly be seen as the cultural result of the impact of microbiological developments in Western science in the last part of the nineteenth century. The theme of heredity . . . is less easily traced back to earlier modes of medical thought and . . . there appears to be a greater readiness to invoke genetic causation in lay culture than in medical science. Patterns of shared illness in families offer a powerful source of ideas of inheritance. However it is unclear how universal such interpretations are. A review . . . of traditional African systems of explaining illness makes little mention of heredity as a form of cause.

Probably one of the most characteristically Western modes of interpreting illness can be found in the variety of related concepts such as 'stress' 'worry', and 'tension' . . .

The Structure of Lay Beliefs

One of the most striking qualities of lay concepts of illness is their very complexity . . . This quality becomes most apparent when some systematic effort is invested in obtaining a number of respondents' ideas about one particular disease. Blumhagen (1980) . . . investigated the views about their disorder of 103 patients attending a clinic for hypertension in the United States. The members of the sample cited an average of thirteen separate items each in their view of what constituted the causes, pathophysiology and prognosis of hypertension . . ., ranging from chronic external stress to heredity, salt, water, and food generally . . .

Although such research suggests a good deal of complexity in the patterns of ideas about illness reported by lay individuals, it may be misleading to talk of such ideas, as some writers have, as lay *theories* . . . Kleinman points out that 'laymen are not concerned with their theoretical rigor so much as the treatment options they give rise to' (Kleinman 1980, p. 93). In other words lay concepts are pragmatic, and are rarely publicly produced for critical scrutiny.

For the same reason, in so far as lay ideas are seldom formalized and normally only emerge as an element of decision-making about actual illness episodes, they are expressed extremely tentatively . . .

One particular way in which lay ideas differ from formal forms of thought is the flexible manner in which ideas respond to experience. Anthropologists and other social scientists normally portray the culture of a society, of which beliefs are an element, as a stable and relatively enduring means by which the society copes with its environment . . . Nevertheless there is a danger of what might be termed *reifying* lay explanations of illness and viewing them as fixed frameworks in terms in which health and illness are experienced. This is the risk attached to any approach to explaining human action which focuses on beliefs and ideas: the very investigation of the beliefs may make them appear more solid and inflexible than in reality they are . . .

Beliefs as a 'System'

Some anthropologists take seriously the term 'system' when they talk of a community's belief system with regard to health and illness. Essentially they argue that the beliefs about illness identified in a community should be analysed in terms of a system in the sense that beliefs are held to be interconnected and structured elements of a whole, rather than a random set of items that a group of people happen to believe in common. An example of the application of this approach to the experience of illness is the work of Helman (1978) who as a general practitioner and anthropologist has examined patterns of ideas about infectious illness in a north London community . . . Patients distinguish the subjectively hot illnesses which are fevers from the cold illnesses which are classified as chills or colds. From a knowledge of which category a set of symptoms indicate, it is possible to read off a set of causes, typical kinds of course, appropriate treatment and also the degree of individual blame attached to the sufferer in contracting the illness. Colds and chills are viewed as the product of the individual's relations with the natural environment, and lower temperatures in the environment can, through dampness, cold winds and draughts, penetrate particularly vulnerable surfaces of the body such as the head and the feet . . . Treatment involves restoring temperature equilibrium by hot drinks or a warm bed . . . Fevers are due to invisible entities − 'germs' or 'bugs' − transmitted from individual to individual. One important treatment is fluid which 'flushes out' germs. The individual is less personally responsible for fevers as they are unavoidably transmitted through social relationships . . .

Helman suggests that this system of beliefs is, at present, unstable: in particular, younger patients tend to view both colds and fevers as due to germs and viruses and less as a results of their own responsible actions. These changes in beliefs are partly due to changes in medicine, especially the growth in availability of antibiotics . . .

Images and Associations in Concepts of Illness

So far lay concepts of illness have been discussed as if they paralleled scientific medicine in concentrating upon the symptoms, causes, and therapies of illness entities . . .

However a different approach suggests that illness concepts, in addition to naming an alternative set of entities and causes to those of medicine, also operate as condensed symbols that refer to a wider variety of experiences contained in a culture. Lay concepts of illness do not merely name entities in the body but are powerful images associated with other realms of life. Good (1977) offers an analysis in these terms of a commonly reported complaint in traditional Iranian communities that he translates as 'heart distress'. It is particularly common in working-class women and frequently presented to the doctor. It is viewed as a disturbance in the heart caused by emotional distress. Traditional Iranians believe the heart to be the source of heat and vitality and the driving force of the body in contrast to Western emphasis on its role in the circulation of blood. At the same time the heart is used linguistically to express emotions . . .

Good argues that 'heart distress' is therefore a powerful idiom to express many female concerns with sexuality and fertility. Another set of associations links heart distress with on the one hand grief and melancholy from the loss of relatives and on the other hand with the anxiety of interpersonal problems and poverty of working-class life. One respondent explained to Good: 'We are poor, we don't have any money, we all have heart problems' (Good 1977, p. 17).

... 'Heart distress' in Iranian culture is not a neatly defined category referring to a specific disorder and may convey any of a variety of symptoms, illnesses, or problems. 'Heart distress is an image which draws together a network of symbols, situations, motives, feelings and stresses which are rooted in the structural setting in which the people ... live' (Good 1977, p. 48). Western-trained doctors are likely to misunderstand patients presenting with heart distress, examining the heart and offering reassurance that there is nothing wrong.

The importance of research by anthropologists such as Good is that we are reminded that lay concepts of illness may have powerful symbolic significance which cannot conveniently be expressed in so many words by the patient or informant but which form an essential element of the meaning of illness experience. They also suggest that we too narrowly limit the search for meaning if we only look for references to bodily symptoms or causes in lay ideas of illness ...

The 'Gulf' between Lay and Medical Concepts

... In order to draw attention to and make sense of problems of communication between health professionals and the public, social scientists have sometimes portrayed in quite dramatic forms the distance between the two modes of thought ...

The analysis of writers such as Freidson is often used to portray a profound gulf between scientific medicine and the majority of lay persons, especially because of the reliance by medicine upon scientific technology to the neglect of those social and psychological aspects of disorders which concern patients ...

Yet there is a risk that the notion of a cultural gulf between lay and professional modes of thought be exaggerated or misunderstood ... Those who have sharply contrasted the medical model with lay perspectives may have failed to recognize the major differences that exist between medicine enshrined in textbooks and clinical practice. Lock (1982) examines the approaches of medicine to the menopause. The subject as treated in textbooks is formal, complex, and replete with unresolved technical controversies. When Lock interviewed practising gynaecologists, their views about menopause were simpler, based on fewer scientific principles, and selective. Also there was a wide variety from very biomedical to very psychosocial approaches amongst clinicians. Lock argues that the doctors' views were best understood as folk models to contrast them with formal textual models. Medical folk models have to be simpler to deal with the practical exigencies of clinical work. There is evidence that doctors retain many lay assumptions and ideas about illness acquired before training and that these assumptions play an important role in clinical practice alongside formal scientific principles . . .

Thus for various reasons an uncritical assertion of 'two worlds of experience' may be misleading. Gulfs of a different kind used to be implied in many early studies of communication between doctors and patients which identified the causes for failures of communication in patients' ignorance of medical terms and in the gaps in knowledge between the two parties. Although much depends on how knowledge is measured, the simple stereotype of the ignorant patient has had to be modified in the light of research . . .

It is possible that the stereotype of the patient with little or no ability to comprehend medical language is self-perpetuating; in other words that doctors, assuming a poorly informed patient, avoid extended discussion in consultations as a result of which their stereotypes are perpetuated. The point argued here is that the idea of unbridgeable gulfs, whether in terms of knowledge versus ignorance or a more cultural theory of separate worlds of experience, may be misleading or damaging. Indeed the major weakness of such views is that they are unable to do justice to the complex processes at work in communication.

References

BLUMHAGEN, D. W. (1980), 'Hypertension: A Folk Illness with a Medical Name', *Culture, Medicine and Psychiatry*, 4(3), pp. 197–227.

CHRISMAN, N. (1977), 'The Health Seeking Process: An Approach to the Natural History of Illness', *Culture, Medicine and Psychiatry*, 1(4), pp. 351–77.

GOOD, B. J. (1977), 'The Heart of What's the Matter', *Culture, Medicine and Psychiatry*, 1(1), pp. 25–58.

HELMAN, C. G. (1978), '"Feed a Cold, Starve a Fever" – Folk Models of Infection in an English Suburban Community', *Community, Medicine and Psychiatry*, 2(2), pp. 107–37.

KLEINMAN, A. M. (1982), *Patients and Healers in the Context of Culture*, University of California Press.

LOCK, M. (1982), 'Models and Practice in Medicine: Menopause as Syndrome of Life Transition', *Culture, Medicine and Psychiatry*, 6(3), pp. 261–80.

33   Graham Scambler

Stigmatizing Illness

Excerpts from Graham Scambler, 'Perceiving and Coping with Stigmatizing Illness', in Ray Fitzpatrick, John Hinton, Stanton Newman, Graham Scambler and James Thompson (eds.), *The Experience of Illness*, Tavistock, 1984, pp. 203–5, 207–12, 215–18, 222–3.

The word 'stigma' is now ordinarily used in a rather broad sense to refer to the disgrace associated with certain conditions, attributes, traits, or forms of behaviour. Precisely which of the latter are publicly regarded as signs or marks of disgrace and to what degree, has of course varied historically and continues to vary between cultures. By way of illustration, consider the divergent experiences of two eminent European philosophers who also happened to be homosexual, Socrates and Wittgenstein. In Greece in the fifth century B.C. homosexuality was an acceptable and expected form of love between normal males, deemed to be most appropriate between youths and older men in a position to set them a good example. We are told that Socrates, 'whose insatiable love of boys is frankly emphasized by his disciples Plato and Xenophon, who were yet at pains to clear him of any charge of corrupting the young, spent much of his time hanging round schools and gymnasia' (Wilkinson 1979). Contrastingly, Wittgenstein, in the very different moral climate of Austria in the first quarter of the twentieth century, was close to despair, even suicide, when he found himself drawn again and again to the dark alleys of towns 'where rough young men were ready to cater to him sexually' ... While Socrates' homosexuality was open and acceptable, Wittgenstein's was clandestine and brought with it the omnipresent threat of exposure and disgrace.

An appreciation of this kind of historical and cultural variability in the criteria of attribution of stigma is important ...

Stigmatizing Illness

Clearly not all those infringements against norms associated with disgrace are wilful, or even avoidable. After studying the lot of the blind in the United States, for example, Scott (1969, 1970) concluded that many were regarded as deviant simply because they could not see. Mankoff (1971) has referred in this context to 'ascribed' as opposed to 'achieved' deviance or rule breaking. An ascribed rule breaker acquires his or her deviant status independently of any purposeful activity: thus, for example, an ugly person might be considered an ascribed rule breaker. By contrast, an achieved rule breaker can be said to have 'earned' his or her deviant status: the young delinquent or the alcoholic have both achieved rule breaking status, at least to some extent, on the strength of their own actions. It has often been assumed that less stigma attaches to ascribed than to achieved rule breaking. However, Albrecht, Walker, and Levy (1982) found that 'the perceived disruption to social interaction a stigma causes, rather than attribution of responsibility, appears to be a better explanation for differential social distance from individuals with various types of stigmas'. For example, individuals with heart disease (and 'ex-convicts') were considered more responsible for their condition than the mentally ill and yet respondents expressed greater social distance from the mentally ill. A recent study ... suggests that people generally tend to have more positive attitudes towards the physically disabled than they do towards the mentally disabled ...

Stigma as a Threat to the Social Order

Scott (1972) has proposed a framework within which he believes a number of theoretical questions concerning both ascribed and achieved deviance might one day be answered ...

Scott interprets 'deviance' as a property of social order. 'This property', he writes, 'is conferred upon an individual whenever others detect in his behaviour, appearance, or simply his existence, a significant transgression of the boundaries of the symbolic universe by which the inherent disorder of human existence is made to appear orderly and meaningful.' Such an individual is perceived and treated as something of an 'anomaly' ...

Every social order ... develops ... 'universe-maintaining mechanisms' as protection against the chaos implied by anomaly. [Scott] goes on to identify and describe several universe-maintaining mechanisms which he regards as common to most modern Western societies. Two of these warrant a mention here. The first is 'normalization', which refers to attempts to force anomalous individuals to change so as to become more like normal people . . . The second is a class of techniques of social control for use against deviants who cannot be changed. 'The symbolic universe may be threatened by a madman but its ultimate superiority may nevertheless be reaffirmed if the social order can render him harmless. There are several ways in which the madman can be "defused", the most common being confinement. By putting the madman or criminal away, a social order removes the symbolically noxious element from its midst and at the same time demonstrates its capacity to master those whom it cannot domesticate.'

It must be stressed that Scott's own account is tentative and replete with statements of qualification and is, hence, less dogmatic and all-embracing than this summary may have suggested. He is well aware, for example, that there can be more than one symbolic universe in a society and that there are often a number of sub-universes of meaning, which may occasionally represent genuine counter-cultures. His limited ambition is to propose a framework for analysing deviance as a property of social order; in his own words, this framework 'only recommends to us the kinds of questions we ought to ask and answer in order to produce a theory to explain this social property' (Scott 1972) . . .

As the focus in this chapter is on ascribed rather than achieved deviance, consideration will be limited here to ways in which people with certain conditions of the body or the mind may be said to threaten the social order. It will be suggested, in fact, that they pose a threat in at least two major ways. They do so, first, by their failure to conform to a particular class of cultural norms – namely, those pertaining to how people should *be* rather than how they should *act* . . . It is not that an individual who infringes against such norms stands condemned for a misdemeanour of some sort – he or she is not *morally* culpable – but rather that that individual is judged an essentially 'imperfect being': the nature of his or her 'offence' is perhaps best characterized as *ontological* (from 'ontology', the study of being). Although it would of course be quite wrong to deny that some stigmatizing conditions – like the sexually transmitted diseases – carry strong connotations of moral failure, it is suggested that it is *generally* the case that such connotations are secondary to those of ontological deficiency.

The second way in which such people jeopardize the social order is by violating cultural norms governing routine social intercourse, by causing ... 'ambiguity in social interaction'. In [a] study of the attitudes of normal people this was the most frequent reason given for distancing from the stigmatized; respondents said things like, 'We are usually afraid of those things which we don't understand and things that are new or foreign to us', The person doesn't know how to cope and feels uncomfortable with the disabled', 'They don't know what, if anything, they should do to help,' and so on (Albrecht, Walker and Levy 1982). Concluding her review of studies of the physically disabled, Safilios-Rothschild comments: 'Interactions between physically disabled and physically normal people are anxiety-laden, tend to cause emotional discomfort and usually take on the form of "stereotyped, inhibited and over-controlled experiences"' (Safilios-Rothschild 1970). In his autobiography *Journey Into Silence*, Labour MP Jack Ashley recalls several unhappy sequelae to his return to the House of Commons after becoming totally deaf. Among these is the following:

On one occasion in the tea-room, I took my cup of tea to a table to join four friends. When one of them asked me a question which I could not understand, the others repeated it for me but I was still unable to lip-read it. They paused while one of them wrote it down and I was aware that the easy-going conversation they had been enjoying before my arrival was now disrupted. When I answered the written question it was understandable that none of them should risk a repeat performance by asking another. Within a few moments two of them had left and after a brief pause the others explained that they had to go because of pressing engagements. They were genuinely sorry and I understood but it was small solace as I sat alone drinking my tea. (Ashley 1973.)

Visibility

... The need for a distinction between a stigma's visibility and whether or not it is known about is readily apparent: an individual's diabetes may be invisible yet widely known about. Of the distinction between a stigma's visibility and its obtrusiveness, Goffman writes: 'When a stigma is immediately perceivable, the issue still remains as to how much it interferes with the flow of interaction' (Goffman 1968). He cites the example of a man in a wheelchair attending a business meeting; his stigma is obvious and yet, around a conference table, unlikely to be obtrusive. Compare his situation with that of another participant with a speech impediment; the latter's stigma is relatively minor but 'the very mechanics of spoken encounters constantly redirect attention to the defect, constantly making demands for clear and rapid messages that must constantly be defaulted'.

The visibility of a stigma also needs to be distinguished from its perceived focus. Goffman points out that normal people tend to 'develop conceptions, whether objectively grounded or not, as to the sphere of life-activity for which an individual's particular stigma primarily disqualifies him'. A facial deformity, for example, might be regarded as imposing an unpleasant burden on face-to-face communication but be considered irrelevant to an individual's employment status or competence. By contrast, a condition like diabetes may be felt to have little or no effect on social interaction but be acknowledged as a proper justification for negative discrimination in employment.

The Discredited and the Discreditable

Clearly, whether or not someone's stigmatizing condition is known about is of fundamental importance. Goffman describes the individual whose stigma is known about as '*discredited*' and the individual whose stigma is not known about as '*discreditable*' . . . Davis, for example, has claimed that people with visible physical handicaps typically pass through three stages when building sociable relationships with normal people: the first is one of 'fictional acceptance' – they find they are ascribed a stereotypical identity and accepted on that basis; the second stage is one of 'breaking through' this fictional acceptance – they have to induce others to regard and interact with them as normal persons; and the third stage is one of 'consolidation' – they work to sustain the definition of themselves as normal. Davis refers to the unfolding of these three stages as a process of 'deviance disavowal' (1964) . . .

Some blind people, whom Scott terms 'true believers', actually come to concur with the verdict reached by the sighted: 'They adopt as part of their self-concept the qualities of character, the feelings and the behaviour patterns that others insist they must have' (Scott 1969). Many others develop and deploy strategies not predicated on an explicit disavowal of their deviance (e.g. they may 'pretend' to comply purely to ease interaction) . . .

Higgins (1980) has shown how the discredited deaf sometimes adopt the expedient of 'avowing' their deviance, and even extending it by acting mute, in order to simplify their dealings with the hearing: written messages can minimize misunderstandings and save time and trauma.

Scott also differs from Davis in stressing the influence of other kinds of factors on impression management. Two are given special emphasis: the fact that, because of the critical importance of eye contact in human communication, personal interaction is deeply disturbed when one of those involved cannot see, and the fact that interactions between the blind and sighted tend to become relationships of social dependency. Scott maintains that these two factors, both of which relate to the mechanics of inter-personal contact, affect the outcomes of socialization in three ways: 'They force upon blind people further evidence of their difference; they deny them the kind of honest, uncluttered feedback about self that is commonplace to the sighted; and they place them in a subordinate position, making it difficult for them to form intimate relationships with those they regard as their intellectual and psychological equals' (Scott 1969).

If one of the primary problems facing the discredited person is the management of impressions, the most pressing problem for the discreditable person is often the 'management of information' about himself or herself. In Goffman's words, the main quandary is: 'To display or not to display; to tell or not to tell; to lie or not to lie; and in each case, to whom, how, when and where' . . .

References

ASHLEY, J. (1973), *Journey into Silence*, Bodley Head.

ALBRECHT, G. L., WALKER, V., and LEVY, J. (1982), 'Social Distance from the Stigmatized: A Test of Two Theories', *Social Science and Medicine*, 16, pp. 1319–27.

DAVIS, F. (1964), 'Deviance Disavowal: The Management of Strained Interaction by the Visibly Handicapped', in H. Becker (ed.), *The Other Side: Perspectives on Deviance*, Free Press, Glencoe, Illinois, pp. 119–37.

GOFFMAN E. (1968), *Stigma: Notes on the Management of Spoiled Identity*, Penguin.

HIGGINS, P. (1980), *Outsiders in a Hearing World: A Sociology of Deafness*, Sage, Beverly Hills.

MANKOFF, M. (1971), 'Societal Reaction and Career Deviance: A Critical Analysis', *Sociological Quarterly*, 12, pp. 214–18.

SAFILIOS-ROTHSCHILD, C. (1970), *The Sociology and Social Psychology of Disability and Rehabilitation*, Random House, New York.

SCOTT, R. (1969), *The Making of Blind Men*, Sage, New York.

SCOTT, R. (1970), 'The Construction of Concepts of Stigma by Professional Experts', in J. Douglas (ed.), *Deviance and Responsibility: The Social Construction of Moral Meanings*, Basic Books.

SCOTT, R. (1972), 'A Proposed Framework for Analysing Deviance as a Property of Social Order', in R. Scott and J. Douglas (eds.), *Theoretical Perspectives on Deviance*, Basic Books, New York, pp. 9–35.

WILKINSON, L. (1979), *Classical Attitudes to Modern Issues*, William Kimber.

Socio-economic Differences in Mortality

Excerpts from R. G. Wilkinson, 'Socio-economic Differences in Mortality', in R. G. Wilkinson (ed.), *Class and Health*, Tavistock, 1986, pp. 1–16.

Prior to the 1980s, it was widely assumed that Britain was becoming a more egalitarian society. The predominant impression was that class divisions and socio-economic inequalities were becoming less important. Although long-term changes in income distribution have been comparatively small, it seemed reasonable to assume that this was compensated for by the growth of welfare services and the increasing volume of protective and regulatory legislation.

In 1980, however, the Black Report – dealing with class differences in health – seemed to cast serious doubt on this picture. Not only did it draw attention to very large differences in death rates between occupational classes but it also suggested that these differences were not declining (DHSS 1980). The crucial figures are reproduced in Table 1. They show that mortality differentials, as measured by age-standardized death rates for occupational classes, have increased

Table 1. *Mortality by social class 1931–81 (Men, 15–64 years, England and Wales)*

Class	1931	1951	1961*	1971*	1981†
I professional	90	86	76 (75)	77 (75)	66
II managerial	94	92	81	81	76
III skilled manual and non-manual	97	101	100	104	103
IV semi-skilled	102	104	103	114	116
V unskilled	111	118	143 (127)	137 (121)	166

*To facilitate comparisons, figures shown in parentheses have been adjusted to the classification of occupations used in 1951.
†Men 20–64 years, Great Britain.
Note: Figures are SMRs – which express age-adjusted mortality rates as a percentage of the national average at each date.
Source: DHSS (1980), Table 3.1.

since the 1930s. What these inequalities amount to can be summed up in terms of differences in life-expectancy. If the 1971 age-specific death rates for classes I (professional occupations) and V (unskilled manual occupations) were applied throughout the lives of a cohort, they would produce a difference in life-expectancy at birth of just over seven years (Registrar General 1978). This amounts to a lower-class disadvantage of about 10 per cent of life . . .

The real size and trends in class differences in mortality are important not only because health matters in itself but also because health serves as a barometer of the social and economic conditions in which people live. Though we can quantify changes in class access to housing, education, jobs, and services, and can also describe some of the wider but perhaps less tangible changes in the social and physical environment in which people live, we do not know what all these changes add up to in human terms. There is no unified summary of changing class differentials in the quality of life and human welfare. Familiar summary measures of changes in the standard of living, such as indices of real income, suffer from a number of important weaknesses. Economic indicators are largely blind to the qualitative changes in the material and social environment, which are so crucial to human welfare. Health, on the other hand, is not only sensitive to qualitative changes in material life but the accumulating research evidence on stress, boredom, inactivity, depression, and lack of close social contact shows that it is also sensitive to many psychosocial aspects of the quality of life . . .

As a record of the social distribution of health in society, there are a number of ways in which the figures in Table 1 may be affected by problems of measurement. An unwary acceptance of the picture they present of the size and trends in social inequalities in health may be unnecessarily alarmist; but if . . . health differences really have failed to narrow, we would surely need to reassess the belief that the burden of socio-economic differentials has narrowed . . .

What, then, does the evidence tell us about the interpretation of the figures in Table 1? A potential weakness of these figures . . . comes from the fact that they depend on dividing the number of deaths in occupations stated on death certificates by the number of people in each occupation as recorded at census: inaccurate occupational descriptions at either point will give rise to a considerable but usually random mismatch. More systematic biases may, however, creep in from sources such as a respectful desire among the next of kin (who are the informants) to 'promote the dead' . . .

By following a 1 per cent sample of people identified at the 1971 census, the OPCS Longitudinal Study (LS) enabled deaths to be classified according to the occupations given at census. Using truly comparable numerators and denominators in the calculation of death rates, the results show 1971 mortality differentials much like those in Table 1 . . .

[In addition] Marmot (1986) provides completely independent evidence of class differences in death rates among a cohort of civil servants classified by their employment grades . . . There is a more than threefold difference in mortality between the lowest and highest grades in the civil service . . . The data on civil servants do not suffer from the problems of relating occupations on death certificates to separately determined population numbers in those occupations . . .

A more difficult question about the way we should interpret the observed class differences in health concerns the possible contribution of social mobility. As early as 1955, Illsley published evidence suggesting that social mobility discriminated in favour of the healthy and against the unhealthy (Illsley 1955) . . . Social class differences in health could occur simply as a result of the healthy moving up and the unhealthy moving down the social scale (Stern 1983) . . . Instead of saying that people are less healthy because they are in lower classes, it suggests that they are in lower classes because they are less healthy.

To analyse this possibility, we must start off by distinguishing between two different ways in which social mobility could be selective in relation to health. A person's chances of upward or downward mobility could be influenced either directly by their current, or manifest, health status, or indirectly through selection according to factors associated with health, such as height or education. In the first case, long-term illness or disability during any period in a person's working life may affect their job prospects. Among young people, it may restrict initial job choices, while later in life it may force people to move to less demanding and perhaps lower-status jobs. The mobility chances of those who suffer from chronic illnesses or disabilities throughout their lives would be most affected . . . Social class at death – based on a person's last full-time occupation as stated on the death certificate – may be substantially affected by the downward mobility of those who are forced by illness to take up less demanding jobs later in life.

Fox, Goldblatt and Jones (1986) . . . using data from the LS . . ., have been able to cut out the effect of mobility during the last 5–10 years of life, when the impact of ill health would be at its maximum . . . [Their] study concludes that social mobility later in life contributes very little to the disparity in death rates between classes. This does not necessarily mean that there is no deterioration in the job prospects of those who do contract chronic illness towards the end of their working lives; it means that the proportion of people affected is too small to have a major influence on the overall figures . . .

Wadsworth (1986) . . . assesses the effects of childhood illness on people's subsequent chances of mobility, based on the cohort of British births born in one week in 1946, and serious illness in childhood is indeed related to subsequent downward mobility . . . To make a rough calculation of the contribution that this amount of illness-related downward mobility might make to the overall class differentials in health . . . it is necessary to know how predictive childhood illness is of poor health in adult life . . . For boys and girls together, the risks of being seriously ill in their early twenties rose from 11 per cent to 25 per cent if they had been seriously ill as children. Applying this increase in risk to the total numbers ill in childhood suggests that some 15 per cent of all serious illness in the early twenties is associated with previous childhood illness . . . To put the arithmetic in a nutshell: the proportion of adult illness which is associated with childhood illness, multiplied by the effect of childhood illness on mobility, gives the effect of the interaction between childhood illness and mobility on the social distribution of adult illness. The result of this calculation suggests that in this population only about 1.5 per cent of those seriously ill in their early twenties have suffered downward mobility as a result of previous childhood illness. Thus, as with the data on selective mobility later in life, this study provides no evidence for thinking that the class distribution of health is noticeably altered by the influence which childhood illness clearly can have on the direction of social mobility in early adulthood.

Having looked at evidence related to the effect of manifest illness on social mobility, we can now turn to the second way in which

Table 2. *Social mobility and perinatal mortality: indices of perinatal mortality rates (births in Aberdeen 1951–80. Mothers classified by their fathers' and husbands' occupation)*

social class of fathers	I–III Non-Manual	social class of husbands III Manual	IV & V	all classes
I–III Non-Manual	73	74	129	81
III Manual	80	107	119	109
IV & V	71	108	138	111
all classes	75	101	129	100

Note: mean = 100 = 24 deaths per 1000 births.
Source: Aberdeen Maternity and Neonatal Data Bank, calculated from Illsley (1983).

social mobility ... might select for characteristics associated with a person's health potential ...

Marmot (1986) ... notes that the heights of civil servants are more closely related to ... their achieved employment grade than to their class of origin. However, much the most important evidence that social mobility may be selective in relation to a prior health potential is provided by Illsley's work on perinatal mortality and the social mobility of mothers in Aberdeen (Illsley 1955 and 1983) ... He was able to look at the social mobility of mothers by comparing the social class of their fathers to that of their husbands. Table 2 shows the relationship between perinatal mortality rates and the social mobility of mothers ... The mortality rates associated with these first births are more closely related to the class mothers marry into than to the class they came from. In effect, the health status (as measured by reproductive performance) of mothers who were upwardly mobile from any given class, is better than that of those who were downwardly mobile from the same class ... Mothers who married upwards were taller, better educated, and probably better fed than other women in their class of origin. Similarly, those who married downwards fared worse than those in their class of origin, on each count. This is important because, in contrast to perinatal mortality rates, a woman's height and school-leaving age are unambiguously determined before marriage ...

There can be little doubt that the Aberdeen data provide evidence that social mobility is selective for characteristics closely related to health ... The fact that height is more closely related to the class into which women marry than to their class of origin is very good evidence that social mobility is selective. Height is not only unambiguously determined before marriage but is also likely to serve as a proxy for nutritional status and is known to be an indicator of reproductive performance ... The Aberdeen data on heights are not only the primary evidence that health selection is involved but are also the best guide as to the extent of its involvement. We can then only assume that selective mobility adds the same 20 per cent to the pre-mobility perinatal mortality differential as it adds to the height differential ... As on this basis the observed perinatal mortality differential more than doubles, expressed as a percentage of this larger differential the selective contribution is more than halved, to just under 10 per cent ...

Before leaving the issue of selection, one difficulty which affects almost all data on intergenerational mobility should be mentioned. It is likely to affect the Aberdeen data as well as Marmot's findings ... Because social mobility is measured by comparing the class of two different people's occupations (intergenerational mobility) or of one person's occupation at two different points in time (intragenerational mobility), inaccurate or inadequate occupational information resulting in misclassification will tend to exaggerate the scale of mobility ...

We can sum up the evidence on selective social mobility by saying that although there is evidence that social mobility is affected by ill-health and/or health potential, its contribution to observed class differences in health is probably always small in relation to the overall size of the mortality differentials. At older ages, the contribution may become almost insignificant.

What does this tell us about the size of the class differences in health that may legitimately be attributed to socio-economic inequalities in society? Selective social mobility has a small inflationary effect on the size of differentials but we have to set against this the failure of the Registrar General's occupational classification to provide a clear rank ordering of the population in terms of socio-economic circumstances. If we take income as a reasonable indicator of people's standard of living, it is clear that there are neither the differences between classes nor the homogeneity within classes that we might expect to find. As Table 3 shows, in 1971 only classes I and II were clearly distinguished from others in terms of their median income. Not only was there no clear gradient across the other four classes but the differences were inconsequential ...

Table 3. *Gross weekly income by social class*

social class	median income (1971)	percentage of social class V
I	£44.14	200
II	£34.02	154
III Non-Manual	£24.12	109
III Manual	£27.05	122
IV	£22.46	102
V	£22.09	100

Source: Registrar General (1978), page 151.

If the variation in incomes, and perhaps by inference in the standard of living, is as great or greater within as between classes, serious problems arise about the uses to which this classification is put. In a great many research reports, occupational class is used as a control for the effects of different socio-economic circumstances. As a result, the researchers almost certainly underestimate the effects of socio-economic factors on the measures they are concerned with and are in danger of attributing them to other variables. In terms of the analysis of health differences, any failure of classification by occupational class to produce a neat ordering of the population in terms of fundamental socio-economic standards will mean that such a classification understates the true impact of socio-economic inequalities on health . . .

Crude though these comparisons are, they confirm that the health differences associated with socio-economic disparities are understated by the heterogeneous nature of the occupational class classification by very much more than they are overstated by selective social mobility. In other words, the true health costs of socio-economic inequalities are likely to be considerably greater than the well-known figures in Table 1 suggest . . .

In interpreting the apparent *trends* in the size of class differences in mortality during recent decades, there are three key issues . . .: first, possible changes in the contribution of selective mobility over time; second, the shift in the population distribution away from class V and towards class I; third, the effects of successive revisions in the classification of occupations and their allocation to classes.

If the rate of social mobility increased, it would be reasonable to suppose that the contribution of selection to observed class differences in health would also have increased. Good evidence on the changing rate of mobility is scarce ... For the period from about 1940 to 1970 the Oxford [Social Mobility Study] figures (Heath, 1981) suggest that there was a rise of only about 6 per cent in the proportion of the population who were mobile. Whatever one's beliefs as to the selectivity of this mobility, such a small increase in mobility would clearly make only a trivial selective addition to the observed class differences in mortality. There is, then, no reason to think that social mobility has adversely affected the trends in the size of class differences in mortality.

The question of the upward shift in the class distribution of the population is quite separate from the issue of the rate of mobility ... During much of this century, net upward mobility has decreased the proportion of the population in classes IV and V and increased the proportion in classes I and II ... In 1931, classes I and II combined contained 14 per cent of the economically active male population (DHSS 1980). In 1971, this had risen to 23 per cent. During the same period the proportion in classes IV and V fell from 38 to 26 per cent.

In which direction will this upward shift in the class distribution of the population have distorted our view of changing class differences in mortality rates? ... An increase in the proportion of the population in classes I and II would, other things being equal, cause an apparent narrowing of mortality differentials, while a decrease in the proportion in classes IV and V would cause an apparent widening ...

Fortunately, Koskinen has recently tackled this problem in an important new analysis using an 'index of dissimilarity' (Koskinen 1985) ... He shows that ... since 1951, class differences seem to have widened in absolute as well as relative terms. In an analysis by separate causes, Koskinen shows that an increasing lower-class disadvantage appears in a wide range of different diseases. The overall picture he provides of widening inequality is confirmed by Pamuk, using a different method for calculating the effects of the changing class distribution of the population (Pamuk 1985) ...

The remaining problem ... is the effect of revisions in the occupational classification and the allocation of occupations to classes ... Taking 143 occupations that she could trace consistently in the five occupational mortality reports 1921–71[, Pamuk] showed that the use of different class classifications had very little impact on the picture of trends in mortality differentials ...

The trends identified by Koskinen and Pamuk inspire confidence not only because of the strength of their methods but also because of the similarity in their results. Both agree that male mortality differentials decreased between 1921 and 1931 and increased both absolutely and relatively in both decades 1951–71 . . . Pamuk also analyses trends in infant mortality and shows that while the rapid decline in infant death rates has produced an absolute decline in differentials, there has been a continuous relative increase since 1931 . . .

Some of the reasons why differentials widened during this decade are not hard to find. Two factors stand out particularly clearly: the first is the gradual downward shift in the class distribution of tobacco consumption (Todd 1976); the second factor is diet. War-time food-rationing resulted in a comparatively egalitarian distribution of many different foodstuffs. It was only after the ending of food-rationing in the early 1950s that the modern inequalities in food consumption grew up. These two factors had a very pronounced effect on the social distribution of heart disease (Marmot et al. 1978), stroke and lung cancer in both sexes: where previously there had been higher death rates in upper classes, the gradient was reversed; where there had been no clear gradient, lower-class rates dramatically increased compared to upper classes. The 1950s also saw a change in the social distribution of sugar consumption, which may well have been part of a longer-term pattern involving other refined foods. In the early decades of the century, it is likely that most refined foods were consumed more by the upper classes. As price differentials changed in the post-war era, refined foods were consumed increasingly by the less well off. The importance of these changes is also reflected in the change in the class distribution of obesity, which probably accompanied the change in the social distribution of heart disease (Wilkinson 1976).

The evidence reviewed . . . provides no support to the assumption that Table 1 gives an unnecessarily alarmist view of the size and the trends in socio-economic inequalities in health.

References

DEPARTMENT of HEALTH and SOCIAL SECURITY (1980), *Inequalities in Health*, Report of a Research Working Group chaired by Sir Douglas Black, DHSS.

Fox, A. J., Goldblatt, P. O., and Jones, D. R. (1986), *Social Class Mortality Differentials: Artefact, Selection or Life Circumstances*, in R. G. Wilkinson (ed.), *Class and Health*, Tavistock, pp. 33–49.

Heath, A. (1981), *Social Mobility*, Fontana.

Illsley, R. (1955), 'Social Class Selection and Class Differences in Relation to Stillbirths and Infant Deaths', *British Medical Journal*, 2, pp. 1520–24.

Illsley, R. (1983), *Social Mobility, Selection and the Production of Inequalities*. Paper presented to an ESRC Conference on Research Priorities in Inequalities of Health (unpublished).

Koskinen, S. (1985), *Time Trends in Cause-Specific Mortality by Occupational Class in England and Wales*, paper at IUSSP 20th General Conference, Florence (unpublished).

Marmot, M. G. (1986), 'Social Inequalities in Mortality: The Social Environment', in R. G. Wilkinson (ed.), *Class and Health*, Tavistock, pp. 21–33.

Marmot, M. G., Adelstein, A. M., Robinson, N., and Rose, G. A. (1978), 'Changing Social Class Distribution of Heart Disease', *British Medical Journal*, 2, pp. 1109–12.

OPCS (annual publication), *General Household Survey*, HMSO.

Pamuk, E. R. (1985), 'Social Class Inequality in Mortality from 1921 to 1972 in England and Wales', *Population Studies*, 39, pp. 17–31.

Registrar General (1978), *Occupational Mortality Tables, 1970–72, Decennial Supplement*, OPCS Series DS No. 1, HMSO.

Stern, J. (1983), 'Social Mobility and the Interpretation of Social Class Mortality Differentials', *Journal of Social Policy*, 12, pp. 27–49.

Todd, G. F. (1976), *Social Class Differences in Cigarette Smoking and in Mortality from Associated Diseases*, Occasional Paper 2, Tobacco Research Council.

Wadsworth, M. E. J. (1986), 'Serious Illness in Childhood and its Association with Later-life Achievement', in R. G. Wilkinson (ed.), *Class and Health*, Tavistock, pp. 50–74.

Wilkinson, R. G. (1976), *Socio-economic Factors in Mortality Differentials*, M. Med. Sci. thesis, University of Nottingham (unpublished).

35   Julian Tudor Hart

The Inverse Care Law

Excerpts from Julian Tudor Hart, 'The Inverse Care Law', in C. Cox and A. Mead (eds.), *The Sociology of Medical Practice*, Macmillan, 1975, p. 205.

In areas with most sickness and death, general practitioners have more work, larger lists, less hospital support and inherit more clinically ineffective traditions of consultation than in the healthiest areas; and hospital doctors shoulder heavier case-loads with less staff and equipment, more obsolete buildings, and suffer recurrent crises in the availability of beds and replacement staff. These trends can be summed up as the inverse care law: that the availability of good medical care tends to vary inversely with the need of the population served.

If the NHS had continued to adhere to its original principles, with construction of health centres a first priority in industrial areas, all financed from taxation rather than direct flat-rate contribution, free at the time of use, and fully inclusive of all personal health services, including family planning, the operation of the inverse care law would have been modified much more than it has been; but even the service as it is has been effective in redistributing care, considering the powerful social forces operating against this. If our health services had evolved as a free market, or even on a fee for item of service basis prepaid by private insurance, the law would have operated much more completely than it does; our situation might approximate to that in the United States, with the added disadvantage of smaller national wealth. The force that creates and maintains the inverse care law is the operation of the market, and its cultural and ideological superstructure which has permeated the thought and directed the ambitions of our profession during all of its modern history. The more health services are removed from the force of the market, the more successful we can be in redistributing care away from its 'natural' distribution in a market economy; but this will be a redistribution, an intervention to correct a fault natural to our form of society, and therefore incompletely successful and politically unstable, in the absence of more fundamental social change.

36 I. K. Zola

Medicine as an Instrument of Social Control

Excerpts from I. K. Zola, 'Medicine as an Instrument of Social Control', in C. Cox and A. Mead (eds.), *The Sociology of Medical Practice*, Macmillan, 1975, pp. 170–73, 175–80.

The theme of this essay is that medicine is becoming a major institution of social control, nudging aside, if not incorporating, the more traditional institutions of religion and law. It is becoming the new repository of truth, the place where absolute and often final judgements are made by supposedly morally neutral and objective experts. And these judgements are made, not in the name of virtue or legitimacy, but in the name of health. Moreover, this is not occurring through the political power physicians hold or can influence, but is largely an insidious and often undramatic phenomenon accomplished by 'medicalizing' much of daily living, by making medicine and the labels 'healthy' and 'ill' *relevant* to an ever increasing part of human existence . . .

An Historical Perspective

The involvement of medicine in the management of society is not new. It did not appear full-blown one day in the mid-twentieth century . . . This interdependence is perhaps best seen in two branches of medicine which have had a built-in social emphasis from the very start – psychiatry and public health/preventive medicine. Public health was always committed to changing social aspects of life – from sanitary to housing to working conditions – and often used the arm of the state (i.e. through laws and legal power) to gain its ends (e.g. quarantines, vaccinations).

Psychiatry's involvement in society is a bit more difficult to trace . . . From its early concern with the issue of insanity as a defence in criminal proceedings, psychiatry has grown to become the most dominant rehabilitative perspective in dealing with society's 'legal' deviants. Psychiatry, like public health, has also used the legal powers of the state in the accomplishment of its goals (i.e. the cure of the patient) through the legal proceedings of involuntary commitment and its concomitant removal of certain rights and privileges.

This is not to say, however, that the rest of medicine has been 'socially' uninvolved . . . Medicine has long had both a *de jure* and a *de facto* relation to institutions of social control. The *de jure* relationship is seen in the idea of reportable diseases, wherein if certain phenomena occur in his practice the physician is required to report them to the appropriate authorities. While this seems somewhat straightforward and even functional where certain highly contagious diseases are concerned, it is less clear where the possible spread of infection is not the primary issue (e.g. with gunshot wounds, attempted suicide, drug use and what is now called child abuse). The *de facto* relation to social control can be argued through a brief look at *whom* they have traditionally treated with *what* – giving *better* treatment to more favoured clientele; and secondly, *what* they have treated – a more subtle form of discrimination, in that with limited resources by focusing on some disease others are neglected. Here the accusation was that medicine has focused on the diseases of the rich and the established – cancer, heart disease, stroke – and ignored the diseases of the poor, such as malnutrition and still high infant mortality.

The Myth of Accountability

Even if we acknowledge such a growing medical involvement, it is easy to regard it as primarily a 'good' one – which involves the steady destigmatization of many human and social problems . . . The assumption is thus readily made that such medical involvement in social problems leads to their removal from religious and legal scrutiny and thus from moral and punitive consequences. In turn the problems are placed under medical and scientific scrutiny and thus in objective and therapeutic circumstances.

The fact that we cling to such a hope is at least partly due to two cultural-historical blind spots – one regarding our notion of punishment and the other our notion of moral responsibility. Regarding the first, if there is one insight into human behaviour that the twentieth century should have firmly implanted, it is that punishment cannot be seen in merely physical terms, nor only from the perspective of the giver. Granted that capital offences are on the decrease, that whipping and torture seem to be disappearing as is the use of chains and other physical restraints, yet our ability if not willingness to inflict human anguish on one another does not seem similarly on the wane. The most effective forms of brain-washing deny any physical contact and the concept of relativism tells much about the psychological costs of even relative deprivation of tangible and intangible wants. Thus, when an individual because of his 'disease' and its treatment is forbidden to have intercourse with fellow human beings, is confined until cured, is forced to undergo certain medical procedures for his own good, perhaps deprived forever of the right to have sexual relations and/or produce children, *then* it is difficult for that patient *not* to view what is happening to him as punishment. This does not mean that medicine is the latest form of twentieth-century torture, but merely that pain and suffering take many forms, and that the removal of a despicable inhumane procedure by current standards does not necessarily mean that its replacement will be all that beneficial . . .

It is the second issue, that of responsibility, which requires more elaboration, for it is argued here that the medical model has had its greatest impact in the lifting of moral condemnation from the individual. While some sceptics note that while the individual is no longer condemned his disease still *is*, they do not go far enough. Most analysts have tried to make a distinction between illness and crime on the issue of personal responsibility. The criminal is thought to be responsible and therefore accountable (or punishable) for his act, while the sick person is not. While the distinction does exist, it seems to be more a quantitative one rather than a qualitative one, with moral judgements but a pinprick below the surface. For instance, while it is probably true that individuals are no longer directly condemned for being sick, it does seem that much of this condemnation is merely displaced. Though his immoral character is not demonstrated in his having a disease, it becomes evident in what he does about it. Without seeming ludicrous, if one listed the traits of people who break appointments, fail to follow treatment regimen, or even delay in seeking medical aid one finds a long list of 'personal flaws'.

The Medicalizing of Society

... Freidson has stated a major aspect of the process most succinctly: 'The medical profession has first claim to jurisdiction over the label of illness and *anything* to which it may be attached, irrespective of its capacity to deal with it effectively.' (Freidson 1970). For illustrative purposes this 'attaching' process may be categorized in four concrete ways: first, through the expansion of what in life is deemed relevant to the good practice of medicine; secondly, through the retention of absolute control over certain technical procedures; thirdly, through the retention of near absolute access to certain 'taboo' areas; and finally, through the expansion of what in medicine is deemed relevant to the good practice of life.

The expansion of what in life is deemed relevant to the good practice of medicine

The change of medicine's commitment from a specific aetiological model of disease to a multi-causal one and the greater acceptance of the concepts of comprehensive medicine, psychosomatics, etc., have enormously expanded that which is or can be relevant to the understanding, treatment and even prevention of disease. Thus it is no longer necessary for the patient merely to divulge the symptoms of his body, but also the symptoms of daily living, his habits and his worries ...

To rehabilitate or at least alleviate many of the ravages of chronic disease, it has become increasingly necessary to intervene to change permanently the habits of a patient's lifetime – be it of working, sleeping, playing or eating. In prevention the 'extension into life' becomes even deeper, since the very idea of primary prevention means getting there *before* the disease process starts. The physician must not only seek out his clientele but once found must often convince them that they must do something *now* and perhaps at a time when the potential patient feels well or not especially troubled ...

Through the retention of absolute control over certain technical procedures

In particular this refers to skills which in certain jurisdictions are the very operational and legal definition of the practice of medicine – the right to do surgery and prescribe drugs. Both of these take medicine far beyond concern with ordinary organic disease.

In surgery this is seen in several different sub-specialities. The plastic surgeon has at least participated in, if not helped perpetuate, certain aesthetic standards. What once was a practice confined to restoration has now expanded beyond the correction of certain traumatic or even congenital deformities to the creation of new physical properties, from size of nose to size of breast, as well as dealing with certain phenomena – wrinkles, sagging, etc. – formerly associated with the 'natural' process of ageing. Alterations in sexual and reproductive functioning have long been a medical concern. Yet today the frequency of hysterectomies seems not so highly correlated as one might think with the presence of organic disease . . . Transplantations, despite their still relative infrequency, have had a tremendous effect on our very notions of death and dying. And at the other end of life's continuum, since abortion is still essentially a surgical procedure, it is to the physician-surgeon that society is turning (and the physician-surgeon accepting) for criteria and guidelines.

In the exclusive right to prescribe and thus pronounce on and regulate drugs, the power of the physician is even more awesome. Forgetting for the moment our obsession with youth's 'illegal' use of drugs, any observer can see, judging by sales alone, that the greatest increase in drug use over the last ten years has not been in the realm of treating any organic disease but in treating a large number of psycho-social states. Thus we have drugs for nearly every mood: to help us sleep or keep us awake; to enhance our appetite or decrease it; to tone down our energy level or to increase it; to relieve our depression or stimulate our interest . . .

Through the retention of near absolute access to certain 'taboo' areas

These 'taboo' areas refer to medicine's almost exclusive licence to examine and treat that most personal of individual possessions – the inner workings of our bodies and minds. My contention is that if anything can be shown in some way to affect the workings of the body and to a lesser extent the mind, then it can be labelled an 'illness' itself or jurisdictionally 'a medical problem'. In a sheer statistical sense the import of this is especially great if we look at only four such problems – ageing, drug addiction, alcoholism and pregnancy. The first and last were once regarded as normal natural processes and the middle two as human foibles and weaknesses. Now this has changed and to some extent medical specialities have emerged to meet these new needs. Numerically this expands medicine's involvement not only in a longer span of human existence, but it opens the possibility of medicine's services to millions if not billions of people . . .

It is pregnancy, however, which produces the most illuminating illustration. For, again in the United States, it was barely seventy years ago that virtually all births and the concomitants of birth occurred outside the hospital as well as outside medical supervision. I do not frankly have a documentary history, but as this medical claim was solidified, so too was medicine's claim to a whole host of related processes: not only to birth but to prenatal, postnatal, and paediatric care; not only to conception but to infertility; not only to the process of reproduction but to the process and problems of sexual activity itself; not only when life begins (in the issue of abortion) but whether it should be allowed to begin at all (e.g. in genetic counselling) . . .

Through the expansion of what in medicine is deemed relevant to the good practice of life

Though in some ways this is the most powerful of all the 'medicalizing of society' processes, the point can be made simply. Here we refer to the use of medical rhetoric and evidence in the arguments to advance any cause . . . Today the prestige of *any* proposal is immensely enhanced, if not justified, when it is expressed in the idiom of medical science . . . In politics one hears of the healthy or unhealthy economy or state. More concretely, the physical and mental health of American presidential candidates has been an issue in the last four elections and a recent book claimed to link faulty political decisions with faulty health . . .

The Potential and Consequences of Medical Control

The list of daily activities to which health can be related is ever growing and with the current operating perspective of medicine it seems infinitely expandable. The reasons are manifold. It is not merely that medicine has extended its jurisdiction to cover new problems, or that doctors are professionally committed to finding disease, nor even that society keeps creating disease. For if none of these obtained today we should still find medicine exerting an enormous influence on society. The most powerful empirical stimulus for this is the realization of how much everyone has or believes he has something organically wrong with him, or put more positively, how much can be done to make one feel, look or function better . . .

The belief in the omnipresence of disorder is further enhanced by a reading of the scientific, pharmacological and medical literature, for there one finds a growing litany of indictments of 'unhealthy' life activities. From sex to food, from aspirins to clothes, from driving your car to riding the surf, it seems that under certain conditions or in combination with certain other substances or activities or if done too much or too little, virtually anything can lead to certain medical problems. In short, I at least have finally been convinced that living is injurious to health.

These facts take on particular importance not only when health becomes a paramount value in society, but also a phenomenon whose diagnosis and treatment has been restricted to a certain group. For this means that that group, perhaps unwittingly, is in a position to exercise great control and influence about what we should and should not do to attain that 'paramount value'.

Reference

FREIDSON, E. (1970), *Profession of Medicine: A Study in the Sociology of Knowledge*, Dodd-Mead, New York.

37   M. Morgan, M. Calnan and N. Manning

The Hospital as a Social Organization

Excerpts from M. Morgan, M. Calnan and N. Manning, 'The Hospital as a Social Organization', in Morgan, Calnan and Manning (eds.), *Sociological Approaches to Health and Medicine*, Croom Helm, 1985, pp. 140–45, 150–52, 157–8.

Hospitals are typically large institutions with a diversity of activities and personnel within them. They have been analysed from a variety of perspectives, such as management structure, staff attitudes and communications, and resource planning . . .

Early analyses of the hospital conceptualize it as a 'formal organization', assuming that it is set up with the intention and design of accomplishing certain goals, and that people who work in an organization believe, at least part of the time, that they are striving towards these same goals through intentionally rational behaviour (Simon, 1955). While the hospital is chiefly a setting for medical practice, it has therefore, by virtue of being an organization, many characteristics of its own . . .

The Hospital as a Bureaucratic Organization

Organization theory has generally employed a positivist approach and views the hospital as consisting of a structured set of relationships which exist independently of the viewpoint of the observer. The primary aim is thus to understand the nature of the organization as it operates in a more or less independent fashion. The classic work for the start of such an analysis is Max Weber's analysis of bureaucracy as a hierarchical system of authority, based on a rational and explicit set of rules . . . (Weber, 1949)

In so far as the hospital is a large-scale organization in modern society, it can be seen to exhibit many aspects of Weber's ideal type of bureaucratic institution. However the hospital also exhibits both general and specific exceptions to Weber's model. These are centred around two areas. First is the modification of these principles, in so far as many hospital personnel are members of a profession which is organized in a different way to a bureaucracy and in particular is characterized by professional autonomy and non-bureaucratic relationships. Second is a related point, that hospital rules do not specify all the possibilities for action for every person in the hospital. Thus staff have to exercise professionally guided discretion from time to time and negotiate these actions with colleagues . . .

The inappropriateness of Weber's bureaucratic model for hospitals has given rise to various reformulations . . .

Etzioni (1975) accepts that organizations have rules, but is concerned with the question of how members of the organization are persuaded to accept the rules and conditions (including technology) of their work . . .

Etzioni suggests members can accept or reject the power position to which they are subjected. Those who reject their position are subject to coercive power; those who accept their position at a price are subject to remunerative power; and those who positively accept their position are subject to normative power. Members of an organization consequently develop a positive or negative emotional commitment giving rise to three related kinds of personal involvement: alienative if their commitment is negative; calculative if their commitment is neutral; and moral if their commitment is positive . . . Etzioni suggests that hospitals are most effective when their members (staff and patients) both accept power exercised over themselves and in addition have a positive moral involvement. However Etzioni provides no criteria by which effectiveness is to be judged and merely assumes that willing compliance by hospital staff and patients to the system of authority is best – an assumption that has been questioned particularly with regard to psychiatric hospitals.

Recognition that hospitals are characterized by two lines of authority, a bureaucratic one represented by the hospital administrators, and a charismatic/traditional one upheld by doctors, with nurses being subject to both systems of authority, has led Bucher and Stelling (1969) to suggest that organizations such as hospitals in which professionals predominate cannot be usefully understood as bureaucracies at all. They argue that such organizations, which they describe as professional organizations, should be understood as unique in their own right . . . They dissolve the problem of alternative lines of authority by considering the general processes through which actions and meanings are agreed upon in the hospital. This conception suggests a much greater fluidity within an organization, with power residing as much in the person as in his or her office . . . Competition and conflict for resources are thus resolved more in the style of a parliamentary political process than a bureaucratic hierarchy.

Stelling and Bucher (1972) reject the notions of authority and hierarchy entirely. Instead they suggest that professional action within hospitals can be better understood in terms of 'elastic autonomy' which is negotiated by each person, and the monitoring of professions by each other to mutually justify the amount of negotiated autonomy exercised. This involves the processing of information rather than the following of rules . . .

The Hospital as a Goal-oriented Organization

A second approach to analysing the nature of the hospital has been to focus on the output or effects of a hospital rather than its internal workings. For example, Parsons (1957) uses functionalist theory to judge the outputs or effects of any social institution by the functions it performs with regard to the achievement of widely shared social values. Parsons suggests that with regard to the hospital there is a widespread expectation that it can provide effective therapy. However, he notes that mental hospitals are also expected to perform additional functions which correspond to other social values. The public expects mental hospitals to provide custody for dangerous or frightening patients, and to protect patients who are vulnerable as a result of their disorder from social demands which they cannot meet and from actions which may be a danger to themselves or to other patients. Finally, Parsons suggests that mental hospitals have the job of re-socializing patients so that they can be returned to normal social roles in the wider society . . .

Parsons' approach has been criticized for focusing too exclusively on factors external to the hospital. Any variation between and within hospitals, particularly in a uniform structure such as the National Health Service, is consequently difficult to explain. In particular his approach has been criticized for ignoring the effects of technology on the organizational structure of the hospital . . .

[Thus] Coser in her classic study of *Life in the Ward* (1962), showed ... that in a general hospital a different social structure corresponded to the different technology used on medical and surgical wards. Surgical wards involved the use of potentially dangerous treatments. Decisions had to be taken unequivocally and obeyed rapidly. Emergencies were not uncommon. This was associated with a social structure resembling Weber's description of an ideal-type of bureaucracy. Social relations amongst the staff, and between staff and patients, were governed by an explicit hierarchy of authority in which the predominant rationale for decisions was based on medical interpretation of the physical needs of the patients. These decisions were arrived at by senior staff and communicated as instructions which junior staff and patients were expected to obey. But in the medical wards treatments were less dramatic, required more thoughtful consideration, and could benefit from the opinions and observations of all grades of staff. The structure of authority was thus more participative on medical wards ...

An important contribution of approaches to hospitals which focus on goals is to draw attention to the existence of basic goal conflicts. Probably the major conflict is between goals focusing on patient care, and those focusing on the control of the patient or the education of the staff. The former are related to the interests of the patient, while the latter are related to the interests of the staff or other people outside the hospital. Of course, these two sets of interests may well overlap ...

A second way of viewing the conflict between care and control is in terms of what Goffman (1961) describes as the tension between 'humane standards' and 'institutional efficiency'. This tension is evident in all people-processing institutions, such as hospitals and prisons, since the objects processed are human beings to whom are attached rights and moral obligations and who possess an ability to react. However, concern with institutional efficiency is most likely to become a paramount and prolonged determinant of the social organization of hospitals where the level of technology is low, and the opportunities for cure and the discharge of patients are limited ...

Coser argues that within medicine there is a similar generalized goal towards curing patients, but again there are various means towards this goal, depending on the nature of the illness and the technology available. Where there is a goal/means disjunction, Coser suggests that a process of alienation develops whereby staff retreat from the goal and merely commit themselves to a ritualistic practice of institutional routines.

Coser's analysis has been extended to include other effects of the disjunction between goals and means in hospital . . . Brown (1973) suggests that the particular reactions of staff members depend crucially on the nature of the reward system in the hospital. In effect, he is suggesting that only if these rewards are high enough, whether financial, intrinsic (such as scientific research) or incidental (easy hours, good accommodation and so on), will staff stay in the job.

There are two further solutions to Brown's dilemma. First, there can develop what Goffman (1961) describes as a moral division of labour. He derived this from Hughes' study of the nature of work (Hughes, 1958). Hughes observed that in work organizations there was very often a division of labour between those who did the 'dirty work', and those who epitomized the higher aspirations of the organization. Goffman suggests that in mental hospitals there is a similar division of labour in that senior staff members, such as doctors, work towards more laudable goals such as therapy, while more junior staff, such as attendants or nurses, are assigned the more unpleasant tasks of managing and controlling patients. In other words, senior staff displace the goals/means disjunction on to junior staff . . .

The Hospital as a Negotiated Order

In contrast to positivist analyses which have emphasized formal structures, the interactionist perspective views organizations as no more than the intentions, actions and meanings of those people within it. Organizations thus become much more flexible and uncertain phenomena, owing any continuity in their existence to continuities in shared meanings. However, these do not arise spontaneously, but are determined largely by those individuals and groups that are successful in getting their own meanings accepted by the rest of the organization. This approach . . . is therefore concerned with the question of how the activities and relationships of the hospital are continually re-created. Thus rather than focusing exclusively on the key professional workers, attention is paid to the interactions and relationships of all its members, regardless of their particular place or position within the organization.

In order to understand this aspect of hospitals, Strauss (1963) introduced the concept of the hospital as a 'negotiated order' ... The analysis of the hospital as a negotiated order is based on the assumption that within hospitals the official rules are rarely specific enough to guide the detailed daily or hourly interactions of people, which are therefore subject to negotiation. Thus Strauss suggests that daily life is organized around a series of bargains, struck and forgotten or renegotiated from time to time, as desired by the individual. One of the most important notions this approach develops is of the ways in which lower level participants within the organization, such as patients, attendants, visitors and paramedical staff, can influence the formal organization through bargaining and negotiation ... An important implication of this is that lower level members of staff have more power than would appear to be the case, given the formal structure of the hospital and their position in the hierarchy of authority ...

Negotiated order theory, although widely regarded as contributing important insights into the working of the hospital, has been criticized for over-emphasizing the fluid nature of negotiations. Bittner (1974) suggests that ordinary staff and patients do in fact adhere to some kind of formal structural description of the organization they are in. They do not necessarily believe the organization is actually like this model, but rather they draw upon such a 'scheme of interpretation' to make sense of that part of the organization out of their reach, so that they may identify with unseen actions elsewhere and gain a sense of uniform purpose ...

Psychiatric Hospitals: Critiques and Alternatives

Sociological interest in hospitals has been particularly strong in the psychiatric field. This has been a result partly of a commitment to analyse and expose oppression in all areas of social life. In addition, psychiatric hospitals have provided a rich source of data about the limits of medical activities in practice, and the social dynamics of organizational life.

Goffman's work combined both an acute eye for detail in noticing the similar structures and processes in mental hospitals, prisons, monastic orders and so on, and an explicit moral condemnation of the impact of those total institutions on the lives of people in them.

His argument was based on the use of ideal-types ... He suggested that the key process – the totality – was established by collapsing the normally separate spheres of work, home and leisure, into one monolithic social experience: a kind of 'batch living' of the kind found in factory farmed animals. The crucial phase in this process is the entry of the patient into hospital. This process shares many similarities with the entry procedures experienced by all clients going into total institutions, from army camps to prisons and hospitals. In essence, this amounts to the common severance of social relations on the outside and the entry into new social relations on the inside. More particularly with respect to hospitals, Goffman referred to this transition as a 'moral career'. He means by this that the changed social relationships resulting from movement into hospital include an important alteration in the patient's own identity, which becomes completely submerged by the requirements of the institution. Goffman identified three distinct aspects of this career in total institutions such as mental hospitals:

Mortification of the Self. This was achieved through the literal degrading of the person's previous status and identity, brought about by the removal of their normal social props such as clothing and personal effects, the restriction of activities and movements and the requirement to engage in various demeaning practices, such as asking permission to smoke or post a letter.

Reorganization of the Self. The hospital replaces those aspects of the patient's identity it has removed: hospital clothes, hospital friends, a new status as patient, etc.

Patient Response. Goffman was well aware that his ideal-type of total institution did not always operate fully. In particular, in his discussion of the 'underlife' of asylums, he acknowledges that there are numerous means of working the system or 'making out' within the officially designated routines. Thus whereas some patients respond to the institution by *colonization*, or the acceptance of their new position without enthusiasm, others become positively identified with their allotted identity in a process of *conversion*, while a third response is to reject the hospital's requirements, and either become *withdrawn* or *intransigent* ...

The reorganized conception of the self which long-stay patients in psychiatric hospitals may come to accept has been termed 'institutionalization' or 'institutional neurosis', which broadly corresponds with Goffman's notion of 'conversion'. Barton (1959) gave the following definition:

Institutional neurosis is a disease characterised by apathy, lack of initiative, loss of interest most marked in things and events not immediately personal or present, submissiveness, and sometimes no expression of feelings of resentment at harsh or unfair orders. There is also a lack of interest in the future and an apparent inability to make practical plans for it, a deterioration in personal habits, toilet and standards generally, a loss of individuality and a resigned acceptance that things will go on as they are – unchangingly, inevitably and indefinitely. (Barton 1959, p. 2.)

References

BARTON, R. (1959), *Institutional Neurosis*, Wright and Co.

BITTNER, E. (1974), 'The Concept of Organisation', in R. Turner (ed.), *Ethnomethodology*, Penguin, pp. 69–81.

BROWN, G. W. (1973), 'The Mental Hospital as an Institution', *Social Science and Medicine*, 7, pp. 407–24.

BUCHER, R., and STELLING, J. (1969), 'Characteristics of Professional Organizations', *Journal of Health and Social Behaviour*, 10, pp. 2–13.

COSER, R. L. (1962), *Life in the Ward*, Michigan State University Press.

ETZIONI, A. (1975), *A Comparative Analysis of Complex Organizations*, Collier-Macmillan.

GOFFMAN, E. (1961), *Asylums*, Penguin.

HUGHES, E. C. (1958), *Men and their Work*, Free Press, Glencoe, Illinois.

PARSONS, T. (1957), 'The Mental Hospital as a Type of Organization', in M. Greenblatt et al. (eds.), *The Patient and the Mental Hospital*, Free Press, Chicago.

SIMON, H. A. (1955), 'Recent Advances in Organization Theory', in *Research Frontiers in Politics and Government*, Brookings Institute, New York.

STELLING, J., and BUCHER, R., (1972), 'Autonomy and Monitoring on Hospital Wards', *Sociological Quarterly*, 13, pp. 431–46.

STRAUSS, A., et al. (1963), 'The Hospital and its Negotiated Order', in E. Freidson (ed.), *The Hospital in Modern Society*, Free Press, New York.

WEBER, M. (1949) *The Methodology of the Social Sciences*, Free Press, New York.

38   Margaret Stacey

Who Are the Health Workers?

Excerpts from Margaret Stacey, 'What is Health Work?' and 'Unpaid Workers: the Carers', in Margaret Stacey, *The Sociology of Health and Healing*, Unwin Hyman, 1988, pp. 4–8, 10–11, 206–7, 209–10.

Health work . . . is a continuous activity . . . Everyone is involved in some aspect of health work. In consequence, when thinking about the division of labour in health care we are thinking about how health-care activities are divided among the total membership of the society. In some societies it is a question as to whether there are any health specialists at all. In other societies, such as advanced industrial societies and in the ancient civilizations such as India and China, there is a highly elaborated division of labour. But we must beware that in consequence of this we do not exclude some important health workers simply because they have not had an elaborate training. Specialists may well be involved, but so are many others.

Many studies in the past have concentrated upon those who are paid for their work in a narrowly defined health-care sector. [I take] a different approach. Whether the society is simple or complex, all those who are involved in health care are taken into account. Ignoring this precept has had the consequence in analyses of advanced industrial societies of distracting analytical attention from the unwaged workers – most often mothers, wives and daughters – although . . . official policy has often relied heavily upon them.

Health production activities begin with the birth of children and maintenance activities with their rearing. Our own care of our bodies and of our life-style is part of health maintenance work. Most important for health production are the activities of the food getters and the food preparers. In highly differentiated societies the former has become a major industry and the latter rests heavily on the activities in the home of those who care for the household, predominantly unwaged women in most societies. Others of their activities, such as cleansing and caring for household members, are also crucial for health maintenance . . .

Using the definition of health work adopted here, it is clear that the entire membership of the society is involved; in market economies this means the unwaged workers in addition to the paid specialists and their waged supporters. In the analysis of the restorative or curative services in such societies all the unpaid workers who help the patient through illness or accident have to be included in the division of labour along with the highly trained salary or fee earners and the waged workers who provide support services. This is also true with regard to the care of the chronic sick and disabled. There are those who are more frequently involved in unwaged health care than others. These are most often women . . .

Health Work is 'People Work'

A large part of health work, particularly the restorative and ameliorative aspects, but also some of the maintenance activities, involves one person or groups of people doing things to or for others (Hughes, 1971). It is 'people work' or 'human service'. It is from this that concepts like the division between professional and client, between doctor or nurse and patient, have become current in societies with highly developed divisions of labour. As biomedicine has developed on a mass scale, health care has come to be looked upon as an industry with the paid workers as 'producers' and the patients as 'consumers' . . .

Patient as Health Worker

Not only is the patient a social actor but s/he is a health worker in the division of health work. This has already become clear as far as the work of health production and health maintenance is concerned. It is also so as far as restorative and ameliorative health work goes . . .

Everett Hughes's proposal (1971) that the patient should be included in the division of health labour flowed from his observations of interactions in health care. Working in the symbolic interactionist tradition, Hughes was not trammelled by preconceptions as to the structure of the social relations he was observing, nor was he seduced by the values of the professional workers involved. He reported what he and his associates saw and he saw that patients were workers . . .

In line therefore with this ineluctable conclusion derived from observation and argument, the analysis in this [Reading] includes the patient in the division of health labour. Further, [I shall] call the suffering person a 'patient', which derives from the Latin *pati*, meaning to suffer . . .

Whether the patient as worker can ever be an equal partner in the health-care enterprise in advanced industrial societies or under what conditions that might emerge is another question which should be kept separate from the observation that the patient *is* a health worker in her/his own case . . .

The Gender Order

All societies, so far as we know, allocate roles and responsibilities differentially between the sexes, although the ways in which this is done are very variable. The notion of the gender order includes more than simple differential allocation of tasks; it implies that there are authority relations and arrogance-deference relations in the sex roles which are the norm in any one society – the relationships between the sexes are systematically ordered. The order is one of gender, not of sex as such, for it is socially constructed and may be constructed in a variety of ways. By far the greater number of societies which we know about have a male-dominated gender order; that is, the men are accorded a superior position . . .

The Generational Order

The generational order also has to be distinguished. Adults have some kind of authority over children in most societies. Women as well as men have authority over children, although each may have a different kind of authority. In some societies the old are venerated, although that tends to occur most commonly in societies with relatively short life expectancies. In industrial societies, whether capitalist or state socialist, the old, no longer producers, tend to be looked down on. Both the nature of the generational order and its relationship to the gender order are critical for an analysis of the health and healing arrangements in any society.

The Public and Domestic Domains

The analysis of the gender order in any complex society requires the use of the concept that the society is divided into public and domestic domains (Stacey and Price, 1981). 'Domestic' is used here rather than 'private' because the crucial reference is to the domain of the home, the arena of reproduction . . .

The domestic and public domains as empirically existing arrangements are not fixed and immutable. The social relations within each domain change, and their relationships with each other change. The boundary of each is never clearly defined, and the distinction between the domains is blurred. A great deal of health work nowadays inhabits an uneasy position between the two domains, but one dominated by men and by public domain values. The understanding of the relationship between the domains is therefore critical for an analysis of health and healing . . .

Nursing, for example, is work done unwaged in the home or for a fee, salary, or wage in the public domain. It is because sociological theory was developed by men in the public domain that sociologists have tended to include in the health division of labour only those who are paid by contract for their work. Thus the unwaged workers and their patients were excluded.

A Question of the Social Structure

In one sense the existence of the public and domestic domains can be said to be a matter of perception; women and men perceive the world differently because of their different locations in the social structure. The central focus of men's work is outside the home, and even today . . . much women's work is still centrally located in the household. Furthermore, the rewards and sanctions of the domestic domain are quite different from those of the public domain. The rewards and sanctions of the public domain are those of the market-place and of bureaucracy; they include wages, salaries, fees and profits and are contract based. In the domestic domain relationships are based on status, not contract, are ascribed rather than achieved; rewards are mostly non-material or take the form of 'gifts'. They take a form which is more akin to the feudal than to the capitalist or the bureaucratic.

Social Structural Changes in and Between the Domains

The nature of the domestic domain has changed; no longer is there an arena in which women have undisputed authority. The so-called 'democratic egalitarian family' has ensured that . . . women have lost that limited area of authority in the domestic domain which they commanded in more highly sex-segregated societies . . . At the same time they have not gained equality of status or of power in the public domain, whether in paid employment or in politics. The domestic domain has also been 'invaded' by the state. The programme to ensure the surveillance of all children's health has, from the beginning of the twentieth century, taken employees of the state into the homes of ordinary people to instruct them how to rear their children. It may still be 'natural' that the mother should also be the child rearer. It is no longer believed that she 'naturally' knows how to do the job properly. The way in which paid women health workers have been used to instruct unpaid women health workers (the mothers) is part of the history of the development of medicine . . .

The Unpaid Carers

. . . Unpaid carers are involved in health promotion, health maintenance, health restoration and caring for the disabled. Most of them are women . . .

Each woman is made responsible for her husband's health also. In order to help him avoid heart disease she should encourage him by stopping smoking herself, replan his diet to make it more healthy, encourage him to take exercise (and join him in it), listen to his worries and take over some of his work, like paying the bills and getting the plumber, according to one advice pamphlet . . . Such advice presumes a woman wants to shape her life-style, and that of her family, around her husband; but, perhaps more important, it also assumes that she is able to do so, which research suggests she may not be (Graham, 1984).

These conflicting role obligations may have deleterious consequences for the women's own health. Devices to help women cope with the labour of caring may bring solace without damage, such as listening to the radio. On the other hand, 'cigarettes, psychotropic drugs, and alcohol offer women this contradictory kind of support, helping and hurting them at the same time' (Graham, 1985).

If women have the primary responsibility for maintaining and promoting the health of their family, it is upon them that the burden of care for the ill and handicapped falls. This development has undoubtedly accelerated since the recent recession and government policies to contain, and now to cut, public expenditure on health. The return of long-stay patients to the 'community' and demands that mothers stay at home with their children or go to hospital with their children have been around since the 1950s . . .

Furthermore, inadequate services have been provided to support the hidden carers who are sustaining chronically ill or handicapped relatives . . . Phillipson, for example, discussed the large amount of women's work which is involved in caring for the elderly:

The caring role which is allocated to women moves from caring for her own children to caring for her parents (or her husband's parents) and back to her grandchildren. Even in her 60s and 70s, a woman may find her life predominantly shaped by the image of her as a caring and mothering figure (Phillipson, 1981).

His research shows that three times as many old people live with married daughters as with married sons. Even those daughters who are not in the same house as their elderly parents are more often called on for help than sons. Hundreds of thousands of single women look after an elderly parent, spending more than eight hours a day on it and at any time of day or night. Such carers frequently have to give up their jobs and also have their own personal and social lives severely curtailed; their situation is much like that of the captive wife at the beginning of the family cycle . . .

State Assumptions about Women as 'Natural' Carers

The assumption in state health and welfare policy has been that women do the caring. In 1982 the Equal Opportunities Commission (EOC) . . . analysed the implications for women of the 'return to the community' policies and also the increasing calls for volunteers to help with day care. These movements made heavy demands on women; the EOC concludes: 'The Government's "community care" policy is revealed as a euphemism for an under-resourced system which places heavy burdens on *individual* members of the community, most of them women. It represents "care on the cheap"'

(EOC 1982, original emphasis). What is more, as the EOC points out, the costs also 'are borne individually and do not figure in any public expenditure account. The price is paid in restrictions on women's opportunities' . . .

Allowances for Caring

Although health and welfare policies assume that health work is women's work, the extra cost has been to some extent recognized of recent years. Allowances may now be paid for 'attendance' upon a handicapped member of the household, and in some cases where the attendance allowance is paid an invalid care allowance may also be payable . . .

The allowances are small when looked at in terms of wages people might get for doing the same work as paid health employment and they appear even smaller when compared with the cost of institutional care . . . Nevertheless they represent a further development of the intermediate zone, between domestic and public domains, in which so much health care takes place and in which the unthinking (and unrecorded) consequences of male-dominated health and welfare policy disadvantage the unpaid carers, be they male or female.

References

EQUAL OPPORTUNITIES COMMISSION (1982), *Caring for the Elderly and Handicapped: Community Care Policies and Women's Lives*, EOC, Manchester.

GRAHAM, H. (1984), *Women, Health and the Family*, Wheatsheaf Harvester.

GRAHAM, H. (1985), 'Providers, Negotiators and Meditators: Women as the Hidden Carers', in E. Lewin and V. Olesen (eds.), *Women, Health and Healing*, Tavistock.

HUGHES, E. C. (1971), *The Sociological Eye*, Aldine, Chicago.

PHILLIPSON, C. (1981), 'Women in Later Life: Patterns of Control and Subordination', in B. Hutter and G. Williams (eds.), *Controlling Women: The Normal and the Deviant*, Croom Helm, pp. 185–202.

STACEY, M., and PRICE, M. (1981), *Women, Power and Politics*, Tavistock.

Part Seven
Community and Urban Life

'Community' is one of the key words in the sociological vocabulary. It is also one of the most frequently used in debates about the use of welfare resources and the care of the socially vulnerable. Words such as 'family', 'heritage', 'community', 'welfare' – used so freely in political debate – have diffuse meanings because they relate to a set of central values in society which, if scrutinized, would lose much of their precision and would look more like myths: i.e. they often express more the way we would like things to be than the way they are. They are therefore imbued with contradictory and emotionally charged beliefs, which might seem to render them valueless as explanatory concepts.

'Community', in particular, has come to carry such a variety of high-flown notions about personal intimacy, emotional depth and political worth – what Emmett, below, terms a 'commitment to romanticism' – that its use in sociology might seem inappropriate. Yet the idea of community does present a challenge to stock theoretical presuppositions and to vested political interests.

'Community' was a key concept in the work of the classical sociologists of the nineteenth century; it was a central theme, in particular, in the counter-reaction to the growing popularity of Marxist and socialist ideas (see Reading 2). 'Community', with its emphasis on the small-scale, on immediate experience, on the strength of affective ties, and on continuity from one generation to the next, was a powerful antidote to 'class', with its emphasis on the national society, on historical knowledge and on rationality and revolution. The most powerful expression of this reaction was that by Ferdinard Tönnies (Reading 39), whose writings influenced the development of sociology in both England and the United States. Tönnies saw intimate experience as *Gemeinschaft*, (usually translated as 'community'), the 'perfect unity of human wills', found, in essence, in the blood-tie. He distinguished Gemeinschaft of locality, based on the use of a common habitat, from Gemeinschaft of mind, found in both religion and friendship. Gemeinschaft, for him, enshrined positive values: he extols the authority of the father; a sexual division of labour in which women are given 'manual labour, the task of execution'; the 'sacred customs' of the village; and the 'natural' authority of the head of state – a clearly conservative philosophy.

In contrast, with urbanization there develops an alternative form of social relationship, based on the money economy, the division of labour and rationality, which he termed *Gesellschaft* (usually translated as either 'society' or 'association'). Gesellschaft, he argued, would eventually replace the older Gemeinschaft relationships of 'mutual affirmation'. This portrayal of life in the modern city was to be further elaborated in 1904 by Georg Simmel, in his *Metropolis and Mental Life*, a bleak portrayal of urban life as inhuman: the constant interaction of strangers.

Such blatantly reactionary and biased arguments were, however, assimilated into the everyday practical use of sociology as a new science of social reconstruction. Louis Wirth's influential essay 'Urbanism as a Way of Life' (Reading 40), written in 1938, summed up several decades of this kind of thinking. He saw the task of sociology as 'to provide a body of reliable knowledge', which would assist those making judgements about poverty, housing, and city planning – an aim which would have been shared by the majority of those studying or teaching sociology, as well as those acting as consultants.

But others were beginning to use the term 'community' in a more limited and less overtly political way. By 1959, for example, Talcott Parsons' definition of community as 'that aspect of the structure of social systems which is referable to the territorial location of persons' was typical of many attempts to remove the normative, emotive and value-loaded elements from what had by then become an everyday term. But a further result of this shift in the use of the term was that the dynamic element in the original concept was also lost. An idea that had once expressed the *social dislocation* of Europe had become restricted simply to territorial *location*. Yet in popular usage, as Raymond Williams has remarked (in Emmett's Reading 44), 'community' is never used pejoratively, or even neutrally. It is always seen as a *benign* condition; its antithesis – the large-scale, industrial, centralized, bureaucratic society – as a malign force in social life.

Throughout the thirties and beyond, however, Wirth's essay, which attempted to link the ideas of Simmel and Tönnies with those developed by the Chicago School of sociology, remained the theoretical basis of urban research. Drawing on demographic and ecological data about the size, density and heterogeneity of the city, he not only retained the dynamic element but tried to translate it into practical urban policy. The theoretical model, however, was riddled with contradictions.

First – with a total disregard for historical evidence or comparative studies – he assumed that what was happening in North America was a universal process. Second, he took the conditions of urban living – size, density, and heterogeneity – to be the *causes* of the social organization he discerned in cities. Third, he confused observation of social life in cities like Chicago with predictions as to what it would become. Fourth, his model of city and community life disregarded empirical evidence (even his own earlier research on the Jewish ghetto). And last, his political ideas coloured his analysis so strongly that, like Tönnies, he inevitably came to deeply pessimistic conclusions about the ways in which urbanization affected political life. His analysis, written as fascism in Europe challenged world democratic values, essentially saw the city as 'mass society'. The 'substitution of secondary for primary contacts, the weakening of the bonds of kinship ... the disappearance of the neighbourhood, and the undermining of the traditional bases of social control' meant that 'it is impossible to appeal individually to the large number of discrete and individuated citizens'. Social control in the city therefore has to be 'proceed through formally organized groups', with the result that 'the masses of men in the city are subject to manipulation by symbols and stereotypes managed by individuals working from afar'.

This denunciation has a modern ring to it, though most writers would now hesitate to speak of 'men', and would refer to corporate and institutional power rather than manipulation by individuals. Yet city life presents both opportunities and challenges: in some circumstances, these are conducive to liberation from conventional restraints, in others, to anomie. The ties of kinship and neighbourhood

are not absolutely binding and unchangeable, but potentially nego-
tiable, as they have been for many centuries in wage-labour economies, even back to medieval times. Political participation, by all but
a minority, is very sporadic, while the legitimacy accorded to state
agencies becomes ever more indirect and impersonal. Accordingly,
political leaders concentrate more on presenting their policies via the
media, the main modern channel through which ideological hegemony is established.

Wirth's arguments have, in fact, been refuted point by point. The
first wave of criticism was directed at his model of human ecology.
Sociologists of his own day, such as Alihan and Firey, argued that
the distribution of population was ultimately dictated by the actions
and the social values of investors and residents. The changes in
social organization that Wirth takes to be a consequence of size,
density and heterogeneity were better conceived of as reflections of a
social system in which great importance was attached to social and
spatial mobility. Comparative criticism came from those with research experience in Latin America and Africa, where kinship and
ethnicity had not disappeared in the cities but persisted as important
bases of social organization, while historical evidence was presented
by writers such as Sjoberg to show that Wirth's model was not valid
for very large preindustrial cities such as Peking. To these arguments
were added criticisms based on empirical research in the USA,
which Greer summarizes in Reading 41. Post-war research showed
that social life in the cities was orderly and that most residents
had achieved a comfortable life-style based on the family household.
People took on 'community' responsibilities only when they sustained
the security and well-being of the household – hence, to use Janowitz's term, these were 'communities of limited liability'. People
knew what they wanted – a secure job, a good house, a safe neighbourhood, and a future for their children – and left politics to the
politicians. It was a complacent, though not unrealistic, image of
urban life which was to be disrupted by the ghetto riots of 1964 and subsequent years, both in the USA and other industrialized countries.

One weakness of the antithesis between traditional community
and modern society was the way this placed 'community' forms of
organization in the past. In the modern city, their survival was in
doubt. Yet one of the contributions of sociological research has been
to demonstrate how migrants and their families have been able to

remake their social worlds in the neighbourhoods of such cities. On the basis on his own research and that of others, American sociologist Suttles (Reading 42) argues that neighbourhoods are a 'creative imposition' by which urban residents bring order into their lives. Defining neighbourhood boundaries, or maintaining a sense of allegiance, were means of screening out undesirables, and of maintaining status and social well-being. More than any other writer, Suttles conveys a sense of the dangers of living in a city of strangers – one of the main sources of insecurity in the modern city – and the utility of the local community as 'the defended neighbourhood which segregates people to avoid danger, insult and the impairment of status claims'.

In this analysis, freedom to move around the city and select associates does not produce 'mass society', but causes the city to become an array of neighbourhoods in which family and property rights are maintained by segregation. Children's safety, the social environment of the local schools, and security of property as well as property values, are protected by the exclusion of groups from a different ethnic background or class status. The neighbourhood boundaries arising from this spatial differentiation are at their most pronounced either in highly unequal societies such as England at the time when Engels wrote *The Condition of the Working Class in England* (1844), or in societies such as the USA or South Africa where there are persistent racial/ethnic divides. At the same time, demands for mobility and access to the freedoms of an urban society persist. Indeed, it can be argued that no modern city – with its dependence on a highly complex division of labour and technical specialization and its promotion of a mass popular culture – can maintain a strict system of segregation. However, as Gilroy argues in Reading 45, segregation in a locality may provide the crucial basis for the transformation of networks of support into 'active communities', thereby giving those who are marginal to the city's labour and housing markets a basis for political mobilization.

Another critique of Wirth's sociological paradigm has come from Marxist writers, notably Manuel Castells. In *The Urban Question* (1972), he objected to any theory of 'the urban' that was not at the same time part of a 'general social theory'. An understanding of 'the urban' had to take into account 'structures of domination' at all levels, including the power structure of society as a whole. A separate 'urban' theory, he said, was 'ideological' in that it abstracted for study only one aspect of urbanization – the conditions of everyday life – thereby providing a rationale for social reform which ignored power and ascribed change in the city merely to changes in land-use. A systematic critique of modern society was then displaced by welfare reforms and/or ecology movements.

The novelty of Castells' approach lay in the way he linked together theories of the state in capitalist society, a view of cities as 'everyday spaces' in which labour-power is reproduced, and local politics. For him, it was the state which guaranteed both the reproduction of labour-power and the reproduction of social relations; urban growth generated demands for new services which could not be provided profitably by the private sector; and local groups were therefore forced into confrontation with the state over this 'collective consumption'. From his experience of the shanty towns of Latin American cities, he was impressed by the political energy of local protests, which he termed 'urban social movements'. In later writing, *The City and the Grassroots* (1983), he collated information about a wide range of local groups, including, for example, the gay movement in San Francisco in the 1970s and the Glasgow rent strikes of 1915. The rationale for categorizing such movements as 'urban' was that they were locally based and territorially defined. In this approach (discussed by Gilroy in Reading 45), urbanization will always give rise to conflict, since the state can never satisfy consumption demands. Though cultural pluralism is generated by the existence of very varied kinds of networks in the large city, it is then blocked by the state. The local determination of needs then comes into conflict with central planning and with the institutions which maintain order in the large city.

Castells' approach caused much controversy. He was accused of isolating consumption, rather than emphasizing production relations as the basis of urban conflict; his concept of collective consumption was said to be unclear (could housing, in particular, be *collectively* consumed?); and in his model, multi-class social movements, not class organizations, were seen as the basis of collective action. How the social base of an urban social movement is converted into a political force was not worked out; there is overemphasis on the welfare function of the state. The police, for example, were included under the rubric of 'collective consumption', not – as many inner-city residents have considered them to be – as a repressive force.

Ultimately, after much discussion, he sees these movements as 'reactive Utopias', and incapable of challenging the political system.

An alternative way of resolving the problem of reconciling traditional Marxist analysis of whole societies with a theory of local urban politics was that of Cockburn (Reading 43). She similarly seeks to develop a perspective which encompasses both class organization and community action. There is, however, a rather different emphasis: on reproduction, not consumption; on organization, not movement; and she is much more conscious, too, of the limitations of local campaigns. She also challenges the notion that 'local' or 'community' ways of thinking and organization can effectively challenge the political system. 'The terrain on which community groups marshal their arguments' she argues, 'is laid out to a state-defined agenda.' Community groupings rarely coincide with political units, since representation in local and national government is ordered on the basis of wards and constituencies, into which plural interests have to be channelled. Ironically, as urban residents become more mobile, and neighbourhoods more heterogeneous, so official bodies attempt to incorporate 'the community' in their management of state services. Local management has to assume that there is, or can be, a 'community' out there, one with a recognized hierarchy and clearly defined interests. They ignore, therefore, that part of Wirth's argument (and that of Greer) which insisted that heterogeneity, mobility and isolation would *limit* popular participation, and thereby render spurious the claims of 'community' leaders that they were putting a 'popular mandate' into action.

It is salutary to read the description presented by Emmett (Reading 44), and to compare it with conditions in the inner wards of cities such as London, where the turnover of population may exceed one household in four per year. The people of Blaenau Ffestiniog live together, belong to the place, and draw immediate boundaries between strangers and those they have known over a lifetime. They are part of an elaborate culture which is renewed every day in the process of living together in a 'knowable' community. Ethnographies of virtually any locality will, of course, reveal some aspects of life which are similar to those of life in big cities. But those who live in cities cannot expect to know others in the same way as people in Blaenau, and there is no overall hierarchy within the community to which they can relate. The promotion of 'community action', and the recognition of 'community' leaders, without the shared knowledge of the isolated small-town community, must raise doubts about the legitimacy of the claim that decisions are being made on behalf of the 'community'.

Questions of accountability like these are particularly evident when groups marginalized by the political process attempt to mobilize on the basis of 'community'. There are indeed localities within the city – especially where there is little movement in and out – where close-knit patterns of life do persist. One of the strengths of the Chicago School in the 1915–1940 period was that it saw the city as differentiated into a 'mosaic of social worlds', mostly of a racial/ethnic kind. Segregation into 'ghettos' made it possible for minorities to be organized into recognized groups within the political system. In Britain, low rates of mobility for the inner-city neighbourhoods where New Commonwealth migrants settled during the post-war expansion of the economy resulted in the formation of similar 'ghettos' and of political groupings based on them. Out of the frequent disputes with local and central government, and with the police and the legal system, hitherto unknown leaders emerge into the public arena in a multitude of localized contexts. These struggles, as Gilroy argues in Reading 45, have allowed Black people to use the idea of 'community' as a basis on which to organize themselves. Such leaders are able to call on real networks of mutual support, and the moral obligations of 'community', as well as what he terms 'racial alterity' – the colour black.

Exclusion from core institutions, dependency, and isolation in slum conditions, are the precipitants of local action in poor neighbourhoods, Black and White, within the inner cities and outside them. 'Ethnic' and 'Black' leaders can appeal to those so categorized in order to mobilize them against 'racial capitalism'. Gilroy argues that out of these cultures of dissent, which condense and symbolize Black people's identity and aspirations, come collective identities 'spoken through "race", community and locality' which are 'powerful means to coordinate action and create solidarity': the history of resistance to colonialism; Rastafarianism; Black music and poetry; as well as local struggles against police practices and for control of Black children's education. In one respect – in asserting the superiority of 'community' and of social movements based on 'affect and kinship' over those of class and formal organization – Gilroy reverts to the outlook formulated by Tönnies a century ago. Urban populations, using modern technology, urban in their work, their consumption and their leisure practices, nevertheless call on the symbolism of 'community' to articulate their interests.

One of the paradoxes of urbanization is that it promotes 'modernity' but does not lead to the loss of 'traditional' social forms such as 'community'. In fact the reverse may be the case, in that the work opportunities and cultural pluralism of the large city make possible what Tönnies called 'intimate, private and exclusive living together'. What research does show is that the acceptance of moral obligations to family, ethnic group, professional body or trade union, or to the local neighbourhood, are situational strategies – ways of coping with specific problems – not, as Suttles puts it, 'universal forms which are required by the mechanisms of life itself'. Another paradox, perhaps, is that groups such as Blacks in Britain, restricted by poverty to life within the local community, exert political energy to escape from these constraints, while those with choice – the affluent of the urbanized world – seek out other people's communities, in villages, or in inner cities, in their search for authenticity. The local community is still a symbol of a preferred social world. From this stems both its inadequacy as a sociological concept, and its vitality in urban life.

39   F. Tönnies
Community and Society

Excerpts from F. Tönnies, *Community and Society*, Routledge, 1955, pp. 33–5, 42–3, 232–3. (First published 1895).

Gemeinschaft (Community) and Gesellschaft (Society)

Human wills stand in manifold relations to one another. Every such relationship is a mutual action, inasmuch as one party is active, or gives, while the other party is passive, or receives ... This study will consider as its subject of investigation only the relationships of mutual affirmation ... The relationship itself, and also the resulting association, is conceived of either as real and organic life – this is the essential characteristic of the Gemeinschaft (community); or as imaginary and mechanical structure – this is the concept of Gesellschaft (society) ...

All intimate, private, and exclusive living together, so we discover, is understood as life in Gemeinschaft (community). Gesellschaft (society) is public life – it is the world itself. In Gemeinschaft with one's family, one lives from birth on, bound to it in weal and woe. One goes into Gesellschaft as one goes into a strange country. A young man is warned against bad Gesellschaft, but the expression bad Gemeinschaft violates the meaning of the word ...

In the most general way, one could speak of a Gemeinschaft comprising the whole of mankind, such as the Church wishes to be regarded. But human Gesellschaft is conceived as mere coexistence of people independent of each other. Recently, the concept of Gesellschaft as opposed to and distinct from the state has been developed. This term will also be used in this book, but can only derive its adequate explanation from the underlying contrast to the Gemeinschaft of the people.

Gemeinschaft is old; Gesellschaft is new as a name as well as a phenomenon ... All praise of rural life has pointed out that the Gemeinschaft among people is stronger there and more alive; it is the lasting and genuine form of living together. In contrast to Gemeinschaft, Gesellschaft is transitory and superficial. Accordingly, Gemeinschaft should be understood as a living organism, Gesellschaft as a mechanical aggregate and artefact ...

The Gemeinschaft by blood, denoting unity of being, is developed and differentiated into Gemeinschaft of locality, which is based on a common habitat. A further differentiation leads to the Gemeinschaft of mind, which implies only cooperation and coordinated action for a common goal. Gemeinschaft of locality may be conceived as a community of physical life, just as Gemeinschaft of mind expresses the community of mental life. In conjunction with the others, this last type of Gemeinschaft represents the truly human and supreme form of community. Kinship Gemeinschaft signifies a common relation to, and share in, human beings themselves, while in Gemeinschaft of locality such a common relation is established through collective ownership of land; and, in Gemeinschaft of mind, the common bond is represented by sacred places and worshipped deities. All three types of Gemeinschaft are closely interrelated in space as well as in time. They are, therefore, also related in all such single phenomena and in their development, as well as in general human culture and its history. Wherever human beings are related through their wills in an organic manner and affirm each other, we find one or another of the three types of Gemeinschaft. Either the earlier type involves the later one, or the later type has developed to relative independence from some earlier one. It is, therefore, possible to deal with (1) kinship, (2) neighbourhood, and (3) friendship as definite and meaningful derivations of these original categories ...

Neighbourhood describes the general character of living together in the rural village. The proximity of dwellings, the communal fields and even the mere contiguity of holdings necessitate many contacts of human beings and cause inurement to and intimate knowledge of one another. They also necessitate cooperation in labour, order, and management, and lead to common supplication for grace and mercy to the gods and spirits of land and water who bring blessing or menace with disaster. Although essentially based upon proximity of habitation, this neighbourhood type of Gemeinschaft can nevertheless persist during separation from the locality, but it then needs to be supported still more than ever by well-defined habits of reunion and sacred customs.

Friendship is independent of kinship and neighbourhood, being conditioned by and resulting from similarity of work and intellectual attitude. It comes most easily into existence when crafts or callings are the same or of similar nature. Such a tie, however, must be made and maintained through easy and frequent meetings, which are most likely to take place in a town ... Those who are brethren of such a common faith feel, like members of the same craft or rank, everywhere united by a spiritual bond and the cooperation in a common task ...

In the earlier period, family life and home (or household) economy strike the keynote; in the later period, commerce and city life. If, however, we investigate the period of Gemeinschaft more closely, several epochs can be distinguished. Its whole development tends toward an approach to Gesellschaft in which, on the other hand, the force of Gemeinschaft persists, although with diminishing strength, even in the period of Gesellschaft, and remains the reality of social life.

The first period is formed by the influence of the new basis of social organization which results from the cultivation of the soil: a neighbourhood relation is added to the old and persisting kinship relations, village to the clan. The other epoch comes into existence when villages develop into towns. The village and town have in common the principle of social organization in space, instead of the principle of time which predominates through the generations of the family, the tribe, and the people. Because it descends from common ancestors, the family has invisible metaphysical roots, as if they were hidden in the earth. The living individuals in the family are connected with each other by the sequence of past and future generations. But in village and town it is the physical, real soil, the permanent location, the visible land, which create the strongest ties and relations. During the period of Gemeinschaft this younger principle of space remains bound to the older principle of time. In the period of Gesellschaft they become disconnected, and from this disconnection results the city. It is the exaggeration of the principle of space in its urban form. In this exaggeration, the urban form becomes sharply contrasted with the rural form of the same principle, for the village remains essentially and almost necessarily bound to both principles.

In this sense, the whole continual development may be considered as a process of increasing urbanization. 'It may be said that the whole economic history of Gesellschaft, i.e., of the modern nations, is in essence summarized in the change in the relationship between town and country' (Karl Marx, *Das Kapital*, I). That is, from a certain point on, the towns by their influence and importance achieve, in the nation, predominance over the rural organization. In consequence, country and village must use more of their own productive forces for the support and furtherance of the urban areas than they can spare for purposes of reproduction. Therefore, the rural organization is doomed to dissolution.

40   Louis Wirth

The Urban Community

Excerpts from Louis Wirth, 'Urbanism as a Way of Life', in R. Sennett (ed.), *Classic Essays on the Culture of Cities*, Appleton Century Crofts, New York, 1969, pp. 150–57, 162–3.

The central problem of the sociologist of the city is to discover the forms of social action and organization that typically emerge in relatively permanent, compact settlements of large numbers of heterogeneous individuals. We must also infer that urbanism will assume its most characteristic and extreme form in the measure in which the conditions with which it is congruent are present. Thus the larger, the more densely populated, and the more heterogeneous a community, the more accentuated the characteristics associated with urbanism will be. It should be recognized, however, that social institutions and practices may be accepted and continued for reasons other than those that originally brought them into existence, and that accordingly the urban mode of life may be perpetuated under conditions quite foreign to those necessary for its origin . . .

A number of sociological propositions concerning the relationship between (a) numbers of population, (b) density of settlement, (c) heterogeneity of inhabitants and group life can be formulated on the basis of observation and research.

Size of the Population Aggregate

Ever since Aristotle's *Politics*, it has been recognized that increasing the number of inhabitants in a settlement beyond a certain limit will affect the relationships between them and the character of the city. Large numbers involve, as has been pointed out, a greater range of individual variation. Furthermore, the greater the number of individuals participating in a process of interaction, the greater is the *potential* differentiation between them. The personal traits, the occupations, the cultural life, and the ideas of the members of an urban community may, therefore, be expected to range between more widely separated poles than those of rural inhabitants.

That such variations should give rise to the spatial segregation of individuals according to colour, ethnic heritage, economic and social status, tastes and preferences, may readily be inferred. The bonds of kinship, of neighbourliness, and the sentiments arising out of living together for generations under a common folk tradition are likely to be absent or, at best, relatively weak in an aggregate the members of which have such diverse origins and backgrounds. Under such circumstances competition and formal control mechanisms furnish the substitutes for the bonds of solidarity that are relied upon to hold a folk society together.

Increase in the number of inhabitants of a community beyond a few hundred is bound to limit the possibility of each member of the community knowing all the others personally ... The multiplication of persons in a state of interaction under conditions which make their contact as full personalities impossible produces that segmentalization of human relationships which has sometimes been seized upon by students of the mental life of the cities as an explanation for the 'schizoid' character of urban personality. This is not to say that the urban inhabitants have fewer acquaintances than rural inhabitants, for the reverse may actually be true; it means rather that in relation to the number of people whom they see and with whom they rub elbows in the course of daily life, they know a smaller proportion, and of these they have less intensive knowledge.

Characteristically, urbanites meet one another in highly segmental roles. They are, to be sure, dependent upon more people for the satisfactions of their life-needs than are rural people and thus are associated with a great number of organized groups, but they are less dependent upon particular persons, and their dependence upon others is confined to a highly fractionalized aspect of the other's round of activity. This is essentially what is meant by saying that the city is characterized be secondary rather than primary contacts. The contacts of the city may indeed be face to face, but they are nevertheless impersonal, superficial, transitory, and segmental. The reserve, the indifference, and the blasé outlook which urbanites manifest in their relationships may thus be regarded as devices for immunizing themselves against the personal claims and expectations of others ...

In a community composed of a larger number of individuals than can know one another intimately and can be assembled in one spot, it becomes necessary to communicate through indirect media and to articulate individual interests by a process of delegation. Typically in the city, interests are made effective through representation. The individual counts for little, but the voice of the representative is heard with a deference roughly proportional to the numbers for whom he speaks . . .

Density

As in the case of numbers, so in the case of concentration in limited space certain consequences of relevance in sociological analysis of the city emerge. Of these only a few can be indicated . . .

On the subjective side, as Simmel has suggested, the close physical contact of numerous individuals necessarily produces a shift in the media through which we orient ourselves to the urban milieu, especially to our fellow men. Typically, our physical contacts are close but our social contacts are distant. The urban world puts a premium on visual recognition. We see the uniform which denotes the role of the functionaries, and are oblivious to the personal eccentricities hidden behind the uniform. We tend to acquire and develop a sensitivity to a world of artefacts, and become progressively farther removed from the world of nature.

We are exposed to glaring contrasts between splendour and squalor, between riches and poverty, intelligence and ignorance, order and chaos. The competition for space is great, so that each area generally tends to be put to the use which yields the greatest economic return. Place of work tends to become dissociated from place of residence, for the proximity of industrial and commercial establishments makes an area both economically and socially undesirable for residential purposes . . . The different parts of the city acquire specialized functions, and the city consequently comes to resemble a mosaic of social worlds in which the transition from one to the other is abrupt. The juxtaposition of divergent personalities and modes of life tends to produce a relativistic perspective and a sense of toleration of differences which may be regarded as prerequisites of rationality and which lead toward the secularization of life . . .

Heterogeneity

The social interaction among such a variety of personality types in the urban milieu tends to break down the rigidity of caste lines and to complicate the class structure; it thus induces a more ramified and differentiated framework of social stratification than is found in more integrated societies. The heightened mobility of the individual, which brings him within the range of stimulation by a great number of diverse individuals and subjects him to fluctuating status in the differentiated social groups that compose the social structure of the city, brings him toward the acceptance of instability and insecurity in the world at large as a norm. This fact helps to account too, for the sophistication and cosmopolitanism of the urbanite. No single group has the undivided allegiance of the individual. The groups with which he is affiliated do not lend themselves readily to a simple hierarchical arrangement. By virtue of his different interests arising out of different aspects of social life, the individual acquires membership in widely divergent groups, each of which functions only with reference to a certain segment of his personality. Nor do these groups easily permit of a concentric arrangement so that the narrower ones fall within the circumference of the more inclusive ones, as is more likely to be the case in the rural community or in primitive societies. Rather the groups with which the person typically is affiliated are tangential to each other or intersect in highly variable fashion.

Partly as a result of the physical footlooseness of the population and partly as a result of their social mobility, the turnover in group membership generally is rapid. Place of residence, place and character of employment, income, and interests fluctuate, and the task of holding organizations together and maintaining and promoting intimate and lasting acquaintanceship between the members is difficult. This applies strikingly to the local areas within the city into which persons become segregated more by virtue of differences in race, language, income, and social status than through choice or positive attraction to people like themselves. Overwhelmingly the city-dweller is not a home-owner, and since a transitory habitat does not generate binding traditions and sentiments, only rarely is he a true neighbour. There is little opportunity for the individual to obtain a conception of the city as a whole or to survey his place in the total scheme.

Consequently he finds it difficult to determine what is to his own 'best interests' and to decide between the issues and leaders presented to him by the agencies of mass suggestion. Individuals who are thus detached from the organized bodies which integrate society comprise the fluid masses that make collective behaviour in the urban community so unpredictable and hence so problematical . . .

Reduced to a stage of virtual impotence as an individual, the urbanite is bound to exert himself by joining with others of similar interest into groups organized to obtain his ends. This results in the enormous multiplication of voluntary organizations directed toward as great a variety of objectives as there are human needs and interests. While, on the one hand, the traditional ties of human association are weakened, urban existence involves a much greater degree of interdependence between man and man and a more complicated, fragile, and volatile form of mutual interrelations over many phases of which the individual as such can exert scarcely any control. Frequently there is only the most tenuous relationship between the economic position or other basic factors that determine the individual's existence in the urban world and the voluntary groups with which he is affiliated. In a primitive and in a rural society it is generally possible to predict on the basis of a few known factors who will belong to what and who will associate with whom in almost every relationship of life, but in the city we can only project the general pattern of group formation and affiliation, and this pattern will display many incongruities and contradictions . . .

Since for most group purposes it is impossible in the city to appeal individually to the large number of discrete and differentiated citizens, and since it is only through the organizations to which men belong that their interests and resources can be enlisted for a collective cause, it may be inferred that social control in the city should typically proceed through formally organized groups. It follows, too, that the masses of men in the city are subject to manipulation by symbols and stereotypes managed by individuals working from afar or operating invisibly behind the scenes through their control of the instruments of communication. Self-government either in the economic, or political, or the cultural realm is under these circumstances reduced to a mere figure of speech, or, at best, is subject to the unstable equilibrium of pressure groups. In view of the ineffectiveness of actual kinship ties, we create fictional kinship groups.

In the face of the disappearance of the territorial unit as a basis of social solidarity, we create interest units. Meanwhile the city as a community resolves itself into a series of tenuous segmental relationships superimposed upon a territorial base with a definite centre but without a definite periphery, and upon a division of labour which far transcends the immediate locality and is world-wide in scope.

41   Scott Greer

The Community of Limited Liability

Excerpts from Scott Greer, *The Emerging City*, Collier Macmillan, 1962, pp. 98–106.

The local area today . . . particularly in the metropolis . . . is necessarily what Janowitz calls a 'community of limited liability'. The individual's investment is relatively small in the interactional network that constitutes the locality group, and if his losses are too great he can cut them by getting out – the community cannot hold him. Even among the most community-oriented, 'small-town-like' areas within the metropolis, there is great variation in the importance of the local area to the individual. The local merchants have more of a stake than the home-owning residents with children, and these have more invested than the couple without children who rent an apartment (though the latter are very rare in such neighbourhoods). However, even the most deeply involved can withdraw from the local community and satisfy all needs elsewhere – and the withdrawal need not be physical.

The older definition of community posited a spatially defined social aggregate that is a powerful social group. Such groups exist only when there is functional interdependence (as the local community in the suburbs is most necessary to its merchants, least so to the childless couple who rent their dwelling). Interdependence, in turn, means commitment to the ongoing social system. Such interdependence and commitment produce intensive participation and the development of common values and norms. Constraint, in this sense, is the key to community.

If this is true, then the great degree of freedom for individual location and action in large-scale society makes the 'primary community' impossible. Exceptions occur only in a few survivals, such as the Appalachian backwoods, or institutional aggregates such as the prison, monastery, and army. Aside from these atypical collectives, however, there *are* groups in which the individual must interact continuously and for a large share of his waking life. Most important is the work organization . . .

Thus, the major organizational segment of society that orders work is unable to supply the basis for primary community. The local area is functionally weak. The kinship system is important, but in a 'privatized' manner. The remaining possible structure for individual participation is the formal voluntary organization. A brief review of the findings cited earlier, however, indicates that such organizations are relatively unimportant at the grass roots. They are arenas for intensive participation to only a small minority of their members; many urban individuals have no formal organizational membership at all . . .

It is apparent that, in a society with a democratic political structure and ideology, democratic social processes are relatively rare. Shared decision-making, control through consent, is probably most common in the kinship and friendship groups, but it is hardly transmitted through them to larger entities. The other areas where individual participation is possible, the local community and the formal organization, engage only a minority in more than token participation, and the organizations of work — most important of all in many respects — are structurally unfit for democratic processes as work is organized in our society. The following picture of participation in metropolitan society results.

There are a plethora of formal organizations, labour, unions, business and professional groups, churches and church–related groups, parent–teacher associations, and the like. They exert pressure and they influence the political party — another formal organization. However, the leadership in such organizations is largely professionalized and bureaucratized, and such leaders become, in effect, oligarchs. At the same time the members participate in an extremely erratic manner, and frequently 'stay away in droves' from the meetings. The organization is a holding company for the members' interests; they exercise an occasional veto right in the plebiscites.

The local area is not a community in any sense, in the highly urban parts of the city; it is a community 'of limited liability' in the suburbs. Communication and participation are as apt to be segmental as in any formal organization that is extraterritorial. And many are utterly uninvolved, even in the strongest spatially defined communities.

Formal government is highly bureaucratized and, aside from votes in national elections and (occasionally) in local elections, the individual participates very little. Most party clubs are made up of professionals, semi-professionals, a handful of actives, and a large majority of paper members.

The organization of work is non-democratic in its control structure and the individual's participation is largely a matter of conforming to directions and implementing decisions made far above him in the hierarchy. This is of basic importance, for, with the rise of professional leadership in all formal organizations – from labour unions to Boy Scouts, the most intense participation in all groups is apt to be that of the official, for whom the organization is his *job* in a job hierarchy.

Thus, interpreting the participation of the average individual in the polity of metropolitan society is a somewhat bizarre experience. By and large he does not participate. Since this is true, it is difficult to make a case for the widespread importance of the democratic processes in the everyday behaviour of most people except in the home and friendship circle. The democracy we inhabit is, instead, largely a democracy of substantive freedoms, or freedom from restraint. Produced by struggles among various professionally directed interest groups, largely quite undemocratic in their control processes, freedom of choice for the individual is something of a by-product. It exists through the balance of countervailing forces, in work, at the market-place, and in government.

This freedom is, however, a considerable area of the average person's life space. It is manifest in the metropolitan resident's ability to choose marriage or single status, children or not, large family or small. It is also apparent in his freedom to choose his local residential area, and his degree of participation in its social structure – his life-style. He may privatize his non-working world and turn inward to his single-family dwelling unit and his conjugal family (which he does); he may refuse to participate in many public activities and yield only a token participation in others (and he does).

Though his commitments to the job and the family are constant and have a priority in time and energy, he exercises freedom of choice – in the market, the large sphere which Riesman calls consumership. He also has a freedom in the symbol spheres that has never been widespread before in any society – the variety of media and of messages are overwhelming. There are some one thousand hours of television available each week to the Los Angeles resident. His relative wealth, literacy, and privacy allow an exploration of meaning never possible before to the rank and file of any society. In his home life he experiments with leisure. The hobby industries, the do-it-yourself industries, the flood of specialized publications and programmes, bear testimony to the increasing use the urbanite makes of this opportunity. He is part of the *nouveaux riches* of leisure.

His wealth is a result of the increasing social surplus, produced by advancing technologies of energy transformation and social organization. It is a surplus of material products, of time, and of symbols. His rise is also a measure of the levelling of the hierarchical orders. Their remnants persist, in the relatively higher rates of competence, participation and leadership for the upper social ranks in most of the formal organizations. Most people, however, are the descendants, and in some respects, equivalents, of the illiterates of a hundred years ago. They have neither the vested interest in, nor the tradition of responsible participation in the life of the polity. And they have great freedom from forced participation in work. They exercise it in fashioning the typical life patterns adumbrated, in avoiding organizations, politely giving lip service to the neighbours and local community leaders, avoiding work associates off the job, orienting themselves toward evenings, weekends, and vacations. These they spend *en famille*, travelling, looking at television, gossiping and eating with friends and kin, and cultivating the garden.

The bureaucratic leadership and the plebiscitary membership, the community of limited liability and the privatized citizen, are not images most Americans hold of a proper democratic society. On the other hand, the picture is less frightening than that of the atomistic man adrift in mass society, anomic and destructive. Furthermore, the ideal picture of participation in the primary political community is a strenuous one. Perhaps a revision downward, toward effective communities of limited liability and effective plebiscites might be more congruent with the organizational structure of large-scale society.

42   G. D. Suttles

The Social Construction of Community

Excerpts from G. D. Suttles, *The Social Construction of Community*, University of Chicago Press, Chicago, 1972, pp. 233–5, 246–7, 256–7, 264–8.

One of the aims of the volume has been to approach the local residential urban community as a response of territorial populations to their environment rather than to look at it as a vestigial remnant of a more fragmented and localized society. This approach takes us in a number of directions, three of which seem most promising: the community as a territorial basis for associational selection; the community as an identity which distinguishes it from the other territorial and non-territorial populations; and the community as an object of administration . . . My hope, however, is not to construct some sharply delineated urban communities but to centre on the processes of community differentiation which do not always yield well-defined territorial units . . .

The Community as a Territorial Basis for Associational Selection

It is probably self-evident that residential proximity creates its own dangers and difficulties of social control. People who are close at hand are impossible to avoid; they can teach your children dirty habits, abuse your daughter, throw cigarette butts in your doorway, or snatch your wife's purse on her way home from downtown. Understandably, people want to live in a 'good area' where they feel reasonably safe and are a known distance from those people they distrust. They also want to know something about how far the 'good area' extends so that they can say something definite about how far their children can go when they play, how far away to park the car for the night, and a multitude of petty day-to-day decisions which require that we break the city up into more or less trustworthy areas.

To arrive at such discrete areas, residents may consult with their neighbours, rely on stereotypes conveyed in the newspapers, or individually foresee the dangers to passage as they cross impersonal domains or no-man's-lands. It does not take a highly imaginative person to invent such boundaries, for they derive from his most primitive notions of how space, distance, and movement have inevitable and universal meanings. Individuals who share an arm's length of space are vulnerable to one another, and this is a lesson learned early and widely. Movement away from or toward one another must be endowed with intent and motive, or else the individual will not survive long in the traffic of life. To openly move closer to one individual than another conveys affect and sentiment, and the person who fails to find this out will certainly fail to express one form of affect which is essential to all societies. It is out of such primitive conceptions of space, distance, and movement that the community – and other spatial groupings – is constructed. We are not speaking here of native or inborn conceptions but of universal cultural forms which are required by the mechanics of life itself. The quest for a good community is, among other things, a quest for a neighbourhood where one does not fear standing an arm's length from his neighbour, where one can divine the intent of someone heading down the sidewalk, or where one can share expressions of affect by the way adjacent residences dress up for mutual impression management.

Decisions like this about an area require us to draw distinctions among areas and ultimately boundaries between them. The ideal boundary is the physical obstruction across which danger and traffic cannot advance at all. There are, of course, no such boundaries in a modern city, but there are fair approximations in some of our expressways, elevated lines, blocks of industry, rivers, and so on. An alternative is to select strips such as vacant land or rail lines where people 'have no business' and, since they are inhabited only by trespassers, are dangerous places to cross. Obviously such obstructions are not always available nor do they always draw a significant boundary between noticeably different populations. What often happens, then, is that rather arbitrary streets, passageways, or some kind of physical marker are hit upon as a point beyond which the gradation in what people are like is said to make a qualitative change. The problem is not too much unlike that of a teacher who must take a continuous sequence of exam scores and decide on a cutting point between those who pass and those who fail. The choice is a familiar one, somewhat arbitrary, but necessary . . .

Community Identity

Elsewhere I have argued that the identities of local neighbourhoods exist in tenuous opposition to one another and that relative rather than absolute differences give them their distinctive reputation. Obviously the main lines of differentiation are the dimensions of stratification which are pervasive to the entire society: race, ethnicity, income, education, and the like. Indeed most communities in the United States can be and are described in these terms. Ethnically and racially homogeneous neighbourhoods are perhaps the most obvious examples, but far less distinctive neighbourhoods find a marginal difference to emphasize and to distinguish between 'us' and 'them'. The difficulty in establishing a neighbourhood's identity, however, is not a shortage of relevant differences but a surplus of them. Even the small list given above shows that the problem is not a simple one and that almost any neighbourhood is distinguished from others on more than one dimension. What I will do here is to map out what seem to be some of the governing conditions for the final determination of a local neighbourhood's reputation . . .

The Community as an Object of Administration

The community is a perennial referent in the rhetoric of politicians, administrators, and sociologists. The politicians pay it eloquent tribute and say that they represent it. Administrators say they serve it. Some sociologists deny the veracity of the politicians and administrators and say only that the community is declining. Is the local community declining and has it lost its *raison d'être*, or has it at least lost out in the power plays which have juxtaposed the state against the community? This is the central question which lumbers throughout most studies of the local community. Before attempting to face the question head on, it is worthwhile to restate a couple of basic observations. First, total societies are not made up from a series of communities, but communities are units which come into being through their recognition by a wider society. Community, then, presumes some type of supracommunity level of organization.

Second, the community is not a little society but a form of social differentiation within total societies, and the problem is how appropriate this type of social differentiation is in modern societies . . .

The Community as Communion

So far I have taken a narrow view of the local urban community by regarding it as the defended neighbourhood which segregates people to avoid danger, insult, and the impairment of status claims. This is, I think, a sufficient basis for explaining community differentiation, but it is not all that communities are or become. Part of my emphasis has been a reaction to the over-romanticization of the local community and the tendency to make sentiments and sentimentalism so basic to it that the community could later be dismissed as only an expressive solidarity without instrumental functions. But, like all other institutions, the local community attracts to itself additional hopes for the expression of self and sentiment. The desire to find a social setting in which one can give rein to an authentic version of oneself and see other people as they really are is not some unanalysable human need but the most fundamental way in which people are reassured of their own reality as well as that of other people. A Goffmanesque world in which people do only what is situationally suitable is ultimately a frightening world, where hypocrisy and insincerity undermine any long-term plans and the people behave as chameleons once backs are turned. Every society rides on the faith that some of the people some of the time really mean what they say and do. The organization man, the other-oriented individual, and a society of labels are insufficient images if people are to trust one another long enough to get through a single day. Presentations of self, then, are not mere ways of letting off steam: they are essential expressive interludes when group members re-establish each other's confidence in the coincidence between subjective and objective realities.

Within this context the local community stands out as a symbol in people's hopes for a collectivity in which they can be rather than seem. Indeed this seems to be a predominant contemporary use of the symbolism of the community and the constant attempts to make other institutions into communities by labelling them as such (the community of scholars, and so forth). Among Americans this quest for community reaches almost pathetic proportions, with people falling victim to the most romantic advertisements for homes which attempt to give an imitation of a bygone age with Tudor cottages, Cape Cod fronts, and plantation porticoes attached to modest bungalows. The search for tree-lined streets, for a small community, and for a quiet place to live are in part a search for collectivities which at least have the earmarks of a place for the authentic moral expression of self. There is a certain irony in this symbolism because the original meaning which Tönnies gave community or *Gemeinschaft* emphasized its ascriptive character and independence of sentiments except as people adapted to necessity. This meaning lingers in sociology, and the freedom of people to move and be indifferent to their residential group seems almost antithetical to the traditional local community. Indeed, community seems to have undergone a transformation in the minds of Americans, and what people see in it is not Tönnies's community but Schmalenbach's communion. The community is a place to share feelings and expose one's tender inner core. The freedom of people (or at least some people) to choose where they live is an essential ingredient to this meaning of the local community. Communion rests on its voluntariness, and as Schmalenbach pointed out, it was antithetical to the traditional community which coerced membership and loyalty. With the loss of the ascribed local community, the entire concept is transformed into a sort of social movement for relations which are intimate enough to be self-revealing.

Although this is a growing symbolic representation of the local community, I suspect that it is poorly realized in most actual communities. To a large extent Americans still live where they have to and, in any case, have to move so often that the community of limited liability is the most prevalent form. The coerciveness of the workplace and other institutions not only creates a yearning for community but makes it difficult to realize in the residential community. Thus people seek for alternatives in other institutions: the student community, the political community, the business community, and so on. The extent to which these other institutions can offer either communion or community is limited by their institutional dependencies. They cannot be fully liberated and continue to function. The focus of the desire for community, then, will probably continue to return to the local residential community, and if people seem shallow and inauthentic elsewhere, the pressure for a community of sentiment may increase . . .

In the context of [the] excessive vision of the local community, it is important to keep in mind the limited role of the local community. The local community can share some of the burden of making available to people the opportunity for communion, but this is a burden widely distributed in any society. It also has the potential to serve as a consolidated, all-purpose, administrative unit which could go far toward rejoining power and responsibility between the various levels of government and their constituencies. As a localized group of people whose placement in a national or local system of stratification warrants mutual trustworthiness, the local community can also give people a sense of security and ease. The local residential group can also be a collective identity, drawing the proofs of its members' pride from the past or the future. I suspect, however, that it is troublesome if not impossible to freeze the local residential group into its present form as dictated by contemporary restrictive residential selection. The local community must remain a partially open institution, and its rights cannot be insured as are those of racial and ethnic groups where membership is fixed and persistent. As a part or the whole of an administrative unit, the local residential community can survive, perhaps even thrive. By acknowledging its limitations, we might be able to use it for what it is: first, as a reflection of our changing system of social stratification so that strangers who are neighbours can trust one another, and second, as a small world within which people who are generally distrusted can find trust on more provincial grounds.

43   Cynthia Cockburn

Community and the Local State

Excerpts from Cynthia Cockburn, *The Local State*, Pluto Press, 1977, pp. 159–64.

'Community' Belongs to Capital

The phrase that has come to be used to describe almost any collective action going on outside the workplace is 'community action'. It rings with implausibility. Why? All through this discussion I've avoided the term, only using the word 'community' where the state has chosen to use it. This was for a reason. It is not the activity, so much as the CATEGORY that needs questioning. It is not just a question of using or not using a form of expression, but of *thinking* with it. I'll suggest four reasons – three of which are fundamental and one tactical. All are related.

First, to think in terms of community action places struggle on ground prepared, over a long historical period, by the state. It takes a shape that is expected, anticipated and even proposed by the state. In a sense (to use an ecological metaphor) the state is the environment that offers a vacant 'niche', a milieu that will reward and foster a certain kind of behaviour, and the fledgling initiatives of struggle step in to fill it.

The local electoral representative system has been, since its inception, based on territorial definition of interest group. The local councillor represents the ward, wards are grouped into constituencies, constituencies into boroughs. More recently the local services of councils, too, have decentralized themselves, partially, into area teams and area offices, again using territory as the basis for this organization. In recent years, and in some boroughs, not only is there a ward councillor and an area housing manager and several other officials on the spot to relate to whatever 'community' may arise – there is a community worker too. They have even revamped the local bobby into the community policeman. When territorial working-class community groups arise there is a set of officers and councillors, in a sense waiting for them, to whom the community group is of vital relevance and who have their own preconceptions which they will bring to bear on its activities.

One effect of the presence of a ward councillor and a community worker in the territory is to encourage the idea that problems arise in 'officialdom' – because this is something that they both know something about and are ready to tackle. 'The expression that workers and peasants initially give to their discontent is generally diffuse and fragmentary and it often moves into a simple anti-authoritarianism such as "dislike of officialdom" – the only form in which the state is perceived.' If discontent is addressed against the local bureaucracy and the top politicians (the Labour leadership) that join with them in urban management, the answer is too easily seen as lying with the ward councillor of left-wing or populist sympathies. And this, as I'll suggest below, has its dangers for collective action.

The second, related, argument, against relying on a concept of 'community action' is that it has been closely connected since its rise to popularity in the late sixties with consumer protection. It tends to cast us in the role of consumers (of capital's products and the state's services), a position that is economically and politically weak. What has been called community action has been rationalized as something that arises NOT from capitalism itself, but from some of the more unfortunate but curable effects of the current stage of technological development. 'We all suffer at the hands of large and insensitive organizations and we are all emotionally stunted by the amorphous uniformity of the cosmopolitan culture to which we belong' – that is the way it is commonly put. Selma James put her finger on what is happening: 'we have inherited a distorted and reformist concept of capital itself as a series of things which we struggle to plan, control or manage, rather than as a social relation which we struggle to destroy'. Community action points not to deficiencies in the mode of production but in the products: the goods or services.

Third, community action is all too often defined as classless. In common usage it is a populist formulation, open to all classes, groups and interests. Where it *is* defined to exclude 'the middle class' it is none the less normally focused not on the working class as such but on 'the deprived', 'the poor' or even the 'poor-poor'. In other words, it bites off what the Victorians called the residuum, the problem-fraction of the people, and distinguishes it from the 'real' working-class. This splintering is reflected in the bourgeois ideology of pluralism and participatory democracy, the essence of which is that no one group in society should be too *big*. There is in the idea of community action the idea of smallness up against bigness. We are asked to think of the David of one small council estate taking on the Goliath of the town hall. 'Small is beautiful.' It is an image which totally rules out the reality of class struggle, in which huge and powerful forces are ranged against each other, not momentarily, but over centuries. It imposes blinkers which stop one working-class group looking to another with similar problems as its natural ally and leads to a situation where groups in neighbourhood territories struggle in competition for the limited resources offered them – a situation often exploited by a local council.

Bernard Greaves, an enthusiast of community action, illustrates this close link between territorial organizations and classlessness. He describes a universal movement, developing as its main power-base residential neighbourhood communities. Among their 'crucial assets' is the following. 'They are socially unifying. Taking over existing power structures is inevitably divisive and leads to such destructive and dangerous concepts as the class war. Building alternative communities enables people of different backgrounds, whether of class, income, employment or whatever, to enter into new relationships on a basis of cooperation deriving from the discovery of a sense of common identity.' The rhetoric of community action here is indistinguishable from the state's own community package. The function of such community action is the maintenance of membership in a capitalist social formation, class positions firmly held though culturally muted.

The fourth (tactical) point is essentially an illustration of the first. The national political parties are now using community action and community politics for competitive *electoral* purposes . . .

If 'community action', then, is not a helpful concept to describe working-class struggle outside the job situation, what is? There have been attempts to place it in a historical situation going back to the Diggers and Levellers of the bourgeois revolution of the seventeenth century, to Tom Paine and to Bakunin and the anarchists. This doesn't get us much further. It identifies these struggles with a particular libertarian tendency in revolutionary socialism. There is an important insistence on experience and autonomy; on 'prefigurative' struggle, including the ends among the means of action; a rejection of leadership and of the imposition of theoretical demands that don't spring from day-to-day working-class understanding . . .

Since many of the issues arising in communities arise in the state services, there is a case for defining our action as anti-state struggles. But to do so deflects attention away from the mode of production, which is the real cause of exploitation. It tends to give the state too much importance and apparent detachment from the economic base.

Shifting the Emphasis to Reproduction

What then? There is no simple catch phrase. I believe we have to rely clearly and simply on the analysis of the local state that we are attempting; we have to see that what we are involved in is *struggle in the field of capitalist reproduction*. We have to recognize that alongside struggle at the point of production, in the mines and factories, there is struggle at the point of reproduction, in schools, on housing estates, in the street, in the family.

This definition is a strong one because it immediately brings into the field of action, alongside 'client' action by residents on housing, patients' action on health services, etc., the *workers employed by the state*, both professional and manual. Furthermore, it identifies the significance of the action of *women in the home*, in privatized reproduction.

A number of other insights follow. Now we see the inseparable nature of production and reproduction in capitalism we can also see the inseparability of industrial struggle and action over reproductive services such as housing. It also shows us ways of making the connections that are so badly needed between the two. Even the male worker now recognizes that, when he went home with his wage packet formerly he was expected to 'reproduce' his own labour power with it – pay his rent, pay his doctor, insure himself through his provident fund. If now the state takes on some of these responsibilities, it is because he has established this right through struggle. The social services have become an intrinsic part of his wage: the social wage. In part, too, the cost of them has been recouped by the state in the increased tax and insurance contributions that he pays. Struggles around housing or benefits or schools are *economic*, as well as 'merely' political. Those things too must be protected against the erosions of inflation and the pressure of profit . . .

Second, it underpins changes in the nature of workplace struggles too. These are coming to be extended to take account not just of wages and conditions but of that part of life where reproduction goes on – life at home. Working mothers are never likely to make the mistake of seeing higher pay as the only, or even the main, demand. For them the most important thing is that the conditions of paid work respond, when necessary, to the needs of children, to take account of sickness and so on. It will force on to the agenda of workplace action the reproductive issues that should be there. An example for instance is agency work by temporary secretaries and agency nurses. Traditional workers' action resists the introduction of agency staff into a firm or institution because their presence weakens the position of employees. Yet these agency staff are often working mothers who are in this form of employment because their re-productive job at home means they *need* flexible hours and terms of work that employers themselves will not provide. What they do *not* need is to be employed in a structure that causes them to compete with organized labour: it is employers alone who benefit from that. Recognition of an issue like this can extend workplace struggle to a wider solidarity.

44 Isabel Emmett
Place and Community

Community as Complexity

The contrast between the man-made scenery of the town [Blaenau Ffestiniog] and the more conventionally acceptable beauty of the mountainous setting is paralleled by a contrast between the rough surface and rich content of the life of the face-to-face community living in it.

The work done by many of the townsmen is heavy and dangerous, and the life of the community has a tough, rough reputation and indeed a tough, rough surface. Beneath that surface lies a living tradition of love of poetry and song, of articulate, often well-read discussions and arguments . . .

The town boasts a music society, band, choirs of renown, discussion groups, clubs for badminton, squash, rugby and Association Football, and the numerous voluntary organizations found in most towns in Britain. In addition, however, here as elsewhere, an important part of the town's life takes place in the pubs. The lack of adequate leisure facilities, the cost and inadequacy of public transport and the nature and history of the town make the pubs the major sociable venue. Some hard drinking takes place, but it is also true that more than one teetotaller frequents them, and drinkers who are not in the mood for alcohol commonly sip orange juice or lemonade, and chat; members of most of the voluntary organizations meet each other and the non-joiners in the pub: all part of the scene.

To incomers, Welsh and English, at least at first, that scene is experienced as relatively simple. The town is a place where a walk along the high street is very likely to involve you in an encounter which is more than a polite passing of the time of day but is part of some continuous sequence of interactions: pursuit of a quarrel, cultivation of a friendship, exchange of gossip, arranging a children's tea party, a meeting, a game or outing or job of work, a purchase, a lift. Terms used to describe the community are 'friendly', 'feel at home', 'feel part of things'.

However, for natives, community is more complex. As Cohen suggests, the way in which sociologists and anthropologists divide societies into complex and simple is misleading. Those who have grown up in the town have such a wealth of knowledge of each other as to make each encounter densely elaborate. Men and women are known as parents, as drinkers or non-drinkers, as singers and speakers, in some version of their work records and in some version of their record as lovers, since in many cases when the affair is over the ex-lovers are likely to continue to come across each other in other roles and other social contexts. Over the course of their lifetime men and women in their seventies will have gone on meeting or passing in the street most of those they have ever kissed, most of those they have ever quarrelled with, and many of those they have ever worked with. Every aspect of their life is used in the picture others have of them, but the knowledge varies from member to member of their community, each of whom has a different composite version of their different facets. Further, the partial nature of the various versions is also known. One women said of another, with whom she periodically played darts, 'Whenever I play darts with her I remember that she pinched my bag when we were in the infants.' It is possible that the second player did not have the same memory when she played darts with the first.

In cities it is relatively easy for men and women to decide on the 'self' they will present to a new lover, friend, colleague or social group. In a face-to-face community fellow actors have so great a hold on one by their knowledge that there is little room for such a manoeuvre.

My first strong sense of this complexity of community life occurred in a grocery shop in which I was one of the dozen or so customers waiting to be served. The shopkeeper, Twm, was serving a young woman, Bethan, who had been 'going with' him some time earlier. At that period Bethan had helped him behind the counter, as most but not all of us knew. Now there was a new young lady 'going with' him and helping him behind the counter, and she was ignorant of

Bethan's significance in Twm's life, having come from outside the district. Bethan asked Twm if he had a certain item, and he replied, both using the formal 'you' rather than the 'thou' of their earlier times together. Then Bethan bent to her shopping basket for her list and Twm looked quickly at her. Those of us in the know read in his look some comparison, some tinge of regret or at least doubt as to whether the change in girlfriends had been for the best. The glances between us showed us, among other things, to be aware of our knowing; aware of some of the customers not knowing; aware of the new young lady not knowing; and conscious of some humour in the situation. And all the 'knowing' was partial, was a version of the records of the two main actors as workers and lovers and other things.

This is a simple and simplified example of the density of community life. In encounter after encounter, in a very large proportion of the talk, the term 'double meaning' is totally inadequate to convey the density of meanings, cross-references, awareness of ignorance here, a layer of knowledge there, and double, triple, quadruple layers of knowledge and understanding. Words can seldom be taken at face value. And of course very much of the communication uses no words.

Those who leave the town enter into social relationships which, in respect of the matters here described, must be relatively flat and shallow.

The degree of knowledge of each other which small-town people have, the lack of privacy, can be and often is oppressive and felt as constraining. At times the anonymity of a large city seems immensely attractive. But the shared knowledge of a particular place and its people enables all members to participate in a continuous fashioning and telling of the story of the place. This cooperative creation of an oral history is one of the important things that is going on, one of the important things that people in a community are doing; that which gives depth and complexity and therefore a particular value to community life. It is not a matter of people preferring to be big fish in a small pond rather than small fish in the big ponds of London or Birmingham . . . Everyone has a part in recognizably the same play which they are jointly performing and making a record of: amending each other's versions, bringing each other up to date, reliving past events, recalling past characters. Blaenau is small and compact, several miles from any neighbouring town; everyone's behaviour, dress and speech are to some degree part of a public performance; the pavements of the high street, the main shops and the pubs part of the stage.

As a member of small networks each man and woman lives and tells sub-plots. The crises of the town — the burning of holiday cottages; the declaration of an expert that half the high street was in danger from rock cliffs above it shifting; the months of immense noise and dust when the rubble of one slate tip was removed and spread on boggy land; the coming of the narrow-gauge railway; the big court cases; the long delays over the opening of the community centre; the fears of an 'Aberfan' catastrophe in the severe floods — evoke opposing reactions and opinions but interest and affect most of the inhabitants.

Gossip and talk and all the non-verbal communication are used not only to create this oral history of the town. They are used to include and exclude; to pass time and entertain; to judge and constrain others; to confer and deny favours; indeed, as precious currency: the commodity exchanged most; a large part of the raw material from which social relationships are created.

To those who regard the use of the word community as a commitment to romanticism it is perhaps worth pointing to the humdrum nature of the content of community life. The content of the story is for the most part as commonplace as the goings on in Ambridge or Coronation Street. In Blaenau the story is of work, courting, singing, fishing, children, drinking, troubles, watching television, journeys by foot, car or bike, politics, struggle, fighting, friendships, birth, death, illnesses and recoveries.

To those who deny any meaning to the word it is worth saying that to live in a community is a very different experience from living in a collection of dwelling places, and in particular to live in a community is to know a more complex meaning in each social encounter than could be known elsewhere. The wit which is thus engendered gives rise to laughter of a different nature from that heard in common-room or city bar. To those who regard the use of the term community as evidence of a desire to 'preserve the *status quo*' I can only say that the *status quo* here and elsewhere both preserves itself and changes itself whatever the feelings of the observer.

Raymond Williams writes:

Community can be the warmly persuasive word to describe an existing set of relationships or the warmly persuasive word to describe an alternative set of relationships. What is most important, perhaps, is that unlike all other terms of social organization (state, nation, society, etc.), it seems never to be used unfavourably, and never to be given any positive opposing or distinguishing term.

In contemporary sociological literature, however, there is an amplification of his point to the degree that the term is seldom used other than unfavourably.

An account of life in a place where plain matters of fact are that people habitually exchange gifts and services without money payment; a strong value is put upon a life in which work, leisure and sociability merge; and in which a large proportion of the inhabitants value their complex familiarity with each other, is *read* and *heard* by many academics as 'romantic and nostalgic'. Equally plain matters of fact relating to high unemployment rates, poor housing, dangerous work, inefficient and/or corrupt local authorities and bleak economic prospects can be spelled out in the same paper, but fail to mend the distorted reception of the message, which as often comes from biased ears as from romantic authors.

Blaenau Ffestiniog, then, is a living community ... The complexity here described colours most of the lives of those who have grown up in the town; it is primarily their community.

P. Gilroy

Race and Community

Excerpts from P. Gilroy, *There Ain't No Black in the Union Jack*, Hutchinson, 1987, pp. 230–37, 246–7.

Manuel Castells' . . . theory of the distinctively urban dimensions of the new social movements which can contribute to the theorization of contemporary 'race' politics in this country . . . argues that urban social movements share some basic characteristics in spite of their obvious diversity. They consider themselves to be urban, citizen or related to the city in their self-denomination; they are locally based, territorially defined and they tend to mobilize around three central goals: 1 collective consumption; 2 cultural identity; 3 political self-management. Collective consumption refers to the goods and services directly or indirectly provided by the state; cultural identity becomes an issue where it is closely associated with a specific territory and is defended on that basis; and political self-management relates to the attempt by urban groups to win a degree of autonomy from the local governments which directly oversee their immediate environments providing use values, income and services.

Each of these features can be found in the recent history of Britain's black communities: struggles over the services provided by the state, particularly the quality of educational opportunities for black children have been intense; the cultural dimensions to the struggle of black inner-city dwellers have already been examined; and the demands of community organizations have repeatedly focused on the need to gain a degree of control over the processes which shape day-to-day experience. Local campaigns for police accountability, prompted by concern about the organization and role of the force in inner-city areas, perfectly illustrate the type of issue which falls in Castells' last category.

There are good grounds on which to argue that the language of community has displaced both the language of class and the language of 'race' in the political activity of black Britain. Though blacks identify themselves as an exploited and subordinated group, there are marked and important differences between the political cultures and identities of the various black communities which together make up the social movement. Local factors, reflecting the class, ethnic and 'racial' composition of any particular area, its political traditions, the local economy and residential structure may all play a decisive part in shaping precisely what it means to be black . . .

According to Castells, it is only when all three of these goals combine in the practice of an urban movement that social change can occur. The separation of any one goal from the others reduces the potential of the social movement and recasts it in the role of an interest group that may be 'moulded into the established institutions of society, so losing its impact'. He views these social movements as precarious, fragile collectivities which may be unable to fully accomplish all the projects promised by their organizational rhetoric. Their specific appeal and the popular power they represent cannot necessarily survive contact with the agencies of the state against which they struggle: 'they lose their identity when they become institutionalized, the inevitable outcome of bargaining for social reform within the political system'.

The theory of urban social movements correctly emphasizes that they are not ready-made agents for structural change but rather 'symptoms of resistance to domination'. They have their roots in a radical sense of powerlessness and though their resistances may have important effects on cities and societies, they are best understood as defensive organizations which are unlikely to be able to make the transition to more stable forms of politics. This lends these movements certain strengths as well as the obvious weaknesses. The Utopian strands in their ideology, which demand the immediate satisfaction of needs, require totalizing, historically feasible plans for economic production, communication and government. The movements are unlikely to be unable to supply these without losing the very qualities which make them dynamic and distinct. Their orientation towards local governments and political institutions, on the immediate conditions in which exploitation and domination are experienced, is a result of the simple fact that those whose grievances give the movements momentum have no other choice. They lack any sense of credible democracy other than the grassroots variety practised in their own organizations. As Castells puts it, 'When people find themselves unable to control the world, they simply shrink the world to the size of their community.' The 'politricks' of the system is replaced by an authentic, immediate politics . . .

For the social movement of blacks in Britain, the context in which these and other similar demands have been spontaneously articulated has been supplied by a political language premised on notions of community. Though it reflects the concentration of black people, the term refers to far more than mere place or population. It has a moral dimension and its use evokes a rich complex of symbols surrounded by a wider cluster of meanings. The historical memory of progress from slave to citizen actively cultivated in the present from resources provided by the past, endows it with an aura of tradition. Community, therefore, signifies not just a distinctive political ideology but a particular set of values and norms in everyday life: mutuality, cooperation, identification and symbiosis. For black Britain, all these are centrally defined by the need to escape and transform the forms of subordination which bring 'races' into being. Yet they are not limited by that objective. The disabling effects of racial categorization are themselves seen as symbols of the other unacceptable attributes of 'racial capitalism'. The evident autonomy of racism from production relations demands that the reappropriation of production is not pursued independently of the transformation of capitalist social relations as a whole. The social bond implied by use of the term 'community' is created in the practice of collective resistance to the encroachments of reification, 'racial' or otherwise. It prefigures that transformation in the name of a radical, democratic, anti-racist populism. [As Calhoun has observed,] this is not so much

a distinct set of political opinions as a mobilization of people who [share] a common understanding of how life ought to be. Not all of the people are mobilized at any one time but the mode of understanding [is] widespread.

The generalization of this mode of understanding coincides with the formation of what has already been called an interpretive community. It has been spread through distinctive communicative networks . . .

[A] cultural focus . . . requires that attention be paid to the symbolic dimensions of community. It is necessary, therefore, to briefly discuss the means by which community is constructed symbolically as part of, or in support of, the collective actions of a social movement. As Anthony Cohen points out:

... community might not have the structure or direction which we associate with social movements, it may nevertheless serve a similar need. It is a largely mental construct, whose 'objective' manifestations in locality or ethnicity give it credibility. It is highly symbolized, with the consequence that its members can invest it with their selves. Its character is sufficiently malleable that it can accommodate all of its members' selves without them feeling their individuality to be overly compromised. Indeed, the gloss of commonality which it paints over its diverse components gives to each of them an additional referent for their identities.

This definition of community depends on the distinction between symbols and meanings. The former are flexible vehicles for a variety of potentially contradictory readings which may be held by a movement's adherents. The idea of a social movement as an interpretive community should not lead to an undifferentiated monadical view of the group from which it wins active support. The strength of symbols is their multi-accentuality and malleability. Sharing a common body of symbols created around notions of 'race', ethnicity or locality, common history or identity does not dictate the sharing of the plural meanings which may become attached to those symbols and cluster around them.

Community is as much about difference as it is about similarity and identity. It is a relational idea which suggests, for British blacks at least, the idea of antagonism – domination and subordination between one community and another. The word directs analysis to the boundary between these groups. It is a boundary which is presented primarily by symbolic means and therefore a broad range of meanings can co-exist around it, reconciling individuality and commonality and competing definitions of what the movement is about. The political rhetoric of leaders is, after all, not a complete guide to the motivations and aspirations of those who play a less prominent role. In Cohen's words again:

just as the common form of the symbol aggregates the various meanings assigned to it, so the symbolic repertoire of a community aggregates the individualities and other differences found within the community and provides the means for their expression, interpretation and containment ... It continuously transforms the reality of difference into the appearance of similarity with such efficacy that people can still invest [their] community with ideological integrity. It unites them in their opposition, both to each other and to those 'outside'.

We [have already] examined some of the points at which closures have been introduced into the symbolic repertoire of black Britain. These can be identified where particular definitions of 'race' and nation or of the meaning attributed to skin colour have been invested with special significance by a group which tries to fix their reading of these symbols as a universal one capable of binding the whole community together. It bears repetition that these tensions are part of a political struggle inside the black communities over what 'race' adds up to.

Such conflicts are possible because black Britain's repertoire of symbols is relatively unfixed and still evolving. It includes the languages of Ethiopianism and Pan-Africanism and the heritage of anticolonial resistances as well as the inputs from contemporary urban conflicts. These diverse elements combine syncretically in struggles to reconstruct a collective historical presence from the discontinuous, fractured histories of the African and Asian diasporas. Multiple meanings have grouped around the central symbol of racial alterity – the colour black – and it is difficult to anticipate the outcome of the political struggle between the different tendencies they represent – ethnic absolutism on the one hand and a utopian, democratic populism on the other. Yet despite their differences, the 'black professional' in a local authority social services department, the Afro-Caribbean ancillary in a hospital and the hip-hopping Asian youth of West London may all discover within that colour a medium through which to articulate their own experiences and make sense of their common exclusion from Britain and Britishness. The actions of organizations of the urban social movement around 'race' may themselves assume symbolic significance. Particularly where people are mobilized to protest, innumerable political and ethical grievances, desires and aspirations may be condensed and unified in the symbolism which dissent provides . . .

In the present, studying the potency of racism and nationalism and observing the capability of movements formed around 'racial' subjectivities involves an examination of the social relations within which people act and their junctions with forms of politics which articulate themselves through historical memory's 'traditional' roots. 'Race' and its attendant imaginary politics of community, affect and kinship provides a contemporary example of how 'traditional' ties are created and re-created out of present rather than past conditions.

Taking on board C. L. R. James's important observation that 'there is nothing more to organize' because 'organization as we have known it is at an end' it is possible to comprehend how people can act socially and cohesively without the structures provided by formal organizations. Collective identities spoken through 'race', community and locality are, for all their spontaneity, powerful means to coordinate action and create solidarity. The constructed 'traditional' culture becomes a means to articulate personal autonomy with collective empowerment focused by a multi-accented symbolic repertoire and its corona of meanings.

Part Eight
Work, Industry and Organizations

Everyday discussions of 'work' typically refer to *paid* work, for an employer or on a self-employed basis. Until recently most sociological discussion has also shared this emphasis: the sociology of work has been predominantly the sociology of employment. During the last decade the limitations of this approach have been widely recognized and employment has come to be seen as only one way in which people's needs for goods and services can be met, a way which has specific features not necessarily shared by all forms of work. This broader definition of 'work', however, raises certain other problems: if almost any activity can be work, can the term be satisfactorily defined and delimited with any precision? Pahl's discussion (Reading 46) clearly places employment in the wider setting, though it also illustrates how varied conditions of employment may be. He shows how the meaning and significance of a simple task like ironing depend on the pattern of social relations in which it is embedded, and argues convincingly that work can only be defined and understood in the light of knowledge of its context.

Braverman (Reading 47) also sees work in this broader context, comparing human work with the instinctual activities of animals so as to identify what he sees as its crucial characteristic: the existence of and possibility of separating the two processes of *conception* and *execution*. Most of Braverman's discussion, however, focuses on the particular form work takes in a capitalist industrial society characterized by the buying and selling of labour power. This term refers to people's capacity to work, something which is variable and can only be realized over time in the process of producing goods or services. This conception of the employment relationship also emphasizes the antagonistic nature of the relations between capital and labour; and although Braverman is solely concerned with capitalist relations of production, such differences of interest between employer and employee over how the potential of human labour power is to be realized are, to a greater or lesser extent, seen as characteristic of all employment. He also draws attention to the fact that employers have to *manage* their employees if they are to secure the work for which wages or salaries are being paid. These two issues, the nature of the conflicting interests of employers and employees, and the problem of management, are developed in the following two readings.

Fox (Reading 48) develops a threefold account of the ways in which employer–employee relations in an enterprise or organization can be interpreted. He dismisses the *unitary* ideology of the enterprise as a 'team' or 'family' as inadequate in assuming common interests, and undesirable if such assumptions lead to the use of coercion to suppress dissent; but he also develops a critique of the more nearly adequate *pluralist* position. Pluralists recognize the diversity of interests contained within an employing organization but argue that such differences can be satisfactorily regulated and contained by mechanisms such as collective bargaining between managers and trade union representatives. The weakness of such an analysis lies in its failure to recognize the major disparities of power between employers and employees. Indeed pluralist arguments are seen by Fox as in part 'ideological', in that they contribute to maintaining the illusion of a balance of power. The *radical* position which is implicit in these arguments is close to the viewpoint taken by Braverman and other Marxists, and it has the merit of directing attention to the need to analyse employment relationships in relation to the class structure and the distribution of power and resources in the wider society.

Burns and Stalker (Reading 49) also emphasize the varied commitments and goals which men and women bring to and develop within an employing organization. They are concerned with the implications of such commitments for the management of the organization, and identify two further considerations which affect this: the external situation of the enterprise, the stability or variability of its markets and/or technology; and the nature and effectiveness of the leadership exercised by the chief executive. In stable situations it may be appropriate for senior management to define employees' contribution to the organization and working relations with others precisely and in a limited way. Such a 'mechanistic' pattern of management (clearly similar to Weber's ideal-type bureaucracy) is however seen as inappropriate in changing or unstable situations where a more wide-ranging commitment is required, with all that that implies for the individual employee; while roles and relationships in such an 'organic' system of management cannot be clearly defined and delimited. As well as exploring the nature of individual–organization relations, Burns and Stalker's argument represents an important contribution to the development of a more satisfactory typology of industrial organizations, one which indicates the ways in which organizations can differ and stresses the influence of the external situation of the organization in bringing about such differences.

Braverman, Fox, and Burns and Stalker all acknowledge the 'subjective' elements in employer–employee (or organization–individual) relations, and the influence of roles and experiences outside the organization on members' participation and action within it. Silverman (Reading 50) develops this important insight into an 'action analysis' of organizations, a perspective which sees an organization as arising from the actions and interactions of its members, and their intended and unintended consequences. Such an approach focuses particularly on employees' 'orientations to work', the priorities they have and the ends they seek in entering employment, which can differ considerably between workers from different backgrounds, at different stages of the life-cycle, and so on. Such an approach is also seen as offering a better basis for explaining change in organizations than those which emphasize the structural and systemic qualities of organizations.

Burns and Stalker's two polar types of organization contribute to a typology of *industrial* organizations. Goffman (Reading 51) ranges more widely to direct attention to a whole range of organizations, only some of which are concerned with the production of goods and services. His category of 'total institutions' incorporates organizations as (apparently) different as prisons, monasteries, ships, boarding schools and long-stay hospitals. They are all organizations whose lower-status members (prisoners, novices, workers, pupils, patients) spend all their time within the organization and have their activities directed by its staff. Goffman emphasizes the implications of such a form of organization for the individual member, the ways in which it can, and often does, change the nature of the 'self'. As we have seen, the experience of working in an organization is likely to affect any employee to some extent, but most 'total institutions' are explicitly and deliberately concerned with this business of 'processing people'.

The final reading by Veronica Beechey (Reading 52) considers directly what has been implicit in many of the others, the processes by which particular individuals come to be employed in specific jobs in particular organizations. She focuses on the position of women in the labour market and the question of why women tend to be found in certain types of work and not others; but the arguments she considers have a general applicability. Explanations which stress the nature and structure of the demand for labour are superior to ones which attribute men's and women's positions in the labour market primarily to personal qualities and/or supposed gender characteristics. But neither dual labour market theory nor a Marxist approach can account satisfactorily for all features of the actual pattern of women's employment. After considering how the actions of male workers and trade unions may influence the employment opportunities of women (in passages not included in this extract), Beechey emphasizes the importance of family situations and familial ideology in channelling women into particular patterns of employment, such as part-time work, and into particular types of work, such as jobs which replicate women's domestic responsibilities. As is the case when analysing organizations, an adequate understanding of the labour market demands consideration of social relations in other areas of social life, and of attitudes and values in the wider society.

Ways of Looking at Work

Excerpts from R. E. Pahl, *Divisions of Labour*, Blackwell, 1984, pp. 121–8.

Exploring the Social Relations of Employment

Employment is the form of work that appears the easiest to understand: in very simple terms, a worker brings his or her skills and strength to an employer and in return receives a wage or salary for the time spent or the task achieved. However, it is not always quite as simple as that, since it would be wrong to see all workers as equally well-placed. Some have conditions of service agreements which give them almost complete security of tenure (such as dockworkers); others, such as contract research workers in universities and elsewhere, have no security and are obliged to waive their redundancy rights. Some employees work for large multinational corporations, whose policy is to provide security and substantial fringe benefits; others work for companies with very uncertain futures, whose concern is to get the maximum return from labour at the minimum cost. Some employees are full-time, some part-time; some have facilities provided at formal workplaces – factories and offices – whereas others are employed on a piecework basis in their own homes.

The state intervenes to a greater or lesser degree to regulate the employer–employee relationship: health and safety regulations, obligatory national insurance contributions, statutory paid maternity leave and so forth. However, there is a wide diversity of practice across the range of employment situations; employers may legally or illegally change the conditions of employment for their own or their employees' benefit. In the case of the former, they may shift from employing male full-time skilled workers to employing part-time semi-skilled married women workers. This strategy may produce a more docile, flexible and cheaper workforce, putting second incomes into some households and reducing some households to having no earners at all. Certain formal employment protection legislation, devised by the state for the protection of the assumed 'normal' male full-time worker, may be avoided. This must be seen as the 'informalization' of formal contractual systems. Whether the employee is male or female will substantially determine levels of pay and conditions of service, irrespective of skill or capacity . . .

There is no need to elaborate the point that the same kind of work – employment for a wage – can range from the stable, protected employment in a large organization to the unstable, informal employment practices of small organizations. Clearly, the social conditions of employment vary substantially, but so long as there is an employer and employee the social relations remain the same. However, the social relations of the self-employed are different.

According to Scase and Goffee, many of those starting an independent business do so as an explicit *rejection* of the capitalist ethic. It 'enables a person to escape from the constraints of authority, the wage–profit relationship and other features of being an employee'. Some can, of course, combine wage labour with self-employment, and this is particularly likely in the building and allied trades. It should be recognized that under certain circumstances informal ties of mutual trust and obligation can bind an employer to an employee far more effectively than formal statutory legislation. However, there is generally a price to be paid in informal sanctions, which of course can work both ways, and the shift from status to contract, from *Gemeinschaft* to *Gesellschaft*, is generally held to be a progressive one.

There is, of course, a range of work where the social relations of the market and of capital do not apply so directly, where transactions take place partly or wholly on the basis of other imperatives such as the need to maintain social solidarity and to confirm the norm of reciprocity. There are many other kinds of work than simply selling labour power to an employer . . .

The Social Relations of Work outside Employment

Let us, by way of illustration, take some relatively simple task – a woman ironing a garment in a domestic dwelling. Viewing that activity on its own, without knowing the social relations in which it is embedded and which to a degree create it, is an inadequate basis for determining the precise nature of the work involved. The various possibilities will be systematically reviewed, providing an alternative typology of work.

The woman could be completing a task for which she is employed as an outworker for a garment manufacturer. This work would be unequivocally *wage labour*. If, on the other hand, the woman was proposing to sell the garment she has just made in her own boutique or market stall, she would be engaged in *petty commodity production* as a self-employed worker, since she would be producing for herself and not for her employer. Both of these forms of work could be undertaken without informing the controlling agencies of the state, which may be referred to then as *shadow wage labour* or *shadow petty commodity production*: the social relations might remain the same, but the system of national accounting would certainly be affected.

The woman could, on the other hand, be ironing a garment for which she received no direct monetary reward. If she is ironing her own blouse in preparation for her next day's wage labour, then she could be said to be engaged in *individual reproduction*. All wage labourers have to be, as it were, reproduced from day to day. Some have much of this activity done for them by others: young wage labourers get the support of their parents; men frequently get the support of their unpaid wives. This work, called *social reproduction*, is to do with the maintenance of existing workers or the reproduction of new ones and is typically done by women: it may be said to be structured by the social relations based on patriarchy, as wage labour is structured by the social relations of capitalism. In both cases, patterns of domination and subordination structure the social relations of the work. However, in the case of social reproduction, while the ironing of the shirt may be described as patriarchally structured social reproduction work, it could also be shared wage labour (the wife is preparing herself for business entertaining on behalf of her husband, for which she gets paid) or shared social reproductive work (tomorrow the husband does the ironing) or undominated subsistence work (the tasks have been equitably divided between all members of the household, none of whom is a wage labourer or self-employed worker, and the woman has agreed to do the ironing as part of her overall contribution).

It would be wrong to assume that all women ironing a garment for another person are constrained to do so by patriarchal values. If the woman were ironing the garment for colleagues in a local dramatic society, it would make a difference if the way the work had been allocated involved a degree of 'friendly coercion' or had been given without question because she was a woman. If, on the contrary, she had *offered* to do this work for her colleagues in the society, or for a neighbour who was sick, then she would be doing what may be described as *social solidarity work*. Such work, based on generalized or specific reciprocity, reflects the social constraints of sharing the same dwelling or locality and is essential if people are to live together reasonably amicably. This is distinct from *voluntary work*, which may be done anonymously and is not based on the constraints of interpersonal interaction or related to any reciprocal recompense.

In all these descriptions of a given task being done, the type of work may be understood by exposing the pattern of social relations in which it is embedded. It is these social relations of work that produce exploitation. The circumstances under which the ironing was agreed to be done and the relative balance of power between the woman doing the ironing and her significant others would need to be known and understood before the particular work task could be appropriately categorized. Such might be an advance in sociological conceptualization, but this intellectual exercise is not self-evidently of any more general significance.

Is All Social Activity or Social Behaviour 'Work'?

The attempt to set out systematically a preliminary typology of work shows that most types of work can be illustrated through the example of ironing, but this possibly supports the position rather too neatly. Some tasks cannot be so easily manipulated in and out of different categories of social relations, yet there are, perhaps, many more tasks in industrial society that could shift out of one category into another. Nevertheless, a valid criticism is that the typology, by attempting to be comprehensive, weakens the distinctive meaning of the word 'work' so that it becomes synonymous with 'activity', or 'task', or simply 'social behaviour'. Since, it may be argued, we live in a capitalist social formation, *all* activities are concerned with the production and reproduction of that system. According to such an extreme position, productive work is seen as central and all other activities as secondary and subservient to it. Thus, people's leisure, free time or play can be seen as recreating the energy and momentum to return to productive work, and, somewhat humourlessly, *re*productive work is seen as serving the function of reproducing the labour power and social relations of the social formation . . .

A number of points need to be made. First, it is clear that domination/subordination-determined social relations occurred in pre-capitalist societies; and, while it may be argued that patriarchal attitudes have been incorporated and 'used' by capitalism, this does not deny that the social relations of, for example, domestic labour or social reproduction pre-date capitalism and are qualitatively different from the class domination associated with capitalist relations of production. Second, all societies require work to maintain the collective conscience, in a Durkheimian sense, and social solidarity has universal significance and importance in a way that cannot be reduced, perhaps over-simply, to another of the 'needs of capitalism'. Third, and perhaps most important, people themselves recognize that work can be qualitatively different and that 'work' for a neighbour, 'work' for oneself or one's spouse and 'work' for an employer are different activities, even though, as shown in the example of ironing, they may involve the same task. Those who wish to reduce the types of work available to a person to simple dichotomies, as being either productive or non-productive, money-generating or non-money-generating, producing either exchange value or use value, do violence to people's experience and make the unwarranted assumption that the social relations of capitalism have become dominatingly all-pervasive. According to this view, principles of social reciprocity have become corrupted by ideas based on market principles, so that the metaphors of exchange infiltrate into personal relationships, with careful calculations of the costs and benefits of various courses of action.

We are now in a better position to answer the question of whether all social activity is 'work'. Quite evidently it is not. But, equally, work cannot be narrowly defined by constraining definitions, which limit it either to employment, or as a result of abstract philosophizing on the nature of 'productive' labour. Work can be understood only in relation to the specific social relations in which it is embedded. Specific people in specific circumstances in specific sets of social relations and social relationships can be described precisely in terms of whether they are engaged in work or play. The word 'work' cannot be defined out of context: that, indeed, is the conclusion and answer to the question.

The Labour Process

Excerpts from Harry Braverman, *Labor and Monopoly Capital*, Monthly Review Press, 1974, pp. 45–58.

→ whole lab. + process debate/school/ discourse

What is important about human work is not its similarities with that of other animals, but the crucial differences that mark it as the polar opposite. 'We are not now dealing with those primitive instinctive forms of labour that remind us of the mere animal', wrote Marx in the first volume of *Capital*. 'We pre-suppose labour in a form that stamps it as exclusively human. A spider conducts operations that resemble those of a weaver, and a bee puts to shame many an architect in the construction of her cells. But what distinguishes the worst architect from the best of bees is this, that the architect raises his structure in imagination before he erects it in reality. At the end of every labour-process, we get a result that already existed in the imagination of the labourer at its commencement. He not only effects a change of form in the material on which he works, but he also realizes a purpose of his own that gives the law to his modus operandi, and to which he must subordinate his will.'

Human work is conscious and purposive, while the work of other animals is instinctual . . . In humans, as distinguished from animals, the unity between the motive force of labour and the labour itself is not inviolable. *The unity of conception and execution may be dissolved.* The conception must still precede and govern execution, but the idea as conceived by *one* may be executed by *another*. The driving force of labour remains human consciousness, but the unity between the two may be broken in the individual and reasserted in the group, the workshop, the community, the society as a whole.

Finally, the human capacity to perform work, which Marx called 'Labour power', must not be confused with the power of any non-human agency, whether natural or man made. Human labour, whether directly exercised or stored in such products as tools, machinery, or domesticated animals, represents the sole resource of humanity in confronting nature. Thus for humans in society, labour power is a special category, separate and inexchangeable with any other, *simply because it is human*. Only one who is the *master of the labour of others* will confuse labour power with any other agency for performing a task, because to him, steam, horse, water, or human muscle which turns his mill are viewed as equivalents, as 'factors of production'. For *individuals who allocate their own labour* (or a community which does the same), the difference between using labour power as against any other power is a difference upon which the entire 'economy' turns. And from the point of view of the species as a whole, this difference is also crucial, since every individual is the proprietor of a portion of the total labour power of the community, the society, and the species . . .

Freed from the rigid paths dictated in animals by instinct, human labour becomes indeterminate, and its various determinate forms henceforth are the products not of biology but of the complex interaction between tools and social relations, technology and society. The subject of our discussion is not labour 'in general', but labour in the forms it takes under capitalist relations of production. (MC?.)

Capitalist production requires exchange relations, commodities, and money, but its *differentia specifica* is the purchase and sale of labour power. For this purpose, three basic conditions become generalized throughout society. First, workers are separated from the means with which production is carried on, and can gain access to them only by selling their labour power to others. Second, workers are freed of legal constraints, such as serfdom or slavery, that prevent them from disposing of their own labour power. Third, the purpose of the employment of the worker becomes the expansion of a unit of capital belonging to the employer, who is thus functioning as a capitalist. The labour process therefore begins with a contract or agreement governing the conditions of the sale of labour power by the worker and its purchase by the employer.

It is important to take note of the historical character of this phenomenon. While the purchase and sale of labour power has existed from antiquity, a substantial class of wage-workers did not begin to form in Europe until the fourteenth century, and did not become numerically significant until the rise of industrial capitalism (that is, the *production* of commodities on a capitalist basis, as against mercantile capitalism, which merely *exchanged* the surplus products of prior forms of production) in the eighteenth century. It has been the numerically dominant form for little more than a century, and this in only a few countries. In the United States, perhaps four-fifths of the population was self-employed in the early part of the nineteenth century. By 1870 this had declined to about one-third and by 1940 to no more than one-fifth; by 1970 only about one-tenth of the population was self-employed. We are thus dealing with a social relation of extremely recent date. The rapidity with which it has won supremacy in a number of countries emphasizes the extraordinary power of the tendency of capitalist economies to convert all other forms of labour into hired labour.

The worker enters into the employment agreement because social conditions leave him or her no other way to gain a livelihood. The employer, on the other hand, is the possessor of a unit of capital which he is endeavouring to enlarge, and in order to do so he converts part of it into wages. Thus is set in motion the labour process, which, while it is in general a process for creating useful values, has now also become specifically a process for the expansion of capital, the creation of a profit. From this point on, it becomes foolhardy to view the labour process purely from a technical standpoint, as a mere mode of labour. It has become in addition a process of accumulation of capital. And, moreover, it is the latter aspect which dominates in the mind and activities of the capitalist, into whose hands the control over the labour process has passed. In everything that follows, therefore, we shall be considering the manner in which the labour process is dominated and shaped by the accumulation of capital.

Labour, like all life processes and bodily functions, is an inalienable property of the human individual. Muscle and brain cannot be separated from persons possessing them; one cannot endow another with one's own capacity for work, no matter at what price, any more than one can eat, sleep, or perform sex acts for another. Thus, in the exchange, the worker does not surrender to the capitalist his or her capacity for work. The worker retains it, and the capitalist can take advantage of the bargain only by setting the worker to work. It is of course understood that the useful effects or products of labour belong to the capitalist. But what the worker sells, and what the capitalist buys, is *not an agreed amount of labour, but the power to labour over an agreed period of time.* This inability to purchase labour, which is an inalienable bodily and mental function, and the necessity to purchase the power to perform it, is so fraught with consequences for the entire capitalist mode of production that it must be investigated more closely . . .

Human labour . . . because it is informed and directed by an understanding which has been socially and culturally developed, is capable of a vast range of productive activities. The active labour processes which reside in potential in the labour power of humans are so diverse as to type, manner of performance, etc., that for all practical purposes they may be said to be infinite, all the more so as new modes of labour can easily be invented more rapidly than they can be exploited. The capitalist finds in this infinitely malleable character of human labour the essential resource for the expansion of his capital.

It is known that human labour is able to produce more than it consumes, and this capacity for 'surplus labour' is sometimes treated as a special and mystical endowment of humanity or of its labour. In reality it is nothing of the sort, but is merely a prolongation of working time beyond the point where labour has reproduced itself, or in other words brought into being its own means of subsistence or their equivalent. This time will vary with the intensity and productivity of labour, as well as with the changing requirements of 'subsistence', but for any given state of these it is a definite duration. The 'peculiar' capacity of labour power to produce for the capitalist after it has reproduced itself is therefore nothing but the extension of work time beyond the point where it could otherwise come to a halt . . .

The distinctive capacity of human labour power is therefore not its ability to produce a surplus, but rather its intelligent and purposive character, which gives it infinite adaptability and which produces the social and cultural conditions for enlarging its own productivity, so that its surplus product may be continuously enlarged. From the point of view of the capitalist, this many-sided potentiality of humans in society is the basis upon which is built the enlargement of his capital. He therefore takes up every means of increasing the output of the labour power he has purchased when he sets it to work as labour. The means he employs may vary from the enforcement upon the worker of the longest possible working day in the early period of capitalism to the use of the most productive instruments of labour and the greatest intensity of labour, but they are always aimed at realizing from the potential inherent in labour power the greatest useful effect of labour, for it is this that will yield for him the greatest surplus and thus the greatest profit.

But if the capitalist builds upon this distinctive quality and potential of human labour power, it is also this quality, by its very indeterminacy, which places before him his greatest challenge and problem. The coin of labour has its obverse side: in purchasing labour power that can do much, he is at the same time purchasing an undefined quality and quantity. What he buys is infinite in *potential*, but in its *realization* it is limited by the subjective state of the workers, by their previous history, by the general social conditions under which they work as well as the particular conditions of the enterprise, and by the technical setting of their labour. The work actually performed will be affected by these and many other factors, including the organization of the process and the forms of supervision over it, if any.

This is all the more true since the technical features of the labour process are now dominated by the social features which the capitalist has introduced: that is to say, the new relations of production. Having been forced to sell their labour power to another, the workers also surrender their interest in the labour process, which has now been 'alienated'. *The labour process has become the responsibility of the capitalist.* In this setting of antagonistic relations of production, the problem of realizing the 'full usefulness' of the labour power he has bought becomes exacerbated by the opposing interests of those for whose purposes the labour process is carried on, and those who, on the other side, carry it on.

Thus when the capitalist buys buildings, materials, tools, machinery, etc., he can evaluate with precision their place in the labour process. He knows that a certain portion of his outlay will be transferred to each unit of production, and his accounting practices allocate these in the form of costs or depreciation. But when he buys labour time, the outcome is far from being either so certain or so definite that it can be reckoned in this way, with precision and in advance. This is merely an expression of the fact that the portion of his capital expended on labour power is the 'variable' portion, which undergoes an increase in the process of production; for him, the question is how great that increase will be.

It thus becomes essential for the capitalist that control over the labour process pass from the hands of the worker into his own. This transition presents itself in history as the *progressive alienation of the process of production* from the worker; to the capitalist, it presents itself as the problem of *management*.

Meaning of Management
(aspect of!)

48   Alan Fox

Perspectives on Industrial Relations

Excerpts from Alan Fox, 'Industrial Relations: A Social Critique of Pluralist Ideology', in John Child (ed.), *Man and Organization*, Allen and Unwin, 1973, pp. 186–96, 206–12.

The Unitary Ideology

We begin, therefore, by recapitulating briefly the main features of the unitary perspective. Perceived through this frame of reference, the 'organizational logic' of the enterprise is seen as pointing towards a unified authority and loyalty structure, with managerial prerogative being legitimized by all members of the organization. This accords with the emphasis that is placed on asserting the common objectives and the common values which unite and bind together all partici-pants.

The assumption of fully shared interests shapes the unitary attitude towards all work group 'custom and practice' or union rules which management experience as seriously irksome. Given that management goals and policies are seen as 'rational', it follows that only in so far as employee behaviour is congruent with those goals and policies is it likewise rational. This view was characteristic of many popularizers and camp-followers of the early Human Relations school, which worked with an ideology strongly unitary in nature . . .

Along with a liberal use of 'team' or 'family' metaphors inspired by this presumed unity is apt to go a strong belief that in a properly ordered world managerial prerogative could always be enforced against the few malcontents by means of coercive power if necessary. The greater the tendency to see the 'true' nature of industrial en-terprise as unitary, and to see any challenge to managerial rule as of doubtful legitimacy, the greater the disposition to view the enforce-ment of prerogative by coercive power as desirable and justified. The time-consuming and patience-straining process of 'winning con-sent' through consultation and negotiation may appear not only burdensome in practice but even pusillanimous in principle. Observation suggests that this stance is apt to predispose its holders to beliefs which may in some circumstances prove to be wishful thinking – that power does in fact lie to hand in sufficient measure not only to make immediate coercion possible, but also to suppress, control, or eliminate any possible adverse long-run consequences which might otherwise outweigh the benefits of applying it. In other words, the notion of the unitary perspective includes the hypothesis that managers holding it are disposed, at times of special stress, crisis, or emergency, to attempt to fall back on coercive means of enforcing their will if challenged . . .

We may hypothesize that the subscriber to the unitary ideology will tend to define transgressors as aberrants. His own conviction of the rightness of management rule and the norms issuing from it may create difficulty for him, not simply in acknowledging the legitimacy of challenges to it, but even in fully grasping that such challenges may at least be grounded in legitimacy for those who mount them . . .

It will be urged that simply by accepting the employment contract, or by signing for a copy of company rules, or by being covered by a collective agreement concluded with a trade union, or even, perhaps, by being subjects of a political regime that has enacted certain legislation by 'democratic' processes, they must be said to be legitimizing the norms that govern them, thereby laying themselves open to justified punishment whenever they need recalling to the paths of righteousness. As we have noted, the unitary frame of reference tends not to promote recognition of the problematical nature of these dynamics of compliance and legitimacy. Fully to accept that the recalcitrants may be nonconformers who totally repudiate the norms in question and see their own repudiation as fully legitimate would be to take the first step away from the unitary pole of the continuum towards the pluralistic pole.

The Pluralist Ideology

. . . Seen from [a] generalized perspective the enterprise is not a unitary structure but a coalition of individuals and groups with their own aspirations and their own perceptions of the structure which they naturally see as valid and which they will seek to express in action if such is required. The term 'coalition' is used, for example, by Cyert and March. It includes the notion that individuals and groups with widely varying priorities agree to collaborate in social structures which enable all participants to get something of what they want. The terms of collaboration are settled by bargaining. Management is seen as making its decisions within a complex set of constraints which include employees, consumers, suppliers, government, the law, the local community, and sources of finance. It is in response to the pressures of these organized constraint mechanisms that management forges its compromises or rises above them with some new synthesis, and in their absence pluralists would be profoundly doubtful if even the roughest of distributive justice would be likely to emerge.

Thus the enterprise is seen as a complex of tensions and competing claims which have to be 'managed' in the interests of maintaining a viable collaborative structure within which all the stakeholders can, with varying degrees of success, pursue their aspirations . . .

To be sure, perceptions by the participants of conflicting interests need not be seen by pluralists as a *logical necessity* of the industrial enterprise. However, even if we consider only the various groups of employees we can see an empirical probability that in a competitive society where, for example, money is universally desired but limited in supply, employee groups will periodically disagree among themselves and with management about what constitutes fair shares. The pluralistic view assumes, therefore, that given the divergent pressures and claims to which managers are subject they may on this and on many other issues be tempted to govern their 'human resources' in ways which one or more subordinate groups experience as arbitrary, summary, or contrary to their own interests, and which they are likely to seek to challenge through independent collective organizations. It therefore sees trade unionism not as a regrettable historical carry-over, but as just another manifestation of one of the basic values of competitive, pressure group, 'democratic' societies of the Western model – that 'interests' have rights of free association and, within legal limits, of asserting their claims and aspirations. It also sees trade unions or organized work groups as being able in some situations to readjust the power balance within the enterprise to such effect as to enable subordinates to impose *their* preferences in ways which *management* finds arbitrary and summary. Trade unions are nevertheless accepted by pluralists as legitimate expressions of legitimate challenges to managerial rule. Indeed they are positively welcomed as giving expression to a mode of joint rule-making by managers and managed which is valued in its own right, simply [in Clegg's words] 'as a method of regulating relationships between people in industry', whether or not it succeeds in 'pushing wages as high as possible' . . .

It is characteristic, therefore, of pluralists to criticize the unitary perspective for failing to analyse carefully enough the distribution of power; for assuming that management or the state has more than may in fact prove to be the case; and for giving too little consideration to the long-term disadvantages of relying on coercion. One would also expect a tendency for those of this persuasion to be doubtful about the efficacy of attempts to apply the law directly to enforce certain patterns of behaviour, on the grounds that if enough people are determined enough to refuse to submit, the law is impotent. They accordingly rest more hope on winning consent to those desired patterns.

It would be regarded as a weakness of the unitary view that, by underestimating the problematical nature of management rule, and overestimating the long-term practicability and net usefulness of prerogative and coercive power as a basis for industrial order in our kind of society, it undervalues the significance of negotiated, agreed, normative codes for coalition-type collaboration, and of the need to explore the dynamics of legitimacy and consent as the stable bases of such codes. Pluralists would see part of the difficulty as lying in the fact that subscribers to the unitary view are reluctant to define the enterprise in coalition terms.

It would also seem plausible to suggest that whereas subscribers to the unitary view may prefer to define transgressors as aberrants who legitimize the relevant norms and can therefore properly (and without adverse consequences) be punished, pluralists are likely to see most transgressors as nonconformers for whom punishment would be futile and indeed counter-productive, and whose repudiation of the relevant norms must be met by a negotiated reconstruction of those norms to the point where they meet at least the minimal needs of all the parties.

Such an approach would hardly make sense without an accompanying assumption that the normative divergencies between the parties are not so fundamental or so wide as to be unbridgeable by compromises or new syntheses which enable collaboration to continue . . .

Pluralists would argue that the situation in most advanced western industrial societies does in fact bear a rough approximation to this picture of a basic procedural consensus. They make, therefore, the working assumption that, given 'good will' and such external stimulus, help, and structural support as may prove necessary, managements and unions will always and everywhere be able ultimately to negotiate comprehensive, codified systems of regulation which provide a fully adequate and orderly context making for the promotion and maintenance of orderly behaviour . . .

Criticisms of Pluralist Ideology

. . . Perhaps the most fundamental reason for rejecting the pluralist position would be a belief that industrial society, while manifestly to some extent a congeries of small special interest groups vying for scarce goods, status, or influence, is more convincingly characterized in terms of the over-arching exploitation of one class by another, of the propertyless by the propertied, of the less by the more powerful. By this view, any talk of 'checks and balances', however apt for describing certain subsidiary phenomena, simply confuses our understanding of the primary dynamics which shape and move society – a useful confusion indeed for the major power holders since it obscures the domination of society by its ruling strata through institutions and assumptions which operate to exclude anything approaching a genuine power balance . . .

The force of this mode of analyses does not depend on accepting the oversimplified terms in which it is sometimes presented or the political prescriptions which sometimes accompany it. There is only space here to note the obvious point that private ownership is not the only source of control over economic resources and therefore not the only source of economic power over people. Nevertheless it is from a perspective similar to this that a radical analysis can be offered which is highly damaging to the generalized pluralist view presented here. It asserts as its starting point a great disparity of power as between, on the one hand, the owners and controllers of economic resources and, on the other, those dependent upon them for access to those resources as a means of livelihood. This power is exercised not only directly in industry, business, commerce, and financial institutions, but also indirectly in a multitude of ways . . .

Such an account contrasts sharply with the one which figures, explicitly or implicitly, in so many pluralist statements, of a rough balance of power among 'the congeries of hundreds of small specialist groups' in society. There is, of course, no question but that, in respect of capital-labour relations, the disparity of power can be, and has been, mitigated. The propertyless are indeed dependent upon the propertied for access to resources, but the latter are also dependent upon the former for getting work done, and combination enables employees to offset somewhat the power of their masters. Yet to enjoy control of resources – a control upheld by the law and in the last resort by the armed forces of the state – seems such a decisive advantage that the fact of many people believing in the existence of a power balance presents us with a puzzle . . .

The power balance illusion . . . rests on the continuing acceptance by the less favoured of social institutions and principles which support wealth and privilege, and which the wealthy and privileged would exert their great power to defend if that acceptance were to pass into attempts at repudiation. But conversely, the illusion contributes towards acceptance, for by veiling gross disparities of power it fosters the belief that all the principal interests, at least, of society compete 'fairly' for its rewards, thereby helping to legitimize the system. Thus does pluralism make its small contribution towards keeping society safe for wealth and privilege.

The critique of pluralist ideology cannot, however, end there. The point was made earlier that for management to concede collective bargaining and other means by which employees or their representatives can participate in the making of some kinds of decision may well strengthen rather than weaken their control. This argument now needs elaboration.

Despite the rejection by some employers and managers of pluralist notions and values, it is not difficult to argue that such an ideology represents, in the context of modern business, a high point in enlightened 'managerialism', in the sense that it serves managerial interests and goals whether pluralists themselves identify with those interests and goals or not. Admittedly it urges the full acceptance by managers of rival focuses of authority, leadership, and claims to subordinate loyalty. It recommends the limited sharing of some rule making and decision taking. It deprives managers of all theoretical justification for asserting or claiming prerogative. Yet the outcome of these concessions is visualized, not as the weakening of managerial rule as we now understand it, but as its strengthening and consolidation. Pluralism would certainly be defended by at least some of its exponents partly on the grounds that it is more likely than the unitary view to promote rational, efficient, and effective management.

PLURALIST IDEOLOGY
CAN AID THE SECURING
OF CONTROL AT CO. LEVEL
(AS WELL AS SOCIETAL)

49 Tom Burns and G. M. Stalker

Mechanistic and Organic Systems of Management

Excerpts from Tom Burns and G. M. Stalker, *The Management of Innovation*, Tavistock, 1961, pp. 97–102, 119–25.

The Working Organization and Private Commitments

An industrial concern exists in order to carry out a specific task. To exist at all, a concern employs a number of people. These are assigned to specific bits of the total task, which is split up according to traditional or rational principles of the division of labour, and according to the technological equipment available. Cooperation between the several members of a concern is achieved by organization. In setting up an organization, the concern confers and defines, for each member, certain rights to control the activity of others (and of himself) and to receive information, and certain obligations to accept control and transmit information. The way in which a concern confers and defines rights and obligations of this kind constitutes the management system. The form of the system varies with the nature of the concern's task.

This task may remain stable in its most important respects, or it may change. The degree of stability or rate of change calls for different systems by which the activities of the concern are controlled, by which information is conveyed throughout the organization, and by which decisions and actions are authorized.

The members of a concern are recruited to be used, by agreement, as resources to achieve its ends. The activities which are directed in this way, *and* the management system in operation, together form the working organization of the concern.

But the men and woman it employs bring in with them other, private purposes of their own. To an extent which varies a great deal from person to person, these purposes may be achieved partly by the return they get from the contract with the employing concern to allow themselves, their physical and mental capacities, to be used as resources. But men and women do not ordinarily yield themselves wholly to use as resources by others; indeed, to do so infringes the human purpose of controlling the situation confronting the individual. In every organized working community, therefore (except those for which religious zeal, political enthusiasm, or some other dedication of the self identifies the personal ends of its members with those they believe to be pursued by the others or by their leader), individuals seek to realize other purposes than those they recognize as the organization's.

Men can attain few of their proximate or ultimate ends by means of their own efforts, unrelated to the conduct of anyone else whatsoever. So that, in addition to the organizational structure of the concern itself, other organizational structures are present through which individuals attempt to realize ends other than those of the concern as such. This private organization is usually called the 'informal structure', to distinguish it from the 'formal structure' of the management system . . .

The presence in a concern of . . . informal structures may exert a decisive influence over the efficiency of the working organization, and particularly over the degree of appropriateness the type of management system has to the external situation, whether stable or changing, which confronts the concern. In pursuing these private purposes which are irrelevant to the working organization, individuals affiliate themselves to groups, and seek to bind others in association. They acquire commitments. These commitments may persist in the face of an express need for the working organization to adapt itself to new circumstances . . .

The Working Organization and its Direction

So far we have treated the concern as an impersonal entity. There is, however, a central source of visible power, so far as the working organization is concerned, in the Chairman of the Board or the Managing Director, or in the Divisional or the Factory Manager, according to the constitution of the concern . . .

He, in fact, whether alone or in association with other members of the concern, directs the use to which the combined resources of people and materials and equipment of the concern are to be put. It is for him to decide the nature of the task to which the concern is being applied, and, in particular, to gauge the rate of change in the conditions of that task. Once the situation is appreciated the resources of the concern can then be strategically disposed in a management system. This function of the head of the concern . . . gives his role a qualitative difference from that of subordinate managers . . .

In our terms, leadership at the top, or 'direction', involves constant preoccupation with the technical and commercial parameters of the situation in which the concern has to operate, and with the adjustment of the internal system to that external situation. It is a different kind of activity from that required in subordinate positions in the management system.

There is a second function of direction, discharged like the first either positively or by default . . . It is the task of the managing director (sc. chairman, factory manager, etc.) to ensure that the bounds of commitment to the working organization are set wide enough – that the resources provided by the individual for use by the working organization are sufficient – to achieve its purposes. This involves a complex social process by which the director of a concern specifies the requirements of the working organization vis-à-vis other private commitments. He 'defines the work situation', displaying in his own actions and expecting in others' (a) the span of considerations, technical, commercial, humane, politic, sentimental, and so forth, which are admissible to decisions within the working organization; and (b) the demands of the working organization for commitment, effort, and self-involvement which the individual should regard as feasible, and should attempt to meet.

These two directive functions each correspond to one of the other two major variables: (i) the rate of change in the external situation, and (ii) the relative strength of the pursuit of self-interest by members of the concern as against their commitment to the working organization. The variable character of this third element lies in the capacity of the director to fit the management system to its task and to define adequately the work situation of himself and his subordinates . . .

We are now at the point at which we may set down the outline of the two management systems which represent for us . . . the two polar extremities of the forms which such systems can take when they are adapted to a specific rate of technical and commercial change. The case we have tried to establish from the literature, as from our research experience ... is that the different forms assumed by a working organization do exist objectively and are not merely interpretations offered by observers of different schools.

Both types represent a 'rational' form of organization, in that they may both, in our experience, be explicitly and deliberately created and maintained to exploit the human resources of a concern in the most efficient manner feasible in the circumstances of the concern. Not surprisingly, however, each exhibits characteristics which have been hitherto associated with different kinds of interpretation. For it is our contention that empirical findings have usually been classified according to sociological ideology rather than according to the functional specificity of the working organization to its task and the conditions confronting it.

We have tried to argue that these are two formally contrasted forms of management system. These we shall call the mechanistic and organic forms.

A *mechanistic* management system is appropriate to stable conditions. It is characterized by:

(*a*) the specialized differentiation of functional tasks into which the problems and tasks facing the concern as a whole are broken down;

(*b*) the abstract nature of each individual task, which is pursued with techniques and purposes more or less distinct from those of the concern as a whole; i.e., the functionaries tend to pursue the technical improvement of means, rather than the accomplishment of the ends of the concern;

(*c*) the reconciliation, for each level in the hierarchy, of these distinct performances by the immediate superiors, who are also, in turn, responsible for seeing that each is relevant in his own special part of the main task;

(*d*) the precise definition of rights and obligations and technical methods attached to each functional role;

(*e*) the translation of rights and obligations and methods into the responsibilities of a functional position;

(*f*) hierarchic structure of control, authority and communication;

(*g*) a reinforcement of the hierarchic structure by the location of knowledge of actualities exclusively at the top of the hierarchy, where the final reconciliation of distinct tasks and assessment of relevance is made;

(*h*)   a tendency for interaction between members of the concern to be vertical, i.e., between superior and subordinate;

(*i*)   a tendency for operations and working behaviour to be governed by the instructions and decisions issued by superiors;

(*j*)   insistence on loyalty to the concern and obedience to superiors as a condition of membership;

(*k*)   a greater importance and prestige attaching to internal (local) than to general (cosmopolitan) knowledge, experience, and skill.

The *organic* form is appropriate to changing conditions, which give rise constantly to fresh problems and unforeseen requirements for action which cannot be broken down or distributed automatically arising from the functional roles defined within a hierarchic structure. It is characterized by:

(*a*)   the contributive nature of special knowledge and experience to the common task of the concern;

(*b*)   the 'realistic' nature of the individual task, which is seen as set by the total situation of the concern;

(*c*)   the adjustment and continual re-definition of individual tasks through interaction with others;

(*d*)   the shedding of 'responsibility' as a limited field of rights, obligations and methods. (Problems may not be posted upwards, downwards or sideways as being someone else's responsibility);

(*e*)   the spread of commitment to the concern beyond any technical definition;

(*f*)   a network structure of control, authority, and communication. The sanctions which apply to the individual's conduct in his working role derive more from presumed community of interest with the rest of the working organization in the survival and growth of the firm, and less from a contractual relationship between himself and a non-personal corporation, represented for him by an immediate superior;

(*g*)   omniscience no longer imputed to the head of the concern; knowledge about the technical or commercial nature of the here and now task may be located anywhere in the network; this location becoming the *ad hoc* centre of control authority and communication;

(*h*) a lateral rather than a vertical direction of communication through the organization, communication between people of different rank, also, resembling consultation rather than command;

(*i*) a content of communication which consists of information and advice rather than instructions and decisions;

(*j*) commitment to the concern's tasks and to the 'technological ethos' of material progress and expansion is more highly valued than loyalty and obedience;

(*k*) importance and prestige attach to affiliations and expertise valid in the industrial and technical and commercial milieux external to the firm.

One important corollary to be attached to this account is that while organic systems are not hierarchic in the same sense as are mechanistic, they remain stratified. Positions are differentiated according to seniority – i.e., greater expertise . . .

A second observation is that the area of commitment to the concern – the extent to which the individual yields himself as a resource to be used by the working organization – is far more extensive in organic than in mechanistic systems. Commitment, in fact, is expected to approach that of the professional scientist to his work, and frequently does. One further consequence of this is that it becomes far less feasible to distinguish 'informal' from 'formal' organization.

Thirdly, the emptying out of significance from the hierarchic command system, by which cooperation is ensured and which serves to monitor the working organization under a mechanistic system, is countered by the development of shared beliefs about the values and goals of the concern. The growth and accretion of institutionalized values, beliefs, and conduct, in the form of commitments, ideology, and manners, around an image of the concern in its industrial and commercial setting make good the loss of formal structure.

Finally, the two forms of system represent a polarity, not a dichotomy; there are, as we have tried to show, intermediate stages between the extremities empirically known to us. Also, the relation of one form to the other is elastic, so that a concern oscillating between relative stability and relative change may also oscillate between the two forms. A concern may (and frequently does) operate with a management system which includes both types.

50   David Silverman

An Action Analysis of Organizations

Excerpts from David Silverman, *The Theory of Organisations*, Heinemann, 1970, pp. 149–54.

Action in Organizations

Many empirical studies have been concerned with linking observable aspects of organizational structure (e.g. technology, nature of authority, promotion opportunities) to the behaviour of those concerned ... Each aspect is associated with the nature and level of rewards offered, for instance opportunity for better-paid work or contact with fellow workers and supervisors. The presence or absence of these will, it is held, *determine* the response of members of the organization. It soon became apparent, however, that knowledge of these objective characteristics of an organization was an inadequate predictor of behaviour ...

An alternative approach, favoured particularly by psychologists, developed out of the work of Morse. She suggested that satisfaction is determined not by the rewards alone but by the extent to which they diverge from what is desired. Expectations thus become of prime importance: where they are very high, one would generally expect satisfaction to be lower than when not very much is expected. Much of the work in this tradition has, however, not sought to relate these expectations to the other orientations of the same people or to examine the extent to which they consider them legitimate. In short, it has failed to take account of the *meaning* attached to the expectation.

This argument has been taken up by Karpik, who has concentrated on what he calls 'social' expectations. These have a variety of subjective meanings depending on their social context, and the impact of experience upon satisfaction is, therefore, very varied. He illustrates his point with a study of several hundred French workers which shows that expectations have different consequences among town and country workers. In the town, high expectation of work signifies a desire for a more interesting and better-qualified job and tends to be associated with low satisfaction. In the country, high expectation implies high satisfaction. This is because in the country a high level of expectation usually means that the worker has accepted an industrial frame of reference as opposed to the prevailing rural values; he finds work satisfying because it offers him a symbolic participation in modern society.

If the social meaning of an expectation cannot be understood, as Karpik puts it, 'independently of the individual's orientations, his social position and the situation within which he acts', it follows that analysis in terms of the actors' expectations, while an advance on positivist assumptions, is still insufficient. It is here that the action frame of reference is so useful. For the action of members of an organization can be explained when their definition of the situation and ends have been understood. The first task of organizational analysis is, then, to distinguish the orientations (finite provinces of meaning) of different members (ideal-typical actors). But why should these orientations differ and what are the consequences of these differences?

Orientations differ, firstly, because actors bring different ends and expectations to their membership of an organization. These derive from their various historical experiences (e.g. unemployment, rural background, experience of a paternalistic management) and from the multiple statuses which they hold at the time (e.g. husband, member or official of voluntary association, member of ethnic or religious minority). These variations arise, secondly, from the different experiences of actors within the organization which encourage or discourage certain ends and expectations and generate others. Chinoy, for instance, has noted a 'chronology of aspirations' held by car-workers: an active concern for self-advancement is held largely by the young, while in a short time the majority of the workers develop goals unrelated to advancement (a 'reasonable' standard of living, a steady, relatively pleasant job).

The consequence of these different orientations is that the nature of involvement in the organization varies considerably among the members and has an impact on the way in which they respond to the behaviour of others, whether equals, subordinates or superiors. It is important, therefore, to distinguish the type of involvement, which can range from moral to alienative [to use Etzioni's terms], and the ways in which it expresses itself, as for instance in [what Dalton describes as] clique membership.

The nature of involvement is likely to be affected by whether authority is maintained by consensus or superior power. Thus the relationship between the junior hospital doctor and the consultant, just as much as that between the prison warder and the inmate or the worker and the manager, need not derive equally from the ends which each is trying to attain. This is not meant to suggest, of course, that all such relationships are based on an element of coercion or that, where coercion is used, it necessarily derives from the superior alone. Warders are dependent on the cooperation of prisoners and, as Eisenstadt has demonstrated, bureaucrats rely on an acceptance of the legitimacy of their position by even the poorest and most illiterate client. All parties must, therefore, use strategies to preserve and enlarge their area of discretion ... The pattern of interaction and related meanings that is then built up (the role-system of the organization) reflects the consequences of the behaviour of the various actors as well as the stock of knowledge that they bring in from outside. Workers expect supervisors to behave in an indulgent, bureaucratic or authoritarian way, not only because their life in the wider society has led them to this expectation but also because what they have expected has or has not been confirmed in their actual experiences of supervisory behaviour in the particular organization. As a consequence, they may or may not attempt to alter the prevailing system of expectations.

The organizational role-system thus denotes the system of institutionalized expectations about the likely action of others without which social life cannot proceed. It expresses the rules of the game which all groups tend to accept for the time being, either because they feel they can do nothing to alter them or, more importantly, because of the rewards which stable group relations offer to all those concerned. Organizations are not, therefore ... merely systems of power. But it is also true that the *values* of actors are involved to a greater or lesser extent in any particular role-system. They may, therefore, be more or less continuously involved in seeking to maintain or to alter the rules of the game ...

It is now possible to suggest the path along which an Action analysis of organizations might proceed. It should look at six inter-related areas in the following sequence:

1. The nature of the role-system and pattern of interaction that has been built up in the organization, in particular the way in which it has historically developed and the extent to which it represents the shared values of all or some or none of the actors.

2. The nature of involvement of ideal-typical actors (e.g. moral, alienative, instrumental) and the characteristic hierarchy of ends which they pursue (work satisfaction, material rewards, security). The way in which these derive from their biographies outside the organizations (job history, family commitments, social background) and from their experience of the organization itself.

3. The actors' present definitions of their situation within the organization and their expectations of the likely behaviour of others with particular reference to the strategic resources they perceive to be at their own disposal and at the disposal of others (degree of coercive power or moral authority; belief in individual opportunity).

4. The typical actions of different actors and the meaning which they attach to their action.

5. The nature and source of the intended and unintended consequences of action, with special reference to its effects on the involvement of the various actors and on the institutionalization of expectations in the role-system within which they interact.

6. Changes in the involvement and ends of the actors and in the role-system, and their source both in the outcome of the interaction of the actors and in the changing stock of knowledge outside the organization (e.g. political or legal changes; the varied experiences and expectations of different generations).

51   Erving Goffman
Total Institutions

Excerpts from Erving Goffman, *Asylums*, Doubleday Anchor, 1961, pp. 4–12, 118–19.

Every institution captures something of the time and interests of its members and provides something of a world for them; in brief, every institution has encompassing tendencies. When we review the different institutions in our Western society, we find some that are encompassing to a degree discontinuously greater than the ones next in line. Their encompassing or total character is symbolized by the barrier to social intercourse with the outside and to departure that is often built right into the physical plant, such as locked doors, high walls, barbed wire, cliffs, water, forests, or moors. These establishments I am calling *total institutions*, and it is their general characteristics I want to explore.

The total institutions of our society can be listed in five rough groupings. First, there are institutions established to care for persons felt to be both incapable and harmless; these are the homes for the blind, the aged, the orphaned, and the indigent. Second, there are places established to care for persons felt to be both incapable of looking after themselves and a threat to the community, albeit an unintended one: TB sanitaria, mental hospitals, and leprosaria. A third type of total institution is organized to protect the community against what are felt to be intentional dangers to it, with the welfare of the persons thus sequestered not the immediate issue: jails, penitentiaries, P.O.W. camps, and concentration camps. Fourth, there are institutions purportedly established the better to pursue some worklike task and justifying themselves only on these instrumental grounds: army barracks, ships, boarding schools, work camps, colonial compounds, and large mansions from the point of view of those who live in the servants' quarters. Finally, there are those establishments designed as retreats from the world even while often serving also as training stations for the religious; examples are abbeys, monasteries, convents, and other cloisters. This classification of total institutions is not neat, exhaustive, nor of immediate analytical use, but it does provide a purely denotative definition of the category as a concrete starting point. By anchoring the initial definition of total institutions in this way, I hope to be able to discuss the general characteristics of the type without becoming tautological.

Before I attempt to extract a general profile from this list of establishments, I would like to mention one conceptual problem: none of the elements I will describe seems peculiar to total institutions, and none seems to be shared by every one of them; what is distinctive about total institutions is that each exhibits to an intense degree many items in this family of attributes . . .

A basic social arrangement in modern society is that the individual tends to sleep, play, and work in different places, with different co-participants, under different authorities, and without an overall rational plan. The central feature of total institutions can be described as a breakdown of the barriers ordinarily separating these three spheres of life. First, all aspects of life are conducted in the same place and under the same single authority. Second, each phase of the member's daily activity is carried on in the immediate company of a large batch of others, all of whom are treated alike and required to do the same thing together. Third, all phases of the day's activities are tightly scheduled, with one activity leading at a prearranged time into the next, the whole sequence of activities being imposed from above by a system of explicit formal rulings and a body of officials. Finally, the various enforced activities are brought together into a single rational plan purportedly designed to fulfil the official aims of the institution.

Individually, these features are found in places other than total institutions. For example, our large commercial, industrial, and educational establishments are increasingly providing cafeterias and free-time recreation for their members; use of these extended facilities remains voluntary in many particulars, however, and special care is taken to see that the ordinary line of authority does not extend to them . . .

The handling of many human needs by the bureaucratic organization of whole blocks of people — whether or not this is a necessary or effective means of social organization in the circumstances — is the key fact of total institutions. From this follow certain important implications.

When persons are moved in blocks, they can be supervised by personnel whose chief activity is not guidance or periodic inspection (as in many employer–employee relations) but rather surveillance – a seeing to it that everyone does what he has been clearly told is required of him, under conditions where one person's infraction is likely to stand out in relief against the visible, constantly examined compliance of the others. Which comes first, the large blocks of managed people, or the small supervisory staff, is not here at issue; the point is that each is made for the other.

In total institutions there is a basic split between a large managed group, conveniently called inmates, and a small supervisory staff. Inmates typically live in the institution and have restricted contact with the world outside the walls; staff often operate on an eight-hour day and are socially integrated into the outside world. Each grouping tends to conceive of the other in terms of narrow hostile stereotypes, staff often seeing inmates as bitter, secretive, and untrustworthy, while inmates often see staff as condescending, high-handed, and mean. Staff tend to feel superior and righteous; inmates tend, in some ways at least, to feel inferior, weak, blameworthy, and guilty.

Social mobility between the two strata is grossly restricted; social distance is typically great and often formally prescribed. Even talk across the boundaries may be conducted in a special tone of voice . . . Just as talk across the boundary is restricted, so, too, is the passage of information, especially information about the staff's plans for inmates. Characteristically, the inmate is excluded from knowledge of the decisions taken regarding his fate. Whether the official grounds are military, as in concealing travel destination from enlisted men, or medical, as in concealing diagnosis, plan of treatment, and approximate length of stay from tuberculosis patients, such exclusion gives staff a special basis of distance from and control over inmates.

All these restrictions of contact presumably help to maintain the antagonistic stereotypes. Two different social and cultural worlds develop, jogging alongside each other with points of official contact but little mutual penetration. Significantly, the institutional plant and name come to be identified by both staff and inmates as somehow belonging to staff, so that when either grouping refers to the views or interests of 'the institution', by implication they are referring (as I shall also) to the views and concerns of the staff.

The staff–inmate split is one major implication of the bureaucratic management of large blocks of persons; a second pertains to work.

In the ordinary arrangements of living in our society, the authority of the work place stops with the worker's receipt of a money payment; the spending of this in a domestic and recreational setting is the worker's private affair and constitutes a mechanism through which the authority of the work place is kept within strict bounds. But to say that inmates of total institutions have their full day scheduled for them is to say that all their essential needs will have to be planned for. Whatever the incentive given for work, then, this incentive will not have the structural significance it has on the outside. There will have to be different motives for work and different attitudes toward it. This is a basic adjustment required of the inmates and of those who must induce them to work.

Sometimes so little work is required that inmates, often untrained in leisurely pursuits, suffer extremes of boredom . . . In other cases, of course, more than a full day's hard labour is required, induced not by reward but by threat of physical punishment . . .

Whether there is too much work or too little, the individual who was work-oriented on the outside tends to become demoralized by the work system of the total institution . . .

There is an incompatibility, then, between total institutions and the basic work-payment structure of our society. Total institutions are also incompatible with another crucial element of our society, the family. Family life is sometimes contrasted with solitary living, but in fact the more pertinent contrast is with batch living, for those who eat and sleep at work, with a group of fellow workers, can hardly sustain a meaningful domestic existence. Conversely, maintaining families off the grounds often permits staff members to remain integrated with the outside community and to escape the encompassing tendency of the total institution . . .

The total institution is a social hybrid, part residential community, part formal organization; therein lies its special sociological interest. There are other reasons for being interested in these establishments, too. In our society, they are the forcing houses for changing persons; each is a natural experiment on what can be done to the self . . .

Recruits enter total institutions in different spirits. At one extreme we find the quite involuntary entrance of those who are sentenced to prison, committed to a mental hospital, or pressed into the crew of a ship. It is perhaps in such circumstances that staff's version of the ideal inmate has least chance of taking hold. At the other extreme, we find religious institutions that deal only with those who feel they have gotten the call and, of these volunteers, take only those who seem to be the most suitable and the most serious in their intentions. (Presumably some officer training camps and some political training schools qualify here, too.) In such cases, conversion seems already to have taken place, and it only remains to show the neophyte along what lines he can best discipline himself. Midway between these two extremes we find institutions, like the Army in regard to conscripts, where inmates are required to serve but are given much opportunity to feel that this service is a justifiable one required in their own ultimate interests. Obviously, significant differences in tone will appear in total institutions, depending on whether recruitment is voluntary, semi-voluntary, or involuntary.

Along with the variable of mode of recruitment there is another variable – the degree to which a self-regulating change in the inmate is explicitly striven for by staff. In custodial and work institutions, presumably, the inmate need only comply with action standards; the spirit and inward feeling with which he goes about his assignment would not seem to be an official concern. In brainwashing camps, religious establishments, and institutions for intensive psychotherapy, the inmate's private feelings are presumably at issue. Mere compliance with work rulings would not here seem to be enough, and the inmate's incorporation of staff standards is an active aim as well as an incidental consequence.

52   Veronica Beechey

Explaining Women's Employment

Excerpts from Veronica Beechey, 'Women's Employment in Contemporary Britain', in Veronica Beechey and Elizabeth Whitelegg (eds.), *Women in Britain Today*, Open University Press, 1986, pp. 103, 108–16, 123–6.

Commonsense and Structural Explanations

Any explanation of women's employment must address the [following] kinds of questions: why women have different patterns of participation in the labour market than men, why women in general and black women in particular are concentrated in particular industries and occupations, why part-time work and home-work are distinctively feminine forms of work in our society, and why women's earnings are systematically lower than men's. A variety of explanations of these phenomena exist in commonsense discourse, in statements like the following, for instance:

(a)   women are better than men at doing boring repetitive work;
(b)   men have an aptitude for mechanical skills;
(c)   women are not interested in career or promotion prospects;
(d)   women cannot lift heavy weights;
(e)   women are not capable of taking responsibility at work.

One of the characteristics of these commonsense explanations is that they explain women's and men's positions within the labour force in terms of characteristics of women and men themselves. For example, the claim that women are not interested in career or promotion prospects assumes that the underrepresentation of women among professionals and managers results from women's lack of interest. And the claim that women cannot lift heavy weights explains women's absence from certain jobs in terms of physiological characteristics. In explaining the characteristic features of women's position in the labour force in terms of characteristics of women themselves, the commonsense explanations are all individualistic forms of explanation. They involve 'blaming the victim'. They explain the position of women in the occupational structure in terms of assertions about women's nature, capabilities or temperament rather than social structures. Individualistic explanations very often implicitly or explicitly involve biologically determinist claims, that is, claims that women's capabilities are determined by their biological attributes . . .

Dual Labour Market Theory

The central focus of dual labour market theory is on the structure of the labour market. [Thus] Barron and Norris do not disregard the impact of the family on the structure of the labour market, but they argue that the sexual division of labour within the family is of less importance in explaining sexual divisions within the labour market than are employers' strategies within the labour market:

The emphasis in this paper is on the structure of the labour market, and the question of men and women's place in the family – the household sexual division of labour – is relegated to the status of an explanatory factor which contributes to, but does not of itself determine, the differentiation between the sexes in their work roles.

Dual labour market theory shares with other economic theories this emphasis upon the labour market. However, it analyses the labour market in a distinctive way. Whereas economists conventionally think of the labour market as a unitary phenomenon, dual labour market theory emphasizes segmentation within the labour market. Barron and Norris outline their perspective on the labour market in the following extract:

There are . . . many ways of characterizing a labour market . . . All of these models have some explanatory value, but this paper concentrates upon one type of segmental model; the 'dual' labour market. A dual labour market is one in which:

1. There is a more or less pronounced division into higher paying and lower paying sectors;
2. Mobility across the boundary of these sectors is restricted;
3. Higher-paying jobs are tied into promotional or career ladders, while lower-paid jobs offer few opportunities for vertical movement;
4. Higher-paying jobs are relatively stable, while lower-paid jobs are unstable.

They argue that the labour market is divided into primary and secondary sectors. This results from the strategies which employers use to tie skilled and technical workers into the firm. Employers offer workers in the primary labour market higher earnings and better career prospects to persuade them to stay in the firm. Barron and Norris suggest a variety of reasons why employers privilege primary sector workers in this way. Among the most important are: the need to have a stable workforce in jobs that require extensive training and investment by the firm; a desire to weaken the unity of the working class, thereby reducing the potential for conflict in the workplace; and a desire to 'buy off' the most militant and well-organized sectors of the working class.

Dual labour market theory argues that employers do not privilege secondary sector workers in this way. These tend to work in unskilled and service jobs which have low skill requirements and require little training. Whereas primary sector workers are tied into the firm's career structure, secondary sector workers tend to move between industries and occupations, between one unskilled or semiskilled low-paying job and another . . .

Barron and Norris suggest that in Britain women comprise the major secondary sector workforce. They argue that employers often use ascriptive criteria in selecting workers – that is, they select workers on the basis of characteristics like age, sex or skin colour, which the individual acquired at birth, rather than on the basis of achievement criteria like educational qualifications . . .

Barron and Norris argue that there are five main attributes that make a particular social group or category a likely source of secondary workers:

1. Dispensability – the ease with which an employee can be removed from a redundant job.
2. Clearly visible social difference – preferably one which emphasizes the relative inferiority of the secondary group.
3. Little interest in acquiring training and experience.
4. Low economism, i.e. little concern for monetary rewards.
5. Lack of solidarism – for instance, relatively low level of trade union or collective strength.

Women, they argue, are likely to score high on each of these criteria, and are therefore commonly used as secondary sector workers. Members of minority ethnic groups, too, often score high on these criteria, and may also be used as secondary sector workers . . .

Dual labour market theory is, however, limited in the extent to which it can explain occupational segregation, because its analysis is derived from an account of employers' strategies in particular kinds of manufacturing industry. The theory is most satisfactory when it deals with industries like the car industry, in which men are employed in skilled and technical jobs. In such industries, it may well make sense to characterize women's work as secondary sector work. However, many kinds of women's jobs do not fit easily into the category of secondary sector work. Some women's work in manufacturing industries is skilled work that is integral to the production process, for example, work in the textiles industry. Although this may be low paid in comparison with men's work, it is not marginal or insecure as secondary sector work is. Much secretarial work throughout all sectors of the economy requires considerable training, and secretarial workers are an integral part of the workforce. Although secretarial work may not be well paid in comparison with some men's jobs, and although it may not actually be defined as skilled, it is not marginal and insecure. Finally, a good number of women are employed in professional and technical jobs, especially in the public sector. The most obvious examples of these are nursing, teaching and social work – all important 'women's professions'. Women are also employed to some extent in some management jobs, especially in these sectors. These require training, they are highly skilled, and are central to the activities of the health, education and social services sectors. Dual labour market theory's conception of women being a secondary sector workforce cannot adequately account for these kinds of women's work. A major problem with dual labour market theory is that it derives its whole conceptual edifice from an account of manufacturing occupations within manufacturing industry, and it generally assumes that women do semi-skilled or unskilled work . . .

Marxist Approaches

A Marxist approach, like dual labour market theory, focuses primarily upon the demand for labour. Marxists have developed a number of theories about the ways in which women workers are employed in advanced capitalist societies, and in this section I shall discuss the argument put forward by Harry Braverman in his book called *Labor and Monopoly Capital*, which has become a classical study of waged work in capitalist societies . . .

Braverman argues . . . that in the form of society which he calls monopoly capitalist – that is, the form of capitalism which exists in twentieth-century Britain and the USA – the economy is more and more dominated by large corporations, and work has become increasingly subdivided so that unskilled labour has been substituted for complex skilled labour. This is because it is cheaper to pay unskilled workers than skilled craftsmen.

Braverman locates his analysis of women's employment within this general analysis of the subdivision of labour, and he argues that there has been a long-term shift in the structure of the working class as a result of this process. Women have been drawn into paid employment mainly in service occupations, which have been expanding under monopoly capitalism, whereas men have been employed in declining manufacturing occupations. There has thus developed a new form of sexual division of labour within the working class, in which women and men are employed in fairly equal proportions, with women being employed in the expanding service occupations like clerical work and retail sales work, and men employed in manufacturing occupations. Braverman thus suggests that a new form of sexual division of labour has developed under monopoly capitalism, and that in the typical working-class family the man is employed as an operative and the woman as a clerical or service worker.

Why, according to Braverman, have women been drawn into work in these service occupations? He points to a number of factors which he thinks have been important in drawing women into paid employment. First, he suggests that, as the capitalist mode of production developed, domestic production within the family was broken down. Women found that they could buy goods and services that they had previously produced within the domestic economy (e.g. cloth, food, clothing) and they thus began to purchase them rather than make them themselves. Second, women were drawn into paid employment to produce the same kinds of goods and services as they had previously produced within the domestic economy. Braverman suggests that women were able to move fairly automatically from working within the domestic economy to working in production outside the home. Third, women have been drawn into paid employment as traditional sources of labour (people migrating from countryside to towns, ex-slaves moving to work in the Northern States, and migrants from Southern and Eastern Europe) have dried up, particularly in the period of expansion since the Second World War. Women have thus become part of the industrial reserve army of labour; this is a reserve of labour which can be drawn on by employers when there is a shortage of labour. Finally, and most importantly, Braverman argues, women are a source of cheap and unskilled labour. This is the major reason why employers hire them . . .

His analysis cannot, however, be used to analyse all forms of women's employment in capitalist societies. It cannot explain women's employment in professional occupations like nursing, teaching and social work (although his deskilling arguments do shed some light on the increasing use of women as unqualified nurses, social workers and teaching assistants to do work which was previously done by qualified professionals). Nor can it easily explain women's employment in jobs which have never been defined as skilled, like much women's work in the service sectors of the economy, nor why many women's jobs are not classified as skilled work when they involve complex competencies. Finally, it cannot explain the reskilling which has occurred in certain kinds of work. Braverman's exclusive emphasis on deskilling ignores, for instance, the fact that the introduction of new technology into the secretarial and clerical fields has created some new skills as well as destroying old ones, as has the use of computerized technology in the health service and in some sectors of manufacturing industry (e.g. telecommunications) . . .

The Family and Women's Employment

Both the family and familial ideology have an important role in determining women's position in the labour market, something which the women's two roles theorists recognized but which generally goes unnoticed in theoretical perspectives which focus on the labour market and the labour process. At the most concrete level, women's participation in the labour force is affected by whether or not they have children, and is most crucially affected by the age of the youngest child. This determines whether or not a woman does paid work, whether she works full-time or part-time (especially if she is white) and the kinds of jobs she does. Furthermore, caring for elderly and handicapped relatives is also becoming increasingly important in preventing some women from doing paid work, especially in mid-life. It is estimated that in London there are more women caring for elderly and handicapped relatives than for children under 16. In the absence of adequate facilities for caring for children, and for elderly and handicapped people in the community, and as back-up facilities like home helps and meals-on-wheels are being cut by many local authorities, it becomes increasingly difficult for women who have responsibilities for caring for others to work full-time.

In addition to determining both the likelihood and the hours of work, home responsibilities influence the type of work undertaken. A study of female factory workers noted that 'employment has to be fitted in with their household duties and childcare arrangements, which they and their families regard as unquestionably their responsibility. Factory work is often seen as the only job possible in the circumstances and entered into more from necessity than from choice.' Similarly, a study of home-workers concluded that 'many mothers gave as their reason . . . the flexibility it gave them to work when it was convenient to them' . . .

Another way in which the sexual division of labour within the family affects women's employment is in the kind of jobs that women do. Many women do jobs that replicate their domestic responsibilities. This has been true historically, and is still true today, and is especially true of black women's jobs . . .

Much women's work, particularly in the Welfare State, involves skills that women learn, at least in part, in the family (e.g. caring, cleaning, preparing and cooking food) – although in non-manual and professional jobs, in particular, these skills are greatly supplemented by formal training programmes. Feminists have also pointed out that women's work often involves other skills and attitudes which are typically 'feminine', particularly in non-manual jobs. These are jobs in which glamour and sexuality are often an integral part of the job (e.g. air hostess, model, and some top-level secretarial jobs). What these share in common with the more domestic and caring jobs first discussed is the incorporation, within the definition of the jobs, of important aspects of women's more general social role . . .

Today women's paid work is becoming more recognized and acceptable. Nevertheless, it is still assumed that a woman's work outside the home should not interfere with her domestic responsibilities in caring for her husband and particularly in caring for her children and other dependent relatives. Women's paid work must fit in with her domestic role and she must be a good wife and mother.

Despite the fact that fewer and fewer families correspond to the nuclear model with male breadwinner, non-working wife and dependent children, familial ideology remains pervasive. It is a crucial element of the dominant ideology. It plays an important role in structuring a woman's participation in the labour market and in restricting opportunities for paid work. It affects her participation in the labour market, deeming it unacceptable for her to work when she should be caring for others. It enters into the construction of certain jobs as 'women's jobs' and other jobs as 'men's jobs' with women's jobs frequently involving caring for and servicing others. It is used to depict women who work full-time (black women in particular) as 'bad mothers'. And finally, it is embedded in the concept of the family wage – the notion that a man's major responsibility is as family breadwinner and that he should provide for a dependent wife and children – which is still prevalent within employers' and trade unions' ways of thinking about wages. When ideologies make differentiations among people on the basis of ascriptive characteristics like age, sex, or race they tend to be particularly pervasive because they represent social relations as though they were natural. Familial ideology, which assumes that women are primarily wives and mothers, plays an important role in the organization of paid employment, while simultaneously portraying the sexual division of labour and women's position in the labour market in quasi-naturalistic terms.

Part Nine
Ethnicity and Race

Sociology emerged as a discipline during the nineteenth century, a period which also saw the rise of modern imperialism and the intellectual victory of Darwinism in biology: events which necessarily impressed early sociologists, some of whom assumed, uncritically, that they were directly interconnected. Thus 'Social' Darwinists tried to explain the success of the West in establishing its rule over the entire world in terms of the assumed superiority of some races and inferiority of others.

Subsequent biological research has rejected the basic assumptions these theories were built on: first, because the way nineteenth-century scientists had gone about defining race – in terms of assumed hard-and-fast physical differences – was itself problematic, since there was often as much, if not more, variation of physical type within populations assumed to constitute distinct 'races' as between them; second, because people who shared one physical characteristic didn't necessarily share others; and third, because the very category of 'race', in its nineteenth-century version, was no longer valid, since modern genetics looked at populations (which might be chosen in the light of *various* criteria) in terms of statistical differences between and within such populations, rather than assuming that every individual member of such a population shared one or more common characteristic.

The principal criticism developed by social scientists focused on the observation that physical differences (hair colour, say, or body size), by no means necessarily gave rise to distinct social groupings, but might be treated as socially irrelevant, while other minimal, even invisible, physical differences might conversely be *thought* to indicate common descent and therefore membership of not only a distinct physical stock but also an inferior one. The crucial issue for social science, then, became the study of racist belief as ideology: how it was that such beliefs came into existence and what sustained them, and the study, too, of the ways in which they were *used* to justify discriminatory social practices. Racist ideologies therefore began to be treated not just as intellectual errors, but 'situated' in terms of their social sources and effects and the varied social contexts in which racism manifested itself, from societal institutions like *apartheid*, designed to keep 'inferior' races subservient, to the myriad *ad hoc* occasions of interpersonal racist behaviour.

An early modern attempt to express the special features of societies overtly based on racial inequality came, not surprisingly, from a student of colonial society, J. S. Furnivall, who formulated the concept of the 'plural society' (Reading 53). Like class societies, plural societies were divided horizontally by differences of property and income. But these economic differences were themselves the outcome of prior divisions along racial lines, divisions brought into being and enforced as a consequence of conquest and rule by foreign colonizers. Between these racial groups, moreover, there was no social intercourse other than that entailed by economic necessity: by the requirements of systems of production and exchange.

There have been many areas of debate among students of race relations, of which the notion of the plural society has been only one, though an important one. Nevertheless, since we cannot cover all these areas in a brief selection, we include three contributions on this particular central theme. M. G. Smith (Reading 54), for instance, drawing on Caribbean research, examined, much more carefully than Furnivall, how each racial group in a plural society had its own complex of culture: different marriage systems, different religions, different languages, etc. Within each of these communities there was, indeed, horizontal class stratification into rich and poor. But overall, the hierarchy that unified the whole was a hierarchy of power: a system of *political* domination.

Rex (Reading 55) later argued that both Furnivall's emphasis on the economy, with the market place as the central institution, and Smith's emphasis upon government as the framework within which all other social relations took place, each capture one, but only one, important aspect of what he calls 'race relations situations': situations which involve *both* the economic exploitation and the political oppression of one group by another (a situation which is extremely common), but where, in addition, these arrangements are 'justified' by appeal to a theory about the believed genetic or biological inferiority of the oppressed group. It is this last factor which distinguished racist societies from other forms of domination, such as the societies of modern capitalist Europe. The presence of highly visible physical differences, especially those of 'colour' (itself a short-hand term for a number of physical differences), also makes it especially difficult for anyone in the minority group to cross social boundaries by 'passing': say by intermarrying or joining the social clubs or political parties, of the dominant group.

These arguments about the concept of the plural society, however, all share in common an approach to the subject of race relations which starts from a societal perspective. Wallman (Reading 56), however, approaches the phenomenon of racial inequality differently: not by examining the structure of the racial system as a whole, but by taking it for granted, and starting instead with what, she suggests, is the reality of social life for Blacks in contemporary Britain, for instance: the necessity of living within a system they can't do much about, while trying, at the same time, to manipulate it to their own advantage. Critics of this approach have objected that the capacity to do this is so circumscribed – by the superior power of the White majority and by the use of colour as a means of allocating people to inferior roles in society – that the whole approach suggests too rosy a view of racial inequality.

The last reading (Reading 57), by Banton, is taken from a distinguished contribution to the theory of race relations. We have selected passages from the conclusions to that work because it uses theory for purposes to which sociologists do not often address themselves: understanding the implications of the various kinds of practical policies commonly advocated as ways of counteracting and eventually abolishing racism.

53   J. S. Furnivall

Plural Economies

Excerpts from J. S. Furnivall, *Netherlands India: A Study of Plural Economy*, Cambridge University Press, 1939, pp. 446–51, 458–9.

Plural Societies. Netherlands India [now Indonesia] is an example of a plural society; a society, that is, comprising two or more elements or social orders which live side by side, yet without mingling, in one political unit. In this matter Netherlands India is typical of tropical dependencies where the rulers and the ruled are of different races; but one finds a plural society also in independent states, such as Siam, where Natives, Chinese and Europeans have distinct economic functions, and live apart as separate social orders. Nor is the plural society confined to the tropics; it may be found also in temperate regions where, as in South Africa and the United States, there are both white and coloured populations. Again, one finds a plural society in the French provinces of Canada, where two peoples are separated by race, language and religion, and an English lad, brought up in an English school, has no contact with French life; and in countries such as Ireland where, with little or no difference of race or language, the people are sharply divided in their religious allegiance. Even where there is no difference of creed or colour, a community may still have a plural character, as in Western Canada, where people of different racial origin tend to live in distinct settlements and, for example, a Northern European cannot find work on the railway, because this is reserved for 'Dagoes' or 'Wops'. And in lands where a strong Jewish element is regarded as alien, there is to that extent a plural society. Thus Netherlands India is merely an extreme type of a large class of political organizations.

The Plural State. Let us turn then to examine some outstanding features of the economic aspect of social organization in such a plural society or, in other words, the distinctive characteristics of plural economy. The most obvious feature is already indicated in the name;

in a plural society there is no common will except, possibly, in matters of supreme importance, such as resistance to aggression from outside. In its political aspect a plural society resembles a confederation of allied provinces, united by treaty or within the limits of a formal constitution, merely for certain ends common to the constituent units and, in matters outside the terms of union, each living its own life. But it differs from a confederation in that the constituent elements are not segregated each within its own territorial limits. In a confederation secession is at least possible without the total disruption of all social bonds, whereas in a plural society the elements are so intermingled that secession is identical with anarchy. Thus a plural society has the instability of a confederation, but without the remedy which is open to a confederation if the yoke of common union should become intolerable . . .

Social Demand. In economic life this lack of a common will, which characterizes plural societies, finds expression in the absence of any common social demand . . . Successive generations of political economists, although prefacing their studies with a definition of political economy as the science dealing with the consumption as well as with the production, exchange, and distribution of wealth, found nothing to say about consumption except, perhaps, a few stale platitudes . . . Problems of demand [were discussed only in terms of] aggregate and joint demand . . . But these are quite distinct from social, or collective, demand; aggregate demand differs from social demand as the will of all differs from the general will, and problems of social demand still await adequate examination. Every political society from the nomad tribe to the sovereign nation, builds up, gradually during the course of ages, its own civilization and distinctive culture, its own ethos; it has its own religious creed or complex of creeds; its own art in all the aspects of literature, painting, sculpture and music; and its own conventions in the daily round of life: part of this large process is the building up of a system of informal education by which each citizen, quite apart from all formal instruction, is moulded as a member of that particular society, and develops social wants, which he experiences only as a member of that society and can satisfy only as a member of that society. Religious, political and aesthetic needs do not, as such, come within the scope of economics; nevertheless, all cultural needs have an economic aspect because they find organized expression only as economic wants, as demand. It is a matter of economic indifference whether a man sings in his bath or says his prayers, but social hygiene and common prayer involve organization and expenditure; we build cathedrals with the same coins that are current in the market place, and the money in the temple treasury bears the image and superscription of Caesar, so that the good housewife, who tries to get marginal value for her expenditure, must be no less careful in her charities and recreations than in buying beef or butter. Every social want, then, has its economic aspect, and in any community the resultant of such social wants is the economic aspect of its civilization or, in other words, the social demand of the community taken as a whole. But, in a plural society, social demand is disorganized; social wants are sectional, and there is no social demand common to all the several elements.

Distinctive Characters. This disorganization of social demand in a plural society has far-reaching effects; it is the root cause of all those properties which differentiate plural economy, the political economy of a plural society, from unitary economy, the political economy of a homogeneous society. Of necessity it raises the economic criterion to a new place in the scale of social values. For there is one place in which the various sections of a plural society meet on common ground – the market place; and the highest common factor of their wants is the economic factor. They may differ in creed and custom, in the kind of music or style of painting they prefer; the members of different sections may want one thing rather than another; but if they want the same thing, they will all prefer to get it for twopence rather than for threepence ... It is common sense to pay twopence rather than threepence, and anyone who can produce a commodity for twopence will be able to undersell competitors who cannot produce it for less than threepence. But, in a unitary society, the working of the economic process is controlled by social will, and if the cheaper vendor cuts the price by methods which offend the social conscience, he will incur moral and perhaps legal penalties; for example, if he employs sweated labour, the social conscience, if sufficiently alert and powerful, may penalize him because aware, instinctively or by rational persuasion, that such conduct cuts at the root of social life. Thus the test of cheapness is valid only in the economics of production and not throughout the whole of social life; it is a standard applicable to supply but inapplicable to demand, and the keenest advocate of cheap production may be equally the stout adversary of sweated labour. Yet in a plural society the economic test is the only test which the several elements can apply in common; all other tests involve considerations transcending common sense and may be regarded as ultimately religious in their character; in the application of such tests reason is no final authority and their validity depends on a conflict of will. Within a society of this type the rules of international morality apply, and the mutual relations of the elements of a plural society tend to be governed solely by the economic process with the production of material goods as the prime end of social life. The fundamental character of the organization of a plural society as a whole is indeed the structure of a factory, organized for production, rather than of a state, organized for the good life of its members . . .

One consequence of the emphasis on production rather than on social life . . . is a sectional division of labour; although the primary distinction between the groups may be race, creed or colour, each section comes to have its own functions in production, and there is a tendency towards the grouping of the several elements into distinct economic castes . . . In Canada an Englishman cannot find work on the railways because this is a prerogative of the peoples of Southern or Eastern Europe . . . thus in Canada there are castes with a double character, racial and economic, much as in British India although, of course, far less sharply defined . . . Similarly in Java, where, even in Hindu times, caste never seems to have been so rigid as in British India, the present distribution of economic functions coincides largely with racial differences, and certain occupations are reserved, partly of deliberate intention but more by the working of the economic process, for Europeans, others for the Chinese and others again for Natives . . .

This distribution of production among racial castes aggravates the inherent sectionalism of demand; for a community which is confined to certain economic functions finds it more difficult to apprehend the social needs of the country as a whole. In a homogeneous society the soldier looks at social problems from the standpoint of the soldier, the merchant looks at them as a merchant and the cultivator as a cultivator; yet at the same time they regard such problems from the standpoint of a common citizenship, and the soldier, merchant or cultivator cannot wholly disregard the views and interests of other classes. In every community there is a conflict of interest between town and country, industry and agriculture, capital and labour; but the asperity of conflict is softened by a common citizenship. In a tropical dependency, however, the conflict between rival economic interests tends to be exacerbated by racial diversity. Thus, in British India, one finds Europeans in the towns, directing industry and owning capital, and Natives up-country, engaged in agriculture and owning little but their labour ... In proportion as conflicting economic interests are complicated by racial diversity, all members of all sections find a greater difficulty in regarding social problems from the standpoint of the common weal, and demand, like production, becomes sectionalized. Plural economy differs then from a homogeneous economy firstly because, in place of a social demand common to the whole society, there are two or more distinct and rival complexes of social demand proper to each constituent element; secondly, by the grouping of production into castes; and, thirdly, by the further sectionalization of demand which follows when the social demand, proper to each constituent element, ceases to embrace the whole scope of social life and becomes concentrated on those aspects of social life falling within its separate province.

There is still a further consequence, that within each section the economic side of life is emphasized. As Dr Boeke writes ... 'there is materialism, rationalism, individualism and a concentration on economic ends far more complete and absolute than in homogeneous Western lands; a total absorption in the Exchange and Market; a capitalist structure, with the business concern as subject, far more typical of Capitalism than one can imagine in the so-called 'capitalist' countries which have grown slowly out of the past and are still bound to it by a hundred roots' ...

In a plural society ... each [community] lives within a closed compartment and life within each section becomes narrower ... The community tends to be organized for production rather than for social life; social demand is sectionalized, and within each section of the community the social demand becomes disorganized and ineffective, so that in each section the members are debarred from leading the full life of a citizen in a homogeneous community ...

54   M. G. Smith

Social and Cultural Pluralism

Excerpts from M. G. Smith, *The Plural Society in the British West Indies*, University of California Press, 1965, pp. 75–6, 79–91.

J. S. Furnivall was the first to distinguish the plural society as a separate form of society . . . He saw clearly that this economic pluralism was simply an aspect of the social pluralism of these colonies . . . [I would also add that] social pluralism is . . . correlated with cultural pluralism, and [that] the plural society itself develops in rather special, although by no means unusual, conditions. Accordingly, I shall begin by considering the most general problems of social science, namely, the nature of culture and society and their interrelation . . .

In my view, only territorially distinct units having their own governmental institutions can be regarded as societies, or are in fact so regarded. Delegation of authority and governmental function is quite general and has many forms, but we do not normally treat an official structure as an independent government unless it settles all internal issues of law and order independently. By this criterion we can identify delegation and delimit societies. It often happens that a subordinate population group is permitted to exercise certain functions of internal administration; one does not thereby distinguish it as a separate society . . .

I hold that the core of a culture is its institutional system. Each institution involves set forms of activity, grouping, rules, ideas, and values. The total system of institutions thus embraces three interdependent systems of action, of idea and value, and of social relations. The interdependence of these three systems arises from the fact that their elements together form a common system of institutions. These institutions are integral wholes, as Malinowski would say, and their values, activities, and social forms are mutually supporting. The institutions of a people's culture form the matrix of their social structure, simply because the institutional system defines and sanctions the persistent forms of social life . . .

It follows from this that a population that shares a single set of institutions will be culturally and socially homogeneous. Provided that it is also politically distinct, it will also form a homogeneous society. The homogeneity of this unit will be evident in the uniformity of its social structure, ideational systems, and action patterns . . .

It also follows that institutional diversities involve differences of social structure, ideational systems, and forms of social action. These differences may conceivably hold for a single institution, such as the family, or for an entire institutional system. Territorially distinct units that practise differing institutional systems and that are politically separate are culturally as well as socially distinct. In short, institutional differences distinguish differing cultures and social units. When groups that practise differing institutional systems live side by side under a common government the cultural plurality of this inclusive unit corresponds with its social plurality, and the network of social relations between these culturally distinct groups is wider and more complex than those within them. In short, culture and society are not always coterminous or interdependent. We do in fact find societies the component sections of which have dissimilar ways of life and modes of social organization. Such societies exhibit cultural and social pluralism simultaneously.

Institutions have been treated as cultural forms by some writers and as social forms by others. Actually, they combine social and cultural aspects equally. Their social aspects consist of set forms of groupings and relations. Their systems of norm and activity, together with their material apparatus, properly belong to culture. Although institutions form the core of culture and society alike, they do not exhaust either. For our purpose, the important thing to note is that a group's institutional homogeneity involves its cultural and social homogeneity, while institutional pluralism involves corresponding cultural and social pluralism. A society the members of which share a common system of basic or 'compulsory' institutions but practise differing 'alternative' and 'exclusive' institutions is neither fully homogeneous nor fully plural. Such units are socially and culturally heterogeneous . . .

Institutions dealing with the same phases of life tend to form a systematic cluster, and to forestall confusion I shall speak of these clusters as sub-systems. Thus marriage, family, levirate, extended kinship forms, and the like, together constitute the kinship sub-system. Likewise, government is the sub-system of explicitly regulative institutions, such as law, parliament, police, and civil and military administration. Each of these institutional sub-systems has many links with the others; thus the kinship institutions have prominent economic, educational, recreative, religious, and governmental aspects. We need not predicate any pre-established harmony of institutions, as functional theory has tended to do. The available evidence suggests that consistency, interdependence, and coherence are necessarily greater within each institutional sub-system than between them. This set of institutional sub-systems forms the institutional system, and this can vary widely in its mode and level of integration and equilibrium. Societies differ in their complement and distribution of institutional forms. Some lack such institutions as the army, the priesthood, chieftainship, markets, or age sets; but any given institutional system tends towards an internal integration and thus some closure. Thus in a culturally divided society, each cultural section has its own relatively exclusive way of life, with its own distinctive systems of action, ideas and values, and social relations. Often these cultural sections differ also in language, material culture, and technology. The culture concept is normally wider than that of society, since it includes conventions, language, and technology, but the presence of two or more culturally distinct groups within a single society shows that these two aspects of social reality may vary independently in their limits and interrelations . . .

It is obvious that modern societies are culturally heterogeneous in many ways. They contain a wide range of occupational specialties, they exhibit stratification and class differences, they often contain ethnic minorities, and their rural and urban populations have somewhat different ways of life. Some writers describe modern society as pluralistic because of its occupational diversity. I prefer to say that it is culturally heterogeneous, and to reserve the term pluralism for that condition in which there is a formal diversity in the basic system of compulsory institutions. This basic institutional system embraces kinship, education, religion, property and economy, recreation, and certain sodalities. It does not normally include government in the full sense of the term for reasons given below. Occupations are simply specialties . . .

The development of occupational groupings and institutions multiplies the host of specialties within the culture, but the resulting diversity leaves the basic institutional system untouched. Such a florescence of alternatives anchored in a common system of basic institutions therefore presents conditions of cultural and social heterogeneity without pluralism.

The same thing is true of class differences, which are differences within a single institutional framework. Their compatibility within this framework is essential for their comparison and ranking . . . Class patterns represent differing styles of life, but the conceptual difference between such life-styles and culture as a way of life is profound. Life-styles can and do change without involving any change in the institutional system. Within class-stratified societies, such as those of the Hausa or of Britain, the various strata or classes hold common economic, religious, familial, political, and educational institutions; but the condition of cultural and social pluralism consists precisely in the systematic differentiation of these basic institutions themselves.

Within each cultural section of a plural society we may expect to find some differences of stratification or social class. These cultural sections themselves are usually ranked in a hierarchy, but the hierarchic arrangement of these sections differs profoundly in its basis and character from the hierarchic status organization within each severally. The distribution of status within each cultural section rests on common values and criteria quite specific to that group, and this medley of sectional value systems rules out the value consensus that is prerequisite for any status continuum. Thus the plurality is a discontinuous status order, lacking any foundation in a system of common interests and values, while its component sections are genuine status continua, distinguished by their differing systems of value, action, and social relations. Accordingly, in so far as current theories assume or emphasize the integrative and continuous character of social stratification, they may apply to each cultural section, but not to the plurality as a whole . . .

It is especially important to distinguish between pluralism and 'class' stratification because of the profound differences that underlie their formal resemblance. Whereas the assumption of integration may be valid for a class system, it cannot normally hold for a plural hierarchy. In general, social stratification occurs without corresponding pluralism as, for example, among the British, the Hausa, or the Polynesians. There is also no inherent reason why all cultural sections of a plural society should be ranked hierarchically ... Cultural difference and social stratification vary independently. Thus they can neither be reduced to one another, nor can they be equated. Cultural pluralism is a special form of differentiation based on institutional divergences. It is therefore a serious error to equate pluralism with 'class stratification' ...

The problems presented by ethnic minorities are somewhat more complex, largely because this term has been ambiguously applied to racial, national, linguistic, and cultural groups. Let us therefore consider specific cases. The Greeks, Italians, and Irish of New York each have their own religious and family practices, perhaps their own languages and sodalities also. If their institutional systems diverge from the general American model so as to be incompatible with the latter, then they must be regarded as cultural sections. Institutional incompatibility is indicated by differences of grouping, norms, activities, and functions. We have simply to ask, for instance, whether the paternal or maternal, the judicial or the priestly status and role have the same definitions and institutional contexts among differing groups, and whether these role incumbents could be exchanged without violating social practice. If they can, the groups share a common institutional system; if they cannot, the groups do not ...

By this criterion, it seems clear that marriage and the family vary among Greeks, Italians, and Irish in content rather than in form, in their affective quality rather than in their social function, sanctions, and norms. Likewise, the Greek, Italian, and Irish variants of Christianity share common basic forms of organization, ritual, and belief ... [But] unless ethnic traditions present incompatible institutional forms, they are, like social class patterns, stylistic variations within a common basic way of life ... Thus ethnic variations, like class styles, may produce cultural and social heterogeneity, but do not involve pluralism ...

American Negroes are culturally diverse and may be subdivided institutionally into two or more sections, the acculturated extreme consisting of those who have adopted white American culture as far as the present colour-caste arrangement permits, while the opposite extreme consists of those whose religious, kinship, economic, and associational institutions are furthest removed from white norms. It follows that the American Negroes do not form a separate cultural section. They are a subordinate social segment of a culturally hetero-geneous society, and may differ among themselves institutionally. Some groups of American Negroes belong to plural communities; others do not. Such a complex situation cannot be handled adequately in terms of race relations alone; pluralism and its alternatives must be defined institutionally rather than in racial or ethnic terms. Cultural heterogeneity has many forms and bases, while cultural pluralism has only one, namely, diversity of the basic institutional system. Plural societies are by no means the only alternatives to homogeneous societies. The United States and Brazil are heterogeneous societies that contain plural communities and evince pluralism without themselves being plural societies. Neither colour-caste nor class stratification implies basic institutional differences and, in my view, the term ethnic minorities should be reserved for those national groups that share the same basic institutions as the host society, but preserve distinctive styles.

Several other points should be made before we leave this subject of institutional variation. As we have seen, each institutional sub-system tends to be integrated with other institutional sub-systems. For this reason, it is rare for the institutional differences between groups to be limited to one particular institution. If these differences are at all significant, they will generally be associated with like differences in other institutions, and the cumulative effect will be basic cultural and social differences between the groups concerned. Such differentiated groups form separate cultural and social sections . . .

Since institutions are integral units, the elements of which are activities, ideas, and social relations, their differences involve differing systems of idea, action, and social grouping. To determine whether such differences exist in a given population is a simple matter of empirical research . . .

Even in a plural society, institutional diversity does not include differing systems of government. The reason for this is simple: the continuity of such societies as units is incompatible with an internal diversity of governmental institutions. Given the fundamental differences of belief, value, and organization that connote pluralism, the monopoly of power by one cultural section is the essential precondition for the maintenance of the total society in its current form. In short, the structural position and function of the regulative system differ sharply in plural and other societies ... The dominant social section of these culturally split societies is simply the section that controls the apparatus of power and force, and this is the basis of the status hierarchies that characterize pluralism ... In such situations the subordinate social sections often seek to regulate their own internal affairs independently of their superiors ... Cultural pluralism is not confined to plural societies, although it is their basis ... In Brazil and the United States the culturally and politically dominant tradition is that shared by the overwhelming majority of the population. Under such conditions, even culturally distinct groups are minorities at the national level, although they may well include some local majorities. As national minorities, they present no threat to the current social order and, as long as their customs are tolerated by the dominant majority, these minorities may persist undisturbed ...

I have tried to show that the institutional system that forms the cultural core defines the social structure and value system of any given population. Thus populations that contain groups practising different forms of institutional system exhibit a corresponding diversity of cultural, social, and ideational patterns. Since any institutional system tends toward internal integration and consistency, each of these differentiated groups will tend to form a closed socio-cultural unit. Such pluralistic conditions are far more widespread than are plural societies, the distinctive feature of which is their domination by a cultural minority. Pluralism is quite distinct from other forms of social heterogeneity, such as class stratification, in that it consists in the coexistence of incompatible institutional systems. Plural societies depend for their maintenance on the regulation of intersectional relations by one or another of the component cultural sections. When the dominant section is also a minority, the structural implications of cultural pluralism have their most extreme expression, and the dependence on regulation by force is greatest. A society whose members all share a single system of institutions is culturally and socially homogeneous. A society having one basic institutional system in a number of styles or one basic system and a number of institutional alternatives and specialties is culturally and socially heterogeneous ...

How do plural societies and other culturally pluralistic units originate? Furnivall thought that they were limited to the modern colonial tropics and were products of Western economic expansion. However, the Norman conquest of Britain, and the Roman conquest before it, certainly established plural societies, and there are many other instances that cannot be attributed to Western economic activity ... Modern economic forces may account for colonial pluralities, but these are not the only ones. Perhaps the most general answer to this question of origin is migration, which also accounts for the development of ethnic minorities. This migration may be forced ... or semi-voluntary ... It may involve conquest and consolidation, but this is not always the case.

It is a major error to conceive the conditions and problems of pluralism directly in terms of race relations ... It often happens that racially distinct groups form a common homogeneous society, as for instance among the Hausa-Fulani of northern Nigeria. Conversely, we sometimes find culturally distinct groups that belong to the same racial stock expressing their differences in racial terms ... History provides us with many other examples, such as the Normans and Anglo-Saxons, the English and the Scots or, most recently and most elaborately, the Nazi ideology. Race differences are stressed in contexts of social and cultural pluralism. They lack social significance in homogeneous units ... The function of racism is merely to justify and perpetuate a pluralistic social order. This being the case, the rigorous analysis of race relations presupposes analyses of their context based on the theory of pluralism.

In class-stratified societies deference is demonstrated or exacted interpersonally, while in plural units it is often generalized by the dominant group and enforced on the subordinate sections. Such generalized obligatory deference is an important mode of social control. Normally, dress, manner, or speech serve to place individuals sectionally but, where racial differences obtain, they usually act as the most general indicators, being the most resistant to change. In this way the dominant minority seeks to perpetuate its dominion and the plural structure simultaneously. Racist ideology seeks to symbolize and legitimize intersectional relations.

Another common sociological error is the reduction of cultural and social pluralism to social stratification. Such equations misstate the character and implications of institutional differentiation where this is not entirely ignored . . . We cannot adequately analyse plurality as an integrated stratification order.

It is also misleading to suppose that the persistence of plural units is due to the predominance of common values between their cultural sections . . . It is especially difficult to isolate the positive effect of common values in culturally split societies that owe their form and maintenance to a special concentration of regulative power within the dominant group . . . Whatever the form of the political system, the differing sectional values within a plural society are a profound source of instability. Since stratification is now assumed to be an integrative order, it is therefore misleading to represent the intersectional relations of a plural society in these terms.

Since the plural society depends for its structural form and continuity on the regulation of intersectional relations by government, changes in the social structure presuppose political changes, and these usually have a violent form.

55   John Rex

Theories of Race Relations

Excerpts from John Rex, *Race Relations in Sociological Theory*, Routledge & Kegan Paul, 1970, pp. 6–23.

A sociology of race relations ... starts with the task of unmasking false biological or related theories ... A few writers have taken the view that beyond this all the sociologist has to do is to show the consequences of such theories being held, so that phenomena like those connected with anti-Semitism in twentieth-century Europe would be seen or studied simply as the consequence of the preaching of racist ideas ... [But] we should surely look ... also at its causes and at its functions ...

Which of the various kinds of social situations, structures and processes which sociologists study belong within the sub-field of the sociology of race relations? ...

There is a particularly difficult problem in defining the field of the sociology of race relations, which arises from the important role of beliefs in the very constitution of the phenomenon in question ... Unlike the natural scientists, who may be thought of as applying concepts to things, the sociologists seek to apply concepts to the understanding of social relations, and social relations in turn depend upon the conceptualizations which actors make of their world and of other actors ...

[One example is] M. G. Smith's treatment of the meaning of colour in intergroup relations in the Caribbean. Smith begins by recognizing that one important subjective dimension in terms of which individuals categorize each other and orient their behaviour towards one another is that of skin colour. On investigation, however, it turns out that if a man has certain other characteristics such as high income, education, or a reputation for associating with people of lighter skin colour, he will be seen as whiter than he is.

Smith uses this fact in support of a general argument that the proper framework for Caribbean sociology is that which is provided by the plural or segmented society concept, rather than that which looks on Caribbean societies as exhibiting patterns of 'race relations'. [But the] bases in terms of which individuals categorize each other . . . involve subjective participant's theories . . .: reputational and other social assessments are translated into a language of colour. Because of this . . . the Caribbean situation [comes] within the purview of race relations studies.

The Caribbean case is a particularly difficult one . . .: men claim that they are classifying each other in terms of colour, when the actual basis on which they make their classifications is not one of colour at all. In some metropolitan societies on the other hand, where liberal ideologies prevent the open confession of colour prejudice and discrimination, men may claim that the discriminations and the classifications which they make have no reference to colour, whereas their practice shows that these classifications are colour-based. Here again, where our interpretation of the meaning of the actor's orientation to his fellows involves reference to colour, we are bound to consider this case as falling within the field of the sociology of race relations.

. . . The sociology of race relations must take account of subjective definitions, stereotypes, typifications and belief systems in the business of defining its field . . .: patterns of social relations may be considerably changed through the causal agency of such belief systems . . . If we are talking about structures in which *alter's* compliance with *ego's* expectations is governed by norms, concepts play a role both in *ego's* classification of *alter*, and in applying moral rules to his behaviour towards *alter*. At the other extreme, where *ego* seeks to gain *alter's* compliance by coercion, however, no such normative element enters in. Between these two extremes one has the case in which *alter* complies because it is in his economic interest to do so . . .

What is sometimes identified as the Marxist position is that which seeks to reduce all social structures to underlying economic forms, that is to say, seeks to reduce them to patterns of social relations in which *alter's behaviour* (and for that matter *ego's*) is seen as being based upon the pursuit of his own economic interest. Not surprisingly it has been possible to demonstrate that many race relations situations cannot be explained in this way . . .

[But] compliance based upon coercion [is] likely to be common where conquest has occurred, and [is] a normal feature of colonial societies ... [where] intergroup relations have the form they do because the two groups involved were not originally one, but have been brought together into a single political framework as a result of the conquest by one of the other.

Thus, although we would not wish to deny that in almost every case of intergroup relations some subjective, conceptual and normative factor enters into the patterning of social relations, we would suggest that social relations in many colonial contexts tend in some degree towards the situation which would be represented by an ideal type of purely coercive compliance. In fact it is this feature of colonial societies, taken together with what we shall later define as racist theories, which defines the central kind of social situation with which we have to deal ...

The biologists, it will be remembered, were simply called upon to pronounce upon the proper use of the concept 'race' in terms of the theory of their discipline. By so doing they might be said to have unmasked racism. The sociologist's task appears to involve unmasking in a more thoroughgoing sense. He has to show the way in which theories and ideas, falsely purporting to be based upon biological science, are built into the structure of social relationships ...

Once we recognize that there may be some functional relationship between theories on the one hand and social structures on the other, the possibility arises that functional substitutes might be found ... the conceptual content of social relations need not always be set out in the form of explicit and well-articulated theories. It may consist of nothing more than stereotypes, proverbs, symbols, folklore and so on, which, while it may be seen to have an internal logic of theoretical assumptions, does not at any point have these assumptions set out ...

[But] are we to take it that any kind of theory may appear in a race relations situation, provided that a certain sort of structure of social relations is present?

Some sociologists would in fact take this step, but by so doing they virtually abolish the sociology of race relations as a special field. It becomes an indistinguishable part of a wider field such as the study of stratification. This is not the position which is taken here ... One group of ... theories is focused on the question of stratification, using that term in a fairly wide sense. The other draws attention to pluralism, i.e. the tendency of social systems to be divided, if not vertically, at least not simply into the sort of horizontal strata which the stratification theorists seem to imply ...

According to [Lloyd Warner] American society includes both class and caste divisions. The white population may be classified as belonging to one of a number of strata (or, as Warner would prefer to say, classes) ... [His] Yankee City studies showed that most European minority groups moved up the stratification hierarchy over two or three generations, but that, so far as the negro population were concerned, however much they might achieve an improved position in terms of such objective status characteristics as income, they still found that there were barriers preventing their free association with whites at an equivalent level ...

Warner suggested that the barrier which thus split the stratification system into two was a caste barrier, at least in an incipient form, and he drew attention to similarities with the Hindu caste system, such as the taboos on intermarriage, eating together, and any other intimate form of association ... Warner's view that these relations cannot be explained in terms of normal stratification models survives, even if his notion of caste is rejected ...

O. C. Cox, approaching the problem of the American negro from a sophisticated Marxist point of view, has sought to show that there are several crucial dissimilarities between intercaste and interracial relations as they occur in the United States, which make the use of the term caste in the latter case impermissible. He believes that a better theoretical construct for explaining race relations is that which may be derived from the Marxist theory of class conflict. Cox notes that the Hindu caste system is one in which there is a large measure of assent to the social inequalities and taboos on association amongst higher and lower castes, and that the central and characteristic feature of the system is the occupational specialization of the castes. Neither of these two conditions prevails in the United States. The position of the negro worker in that society is that of the most exploited worker within a capitalist system of social relations of production ...

Clearly the difficulty in sustaining Cox's theory is to show why it is that white workers are not in the same position as negro workers. The simplest Marxist way out of this is simply to attribute the subjectively felt divisions within the working class to a state of 'false consciousness' fostered in its own interest by the bourgeoisie. A non-Marxist alternative would [argue] that a prior distinction had been made as to who should fill inferior working-class roles, and that this distinction was based upon non-economic criteria . . .

The most influential theory of social stratification in the United States today, that of Talcott Parsons, as set out in his 'Revised Analytic Approach to Social Stratification', treats the problem of ethnic differences as a factor which modifies the stratification system . . .

In American society Parsons has to admit that ethnicity provides an exception to the general pattern of stratification. But there clearly are a number of societies in which the fact of ethnic pluralism makes the application of the Parsonian type of stratification model quite impossible . . .

What Parsons assumes is that . . . a social system involves some roles which are economic, technical or adaptive, some of which are directed towards ensuring that the system as a whole attains its end, some of which are concerned with preventing interests from clashing and thus holding the system together, and some of which are concerned with socialization and social control . . .

The plain fact about many colonial societies however, is [that] there just *is* no common pattern. What one finds instead is that a number of groups have been brought together from different societies and that . . . there is no shared value system on which an agreed pattern of stratification, either of all groups, or of all individuals within the society, could be based . . .

As against these attempts to reduce race relations theory to stratification theory we must now consider another influential tradition which reduces it to the theory of the plural society. According to this tradition, what we are concerned with in the study of race relations and of the plural society are neither hierarchically arranged castes, nor classes in conflict, nor a system of roles arranged hierarchically according to their evaluation in terms of some set of ideal values [but] segments which cut across the strata, producing vertical rather than horizontal divisions within the society . . .

Furnivall has been thought of as describing a state of affairs in which there is an almost total disjunction between the various ethnic groups. Real social life, according to this interpretation, is what goes on round the camp-fires of the separate communities when they are

separated from one another. Their contact is a marginal business
which takes place only in the market place and since this produces
no common will, no normative order, is of little interest to the sociologist.

In fact Furnivall specifically mentions three types of social bond
. . .: the 'religion, culture and language, ideas and ways' of the
separate groups . . . But he also speaks of a single 'political unit' thus
recognizing coercive ties and of 'a division of labour on racial lines'
recognizing utilitarian and economic bonds.

Smith reads Furnivall as arguing that the 'plural economy' of
South East Asia rests upon an underlying social pluralism. He himself
prefers to 'take the argument back one step further' and to look at
what to him as an anthropologist is the most fundamental thing of
all, namely cultural pluralism. The core of any culture is its 'institutional system' and what characterizes a plural society is that its
different segments have different institutional systems. Such institutional systems [include] 'kinship, education, religion, property and
economy, recreation and certain sodalities' . . . [But] without a single
governmental institution we should not have a society at all. We
should have several coexisting societies . . . Smith goes further than
merely saying that there should be a shared governmental institution
. . .: 'Given the fundamental differences of belief, value and organization that connote pluralism, the monopoly of power by one cultural
section is the essential precondition for the maintenance of the total
society in its current form.'

Pluralism in a society is not to be confused with stratification [or]
reduced to the study of race relations . . . So far as we are concerned
the social myth is part of the reality . . . , a situation in which two
distinct groups are held together within a single political framework,
in which there is an unequal apportionment of rights between these
groups, and in which, finally, the system is justified by appeal to
some kind of deterministic theory such as a racial one . . . [Smith
argues that] the segments [are] bound together through political
domination by one of them rather than through any kind of overall
consensus as to the qualities meriting higher or lower prestige . . .

[He] leans very heavily upon Malinowski's definitions of 'culture'
and 'institution' . . . [Yet] Malinowski suggests that, in listing the
institutions in the plural society, one should not merely list those of
each of its component sections, but should add a 'third column' to

include institutions which arise within the process of culture contact. Such an institution according to Malinowski is the system of compound labour, found within South African society, but having no parallel either in English or Dutch society on the one hand, or in African societies on the other . . .

Whatever our interpretation of slavery or of compound labour in South Africa, it must surely be agreed that these are institutions of the whole society and not simply of one cultural or social segment . . . forms of 'property and economy' [cannot be treated, as Smith does, as] institutional sets which are said to pertain to the separate segments . . .: the segments are bound together economically as well as politically . . .

56   Sandra Wallman

Ethnicity and the Boundary Process

Excerpts from Sandra Wallman, 'Ethnicity and the Boundary Process in Context', in John Rex and David Mason (eds.), *Theories of Race and Ethnic Relations*, Cambridge University Press, 1986, pp. 226–34.

Ethnic categories are organizational vessels that may be given varying amounts and forms of content in different sociocultural systems. They may be of great relevance to behaviour but they need not be; they may provide all social life, or they may be relevant only in limited sectors of activity (Barth 1969).

Relative to other social scientists, anthropologists are seldom professionally concerned with vertical relations between ethnic groups and macro-state structures, and they rarely undertake studies of social stratification and minority status as such ... Some anthropologists doubt that ethnic relations can be separated out from the general range of social interactions. 'Us'/'them' distinctions, after all, are essential to social grouping of any sort. If there are definitely *ethnic* social relations, they must occur between members of different ethnic groups as such – i.e. there must be a specifically ethnic dimension to social life ...

One is the comparative perspective: it is to us axiomatic that not everyone classifies the same event in the same way; and that 'our' view of it is no less exotic/contingent/problematic than 'theirs'. The other is a model of the social system which identifies separate domains of activity or exchange or meaning within it, which recognizes that different resources or kinds of resources pertain to each of them and [in] which ... each of those resources is regularly 'converted' into others, and may be transposed from one domain to another ... In fact it is arguable that boundary definition is the central concern of anthropology – whether the limits of nation and culture, of structure and context, of resources and their value, of exchange systems and networks, or of a particular 'us' are in question

... Since in cities he encounters different kinds of difference, ethnic boundaries soon came to be recognized as a problematic feature of the migrant's experience of poly-ethnic urban life. [And if] race has lost its scientific credibility [this] is not to say that the concept is no longer current. On the contrary: ordinary discourse reveals a gap between scientific and folk models that has implications for policy as well as for social analysis. The word 'race' is still used when the speaker wishes to indicate objective and immutable differences between human groups or individuals, i.e. it continues to denote difference that *seems to be* immutable. In the same popular language, 'ethnicity' is apparently of a different order. Usage changes over time and varies from one country to another ... In Britain it signifies allegiance to the culture of origin and implies a degree of choice and a possibility for change which 'race' precludes ... In both cases it is the classifier's *perception* of choice or immutability which is decisive ... It is [this] variability of ethnic boundaries which catches the anthropologist's eye, and the logic of ethnic boundary processes ...

All the issues can be summarized under three headings: the nature of the boundary; the dynamics of the relation between its two sides; and the context or 'structural ecology' of the boundary process. The debate begins with the premise stated in Fredrik Barth's 1969 essay: all kinds of items are sometimes used to mark ethnic difference, but they are not used consistently. The bases of boundedness can be visible or invisible, symbolic or real. Those most often converted into ethnicity are territoriality, history, language, economic considerations, and symbolic identifications of one kind or another, but there is no logical limit to their number: ... the problem of predicting whether the actors will 'use' them, or which they will choose at any one time remains ...

Other writers doubt that ethnicity has [any] value [at all.] When people are not acting ethnic, not actually beating the boundary, how can we assume they are identifying ethnically? And if they are not themselves involved in the boundary process, who is the observer to say that ethnicity is there at all? ... All the elements of shift and change pertaining to the first side pertain also to the second, but each side is [also] affected by the dynamic of the relationship between them.

Equally, the transparency and permeability of the boundary affect the whole system, although of course they do not always affect both sides equally . . . The more opaque the boundary, the more chance an ethnic group has to manipulate others' perception of it, or to stay invisible when it chooses. Permeability certainly governs the kinds of items, influences or people that can cross from one side of the boundary to the other, and may possibly also affect its resilience . . .

[Another] strand of anthropological theory . . . deals explicitly with the relation between structure and process. The strand begins with Raymond Firth's distinction between social structure and social organization. Structure in this sense is the shape of the social system. It constrains the people who make up that system because it constitutes the framework of behavioural/institutional/symbolic options available to them. Social organization in the same model is a product of the choices people make from among those options – i.e. from among the possibilities that the structure allows. In sum, structure is the form and organization the process. Barth carries the same reasoning a step further. He too conceives of social organization in terms of choices made among options available, but he goes on to describe how the choices accumulate to generate new kinds of structure . . .: individual choices are converted into (new) group structures . . . The combined realities [are those of] choice and constraint. Whatever you choose, your self-interest is limited by other people's interests and by environment, climate, opportunity structure and the like . . .

The practical limitations of a process view are clarified when it is compared with models in which ethnicity is ascribed by a categorical marker of some sort – colour, religion, immigrant status, birthplace or the like . . . Any once-for-all typology of people is necessarily tidier than life and . . . can take no account of whether, when and how far the actor identifies with those who share the same categorical status. [But] official purposes demand fixed classifications. Whether a government intends to make a demographic census, to legislate for 'multi-cultural' development or to correct economic disadvantage, it needs to be able to assign each person or group to one population category and to know that each category is distinct from every other. In the face of this bureaucratic need, anthropological models of boundary process tend to look untidy and rather vague. Even bureaucrats 'know' that social boundaries are fluid because they too have experienced the face that the same difference can have a different meaning in another context, but in the official domain process models are not helpful. Consequently they have little general application and only limited relevance to public policy . . .

[Yet] the only course is for us to make explicit the perspectives of the discipline which are implicit among its members ... Not all research problems or agendas lend themselves to a test procedure.

Reference

F. BARTH (1969), *Ethnic Groups and Boundaries*, Universitets Forlarget.

57　Michael Banton

Policy Implications

Excerpts from Michael Banton, *Racial and Ethnic Competition*, Cambridge University Press, 1983, pp. 390–407.

There is scarcely any discussion of what constitutes good racial relations, yet if policies are to be designed to improve such relations there must be some conception of the goal towards which efforts are to be directed.

One answer is that good racial relations will exist when each racial group has the same share of the desirable positions in society. Another answer is that good racial relations will exist when racial criteria have become socially insignificant and the desirable positions are distributed according to individual merit. These two may be identified as the 'fair shares for groups' and the 'fair shares for individuals' arguments . . .

The first argument soon runs into serious difficulties. This can be appreciated by imagining a society divided into several racial groups in such a way as to achieve equality or privilege between groups: each group gets the same share of rewards and the average income in each group is the same. The idea of racial equality does not imply that people should be paid the same for doing different work, so aircraft pilots could continue to be paid more than baggage handlers. To maintain inter-group equality in this society it would be necessary, firstly, to prevent anyone changing groups or forming new ones; secondly, to keep each group the same relative size; thirdly, to operate quotas to ensure that the same proportions of each group become pilots and baggage handlers. The principle of group equality would come into conflict with the principles of individual freedom and of fair treatment for individuals. On the other hand, a society constructed on the basis of these two last principles could perpetuate inequality between groups because of the transmission of privilege from one generation to the next . . .

'Economic progress' [, it has been argued,] 'is an inter-generational relay race.' Rich parents can give their children many advantages that will help them in competition with their peers. The analogy can be used to raise some further questions, for, if the rules allow one team to build up an unassailable lead, members of the other teams may lose interest and refuse to continue the competition unless the rules are revised to give them a better chance. One of the main motivations behind revolutionary movements is the desire to eliminate inherited inequality and allow all the teams to go back to the same starting line. Since revolutions occur in racially homogeneous societies, there is more reason to expect them when the competing groups are physically distinguishable and there is an extra barrier to inter-group mobility.

The most familiar form of the 'fair shares for individuals' argument is that everyone in society benefits when positions are filled by the most competent individuals, and it is therefore desirable to ignore the advantages that some competitors bring with them to the starting line. The alternative argument accepts this as one criterion, while adding that it is also in the social interest to motivate the less gifted individuals to compete to their full potential . . .

The argument that each group should receive a fair share of the rewards states the case for the equality of outcomes, whereas the argument that individuals are entitled to fair shares advocates equality of opportunities . . . The group argument is advanced in support of short-term policies while the individual argument has most force in relation to the long term . . .

One of the difficulties with any policy of group compensation is that of determining just who is a member of the category which is to receive the benefit . . . The Singapore government [for example,] has pursued a policy of 'multi-racialism'; this accords equal status to the cultures and ethnic identities of the four main 'races' which compose the population. It is symbolized by the picture of four interlinked but differently coloured hands that appears on the back of Singapore's ten-dollar currency note . . . When the birth of a baby is registered, entries are made specifying the race and mother tongue of the child . . . [The idea] that one day Singapore's sample of elements from these four cultures will merge into a single new culture . . . is [, however,] implemented in a way which stresses the distinctiveness of the four cultures and therefore erects obstacles to any merging . . . So members of each group are supposed to cultivate the features which differentiate them from other groups, even if they do not wish to do so [and even though] others are potentially sources of political embarrassment. The Chinese speak so many dialects that the development of a group identity might best be done through Mandarin-language education; yet this would conflict with the use and official encouragement of English as the civic language. The main feature the Indians have in common is the caste system, but that is something they do not wish to discuss and which clashes with the Republic's meritocratic egalitarianism. That which most distinguishes the Malays is their profession of Islam, but for them to stress this could cause difficulty since Singapore is a secular state . . .

In the creation of a new national culture children of cross-ethnic marriages could play an important part, yet these children are assigned to the ethnic group of one of the parents only, usually the father. They are similarly assigned to a mother tongue irrespective of whether that is the language spoken in the home . . . Children are supposed to learn a second language at school but this is based on the assumption that their first language is the mother tongue on their identity card; if this is not the case such a child will have to struggle with a third language . . .: the policy presses the Chinese to become more Chinese, the Indians more Indian and the Malays more Malay . . . Cultural characteristics are assumed to derive from distinctive genetic backgrounds and therefore to change only very slowly indeed. In reality people of all groups are changing as they adapt to the opportunities provided by a bustling commercial city, and this is the real basis for a commonality of culture which is growing rapidly . . .

If the customs of a particular minority are different in ways that put them at a competitive disadvantage or result in their breaking the laws of the majority society . . . the rules may either be drawn in such a way that individuals are left with discretion as to their implementation, or they may specify the extent of the allowance that is to be made. An example of a discretionary allowance would be that permitting the admission to university of a minority student with slightly lower grades if that student had obtained those grades under adverse circumstances and might therefore be expected to perform better once he or she was able to study in the same environment as majority students. An example of a regulated allowance would be one which established the qualifying grade for minority students at a lower level and left little to the judgement of the person responsible for admissions. If this latter course is followed then an immediate problem is the definition of the category of persons to benefit from the regulation. Unless the policies of Singapore and South Africa are followed, whereby category membership is a matter of official record on a person's identity card, there must be some other clear-cut, administratively viable, procedure for determining whether a person who, for example, has a majority father and a minority mother counts as a member of the minority. This cannot be left to the discretion of officials . . .

Singapore's 'multi-racialism' is relatively benign in that, unlike South Africa's, it does not greatly affect the access of individuals to jobs and economic opportunities . . .

Some states, struggling to hold together a heterogeneous population, have adopted special rules or conventions for the distribution of political offices, or to regulate the balance of political power. Lebanon provides a striking example. There it was agreed that the president should be a Maronite, the prime minister a Sunni, the speaker of the house a Shi'ite, the vice-speaker a Greek Orthodox, and so on; the ethnic composition of the legislature was prescribed by law. For over thirty years these arrangements were a foundation for internal peace and a substantial measure of prosperity . . . No one [was] obliged to subscribe to a particular religious faith . . .

The main characteristic of racial relations, however, is that it is exceedingly difficult for an individual to change groups. The argument in favour of fair shares for individuals starts from this. It holds that the objective of public policy should be to eliminate any unfavourable treatment of individuals based on their assignment to particular categories when membership is not a justifiable ground for differential treatment. If a man wishes to identify himself as a Jew, a gypsy, or an Arab, he will know that this may make him unwelcome in some circles and will accept these consequences of his decision. It is quite another matter for him to be assigned to such a category when he does not identify with it, or for his presumed membership in a private group to be used as a reason for denying him equal treatment in the public domain . . .

One way of transcending racial categories is to support any tendencies that lead to their multiplication. If people who occupy an intermediate position between two categories want to be recognized as a distinct group, then a policy which permits them to be so classified weakens the element of constraint that would otherwise force them into categories with which they did not identify. So long as there is one option open which an individual considers acceptable, freedom of choice can serve as a criterion for deciding what good racial relations would be. [A] person of Jewish origin who rejects the Jewish faith . . . should be free to identify as a member of the Jewish minority or as a member of the majority. The American male with a brown complexion is not free to choose between being an Afro-American and being a majority member because, whatever his wishes, whites will assign him to a racial category. His freedom is restricted by others' definitions as well as by the consequences of any choices he has made . . .

The prime motivation behind the actions of those who mark off physically distinguishable people as constituting separate racial categories is the defence of privilege, though the privilege is not necessarily economic; people who draw a psychological satisfaction from a feeling of belonging to a group could not draw so much satisfaction if everyone could be a member. Social exclusiveness can create a privilege irrespective of whether the group is economically privileged, indeed exclusiveness on the part of a minority can be important to an ethnic revaluation movement . . . Economic inequalities, if they are allowed to get too large, occasion disruption if not revolution. If the economic inequalities between racial groups are reduced, there will be less incentive to maintain racial categories. People will have more freedom to gain entry to groups on their individual merits rather than on their complexion, and competition will be more on an individual rather than a group basis . . . Colour would still be an element in the assessment of an individual's claims to status but it would be just one item among many and, as . . . in Brazil and Puerto Rico . . . change would be slower in respect of a physical characteristic like colour than a cultural one because colour is transmitted genetically and identifies one generation with its predecessor. In most parts of the United States a substantial measure of intermarriage would have to occur before colour could lose its salience.

If this process were carried to its logical conclusion every adult could seek membership of any group, just as he or she can change his or her religion and seek recognition by others who profess his or her chosen faith. The only groups (at any rate groups of this general kind, since other considerations arise with respect to families) would then be voluntary groups resulting from inclusive processes ... Ethnic groups ... [are groups] in which beliefs about a common heritage are used to create identities ...: good racial relations [, then,] would be ethnic relations.

Strategies for Governments

... The case for governmental action to promote fair competition by eliminating restrictive practices and monopolistic organization ... has to be reviewed continuously [as] part of a general policy for regulating social inequality ...

Governments in the United States have been the pioneers in the use of legal measures to combat discrimination. For example, after the enactment of laws against discrimination in housing, the state of Massachusetts in 1946 established a Fair Employment Practice Commission ... Its impact was limited because the Commission took action only on the receipt of complaints and not all of these opened up situations strategically important to the attack on prevailing practices. The typical complaint about discrimination in employment alleged unequal treatment on the job ... The position was different in housing where the typical complaint was brought by a middle-class Afro-American against someone who had refused to rent an apartment ... In housing, discrimination was more flagrant, the justice of a complaint was easier to prove and, if proven, could be resolved more simply ...

The first big step in this direction is for such bodies to have the legal powers and the resources to investigate practices in the areas they consider important without having to wait for complaints. The next big step is for them, or some other body, to impose quotas. A company – or, for example, a police department – may be ordered to recruit one minority employee for every majority person engaged until it has attained a stipulated quota of minority employees. In support of such actions it can be argued that statistical discrimination in hiring ... can rarely be modified by the investigation of individual complaints. It is a malady which requires a statistical remedy even if the treatment has some undesired side-effects. Whether it is necessary, or morally justifiable, for governments to authorize the imposition of quotas and indeed whether such policies are actually effective in attaining their goals have been matters of bitter dispute.

Broadly speaking, there are two contrasting arguments, one future-orientated and one past-orientated . . . A future-oriented argument might say that members of a minority suffer peculiar disadvantages such that without special assistance they will not catch up within the foreseeable future. In some circumstances it could go on to maintain that since many (but not all) young people in that group are unable to compete effectively, they take to anti-social behaviour and to crime. Their anti-social behaviour damages the reputation of their group, lowers morale, increases friction within their group, and in many ways makes it more difficult for other members of the minority to compete effectively with majority members. Their criminal behaviour necessitates greater expenditure on the police, the courts, the probation service, the prisons, and all the social agencies that assist the dependants of people in prison and help prisoners on release. Their criminality also entails costs for the victims, increases insurance rates and so on . . .: it is cheaper to spend money on programmes that will prevent anti-social behaviour and crime than on dealing with their consequences. Such programmes could be either discretionary – such as spending more money on schooling in particular localities – or be based upon a legally enforceable rule – such as one stating that only employers with a particular quota of minority employees will be eligible to tender for government contracts. [Either way,] the distinctive characteristic of the argument is that such a policy is justified by the case for achieving a particular future outcome.

A past-orientated argument might say that members of a particular minority are at a disadvantage because of past injustices to them which have had a cumulative effect in reducing their competitive ability. As a consequence many, but not all, young people in that group take to anti-social behaviour and to crime, with the results just mentioned. To rectify the disadvantages suffered (though not evenly) by the minority as a group, they should be compensated for past exploitation (in the way, for example, that Germany was required to pay reparations to the Allies after the First World War). Compensation might take the form either of payments or of preferential policies designed to permit minority members to recover from past disadvantage.

Each of these two kinds of argument has its special difficulties. One based upon the desirability of attaining a particular state in the future is dependent upon very unreliable estimates about the amount of expenditure required, and about the probability of that expenditure having the desired result. [And some majority members] are likely to see members of the minority as morally undeserving of preferential treatment.

Where a future-orientated argument is based upon the interest of the public in bringing about a new state of affairs, a past-orientated argument can appeal to the duty of the public to make good past injustice . . . from the sense of guilt many members of the majority feel about features of their society's history . . . Yet such a policy encounters two special difficulties: firstly, that of deciding how much recompense is sufficient; and secondly, that of establishing a transfer mechanism consistent with the rationale of the policy . . . The descendants of immigrants who entered in the twentieth century [have objected to having] to pay for injustices committed to Afro-Americans in earlier historical periods. [Others argue] that benefits should be made available only to those minority members who can show that they have been disadvantaged by the historical injustices.

The federal government in the United States started at least as early as 1941 to pursue policies based upon the future-oriented argument and to promote equality of opportunity. [Under] Presidents Kennedy and Johnson, 'affirmative action' . . . suggested that employers should advertise that they were equal-opportunity employers, should seek out qualified job applicants from all likely sources, and should treat them without discrimination. In 1968 the Department of Labor started to require every major contractor and sub-contractor for federal contracts to submit an affirmative action compliance programme, showing what they were doing to utilize minority-group personnel . . . The federal courts were increasingly involved in themselves setting standards about the hiring and promotion of employees, qualifications for being able to register as voters, and the adequacy of plans to desegregate schooling . . .

Affirmative action policies started as the promotion of equal opportunity – showing preference to minority job applicants whose qualifications were comparable with those of majority applicants – changed into one by which employers had to be able to show that they had taken all reasonable steps to meet targets for employing given quotas of minority employees. Equality of opportunity gave place to a test which required equality of results or outcomes . . .

In recent years black earnings have been improving relative to those of whites and the increase has been greatest for the better educated blacks . . . Over the period 1973–8 the percentage of appointments to management positions obtained by black males rose from 2.3 to 4.9; by black females from 2.9 to 6.0; and by white females from 34.4 to 37.4 . . . Neither equal-opportunity policies nor quota policies [, however,] have helped the black poor [whose] problems are so much more complex. In 1978, 74 per cent of all poor black families had female heads [, a] family form . . . less able to foster social mobility . . . Among blacks who failed to pass army I.Q. tests three quarters were from families of four or more children and one-half from families of six or more children. No policy package is likely to have much impact upon such a set of conditions unless it can improve male employment, relieve poverty, and promote family stability . . .

In the conditions in which most poor Afro-American children grow up, the parents' problems are magnified by the incidence of crime (of which blacks are most often the victims) and the glamour which seems to attach to many deviant life-styles. If it is the accumulation of human capital that enables immigrant minorities to climb the ladder, what is to happen in connection with drug addicts and criminals who, far from accumulating any capital themselves, only destroy that which is accumulated by others? . . .

Formal controls of codes, courts and constables . . . are never quite as effective as informal controls. They can restrain deviant behaviour but they rarely bring people to un-learn the lessons they learned about social relations during their early years. The criminal justice system is supposed to constitute a framework permitting exchanges to take place freely between individuals, by providing and enforcing sanctions upon people who break the rules about what may be exchanged and how . . . In practice, however, laws often reflect the interest of particular groups within society: the laws about slavery in the United States reflected the interests of the slave-owners and not the slaves. The judges who interpret and enforce the laws are members of the society and they are likely to sympathize with the views prevailing in the groups from which they are recruited and among the persons with whom they associate. Similar observations can be made with respect to the police . . .

[Yet] the criminal justice system can be used both to protect and to undermine minority interests. The civil courts can be used ... to solve problems about the distribution of resources ... But they can contribute little to policies directed to the wantonly anti-social and criminal behaviour ... In the United States that problem is more acute at the present time because of the ready availability of deadly weapons, the lower level of informal social control and the greater pressures of a more competitive social order ... In New York City in the 1970s a minority of Afro-Americans and a minority of Cubans followed crime as a way of life with a callousness that has little precedent. Of every twenty criminal homicides for which a black person is responsible, in nineteen cases the victim is another black. Afro-American communities are terrorized and gravely handicapped by the violence in their midst. The people who live in them will not be able to improve their economic position until the level of violence has been greatly reduced and they have some expectation that they will be able to enjoy the fruit of their labours ...

Minority criminality is in no sense a racial problem ... The problems which have been loosely called racial are economic, social, psychological and political problems, each one of which is to be analysed in ways appropriate to its peculiar character. Policies for dealing with these problems do not have to be of a special kind.

Strategies for Minorities

No minority has to contend with precisely the same problems as any other ... However, they do have to contend with the two main kinds of discrimination on the part of the majority: ... price discrimination and exclusion. Minority members may be able to secure employment only by working for lower pay or by being more accommodating to an employer's demands. In the respect of housing, they may be able to rent the rooms or buy the properties they want only by paying a premium as a 'colour tax', that is, paying more than a member of the majority would have to. Minority members can also be excluded altogether from certain kinds of employment, by either employers or unions, irrespective of wage levels. In the public sector, official policies may neglect their interests or administrators use discretionary powers to their disfavour. In the private sector, vendors, real-estate agents, finance companies and landlords can combine to exclude them from certain residential neighbourhoods while any family that slips through the net can be subject to intimidation . . .

In general, a low-profile strategy will be best for countering price discrimination and a high-profile strategy for countering exclusion. [An] example of low-profile strategies is that of Britain's Jewish minority which has never organized as a political group. Jews have entered all political parties; they have held more seats in the House of Commons than might have been expected on the basis of their proportion in the total population and have often attained high office, Benjamin Disraeli being an early example of such success . . .

The most striking example of a high-profile strategy is that followed by the black political movement in the United States during the mid and late 1960s. It was directed primarily towards Afro-Americans, trying to mobilize them politically and persuade them to abandon attitudes of deference towards whites and of resignation to subordination . . .

Any strategy's chance of success will be affected by the extent to which the majority regards minority ethnicity as a legitimate basis for pressing a political claim. Majorities often see themselves as committed to universalist values and deny claims which they interpret as particularistic and sectional. It is difficult for majority representatives in the United States to argue in such a vein given the long history of legal discrimination against blacks and the legitimacy that has been accorded to white ethnic organizations.

[But] in Great Britain, the argument from universalism can be more persuasive. Ethnic minority organization in England . . . is regarded as legitimate and expected in the social sphere. It is not used as a basis for claims to resources. The whites can make use of a potent past-oriented argument which presents the country as the historical patrimony of a white English nation. This constrains any attempt on the part of the ethnic minorities to follow the political example of the black movement in the United States since, apart from the difference in size of the two minorities, any use of a high-profile strategy has to be based upon moral claims of a kind that the majority cannot successfully deny.

When minority members follow a low-profile strategy, they present themselves as individuals ready to compete with others on equal terms and do nothing which attracts attention to their membership of a distinctive group . . . As majority people become acquainted with minority members any disposition to discriminate purely on a group basis can be expected to decline . . . Individual success has the advantage of minimizing hostility towards the minority as a group.

When minority members follow a high-profile strategy they present themselves as members of a group rather than as individuals. They draw attention to any injustices from which their group has suffered and which still handicap them. They know that by so doing they are likely to increase hostility from some sections of the majority but assume that these costs will be outweighed by the likely long-run benefits. Since they are being excluded from the possibility of equal competition there is little chance of their being able gradually to prove themselves, so there is little attraction in continuing as they have been doing. They have to take political action, threatening to increase costs to the majority by disruptive activity unless the rules on which the market operates are changed. This can be done most easily by a fairly powerful minority whose members do not feel that they have too much to lose by running the risks that come from raising the political temperature.

Part Ten
Class

To explain how societies with sharp social divisions persist at all is a major problem in sociological debate. So is the analysis of what nevertheless causes some of them to collapse.

In European industrialized societies we tend to think of class divisions as the most significant kind, though Americans do not. Historically speaking, in Europe classes only took on their modern importance within the last two hundred years. Before that, and in other parts of the world, other kinds of stratification – in medieval Europe, into estates, in Hindu India, into castes – were more important, while societies were also divided vertically by religion and by ethnicity.

In the nineteenth century it was commonly assumed that older kinds of divisions would disappear as class became the main basis of social organization and identity. This assumption was made both by those who thought that the new capitalism was the beginning of a new kind of 'positive' society and by its critics, notably Karl Marx. As we have seen in Part Four, however, gender divisions, much older than industrialized society, not only persist but have also become entrenched in new ways. The division of the entire globe into colonizers and colonized in the nineteenth century, too, has left a permanent stamp on the modern world, both in terms of the legacy of underdevelopment in the Third World and of a racial division of labour (and of unemployment) within the developed world as a consequence of the large-scale mobility of labour, from migrant labour to forced labour, during the colonial and post-colonial periods.

The most influential critique of the new world order came from Marx, whose theories have inspired resistance and revolution ever since. Class struggle was so central to his analysis of 'all hitherto existing society' that we have placed the crucial statement on the subject (Reading 72) in Part Twelve, which deals with the major theoretical schools of sociology, rather than simply under 'class', though three other short passages are included in Reading 58 in this chapter. Ever since then, even such great subsequent theorists as Max Weber (Reading 59) have felt obliged to engage in what has been called a 'debate with the ghost of Marx' on the subject, above all, of class.

Weber does not dispute the centrality of ownership of the means of production or the political power this carries with it. Indeed, he argues that the economic roots of class are even wider than this. They are not restricted to the sphere of production and ownership, but also derive from differences of position in the market: as consumers; as owners of different kinds of wealth (financial capital, land, etc); as between those who own their houses and those who rent; or as between those employed in the public sector and those who work in private industry, and so on. But, he argues, stratification is in any case not simply economic, but social, and differences of social status – not just in ownership of wealth – are significant bases of social prestige and of power in their own right, which can also get out of kilter with a person's actual economic position. Finally, he argues, the very process of mobilizing a political following – in modern democracies, notably via the political party – constitutes yet another basis for the exercise of power which does not derive simply and directly from ownership of wealth or from having an established position in society.

In Reading 60, Frank Parkin develops a similar approach. He argues that there is indeed a 'material basis' to class inequality, but rather than discovering a general social consensus, he insists that 'there is more than one way in which [class inequality] can be interpreted'.

In Part Five, we discussed the role of the educational system as one major avenue of social mobility in this century. In Reading 61, Halsey summarizes what the major changes in British class structure have been; changes in the occupational structure; in women's position in the economy; in the distribution of wealth and of access to other social 'goods', and the extent to which there has been any significant redistribution of wealth with the rise of the Welfare State.

Mack and Lansley (Reading 62) focus on one major segment of

the class structure: the poor. They begin by examining the classic definitions of what constitutes poverty developed by the major researchers in the field from Rowntree to Townsend. The conclusion that those scholars reached – that poverty is not an absolute, since it is something that is 'socially perceived' and changes over time – obliged Mack and Lansley to look into the conceptions of poverty held not just by scholars, but by people in all walks of life. They found a surprising degree of consensus – a 'general cultural ethos' – about what the minimal necessities for a 'decent and proper' existence were today, including items such as heating and a bath, which would have been unimaginable luxuries for poor people at the beginning of the century.

Marshall, Rose, Newby and Vogler (Reading 63) undertake the formidable task of empirically investigating this variety of interpretations. They begin where the Oxford Social Mobility Study of the 1960s, carried out by Goldthorpe and his colleagues – discussed in Chapter 10 of *Introducing Sociology* – left off. It was not just a question of collecting more 'facts': the major theories about changes in class structure and consciousness had to be rigorously examined, and the often dubious categories used in very different influential surveys critically scrutinized – from those carried out by market-research organizations and by the Registrar-General in Britain to Erik Olin Wright's Marxist study of the USA and Sweden.

They begin by examining the widespread idea that 'Thatcherism' is the expression at the level of politics of the replacement of traditional working-class solidarity by sectional divisions within that class, by individualism and privatism, and that these, in turn, derive from changes in the occupational structure of modern society brought about by modern technology and the declining importance of manufacture in a 'post-industrial' epoch. Yet they found 'no evidence that class has lost its salience as the foremost source of social identity'. Sectionalism and privatism are nothing new in the life of the working class, which had nevertheless, historically, created institutions to defend and extend their common interests; people in all classes found satisfaction in their work, and friendships formed at work were carried over into non-work contexts too.

And when they turned to the political implications of these economic changes they found the idea of 'the demise of class politics' unproven. Nearly two out of every three people in their sample thought that the main social conflict in Britain today was between those who run industry and those who work for them; two out of five that the gap between the 'haves' and the 'have nots' is too wide; and a further one in ten believed that there is too much poverty, that wages are too low, and that too many people are reduced to welfare.

Yet this is not necessarily an expression of class consciousness in the classical Marxist sense: that people with these views will sooner or later become activists, and come to seek a collective solution to their present problems, even less that they will begin to think and act in terms of creating a different kind of society altogether. Two thirds *also* saw the two sides of industry as sharing a number of interests in common. They also thought that there was little, realistically, that people like them could do about changing things. Even then, though, almost three quarters thought that something *could* be done, though what this something was varied a lot: some emphasized changing individual attitudes, some changing the government; some increasing national self-sufficiency. But few thought that governments would in fact do much for them, whatever political party was in power. Fatalism is widespread, though it is 'a fatalism informed by an awareness of distributional injustice'. 'People', then, 'are no more wholeheartedly "fatalistic" than they are 'class conscious"'; few of them 'subscribe to ... uncomplicated or one-sided worldviews rooted in any single principle of social organization'. Rather, 'the "class consciousness" of the majority ... is characterized by ... complexity, ambivalence, and occasional contradictions'.

There have been methodological criticisms of this study: the fact that one third of the males in Class I started life in the working class, and only one quarter of men in Class I had been born into that class represents, by any yardstick, a substantial amount of upward social mobility. And the strong emphasis which interviewees put upon class, it has been argued, reflected the structure of the questionnaire, which began with a battery of questions about the class system. Furthermore, the timing of the research, when a very bitter national miners' strike was in progress, was likely to put class issues at the forefront of people's consciousness which might have been much less salient at other times. Nevertheless, the findings of this study seem to be strongly supported by re-analysis of other surveys in the same field.

The political expression of these complex attitudes is difficult to predict, and is liable to change swiftly when latent popular resentments are more effectively articulated by political leaderships. It may therefore come as a surprise that what most people, including political scientists, psephologists, etc., take to be a 'sociological' explanation of changes in voting behaviour – explanation in terms of changes in occupational structures and in ideologies – are rejected by this study. Instead, their conclusion is that 'class politics is far from exhausted'. Shifts in voting reflect the success or failure of rival political parties in developing an appeal appropriate to their 'natural' supporters among the electorate – a conclusion almost universally rejected by those who assumed that 'regression to the centre' was not only a straightforward reflection of changes in social structure but also an irreversible fact of life. It is a conclusion, however, which would have made sense to Max Weber, with his emphasis upon the relative autonomy of the political, and seems, too, to make sense of the eclipse of the centre in recent years.

58 Karl Marx on Class

(a) The Historical Tendency of Capitalist Accumulation

Excerpt from Karl Marx, *Capital*, reprinted in L. S. Feuer (ed.), *Marx and Engels: Basic Writings*, Collins, 1959, pp. 205–8. (First published in German in 1867.)

Private property, as the antithesis to social, collective property, exists only where the means of labour and the external conditions of labour belong to private individuals. But according as these private individuals are labourers or not labourers, private property has a different character. The numberless shades that it at first sight presents correspond to the intermediate stages lying between these two extremes. The private property of the labourer in his means of production is the foundation of petty industry, whether agricultural, manufacturing or both; petty industry, again, is an essential condition for the development of social production and of the free individuality of the labourer himself. Of course, this petty mode of production exists also under slavery, serfdom and other states of dependence. But it flourishes, it lets loose its whole energy, it attains its adequate classical form only where the labourer is the private owner of his own means of labour set in action by himself, the peasant of the land which he cultivates, the artisan of the tool which he handles as a virtuoso. This mode of production presupposes parcelling of the soil and scattering of the other means of production, so also it excludes cooperation, division of labour within each separate process of production, the control over and the productive application of the forces of nature by society and the free development of the social productive powers. It is compatible only with a system of production, and a society, moving within narrow and more or less primitive bounds. To perpetuate it would be, as Pecqueur rightly says, 'to decree universal mediocrity'. At a certain stage of development it brings forth the material agencies for its own dissolution. From that moment new forces and new passions spring up in the bosom of society, but the old social organization fetters them and keeps them down. It must be annihilated; it is annihilated. Its annihilation, the transformation of the individualized and scattered means of production into socially concentrated ones, of the pygmy property of the many into the huge property of the few, the expropriation of the great mass of the people from the soil, from the means of subsistence, and from the means of labour, this fearful and painful expropriation of the mass of the people forms the prelude to the history of capital. It comprises a series of forcible methods, of which we have passed in review only those that have been epoch making as methods of the primitive accumulation of capital. The expropriation of the immediate producers was accomplished with merciless vandalism, and under the stimulus of passions the most infamous, the most sordid, the pettiest, the most meanly odious. Self-earned private property which is based, so to say, on the fusing together of the isolated, independent labouring individual with the conditions of his labour, is supplanted by capitalistic private property, which rests on exploitation of the nominally free labour of others, i.e. on wage labour.

As soon as this process of transformation has sufficiently decomposed the old society from top to bottom, as soon as the labourers are turned into proletarians, their means of labour into capital, as soon as the capitalist mode of production stands on its own feet, then the further socialization of labour and further transformation of the land and other means of production into socially exploited and, therefore, common means of production, as well as the further expropriation of private proprietors take a new form. That which is now to be expropriated is no longer the labourer working for himself, but the capitalist exploiting many labourers. This expropriation is accomplished by the action of the immanent laws of capitalistic production itself, by the centralization of capital. One capitalist always kills many. Hand in hand with this centralization, or this expropriation, of many capitalists by few, develop, on an ever extending scale, the cooperative form of the labour process, the conscious technical application of science, the methodical cultivation of the soil, the transformation of the instruments of labour into instruments of labour usable only in common, the economizing of all means of production by their use as the means of production of combined, socialized labour, the entanglement of all peoples in the net of the world market, and this, the international character of the capitalistic régime. Along with the constantly diminishing number of the magnates of capital, who usurp and monopolize all advantages of this process of transformation, grows the mass of misery, oppression, slavery, degradation, exploitation; but with this too grows the revolt of the working class, a class always increasing in numbers, and disciplined, united, organized by the very mechanism of the process of capitalist production itself. The monopoly of capital becomes a fetter upon the mode of production which has sprung up and flourished along with and under it. Centralization of the means of production and socialization of labour at last reach a point where they become incompatible with their capitalist integument. This integument is burst asunder. The knell of capitalist private property sounds. The expropriators are expropriated.

The capitalist mode of appropriation, the result of the capitalist mode of production, produces capitalist private property. This is the first negation of individual private property, as founded on the labour of the proprietor. But capitalist production begets, with the inexorability of a law of nature, its own negation. It is the negation of negation. This does not re-establish private property for the producer, but gives him individual property based on the acquisitions of the capitalist era, i.e. on cooperation and the possession in common of the land and of the means of production.

The transformation of scattered private property, arising from individual labour, into capitalist private property is, naturally, a process incomparably more protracted, violent and difficult than the transformation of capitalistic private property, already practically resting on socialized production, into socialized property. In the former case we had the expropriation of the mass of the people by a few usurpers; in the latter we have the expropriation of a few usurpers by the mass of the people.

(b) The Class Struggles in France, 1848 to 1850

Excerpts from Karl Marx, *The Class Struggles in France, 1848 to 1850*, reprinted in L. S. Feuer (ed.), *Marx and Engels: Basic Writings*, Collins, 1959, pp. 322–3, 353–4. (First published in 1850.)

After the July revolution [of 1830], when the liberal banker Laffitte led his godfather, the Duke of Orleans, in triumph to the Hôtel de Ville, he let fall the words: '*From now on the bankers will rule.*' Laffitte had betrayed the secret of the revolution.

It was not the French bourgeoisie that ruled under Louis Philippe, but *one section* of it: bankers, stock-exchange kings, railway kings, owners of coal and iron mines and forests, a part of the landed proprietors that rallied round them – the so-called *finance aristocracy*. It sat on the throne, it dictated laws in the Chambers, it distributed public offices, from cabinet portfolios to tobacco bureau posts.

The *industrial bourgeoisie*, properly so called, formed part of the official opposition, i.e. it was represented only as a minority in the Chambers. Its opposition was expressed all the more resolutely the more unalloyed the autocracy of the finance aristocracy became, and the more it itself imagined that its domination over the working class was ensured after the mutinies of 1832, 1834 and 1839, which had been drowned in blood . . .

The *petty bourgeois* of all gradations, and the *peasantry* also, were completely excluded from political power. Finally, in the official opposition or entirely outside the *pays légal*, there were the *ideological* representatives and spokesmen of the above classes, their savants, lawyers, doctors, etc. – in a word, their so-called *men of talent* . . .

The most comprehensive contradiction of this constitution, however, consists in the following: the classes whose social slavery the constitution is to perpetuate, proletariat, peasantry, petty bourgeoisie, it puts in possession of political power through universal suffrage. And from the class whose old social power it sanctions, the bourgeoisie, it withdraws the political guarantees of this power. It forces the political rule of the bourgeoisie into democratic conditions, which at every moment help the hostile classes to victory and jeopardize the very foundations of bourgeois society. From the former classes it demands that they should not go forward from political to social emancipation; from the others that they should not go back from social to political restoration.

(c) The Eighteenth Brumaire of Louis Bonaparte

Excerpt from Karl Marx, *Eighteenth Brumaire of Louis Bonaparte*, reprinted in L. S. Feuer (ed.), *Marx and Engels: Basic Writings*, Collins, 1959, pp. 377–9. (First published in 1852.)

Only under the second Bonaparte does the State seem to have made itself completely independent. As against civil society, the State machine has consolidated its position so thoroughly that the chief of the Society of December 10 suffices for its head, an adventurer blown in from abroad, raised on the shield by a drunken soldiery, which he has bought with liquor and sausages, and which he must continually ply with sausage anew. Hence the downcast despair, the feeling of most dreadful humiliation and degradation that oppresses the breast of France and makes her catch her breath. She feels dishonoured.

And yet the State power is not suspended in mid-air. Bonaparte represents a class, and the most numerous class of French society at that, the *small-holding* [*Parzellen*] *peasants*.

Just as the Bourbons were the dynasty of big landed property and just as the Orleans were the dynasty of money, so the Bonapartes are the dynasty of the peasants, that is, the mass of the French people. Not the Bonaparte who submitted to the bourgeois parliament, but the Bonaparte who dispersed the bourgeois parliament is the chosen of the peasantry. For three years the towns had succeeded in falsifying the meaning of the election of December 10 and in cheating the peasants out of the restoration of the empire. The election of 10 December 1848 has been consummated only by the *coup d'état* of 2 December 1851.

The small-holding peasants form a vast mass, the members of which live in smaller conditions but without entering into manifold relations with one another. Their mode of production isolates them from one another instead of bringing them into mutual intercourse. The isolation is increased by France's bad means of communication and by the poverty of the peasants. Their field of production, the small holding, admits of no division of labour in its cultivation, no application of science and, therefore, no diversity of development, no variety of talent, no wealth of social relationships. Each individual peasant family is almost self-sufficient; it itself directly produces the major part of its consumption, and thus acquires its means of life more through exchange with nature than in intercourse with society. A small holding, a peasant and his family; alongside them another small holding, another peasant and another family. A few score of these make up a village, and a few score of villages make up a Department. In this way the great mass of the French nation is formed by simple addition of homologous magnitudes, much as potatoes in a sack form a sack of potatoes. In so far as millions of families live under economic conditions of existence that separate their mode of life, their interests and their culture from those of the other classes and put them in hostile opposition to the latter, they form a class. In so far as there is merely a local interconnection among these small-holding peasants and the identity of their interests begets no community, no national bond and no political organization among them, they do not form a class. They are consequently incapable of enforcing their class interest in their own name, whether through a parliament or through a convention. They cannot represent themselves, they must be represented. Their representative must at the same time appear as their master, as an authority over them, as an unlimited government power that protects them against the other classes and sends them rain and sunshine from above. The political influence of the small-holding peasants, therefore, finds its final expression in the executive power subordinating society to itself.

Historical tradition gave rise to the belief of the French peasants in the miracle that a man named Napoleon would bring all the glory back to them. And an individual turns up who gives himself out as the man because he bears the name of Napoleon ... After a vagabondage of twenty years and after a series of grotesque adventures the legend finds fulfilment and the man becomes Emperor of the French. The fixed idea of the nephew was realized because it coincided with the fixed idea of the most numerous class of the French people.

59   Max Weber on Class and Status

(a) Social Status

Excerpt from Max Weber, *The Theory of Social and Economic Organizations*, translated by A. M. Henderson and Talcott Parsons, revised and edited by Talcott Parsons, Oxford University Press, Inc., 1947. Reprinted in Hans H. Gerth and C. Wright Mills (eds.), *From Max Weber: Essays in Sociology*, Oxford University Press, Inc., 1946, p. 428. (First published in German in 1922.)

The term of 'social status' will be applied to a typically effective claim to positive or negative privilege with respect to social prestige so far as it rests on one or more of the following bases: (a) mode of living, (b) a formal process of education which may consist in empirical or rational training and the acquisition of the corresponding modes of life, or (c) on the prestige of birth, or of an occupation.

The primary practical manifestations of status with respect to social stratification are connubium, commensality and often monopolistic appropriation of privileged economic opportunities and also prohibition of certain modes of acquisition. Finally, there are conventions or traditions of other types attached to a social status.

Stratificatory status may be based on class status directly or related to it in complex ways. It is not, however, determined by this alone. Property and managerial positions are not as such sufficient to lend their holder a certain social status, though they may well lead to its acquisition. Similarly, poverty is not as such a disqualification for high social status though again it may influence it.

Conversely, social status may partly or even wholly determine class status, without, however, being identical with it. The class status of an officer, a civil servant and a student as determined by their income may be widely different while their social status remains the same, because they adhere to the same mode of life in all relevant respects as a result of their common education.

(b) Class and Market Situation

Excerpts from Max Weber, 'Class, status, party', published posthumously in Hans H. Gerth and C. Wright Mills (eds.), *From Max Weber: Essays in Sociology*, Oxford University Press, Inc., 1946, pp. 182–8, 193–4. (First published in German in 1922–3.)

In our terminology, 'classes' are not communities; they merely represent possible, and frequent, bases for communal action. We may speak of a 'class' when (a) a number of people have in common a specific causal component of their life chances, in so far as (b) this component is represented exclusively by economic interests in the possession of goods and opportunities for income, and (c) is represented under the conditions of the commodity or labour markets. (These points refer to 'class situation', which we may express more briefly as the typical chance for a supply of goods, external living conditions and personal life experiences, in so far as this chance is determined by the amount and kind of power, or lack of such, to dispose of goods or skills for the sake of income in a given economic order. The term 'class' refers to any group of people that is found in the same class situation.)

It is the most elemental economic fact that the way in which the disposition over material property is distributed among a plurality of people, meeting competitively in the market for the purpose of exchange, in itself creates specific life chances. According to the law of marginal utility this mode of distribution excludes the non-owners from competing for highly valued goods; it favours the owners and, in fact, gives to them a monopoly to acquire such goods. Other things being equal, this mode of distribution monopolizes the opportunities for profitable deals for all those who, provided with goods, do not necessarily have to exchange them. It increases, at least generally, their power in price wars with those who, being propertyless, have nothing to offer but their services in native form or goods in a form constituted through their own labour, and who above all are compelled to get rid of these products in order barely to subsist. This mode of distribution gives to the propertied a monopoly on the possibility of transferring property from the sphere of use as a 'fortune', to the sphere of 'capital goods'; that is, it gives them the entrepreneurial function and all chances to share directly or indirectly in returns on capital. All this holds true within the area in which pure market conditions prevail. 'Property' and 'lack of property' are, therefore, the basic categories of all class situations. It does not matter whether these two categories become effective in price wars or in competitive struggles.

Within these categories, however, class situations are further differentiated: on the one hand, according to the kind of property that is usable for returns; and on the other hand, according to the kind of services that can be offered in the market. Ownership of domestic buildings; productive establishments; warehouses; stores; agriculturally usable land, large and small holdings – quantitative differences with possibly qualitative consequences; ownership of mines; cattle; men (slaves); disposition over mobile instruments of production, or capital goods of all sorts, especially money or objects that can be exchanged for money easily and at any time; disposition over products of one's own labour or of others' labour differing according to their various distances from consumability; disposition over transferable monopolies of any kind – all these distinctions differentiate the class situations of the propertied just as does the 'meaning' which they can and do give to the utilization of property, especially to property which has money equivalence. Accordingly, the propertied, for instance, may belong to the class of rentiers or to the class of entrepreneurs.

Those who have no property but who offer services are differentiated just as much according to their kinds of services as according to the way in which they make use of these services, in a continuous or discontinuous relation to a recipient. But always this is the generic connotation of the concept of class: that the kind of chance in the *market* is the decisive moment which presents a common condition for the individual's fate. 'Class situation' is, in this sense, ultimately 'market situation'. The effect of naked possession *per se*, which among cattle breeders gives the non-owning slave or serf into the power of the cattle owner, is only a forerunner of real 'class' formation. However, in the cattle loan and in the naked severity of the law of debts in such communities, for the first time mere 'possession' as such emerges as decisive for the fate of the individual. This is very much in contrast to the agricultural communities based on labour. The creditor–debtor relation becomes a basis of 'class situations' only in those cities where a 'credit market', however primitive, with rates of interest increasing according to the extent of dearth and a factual monopolization of credits, is developed by a plutocracy. Therewith 'class struggles' begin.

Those men whose fate is not determined by the chance of using goods or services for themselves on the market, e.g. slaves, are not, however, a 'class' in the technical sense of the term. They are, rather, a 'status group' . . .

Every class may be the carrier of any one of the possibly innumerable forms of 'class action', but this is not necessarily so. In any case, a class does not in itself constitute a community. To treat 'class' conceptually as having the same value as 'community' leads to distortion. That men in the same class situation regularly react in mass actions to such tangible situations as economic ones in the direction of those interests that are most adequate to their average number is an important and after all simple fact for the understanding of historical events. Above all, this fact must not lead to that kind of pseudoscientific operation with the concepts of 'class' and 'class interests' so frequently found these days, and which has found its most classic expression in the statement of a talented author, that the individual may be in error concerning his interests but that the 'class' is 'infallible' about its interests. Yet, if classes as such are not communities, nevertheless class situations emerge only on the basis of communalization. The communal action that brings forth class situations, however, is not basically action between members of the identical class; it is an action between members of different classes. Communal actions that directly determine the class situation of the worker and the entrepreneur are: the labour market, the commodities market and the capitalistic enterprise. But, in its turn, the existence of a capitalistic enterprise presupposes that a very specific communal action exists and that it is specifically structured to protect the possession of goods *per se*, and especially the power of the individuals to dispose, in principle freely, over the means of production. The existence of a capitalistic enterprise is preconditioned by a specific kind of 'legal order'. Each kind of class situation, and above all when it rests upon the power of property *per se*, will become most clearly efficacious when all other determinants of reciprocal relations are, as far as possible, eliminated in their significance. It is in this way that the utilization of the power of property in the market obtains its most sovereign importance . . .

In contrast to classes, *status groups* are normally communities.

They are, however, often of an amorphous kind. In contrast to the purely economically determined 'class situation' we wish to designate as 'status situation' every typical component of the life fate of men that is determined by a specific, positive or negative, social estimation of *honour*. This honour may be connected with any quality shared by a plurality and, of course, it can be knit to a class situation: class distinctions are linked in the most varied ways with status distinctions. Property as such is not always recognized as a status qualification, but in the long run it is, and with extraordinary regularity. In the subsistence economy of the organized neighbourhood, very often the richest man is simply the chieftain. However, this often means only an honorific preference. For example, in the so-called pure modern 'democracy', that is, one devoid of any expressly ordered status privileges for individuals, it may be that only the families coming under approximately the same tax class dance with one another. This example is reported of certain smaller Swiss cities. But status honour need not necessarily be linked with a 'class situation'. On the contrary, it normally stands in sharp opposition to the pretensions of sheer property.

Both propertied and property-less people can belong to the same status group, and frequently they do with very tangible consequences. This 'equality' of social esteem may, however, in the long run become quite precarious. The 'equality' of status among the American 'gentlemen', for instance, is expressed by the fact that outside the subordination determined by the different functions of 'business', it would be considered strictly repugnant – wherever the old tradition still prevails – if even the richest 'chief', while playing billiards or cards in his club in the evening, would not treat his 'clerk' as in every sense fully his equal in birthright. It would be repugnant if the American 'chief' would bestow upon his 'clerk' the condescending 'benevolence' marking a distinction of 'position', which the German chief can never dissever from his attitude. This is one of the most important reasons why in America the German 'clubby-ness' has never been able to attain the attraction that the American clubs have.

In content, status honour is normally expressed by the fact that above all else a specific *style of life* can be expected from all those who wish to belong to the circle. Linked with this expectation are restrictions on 'social' intercourse (that is, intercourse which is not subservient to economic or any other of business's 'functional' purposes). These restrictions may confine normal marriages to within the status circle and may lead to complete endogamous closure. As soon as there is not a mere individual and socially irrelevant imitation of another style of life, but an agreed-upon communal action of this closing character, the 'status' development is under way.

In its characteristic form, stratification by 'status groups' on the basis of conventional styles of life evolves at the present time in the United States out of the traditional democracy . . .

With some over-simplification, one might say that 'classes' are stratified according to their relations to the production and acquisition of goods; whereas 'status groups' are stratified according to the principles of their *consumption* of goods as represented by special 'styles of life'.

An 'occupational group' is also a status group. For normally, it successfully claims social honour only by virtue of the special style of life which may be determined by it. The differences between classes and status groups frequently overlap. It is precisely those status communities most strictly segregated in terms of honour (viz., the Indian castes) who today show, although within very rigid limits, a relatively high degree of indifference to pecuniary income. However, the Brahmins seek such income in many different ways.

As to the general economic conditions making for the predominance of stratification by 'status', only very little can be said. When the bases of the acquisition and distribution of goods are relatively stable stratification by status is favoured. Every technological repercussion and economic transformation threatens stratification by status and pushes the class situation into the foreground. Epochs and countries in which the naked class situation is of predominant significance are regularly the periods of technical and economic transformations. And every slowing down of the shifting of economic stratifications leads, in due course, to the growth of status structures and makes for a resuscitation of the important role of social honour.

60 Frank Parkin

Meaning-Systems and Class Inequality

Excerpts from Frank Parkin, *Class Inequality and Political Order*, Paladin, 1972, pp. 79, 81–4, 88–91.

Sociological accounts of the normative aspects of inequality reveal the absence of any general agreement concerning the distribution of values in the class hierarchy. One school of thought maintains that the values underlying major social institutions are held in common by all social classes, though perhaps with varying degrees of commitment. A different school of thought argues that values vary sharply and systematically between classes, so that one cannot speak of a unified moral order . . .

It might be helpful if we approach this complex issue by looking at the normative order as a number of competing meaning-systems. Although there is a factual and material basis to class inequality, there is more than one way in which it can be interpreted. Facts alone do not provide meanings, and the way a person makes sense of his social world will be influenced by the nature of the meaning-systems he draws upon. So far as class stratification in Western societies is concerned it seems that we can quite usefully distinguish three major meaning-systems. Each derives from a different social source, and each promotes a different moral interpretation of class inequality. These are:

1. The *dominant* value system, the social source of which is the major institutional order. This is a moral framework which promotes the endorsement of existing inequality; among the subordinate class this leads to a definition of the reward structure in either *deferential* or *aspirational* terms.
2. The *subordinate* value system, the social source or generating milieu of which is the local working-class community. This is a moral framework which promotes *accommodative* responses to the facts of inequality and low status.

3.   The *radical* value system, the source of which is the mass political party based on the working class. This is a moral framework which promotes an *oppositional* interpretation of class inequalities.

In most Western societies all three meaning-systems tend to influence the social and political perceptions of the subordinate class. Variations in the structure of attitudes of groups or individuals within this class are thus to some extent dependent upon differences in access to these meaning-systems. Any discussion of working-class values regarding the reward structure must thus concern itself both with the types of major meaning-systems 'available', and with social factors which help to account for variations in their adoption. Clearly, values are generally not imposed on men in any crudely mechanistic way. Men also impose their will by selecting, as it were, from the range of values which any complex society generates. At the same time, individuals do not construct their social worlds in terms of a wholly personal vision, and without drawing heavily upon the organizing concepts which are part of a public meaning-system . . .

The concept of a dominant value system derives from Marx's celebrated statement that 'the ideas of the ruling class are, in every age, the ruling ideas'. This proposition rests on the plausible assumption that those groups in society which occupy positions of the greatest power and privilege will also tend to have the greatest access to the means of legitimation. That is to say, the social and political definitions of those in dominant positions tend to become objectified and enshrined in the major institutional orders, so providing the moral framework of the entire social system. It is not of course necessary to posit any monolithic social or normative unity to the groups which cluster at the apex of the dominant class. Undoubtedly they display variations in political and social outlook – as, for example, between aristocratic or traditional élites on the one hand and managerial or entrepreneurial élites on the other. However, these differences are not likely to be fundamental with regard to the values underlying class inequality and its institutional supports. With the partial exception of that group or stratum loosely defined as the intellectuals, almost all groups within the dominant class tend to define the reward system as morally just and desirable. Dominant values are in a sense a representation of the perceptions and interests of the relatively privileged; yet by virtue of the institutional backing they receive such values often form the basis of moral judgements of underprivileged groups. In a way, dominant values tend to set the standards for what is considered to be objectively 'right'. This holds not only for the rules governing the distribution of rewards but also for many other aspects of social life. In the sphere of culture, for example, the musical, literary and artistic tastes of the dominant class are accorded positive evaluation, while the typical cultural tastes and pursuits of the subordinate class are negatively evaluated. Thus in the allocation of national resources to the arts, or of honours to their practitioners, the claims of 'élite' culture will tend to have precedence over the claims of 'mass' culture. To take a somewhat similar example, the characteristic speech-patterns and linguistic usages of the dominant class are generally regarded as 'correct', or what counts as the grammar of the language; the usages of the subordinate class are often said to be 'incorrect' or ungrammatical where they differ from the former, even though such usages may represent the statistical norm. These examples serve to illustrate that what is essentially an *evaluative* matter can be transformed into an apparently *factual* one by virtue of the legitimating powers of the dominant class . . .

Now the more completely the subordinate class comes to endorse and internalize the dominant value system, the less serious will be the conflicts over existing inequalities . . .

This phenomenon of a class, or at least a large segment of it, endorsing a moral order which legitimizes its own political, material, and social subordination is open to somewhat different assessments. On the one hand, it can be taken as evidence of a socially desirable political consensus – a social order free from disruptive class conflicts. Or, on the other hand, it can be understood as an example of a society in which the dominant class has been especially successful in imposing its own definitions of reality on less privileged groups. Thus, to equate political and social consensus with the good society, as so many contemporary writers do, is really to state a concealed preference for a system in which the dominant class has effectively translated its own values into a factual moral order binding on all . . .

The *subordinate* value system; the generating milieu of this meaning-system is the local working-class community. There is an abundance of studies of the patterns of attitudes and beliefs typifying what is sometimes called the working-class or lower-class subculture.

In so far as it is possible to characterize a complex set of normative arrangements by a single term, the subordinate value system could be said to be essentially *accommodative*; that is to say its representation of the class structure and inequality emphasizes various modes of adaptation, rather than either full endorsement of, or opposition to, the *status quo*. Hoggart portrays this underlying theme of the subordinate value system as follows:

When people feel that they cannot do much about the main elements in their situation, feel it not necessarily with despair or disappointment or resentment but simply as a fact of life, they adopt attitudes towards that situation which allow them to have a liveable life under its shadow, a life without a constant and pressing sense of the larger situation. The attitudes remove the main elements in the situation to the realm of natural laws . . .

The subordinate value system tends to promote a version of the social order neither in terms of an open opportunity structure nor as an organic unity; rather, strong emphasis is given to social divisions and social conflict, as embodied in the conceptual categories of 'them' and 'us'. This power or conflict model of the reward structure is clearly different from any which could be derived from outright endorsement of the dominant value system. Indeed, it is a general perspective which casts some doubt on the morality of the distributive system and the persistent inequities it generates. At the same time, however, it would be misleading to construe the subordinate value system as an example of normative opposition to the dominant order. Least of all, perhaps, should it be understood as exemplifying class-consciousness or political radicalism . . .

To begin with, Hoggart's catalogue of working-class usages (which is the main empirical source of the power model so far as England is concerned) refers primarily to the experience of authority relations which such diverse figures as policemen, civil servants, local government officials, and petty bureaucrats, as well as with employers. Now resentment at bureaucratic officialdom is certainly likely to be more sharply felt among the subordinate than the dominant class. But this is hardly to be equated with political class consciousness in the usual meaning of that term. Nor, again, is the pervasive sense of communal solidarity which is typically found in the underclass milieu to be equated with a class outlook on politics and society. As Hoggart himself points out, the communal or solidaristic aspect of working-class life is largely confined to *interpersonal* relationships, and for 'most people it does not develop into a conscious sense of being part of the "working-class movement"'. Conventionally, to describe workers as class conscious is to refer to their commitment to a radical or oppositional view of the reward structure of capitalist society. Typically, of course, this type of outlook is associated with Marxist or socialist movements, and does not emerge of its own accord from the underclass milieu. Indeed, it could be said that the subordinate value system represents something of a bulwark to political class consciousness, in so far as it entails adaptive rather than oppositional responses to the *status quo*. As Westergaard has argued, the solidarities of class and the solidarities of community are antithetical rather than complementary. Subordinate class communities throw up their distinctive value systems more or less independently of one another; there is no 'national' subordinate value system in the way that there is truly national or societal dominant value system. The similarity in the normative patterns of working-class communities derives largely from the similarity of the conditions they are exposed to. They generate a meaning-system which is of purely parochial significance, representing a design for living based upon localized social knowledge and face-to-face relationships. A class outlook, on the other hand, is rooted in a perception of the social order that stretches far beyond the frontiers of community. It entails a macro-social view of the reward structure and some understanding of the *systematic* nature of inequality. In a way, becoming class conscious, at least in the ideal-typical sense, could be likened to learning a foreign language: that is, it presents men with a new vocabulary and a new set of concepts which permit a different translation of the meaning of inequality from the encouraged by the conventional vocabulary of society. In some social settings, and for many individuals, becoming class conscious must often amount to what is virtually a normative transformation; at any rate, it draws upon a meaning-system which is far removed from that embodying accommodative or adaptive responses to the facts of subordinate status.

   In certain respects, accommodation to material insecurity or deprivation betokens a kind of fatalistic pessimism. Hoggart catalogues some of the many working-class expressions indicating the necessity for making mental adjustments to material hardship: 'What is to be will be'; 'that's just the way things are'; 'grin and bear it'; 'y've got to tek life as it comes'; 'it's no good moaning'; 'mek the best of it ... stick it ... soldier on ...' etc., etc. Although fatalism and the reluctant acceptance of one's lot is a prominent theme of the subordinate value system, it is by no means the only major response compatible with adaptation. A no less important element in the accommodative outlook is the 'instrumental collectivism' typified by the trade union movement. Trade unionism is one of the few forms of socio-political organization which is indigenous to the subordinate class, and yet based upon society rather than community. And, in so far as men combine in the attempt to improve their material situation they could not be said to have a purely fatalistic outlook; commitment to trade unionism implies a belief that conditions should and can be improved, which is quite different from the pessimistic resignation enshrined in the popular sayings quoted above. However, the fact that unionism is closely geared to the moral framework of the subordinate value system is reflected in the movement's aims regarding the distribution of rewards. Collective bargaining and its attendant strategies imply a general acceptance of the rules governing distribution. Organized labour directs its main efforts towards winning a greater share of resources for its members – not by challenging the existing framework of rules but by working within this framework.

A. H. Halsey

A Class-Ridden Prosperity

Excerpts from A. H. Halsey, *Change in British Society*, 3rd edition, Oxford University Press, 1986, pp. 31–3, 36–42, 45.

At the beginning of the century the occupational division of labour in Britain was such that over three quarters of the employed and self-employed population were engaged in manual work. Of these, 28.7 per cent were skilled, 34.3 per cent semi-skilled, 9.6 per cent unskilled, and 1.8 per cent were self-employed artisans in 1911. Above these manual workers stood a white-collar and professional class, more confidently divided then than now into the upper-middle class and lower-middle class. And above these stood the tiny group of a few thousand – the group which Lord David Cecil ... termed 'the governing class' of his grandfather's day. By mid-century the proportion of manual workers had fallen below two thirds and since then it has fallen still further to roughly a third. So the first impression is of a gradual movement away from what might be called a proletarian society: and this transformation has been gathering pace in recent decades. Thus between the 1971 and 1981 Censuses the proportion of employed people in manual work fell from 62 to 56 per cent from men, and from 43 to 36 per cent for women.

By 1971, as John Goldthorpe and Catriona Llewellyn have described it the occupational structure was more differentiated and more balanced. In the middle there were now three main blocks of comparable size, each accounting for one fifth to one quarter of the total. There were first the semi-skilled manual workers, second the skilled manual workers, and third the clerical and sales workers. Flanking these three groups were three other small groups, each between 7 and 15 per cent of the total – on the one side the unskilled workers, and on the other the professional and technical workers and the administrative, managerial, and supervisory staff.

These shifts of occupational structure in the first three quarters of the twentieth century, from the shape of a pyramid to that of an electric light bulb are characteristic of advanced industrial societies in general . . . Behind them lies economic transformation: from small to large scale; from manufacturing to so-called tertiary-sector activity; from personal dealing to bureaucracy: from handling things to manipulating words and numbers; and from private to public organizations.

Some sociologists interpreted these trends as involving the development of a middle mass of technical and clerical employees with a consequent decline of class antagonisms, and with the spectre of polarized capitalist society in retreat . . . The end of the post-war period and the resurgence of economic liberalism with high unemployment and privatization raise again the problem of class polarization.

But in any case, before drawing such inferences about Britain, it is prudent to notice what is perhaps the outstanding feature of occupational change, namely the growth of women's employment outside the home. Male and female involvement in the economy have run different courses over the period we are considering . . . In 1911 both sexes were divided between manual and non-manual jobs three quarters to one quarter. Subsequently, the female labour force has both grown and shifted substantially into non-manual work, so that by 1981 three fifths of the employed women were non-manual while over half of the men were still manual workers. And even the shift to non-manual jobs among men has mostly taken place since the Second World War. What is more important about it is that the increasing numbers of higher-level professional and managerial positions have largely gone to men, while women have filled the even faster expanding array of lower white-collar jobs.

This development of the pattern of male and female employment raises two important issues, one with respect to the Marxist two-class model, the other concerning the relation of women to the class structure. The two-class model has to be adapted to take account of the expansion of professional and managerial occupations. Marxists have argued that these middle classes are in a contradictory class position. They exercise control over the productive powers but most of them own no capital. Ralf Dahrendorf and other liberal analysts have called them the 'service class' – those who provide a bridge between the rulers (capitalists) and the masses (workers) by acting as the agents of public and private authorities. From a Marxist standpoint these groups are explained as functionaries serving the owners of capital which has brought them into existence as a consequence of concentrations into larger enterprises. Large scale necessitates delegation of capitalist control to bureaucratic managers and professional experts. The capitalist development of production, on this view, determines the division of labour.

Women and the Class Structure

The second point – women and class – is still more important and has occasioned lively recent debate. Are women a class? My answer is no; but explanation is needed. Married women's paid employment has certainly increased from about a tenth at the beginning of the century to roughly half now: but employment outside the home is not only largely treated as additional to retaining the major responsibilities for domestic work but is also characteristically intermittent, part-time, and secondary to male employment. The typical case remains that the 'head' of a family determines the class of its members, including wives, by his labour-market role. The restricted and conditional nature of women's participation in the labour market also largely deprives them of the essential capacity for class action, i.e. the power to disrupt the productive process in any serious or effective manner. Instead, as Parkin has argued, women, like other groups with status or 'party' disadvantages, 'are forced to rely far more heavily upon collective mobilization of a purely social and expressive kind in order to press their claims'.

Most certainly the evidence is overwhelmingly that women suffer systematic inequalities of power and advantage as against men. But, while warranting full recognition, these inequalities are more adequately explained as inequalities of status, party (organization), and kinship than as class phenomena, even though their character is related to class . . . Nevertheless, it should be remarked at this point that sexual stratification is a fundamental feature of the social division of labour in all complex societies and that the increasing involvement of women in the occupational (i.e. labour market) division of labour in the twentieth century has had important consequences for class structure. Sexual inequality is a dimension of social stratification in its own right. But its impact on class inequality, as Westergaard and Resler have suggested, is to sharpen class division. Socially assortative mating increases the spread of income and wealth *between* families 'headed' by individuals (usually males) of different occupational class. Significantly also there is a high correlation between husband's and wife's unemployment.

The Wealth of the Nation

. . . Now let us look at collective prosperity. At the outset, the reader should be warned against taking official estimates of the national income or the gross national product — those modern talismans of national virility — as ultimate measures of the wealth of a nation. They are the gifts of bureaucracy rather than social science. These economists' sums tell us roughly what are the products of the *occupational* division of labour: but there is a larger *social* division of labour which includes the exchanges in families, and the services of the Samaritans, as well as the fiddles unrecorded by the Inland Revenue. There is, in short, another economy of vast dimension. It was, for example, only by the fiat of the Victorian economist Alfred Marshall that the paid labour of charwomen is counted as part of the national product, while the work of housewives is not. If we were to reckon the whole output of the social division of labour it is most likely that our sterling numbers would be more than doubled. Nevertheless, if we assume that outputs from the two economies are in less than completely inverse relation, the official figures can be used to indicate trends. They tell us that since 1900 the United Kingdom has at least tripled its gross national product in real terms.

In any case, there is general agreement that British levels of living rose throughout the century until the late 1970s and even in the 1980s for those in secure employment. If the word 'living' is taken quite literally, it may be noted that, compared with a hundred years ago, the average Briton lives thirty years longer, mainly because of a reduction in infantile mortality. In the childhood of the oldest readers the death of a baby in the house was a grim commonplace: now, less than two in a hundred die in infancy. A narrower and more conventional measurement of living standards, by income, yields a similar ameliorative story. The median earnings of male manual workers rose from just over £1.00 a week in 1905 to £122 a week in 1983. While it is difficult if not impossible to translate these money figures into real purchasing power by discounting for inflation, we can

safely say that they also represent at least a tripling of real income
. . . Hours of work have been steadily reduced (from 54 to 43 between
1900 and 1980). After the Second World War, paid holidays became
common and four weeks is now the norm. The official statistics for
1983 record 48 million holidays by residents of Great Britain. This is
a far cry from the experience of many, if not most, ordinary children
between the wars – the annual charabanc trip to Blackpool or
Skegness.

Yet inequality persists after a long period of economic growth.
From this point of view the picture of prosperity looks very different,
especially since the end of the 1970s and the arrival of a government
determined to press policies of economic liberalism. The assumption
of growing affluence is not beyond question. The old poverties of
lack of property, low pay, poor health, inadequate education, and
bad housing still disfigure, and many would say disgrace, the powerful engine of production which we call industrial society. The official
rate of registered unemployment doubled from the beginning of the
Thatcher administration to over 13 per cent of all employees in
1983. Unemployment is heavily concentrated in the working class,
and within that class among the young, the old, the sick, and the
disabled. Over seven million Britons depend on the Supplementary
Benefits Commission. In other words, over seven million are living
on the government's own estimate of the poverty line. And there are
more below it who do not claim their due . . .

How, then, are income and wealth shared among the population?
Let us begin with two relatively simple statistics. In Britain now the
richest 5 per cent still own 41 per cent of all marketable wealth.
Income is less unequally distributed, but here again the richest 1 per
cent take home about the same amount as the poorest 20 per cent.
They each have, in other words, more than twenty times as much
income. These are quite spectacular inequalities.

The Distribution of Market Income

From the First World War to the 1970s there was slow and unsteady
progress towards a more equal distribution of personal income. By
the early 1970s the top 10 per cent of income receivers were taking
about one quarter of total income, and this one-quarter share was
also the amount being taken by the bottom half of income receivers.

Comparing manual and non-manual earnings a trend towards decreasing inequality can be traced at least as far back as the 1920s. In 1978 the ratio of non-manual to manual earnings was 1.25 . . .

These equalizing tendencies in the market fortunes of occupational classes came to a halt with the passing of the post-war period. Between 1976 and 1982 the distribution of market incomes became more unequal. The top one fifth of households increased their share from 44 to 47 per cent, while the bottom one fifth sank from a share of 0.8 per cent to one of 0.4 per cent.

Redistribution by the State

The impact of taxes and transfers is a complicated one and much debated. It operates, as R. M. Titmuss pointed out, through three loosely related systems of state intervention – fiscal policy, the social services, and occupational welfare. Essentially these political interventions can only be understood as collective action to change the unacceptable outcome of market exchanges: and that means the outcome of class. Historically, the development of these elements of social policy starts from the Liberal governments before the First War. Their complexity mirrors the increasing complexity of the division of labour. They give Britain now a social division of welfare which is not by any means simply a political antidote to class distribution of what is produced by collective labour. On the contrary, social policy itself has been powerfully shaped by class. For example, the fiscal system has been no simple extension of progressive taxation from its introduction in 1907. We have noticed that the richest one fifth of households in 1982 took 47 per cent of the nation's income. After taxes and benefits that share was reduced to 39.4 per cent. The poorest one fifth of households had taken 0.4 per cent of market income. Taxation and benefits raised that share to 6.9 per cent. These figures can scarcely be interpreted as evidence of a hugely redistributive 'welfare' state. Welfare, it would appear, is largely self-financed for the bulk of the population. The activity of the state makes for no dramatic reduction of market inequalities.

Similarly, the social services are not to be thought of as a steady development of 'class abatement' through politics. In education, for example, throughout the twentieth century, a policy of expansion has been frequently justified as a means to equality of opportunity. But in spite of a slight tendency to more equal investment in the school education of children from different classes, the development of further education more than counterbalanced this equalizing effect because it was concentrated on middle-class children. If we compare boys born between 1913 and 1922 with those born between 1943 and 1952 (and standardize the figures by putting them into 1958 prices), it turns out that the average son of a professional or managerial family had seven times as much spent on him as the son of an agricultural labourer in the earlier period, and six times as much in the later period. A comparison of these First War and Second War children in absolute terms shows that the average professional son got an extra £566 a year for education after school, and the agricultural labourer's son an extra £103 a year as a result of the intervening expansion of educational opportunity.

Inequality of Wealth

Again, the third system of occupational welfare is more of a complement than a counterweight to class inequality. Occupational pensions are earnings-related. Sick pay and pension arrangements are better for non-manual than for manual workers. And there has been a considerable growth of tax-deductible fringe benefits since the war with the effect of increasing inequality between highly paid executives and the rest . . .

Professor Westergaard and Miss Resler, who have produced a voluminously and soberly argued empirical account from the Marxist standpoint, conclude that it was the exceptional circumstances of war which produced lasting effects on the contrasts in income and wealth . . . [Yet, they say,] 'capitalism can make no claim to a steadily more equal spread of wealth. Inequality is entrenched in its institutional structure.'

Liberal theorists, for their part, do not deny the inequality of distribution of personal wealth . . . Instead, they begin by arguing the significance of trends towards a more equal spread of both wealth and income. Argument about the exact measure of the distributions themselves is relatively unimportant. The various authorities would agree that the proportion of personal wealth held by the richest 1 per cent of the population before the First World War was about 70 per cent. By the mid-1930s it was reduced to 56 per cent, and by 1960 to 42 per cent. Subsequent official figures are on a slightly different basis. They show the percentage held by the top 1 per cent of people as moving down from 37 per cent in 1962 to 24 per cent in 1977 ... At first glance, then, these figures would appear to contradict Westergaard and Resler, and to show a strong and steady trend towards equality. But essentially Westergaard is right because the redistribution has very largely been a spread of wealth to the richest 5 per cent instead of 1 per cent, and much of it reflects arrangements for gifts *inter vivos* – gifts between the living as distinct from those bequeathed at death. In this way rich families have passed on their wealth and legally avoided tax ... If, following R. H. Tawney, we distinguish between property for power, by which I mean property that carries with it control over the lives of other people, and property for use, possessions that free a man from other people's control, then we can reasonably say that, throughout the period we can collectively remember, three quarters of the British have been virtually property-less in that area which covers the central part of life and occupations – how men and women earn a living and how they relate themselves most fully and creatively to their fellows. A minority has monopolized wealth, and an even tinier minority of that minority has monopolized property for power.

At the same time, of course, harking back to the fact of rising affluence, we should not ignore the social significance of the spread of property for use. Most of the under-40s take a wide range of amenities and consumer durables for granted. Only the over-40s remember those primitive instruments of washing day – the poss-stick and the dolly-tub.

To sum up a formidable ledger of evidence, we can say that distributions through the capital and labour markets were dramatically unequal at the opening of the century. Wealth, part of which is property for power, was always more unequally spread than income. And both distributions have remained unequal around a rising average level. Over and above such wealth for use as housing and personal possessions, property for power still has a most impressively unequal distribution. But the trend to a relatively more equal sharing of income has increasingly dominated the structure of inequality as a whole because the labour market distributes much more income than does the capital market. In 1976 income from employment accounted for well over two thirds of all income. The self-employed accounted for less than one tenth, and so did unearned income from rent, dividends, and interest payments.

How Poor is Poor?

Excerpts from Joanna Mack and Stewart Lansley, *Poor Britain*, Allen & Unwin, 1985, pp. 26–9, 44–5, 53, 55–7, 86.

How Poor is Too Poor?

There has been a long tradition that has tried to define poverty narrowly in terms of health, aiming either for a universal standard or for a standard relative to a particular moment in time. There has been an equally long tradition that has seen a person's needs as being culturally and socially, as well as physically, determined. It is a view that recognizes that there is more to life than just existing. Two hundred years ago the economist Adam Smith wrote:

By necessaries, I understand not only commodities which are indispensably necessary for the support of life but whatever the custom of the country renders it indecent for creditable people, even of the lowest order, to be without. A linen shirt, for example, is strictly speaking not a necessity of life. The Greeks and Romans lived, I suppose, very comfortably though they had no linen. But in the present time . . . a creditable day-labourer would be ashamed to appear in public without a linen shirt, the want of which would be supposed to denote that disgraceful state of poverty.

This theme was adopted and first used for a more practical purpose by Charles Booth in his pioneering surveys of poverty in London from the late 1880s to the turn of the century. He defined the very poor as those whose means were insufficient 'according to the normal standards of life in this country'.

Even Seebohm Rowntree, the man who had developed the idea of 'primary' poverty, had, by the time of his second survey of York in 1936, incorporated into his definition of poverty some needs that were not related in any way to the maintenance of physical health. His 1936 definition allowed for items such as a radio, books, newspapers, beer, tobacco, presents and holidays. Although the amounts allowed were small – and largely arbitrary – Rowntree had conceded the importance of a wide range of aspects of a person's standard of living – from consumer durables to leisure activities and social participation.

The essentially relative nature of poverty is immediately obvious when viewing people's standards of living in these broader terms. Purchases of consumer durables are specific to each generation, or even each decade, and activities involving social participation have no meaning outside the society in which people live . . .

To view necessities as socially determined is explicitly to view poverty as relative. For this reason this concept is often called 'relative poverty' . . . During the 1960s this view became widely accepted as a result – at least in part – of the work of Professor Peter Townsend. For the last thirty years, Townsend has argued that poverty can only be viewed in terms of the concept of 'relative deprivation' . . . In his 1969 survey of living-standards . . . Townsend defined poverty as follows:

Individuals, families and groups in the population can be said to be in poverty when they lack the resources to obtain the types of diet, participate in the activities and have the living conditions and amenities which are customary, or at least widely encouraged or approved, in the societies to which they belong.

Although something like this definition of poverty would now be widely accepted, there remains immense room for debate about what exactly it means . . .: Lack of which living conditions and amenities constitutes poverty? What types of diet are we talking about? Lack of participation in which activities distinguishes the poor from the non-poor? Behind these question lies a more fundamental question: on what basis should such decisions be made? The definition in itself provides little guidance. Are activities that are 'customary' those carried out by, say, 51 per cent of the population or 90 per cent? Are those that are customary the same as those that are 'widely encouraged or approved'? . . .

This study proceeds, therefore, by attempting to identify a minimum standard of living *directly*. We asked a representative sample of people to judge the *necessities* for living in Britain in the 1980s. To our knowledge, this approach is original. It should be stressed, at this point, that an important component of any definition of poverty is that the deprivations suffered spring from lack of resources . . . Only those who face what we have termed 'an *enforced* lack of necessities' are classed as living in poverty . . . We decided that only those aspects of life facilitated by access to money should be tested . . . The method adopted was to select a range of items indicative of various aspects of our way of living and to ask people whether these items were necessities. The survey concentrated on individual or personal aspects of behaviour, which were seen not only in terms of personal 'consumption' but also, following Townsend, in terms of *social* activities. The areas covered were food, heating, clothing, consumer durables, entertainment, leisure activities, holidays, and social occasions and activities. Two services that are provided at least in part by the public sector were also included: housing and public transport. Most housing is provided through the market, but even where it is provided through public services it is paid for directly. While the use of public transport is affected by the degree of subsidy, it remains a service that is primarily paid for.

Other public services were excluded – most significantly, health care and education. Such services are an important influence on each individual's quality of life, but they are not in the main paid for. Of course, the divisions are not clear-cut: a few do pay directly for health care and education and for the rest who use the public services there are often hidden costs. But in general, where such services are facilitated by access to money, it is on the margins or indirectly. Nor did it seem appropriate to include conditions at work. While we recognize that poor working conditions are concentrated among the low-paid, it is not an aspect of life that could readily be improved by higher pay. Similarly, various environmental factors, such as safety on the streets, were excluded, although again these aspects of life are generally worse for the poor than for others.

We accept that each individual's quality of life is affected by a whole range of public services, from sports centres to health care, from an emptied dustbin to education . . . [Yet] while public squalor diminishes the lives of everyone in a community, poverty affects the individual and stems from that individual's lack of resources . . .

In summary, this study tackles the questions 'how poor is too poor?' by identifying the minimum acceptable way of life for Britain in the 1980s. Those who have no choice but to fall below this minimum level can be said to be 'in poverty'. This concept is developed in terms of those who have an enforced lack of *socially perceived* necessities. This means that the 'necessities' of life are identified by public opinion and not by, on the one hand, the views of experts or, on the other hand, the norms of behaviour *per se*.

The survey established, for the first time ever, that a majority of people see the necessities of life in Britain in the 1980s as covering a wide range of goods and activities, and that people judge a minimum standard of living on socially established criteria and not just the criteria of survival or subsistence ... Over nine in ten people are agreed about the importance of the following basic living conditions in the home:

- heating,
- an indoor toilet (not shared),
- a damp-free home,
- a bath (not shared), and
- beds for everyone.

... The survey also found a considerable degree of consensus about the importance of a wide range of other goods and activities. More than two thirds of the respondents classed the following items as necessities:

- enough money for public transport,
- a warm water-proof coat,
- three meals a day for children,
- self-contained accommodation,
- two pairs of all-weather shoes,
- a bedroom for every child over 10 of different sex,
- a refrigerator,
- toys for children,
- carpets,
- celebrations on special occasions such as Christmas,
- a roast joint or its equivalent once a week, and
- a washing machine.

This widespread consensus on what are necessities clearly reflects the standards of today and not those of the past. In Rowntree's study of poverty in York in 1899, for a family to be classed as poor 'they must never spend a penny on railway fare or omnibus'. In

Britain in the 1980s, nearly nine in ten people think that such spending is not only justified but a necessity for living today.

The importance of viewing minimum standards in terms of contemporary living conditions is highlighted most forcefully by the impact of labour-saving household goods. A large majority of people think that a refrigerator and a washing machine are necessities – items that were unknown to the Victorians and even twenty years ago would have been seen as a luxury. In part, this reflects shifting standards and expectations; but it also reflects the fact that, in a practical sense, items that become customary also become necessary because other aspects of life are planned and built on the very fact that these items are customary. For example, many single elderly people have commented to us that, whereas once they could manage without a fridge, it is now so difficult to buy perishable food in small quantities that they find they need one . . .

While these trends are of great importance, the survey also shows that people do not judge necessities, directly or indirectly, simply on the criterion of subsistence. It is not just that a new range of goods have become critical to coping; people also classed as necessities items that solely add to the quality of life. Included in the items that over two thirds of people class as necessities are goods that add to one's comfort (such as carpets) and those that add to one's enjoyment (celebrations or a roast joint).

The rejection of an 'absolute' or 'subsistence-based' approach to determining necessities is seen more clearly in the items that over half of the respondents, but under two thirds, viewed as necessities:

- new, not second-hand, clothes,
- a hobby or leisure activity,
- two hot meals a day (for adults),
- meat or fish every other day,
- presents for friends or family once a year,
- a holiday away from home for one week a year,
- leisure equipment for children,
- a garden, and
- a television.

All these items are primarily to do with the quality of life, with enjoyment and with joining in social activities . . . There is virtually no disagreement that there should be more to life than just existing . . .

The survey [also] found widespread agreement between all groups in society about the items that are classified as necessities. The homogeneity of views is striking. People from all walks of life, from across the generations, from widely varying family circumstances, and with fundamentally opposed political beliefs, share the same view of the kind of society Britain should be in terms of the minimum standards of living to which all citizens should be entitled. Their views are based, it seems, on a general cultural ethos of what is decent and proper. This suggests that these views are deeply held. They are unlikely to fluctuate rapidly or to be affected by the kinds of changes in political climate that influence the public's views on policies.

Gordon Marshall, David Rose, Howard Newby and Caroline Vogler

Goodbye to Social Class?

Excerpts from Gordon Marshall, David Rose, Howard Newby and Caroline Vogler, *Social Class in Modern Britain*, Unwin Hyman, 1989, pp. 196, 202–3, 207–8, 210, 212, 214–16, 219–20, 225, 259–260.

It is commonly argued nowadays that decisive shifts in the structuring of social inequalities have generated original forms of sectionalism to replace the long-standing solidarities associated with social class. Accompanying shifts in values and life-styles allegedly have encouraged individualism and privatism. Both processes are said to be discernible in a decline of class-based politics in Britain since 1979. Class analysis, according to its many critics, will therefore prove to be increasingly bankrupt in the explanation of social inequalities and schisms . . .

The watchwords in the thesis of restructured distributional conflict are sectionalism, egoism and privatism. Although proponents of the argument interrelate these in different ways their common perception is one of recent changes in social hierarchy (in particular the occupational structure), and in social values, each associated with the rise of a diffuse individualism embracing life-styles, politics, and ideology. The heterogeneous working class of contemporary Britain has absorbed capitalist economic values; it takes an instrumental stance towards class organizations so that pecuniary collectivism based on sectional self-interest has undermined worker solidarity; and it has retreated from class politics into the private world of home and family. Distributional dissent now centres on consumption and status rather than production and class. In this way sectionalism and privatism emerge as the obverse of class consciousness. The assumption is that they are not and cannot be associated with solidaristic or inclusionary forms of class-based distributional conflict.

This contrast forces the history of British labour into an implausible dualistic mould: solidaristic and class versus sectional and privatized. The reality is more complex. Consider, for example, the evidence from studies of the mid nineteenth-century work-force in rapidly industrializing Britain. Sectionalism is already evident, most obviously in the existence of a 'labour aristocracy' of traditional artisans and skilled manual workers, but for both groups the emergence of a culture of domesticity centred on the home and on privatized life-styles co-existed with solidaristic and class-based political activity in the context of the trades union movement . . .

A common starting point is the observation that the culture of the artisan in the immediate pre-industrial era was trade-based, work-centred, and male-dominated. During the first half of the nineteenth century, for example, most London trades worked a twelve-hour day, six days each week, with people residing in the immediate vicinity of their work. Spare-time association, conviviality, and political discussion were centred on the workplace or an associated local hostelry, which served also as a house of call and centre of craft organization. Trade feasts, carnivals, intermarriage, and hereditary apprenticeships all served to reinforce trade solidarity. Homes were cramped, uncomfortable and, where they were not places of work, served as little more than somewhere to eat and sleep.

During the second half of the century, however, home and family became increasingly important both for artisans and the newly emerging skilled workers in the capital goods sector. For those who enjoyed secure employment and were able to restrict entry to the trade via apprenticeships the mid-Victorian economic boom brought a new prosperity. Rising real wages and falling prices saw the emergence of a margin of comfort over subsistence. The rise in living standards was, in turn, associated with a shortening of the working week, improved housing, suburbanization, home-centred patterns of consumption, and new forms of 'family leisure', all of which increased the importance of home and family in working men's lives. Robert Gray, for example, documents the emergence of a 'culture of domesticity', of 'domestic responsibility', and the shifting focus of artisanal life away from work towards home-centred and family-centred life-styles. This period also sees the emergence of specifically artisanal housing areas as skilled workers moved away from the courts and alleys of the slums, where they shared facilities with unskilled and casual labour, to the often badly built but nevertheless self-contained houses in superior suburbs. By 1870 the majority of skilled workers already commuted to work by tram or workers' train.

The concern for better housing was not simply a reflection of the desire for improved physical amenities. It was also an attempt to escape identification with the inhabitants of the older central slums and reflected the revaluation of home and family as a haven from work, source of dignity, and centre of recreation . . .

This does not mean that there was wholesale conformity to middle-class ideals of domesticity. The outlook of the labour aristocracy was an ambivalent one. 'Dominant values changed their meaning as they became adapted to the conditions of the artisan world and mediated through autonomous artisan institutions.' But a distinctively working-class conception of respectability did emerge and this was closely tied to a developing domestic ideal.

One consequence of this revaluation of family life that did in fact diffuse down the class structure was the emergence of a much stricter sexual division of labour, under which married women withdrew from paid employment outside the home. Men bargained for, and in effect secured, a 'family wage'. Wives who remained in paid labour shifted to 'genteel' occupations like shopkeeping or did homework such as laundering. The new division of labour was reinforced by the Education Act of 1870 which forced children into schools and left all household tasks in the hands of adult women. In due course the interiors of skilled working-class homes were transformed by cheap factory-produced commodities for home-based consumption. Wallpaper, floor coverings, furniture and ornaments turned front parlours everywhere into shrines of respectability. Finally, rising living standards and shorter working hours saw the development of new forms of family-centred recreation, including excursions and seaside holidays, although there remained considerable regional variation in this sphere with mining and heavy industry areas tending to retain more traditional sex-segregated patterns of associational activity.

These evolving home-centred and privatized life-styles nevertheless co-existed with high levels of participation in a range of voluntary associations, from sport clubs and churches to working men's clubs and trade unions. The labour aristocrats were unified outside family and workshop through their participation in local associations that were linked to claims both for respectability and citizenship rights. Skilled workers in particular were dependent on collective forms of organization and especially on the trades unions . . .

The instrumental use of trades unions by the skilled elite of manual workers differed from the individualistic instrumentality typical of the Victorian middle class in that the latter was concerned solely with personal or family benefit whereas the former rested principally on collective self-help. There was, in other words, an identification with craft or stratum, a feeling of mutuality and collective strength, a shared aspiration for economic betterment and social respectability to be achieved by the group as a whole. But this was, nevertheless, still instrumentalism. Many trades union struggles during the period were therefore exclusionary; that is, sectional and conventional. Their objective was to advance the interests of members in the areas of pay, hours, craft privileges, conditions of work and social benefits. At another level, however, these same craft unions were engaged in strenuous attempts to extend industrial and social citizenship by petitioning parliament on such issues as the ten-hour day, health and safety at work, formal rights for trades unions, and the vote for working men. Narrowly instrumental in pursuing sectional wage demands, the labour aristocracy in mid-Victorian Britain was also considerably more radical than any other section of the working class, both in its class and its status aspirations ... Among nineteenth-century labour aristocrats, therefore, sectionalism and privatism co-existed with solidarism and the growth of class institutions (trades unions, trades councils, the Trades Union Congress) which were commonly engaged in pursuit of civil, political, and social rights of citizenship that extended beyond particular crafts to the working class as a whole ...

One established way of broaching arguments about privatism as culture or consciousness is simply to ask people about central life interests and report their assessments of these. Respondents in our study were asked how they viewed their work ... Only 34 per cent of those in employment at the time of the survey saw their present job as nothing more than a means of earning a living. Sixty-six per cent claimed it meant more to them than that – and were then asked to explain why this was so. A variety of answers were offered, the most popular being that the work in question was somehow fulfilling or enjoyable (82 per cent of interviewees asked the question included this among their answers), that it offered sociability with colleagues, or that it provided an opportunity for using specific skills ... On the other hand, only 11 per cent of employees who claimed that work meant more than simply a means of earning a living went on to say that it was 'central to their life', so the argument can always be put that many of the seemingly positive attributes mentioned in this context are testimony to after the event rationalization rather than non-pecuniary attitudes to work. In other words, they are evidence merely of the extent to which people reconcile themselves to an unalterable and relatively unpleasant fact of life, literally by making the best of a bad job. In some instances this will undoubtedly be true. However, this does not seem to be generally the case, since our data also show that, among employees who stated that their jobs *were* simply a means of earning a living, only 36 per cent claimed that they would feel this way about *any* job they obtained. Other non-pecuniary explanations (relating to the character of the local labour market and limited skills of the respondent) were, by comparison, proffered by 31 per cent and 33 per cent respectively of these employees . . .

Women across all class locations are much more likely than men to emphasize the sociability of formal employment as one of its rewards. Elsewhere in this table the expected class differences also materialize: service-class respondents can see more of value to the country in their work than can other employees, are more likely to experience the rewards of using their own initiative, and more commonly enjoy the variety in the work itself. Working-class respondents, on the other hand, tend to emphasize the sociability of work and, among males at least, the opportunity it offers to use or develop particular work skills. None of these findings are exceptional since all are consistent with data reported extensively elsewhere . . .

In general, then, these findings lead us to conclude that only a relatively small minority of people are *strict* pecuniary instrumentalists with respect to their employment. Most people find some reward other than money in what they do. Of course these rewards are not evenly distributed since proportionately many more employees among the working classes are trapped in jobs that offer nothing other than a source of income to the incumbents . . .

Very few people could think of some other aspect of their lives that was obviously 'more important' to them than work. Twenty-three per cent of the sample did give priority to such an item, but 73 per cent thought work was at least as important (or more so) than any non-work activity they had listed, with the remainder unsure.

Employees showed no variation by social class on this pattern, with at minimum 16 per cent, and at most 24 per cent in any one class deeming some other activity to be more important to them than work . . .

There is . . . no systematic tendency among the working classes to 'retreat into the home' as some sort of private haven from communal and other sorts of social activities . . .

About half of all employees (46 per cent) stated that none of those whom they would number among their friends actually worked alongside them at the present time. But no less than 82 per cent of those claiming to have some friends at work also met these individuals socially in other contexts . . . Half of those in employment can number friends among their workmates, and . . . over 80 per cent of these friendships are subsequently pursued in non-work contexts. There is scant evidence for structural privatism in this finding at least . . . Class action is not an automatic by-product of economic developments. It is not simply a function of changes in the structure of occupation or income. Class actions are shaped, not only by political and ideological as well as economic considerations, but also by the institutional frameworks of political democracy within which they occur. The various working-class organizations operating within this framework themselves help shape class conflicts . . .

We have argued that the 'demise of social class' is a thesis not well supported by the evidence from the British survey of class structure and class consciousness. Sectionalism associated with possible sectoral cleavages is relatively unimportant when set alongside class phenomena, in particular the persistence of class identities, and the unequal class mobility chances associated with unchanging 'social fluidity' over the past half-century or so. To the extent that our respondents are instrumental in their attitudes to class organizations and privatized in their life-styles – and our evidence suggests that such claims must be qualified in important respects – then these are hardly novel developments somehow to be attributed to recent changes in the economic or social structure of this country. Studies undertaken by historians suggest that sectionalism, privatism, and instrumentalism are longstanding characteristics of British working-class life, yet have not prevented working-class organizations from pursuing class as well as sectional objectives. This suggests that class action is but partly a function of the 'social consciousness' of class members.

Specific outcomes depend also upon the attributes of the organizations that represent class interests in the economic and political spheres. Class analysis should be extended to embrace this institutional level . . . We can find no evidence in our survey that class has lost its salience as the foremost source of social identity . . . There is a tendency to connect changes in electoral behaviour directly to putative shifts in the class structure and to associated alterations in values, consciousness, or culture . . .: this tendency to trace each and every transitory movement in the electoral landscape to major upheavals in the class structure displays unwarranted contempt for important issues that arise at the level of organizational capacity and political mobilization. Most obviously it neglects the lesson taught by Michels; namely, that organizations count. Between the perception of common interests or consciousness of shared values, and joint pursuit of these in coordinated action, lies the necessity of collective organization . . . The organizational process intervenes between tendencies immanent in social structures and whatever patterns of social action are consequent upon these . . .

There is nothing in our data to support Crewe's thesis that there has been a 'sea-change of attitudes among the proletariat'. Social class and social class identities are no less salient today than during earlier periods commonly acknowledged as being characterized by 'class voting' . . . Contemporary sectional struggles are, instead, testimony to the failure of national class organizations to mobilize members behind centrally organized initiatives on behalf of general rather than particular interests.

Part Eleven
Crime and Deviance

If you are ever locked away for a long prison sentence, take this book with you and read this section carefully. It won't make the spell in prison any more pleasant, but it might help you understand how you got there in the first place.

For the sociology of crime and deviance tries to explain the causes of crime. It will not, however, provide you with a single clear-cut explanation, for there are many different types of crime and many different theoretical approaches. Many people, for instance, both researchers and ordinary members of society, assume that we should begin with the individual. Others start with society in general, or with the component parts of society. For those who adopt an historical approach, similarly, there is a division between those who concentrate on the very varied forces in society which bear upon the individual and those who take as their starting-point the life-history of the individual. Formulating these approaches clearly, comparing them one with another, and teasing out their underlying (and often only implicit) assumptions will help us in our search for the causes of crime.

All sociological approaches to crime, whatever their other differences, are necessarily concerned with the problem of social control, as Cohen and Scull (Reading 64) point out. Thus such great pioneer nineteenth-century writers as Marx and Durkheim (see Reading 65) shared this preoccupation in common, though their conclusions were very different. Yet this early emphasis upon social control and upon the institutions used to maintain social order, has tended to be neglected in this century; as Box shows (Reading 66), these issues have only begun to be debated once more in quite recent years.

So he raises again the question Durkheim asked a century ago: not why it is that some people break the law, but why most people do not. The answer to that question requires not only that we make some assumptions about human nature but also assumptions about the mechanisms that induce social conformity. These are very ancient questions. Aristotle, for instance, focused upon non-conformity to the law: 'It is in the nature of men,' he argued, 'not to be satisfied.' Hobbes concentrated on the second aspect of the problem, conformity. People obey, he said, either because they fear the consequences if they don't or because they are rewarded when they do.

These debates about social control are quite different in kind from research that assumes that the way to go about isolating the essence of criminality is to identify the criminal personality. This kind of approach has a long history. The nineteenth-century biologist Cesare Lombroso, in particular, is often regarded as the first criminologist because his work was directed towards establishing the criminal personality type through the study of the shapes of skulls and variations in cranial capacity. Sapsford's discussion (Reading 67) examines not only his theories but also more modern research based upon the idea that a proclivity to commit crime might be genetically determined: an approach which cannot be ignored even though sociologists usually reject it.

Most research into criminal and deviant behaviour has been carried out in Western industrial societies, and it is often uncritically assumed that what has been found valid in studies of Britain or the USA will be applicable to the rest of the world. But quite different patterns might be found when we start looking at different 'worlds': at the USSR, for instance (Reading 68), or at crime and deviance in the Third World (Reading 69).

Another neglected area that has only begun to receive attention in recent years is that of female crime. Campbell's study of delinquent girls (Reading 70) begins with some critical remarks about what she calls 'second-rate theories for the second sex', in particular the assumption that female and male crime patterns are necessarily fundamentally different: for the female offenders she studied shared in common the values of their families and subcultures, especially the value placed upon physical toughness as a mode of asserting one's individuality.

This kind of law-breaking behaviour is highly public. Other kinds, for instance white-collar and 'upperworld' corporate crime, are so highly concealed that Levi has dubbed their practitioners 'phantom capitalists', since they operate most effectively when left well alone. The classic study of these up-market deviants with low profiles was carried out by Sutherland as long ago as 1949. But few have followed him up. Fraud, studied by Levi in Reading 71, is only one form of this kind of criminal activity, which is not only under-studied but is also notoriously under-policed, despite the fact that it costs society vastly more than the bulk of crimes which absorb police effort and public expenditure.

Social Control in Sociology

Excerpt from Introduction to S. Cohen and A. Scull (eds.), *Social Control and the State*, Blackwell, 1985, pp. 5–7.

In the classical nineteenth-century sociological tradition, the concept of social control was at the centre of the enterprise – both in relating sociology to political philosophy and in solving the emergent debates of macro-sociology. The unit of analysis was the whole society, and the question posed was how to achieve a degree of organization and regulation consistent with certain moral principles, but without an excessive degree of purely coercive control.

This was the great problem of 'social order' – posed most explicitly, of course, by Durkheim and his functionalist inheritors and understood in different ways by Weber and Marx. An examination of the continuities and discontinuities from this classical lineage is a rewarding exercise. What largely happened in the twentieth-century development of sociology in America was that the concept of social control lost its original connections with the classic macro-sociological questions of order, authority, power and social organization. It was not that the concept became unimportant. Indeed, in the first indigenous American sociological tradition – the Chicago School of the 1920s – the concept of social control was much more central than is usually recognized. In Park and Burgess's famous text, 'All social problems turn out finally to be problems of social control.' Social control should be '. . . the central fact and the central problem of sociology'.

But the way this sociological task was interpreted gave the clue to how the concept of social control was later to be used. Sociology was to be '. . . a point of view and method for investigating the processes by which individuals are inducted to and induced to cooperate in some sort of permanent corporate existence we call society' (Park and Burgess). Whether functionalist or interactionist, this essential social psychological perspective on social control was to remain dominant. The emphasis was on the *process* of the individual's induction into society – that is, the problem of socialization.

Pick up now any sociological dictionary, encyclopaedia or first-year textbook – the sources of the discipline's folk wisdom – and this picture of social control still remains. Here is an example from a standard American introductory textbook: 'Sociologists use the term social control to describe all the means and processes whereby a group or society secures its members' conformity to expectations' (Horton and Hunt). On the basis of such definitions, the standard method of interpreting the concept of social control is then to erect a typology of the 'means and processes' by which social conformity is achieved. Typically, the first and most basic process is seen as 'internalization' or socialization; then, second, there are the 'informal' means of social control such as social pressure, peer group opinion and so on; finally, there are the 'formal' methods of social control – those 'elaborated and specialized mechanisms', as Parsons blandly termed them, such as the police, the legal system and 'force'. Typically, little attempt is made to distinguish between the relative importance of these processes, except to assume that socialization (teaching the individual to *want* to follow norms) is the most effective process. Only if it fails are rewards and punishments by external agencies brought into the picture.

This is not the place for general comment on the weakness of such formulations; they have been well exposed in the broader 'crisis' of sociology in the last two decades. This is social control without history and politics, a concept severed from its original organic connection in the project of classical sociology. Little wonder that, when historians came to look at such formulations, they found so much to criticize.

Paradoxically, it took a number of related developments in the sociology of crime and deviance from the late 1960s onwards to reconnect the study of social control with its original connotations: paradoxically, because these were the most theoretically impoverished sub-fields of sociology. Not only were they identified fully with the simple-minded reform view of the history of control, but they carried to its extreme the separation of formal organized social control from the general question of conformity (a separation defensible perhaps only for definitional purposes). Criminological positivism, as Matza so clearly showed, achieved the astonishing task of separating the study of crime from the study of the state. The reconnections came from many diverse sources. First, there was labelling theory, which – whatever its ultimate theoretical limitations – forced a reconsideration of social control not just as a reactive, reparative mechanism when other measures 'fail' but as the active force in shaping the very stuff of crime and deviance. As Lemert expressed it in his famous formula, 'Older sociology . . . tended to rest heavily upon the idea that deviance leads to social control. I have come to believe that the reverse idea (i.e. social control leads to deviance) is equally tenable and the potentially richer premise for studying deviance in modern society.'

This ironical world view of labelling theory was to find resonances from many other directions. Such social movements as anti-psychiatry, radical social work, de-medicalization and de-schooling both fed from and contributed to an image of social control quite different from the bland textbook formulations. At its extreme, all state social policies began to be seen as forms of social control, all ameliorative and progressive reforms as merely a subtle camouflage for further repression.

But rhetorical extremes aside, the key theoretical development was to rebuild labelling theory's limited studies of social control 'culture' or control agencies on to a more politically and historically informed map. Ethnography gave way to history. An emerging Marxist criminology and sociology of law returned the state to the centre of the drama. This was the point at which sociologists of crime and deviance 'rediscovered' history and were the diverse revisionist writings we mentioned earlier – those of Rothman, of E. P. Thompson's school, of Foucault and the French neo-structualists – began having the type of influence that this volume records. What became recognized is that matters of crime, deviance, delinquency, illness and madness don't just every now and then touch on wider issues of politics, economics and power. They are intimately related – and, indeed, these very categories are politically defined.

65   William Chambliss

Marx and Durkheim on Crime

Excerpt from William Chambliss, 'Functional and Conflict Theories of Crime' in W. Chambliss and M. Mankoff (eds.), *Whose Law? What Order?* Wiley & Sons, 1979, pp. 3–7.

Marx and Durkheim both addressed the dual problem of explaining the causes and the consequences of crime and criminal law.

Durkheim postulates the presence of a set of customary beliefs which permeate 'all healthy consciences' in every society. Crime is best understood as behaviour which occurs because one part of society (for example, the family, the schools, the division of labour, or the neighbourhood) is not adequately instilling the society's agreed-upon customs into some of its members. The criminal law is explained as a reflection of the society's customary beliefs. Thus both criminal behaviour and criminal law have their roots in the customs of the society.

From the functional perspective:

The law represents the value consensus of the society.

The law represents those values and perspectives which are fundamental to social order.

The law represents those values and perspectives which it is in the public interests to protect.

The state as represented in the legal system is value-neutral.

In pluralistic societies the law represents the interests of the society at large by mediating between competing interest groups.

Durkheim stated his central thesis quite clearly: for an act to be a crime that is punishable by law, it must be (1) universally offensive to the collective conscience of the people, (2) strongly opposed, and (3) a clear and precise form of behaviour. In his words:

. . . the only common characteristic of crimes is that they consist . . . in acts universally disapproved of by members of each society . . . Crime shocks sentiments which, for a given social system, are found in all healthy consciences. . . .

The collective sentiments to which crime corresponds must, therefore, singularize themselves from others by some distinctive property; they must have a certain average intensity. Not only are they engraven in all consciences, but they are strongly engraven.

The wayward son, however, and even the most hardened egotist are not treated as criminals. It is not sufficient then, that the sentiments be strong; they must be precise.

. . . An act is criminal when it offends strong and defined states of the collective conscience.

[Those acts, to offend the common conscience, need not relate] . . . to vital interests of society nor to a minimum of justice.

Durkheim argues that a single murder may have less dire social consequences than the failure of the stock market, yet the former is a crime for the reasons stated and the latter is not.

Durkheim distinguishes two types of law: restitutive and repressive. Restitutive law 'is not expiatory, but consists of a simple return to [a normal] state'. Repressive law is that which 'in any degree whatever invokes against its author the characteristic reaction which we term punishment'. Restitutive laws, or as he sometimes says, 'cooperative laws with restitutive sanctions', are laws that invoke rule enforcement but (a) do not reflect the collective conscience (they reflect only the opinions of *some* of the members of society) and (b) do not reflect sentiments which are strongly felt. Therefore, these laws do *not* invoke penal sanctions but only rule-enforcement. The more specialized the functions of law the less the law represents the common conscience. As a result, they cannot then offend the common conscience since they are in fact marginal and not common to all. Thus expiatory responses are likely. 'The rule which determines them cannot have the superior force, the transcendent authority which when offended, demands expiation.'

For Durkheim, crime's most important function (i.e., consequence) in society was its role in establishing and preserving the moral boundaries of the community:

Crime brings together upright consciences and concentrates them. We have only to notice what happens, particularly in a small town, when some moral scandal has just been committed. They stop each other on the street. They visit each other. They seek to come together to talk of the event and to wax indignant in common. From all the similar impressions which are exchanged, for all the temper that gets itself expressed, there emerges a unique temper . . . which is everybody's without being anybody's in particular. That is the public temper.

From the perspective of the conflict paradigm [notably that of Marx], customs explain little and are only a reflection of economic realities. In capitalist societies customs may be merely 'false consciousness', rather than the glue that holds society together. Crime and criminal law are not universal forms comparable between 'primitive' and 'civilized' societies; rather these phenomena have unique characteristics depending on their particular historical period.

Capitalist societies are class societies within which the most fundamental division is between the class that rules (in Marx, through ownership and control of the means of production) and the classes that work for those who rule. The criminal law is seen as a set of rules which come about as a result of the struggle between the ruling class and those who are ruled. The state, which is the organized reflection of the interests of the ruling class, passes laws which serve the ruling-class interests. The laws are then enforced primarily against those classes who are struggling to overthrow the ruling class.

Criminal behaviour is explained by the forces of class interests and class struggle, and most fundamentally by the contradictions inherent in the social relations created by the society's particular mode of production. In capitalist societies crime and criminal law are the result of the social relations created by a system which expropriates labour for the benefit of a capitalist class. The division of a society into a ruling class that owns the means of production and a subservient class that works for wages *inevitably* leads to conflict between the two classes. As those conflicts are manifest in rebellions and riots among the proletariat, the state, acting in the interest of the owners of the means of production (the 'ruling class'), will pass laws designed to control, through the application of state-sanctioned force, those acts of the proletariat or of segments of the bourgeoisie which threaten the interests of the capitalist class.

It follows that as capitalism develops and conflicts between social classes continue to become more frequent or more violent (as result, for example, from increasing proletarianization) more acts will be defined as criminal.

There are, then, at the outset, important disagreements between the functional and conflict paradigms. The functional paradigm sees the criminal law as a reflection of those customs most strongly held in the society; criminal behaviour is behaviour which is in violation of those customs which are felt to be most important; criminal behaviour is caused by the fact that some members of the society are not properly socialized into the customary patterns; and criminal behaviour, when it occurs, reinforces the sacredness of the customs within the society.

The conflict perspective takes issue with each of these suppositions. According to it, criminal law is *not* a reflection of custom but is a set of the rules laid down by the state in the interests of the ruling class and resulting from the conflicts inherent in class-structured societies; some criminal behaviour is no more than the 'rightful' behaviour of persons exploited by the extant economic relations – what makes their behaviour criminal is the coercive power of the state to enforce the will of the ruling class; criminal behaviour results either from the struggle between classes wherein individuals of the subservient classes express their alienation from established social relations or from competition for control of the means of production; criminal behaviour is the product of the economic and political system, and in a capitalist society some of its principal consequences are the advancement of technology, use of surplus labour, and generally the maintenance of the established relationship between the social classes. Marx says, somewhat facetiously, in response to the functionalism of bourgeois social scientists:

... crime takes a part of the superfluous population off the labour market and thus reduces competition among the labourers – up to a certain point preventing wages from falling below the minimum – the struggle against crime absorbs another part of this population. Thus the criminal comes in as one of those natural 'counter-weights' which bring about a correct balance and open up a whole perspective of 'useful' occupations ... The criminal ... produces the whole of the police and of criminal justice, constables, judges, hangmen, juries, etc.; and all these different lines of business, which form equally many categories of the social division of labour, develop different capacities of the human spirit, creates new needs and new ways of satisfying them. Torture alone has given rise to the most ingenious mechanical inventions, and employed many honourable craftsmen in the production of its instruments.

Paradigms do much more than simply supply specific causal explanations. They lead us to emphasize certain features of social reality and to ignore or at least de-emphasize others. The functionalist perspective emphasizes the acquisition of norms and values and the social psychological experiences of individuals that lead to this acquisition as the most important feature of social relations in understanding crime. The conflict perspective emphasizes the institutional patterns – particularly the economic system – and how these patterns affect the distribution of criminality. The functionalists accept criminal law as a given – a standard reflective of the 'agreed-upon values' of 'the society'; the conflict perspective assumes that the criminal law is problematic and must be studied to determine how it is shaped and who gets processed as a criminal.

The accompanying propositions highlight the most important areas of disagreement between the functional and conflict paradigms of crime.

	Criminal Law		Criminal behaviour	
	Cause	Consequence	Cause	Consequence
Conflict paradigm	Ruling class interests	Provide state coercive force to repress the class struggle and to legitimize the use of this force	Class divisions which lead to class struggle	Crime serves the interests of the ruling class by reducing strains inherent in the capitalist mode of production
Functional paradigm	Customary beliefs that are codified in state law	To establish procedures for controlling those who do not comply with customs	Inadequate socialization	To establish the moral boundaries of the community

Control Theory

Excerpt from Steven Box, *Deviance, Reality and Society*, 2nd edn, Holt, Rinehart & Winston, 1981, pp. 122–32.

'Why don't we all break the law?' To anticipate the conclusion of our inquiry, the answer, in the briefest possible terms, is 'We all would' if only we dared, but many of us dare not because we have loved ones we fear to hurt and physical possessions and social reputations we fear to lose.

It is not part of control theory that human beings are born wicked or evil – these are evaluative labels others may choose to attach to some individual's behaviour. Instead, people are perceived as being by nature morally neutral. They are born capable of engaging in an extremely wide diversity of acts. Thus, in moral innocence, their reasons or passions could lead them into all manner of behavioural experiments. Left alone, a human being would know no moral boundary save that which s/he might wish to impose.

Unfortunately, society, and those who already have a stake in its continuity, cannot tolerate such diversity, for it is incompatible with orderly and predictable patterns of social interaction. Consequently, attempts are made to persuade youths and newcomers that they should restrict their potentially infinite activities to a comparatively small bundle which have already been recognized in that society as 'proper'. These appropriate behaviours are initially justified by reference to customs, morals and the legal systems, but since to each of these the stranger could ask 'Why should I obey?' they are normally further legitimized by reference to some supra-natural authority. Thus human sexual energy could be directed towards many animate and some inanimate objects. However, in societies like ours, citizens are encouraged to confine their sexual outlets to one legally recognized heterosexual partner. Such institutional arrangements have been initially justified in terms of their benefits to individuals and their functionality to the social order, but ultimately they have been legitimized as the manifestation of Divine Will or the Natural Order of Things.

To facilitate such social learning, society, through social interaction, attempts to seduce individuals with affection, trap them with physical and social possessions, and threaten them with sanctions. Rather than assume that this human miracle invariably works, control theorists view its outcome as extremely problematic, and even if 'success' is achieved it is seen as tenuous and fragile rather than permanent and invulnerable. Only to varying degrees do individuals, at least temporarily, surrender their option to engage in diverse behaviours (including many outside legal and moral codes). Their preparedness to make this surrender depends upon the *attachments* they form, the *commitments* they develop, and the *beliefs* they accept. These three elements – *attachment*, *commitment* and *beliefs* – can be conceptualized as the bonds which tie an individual to the 'conventional order'. If they are not made, or are broken, then the individuals remain free or regain their freedom to engage in law-violating behaviour. However, freedom to do something does not necessarily mean that the option will be exercised. Individuals may not be *able* or *want* to take up that option. Control theory seeks to map out the conditions under which individuals who are free to break the law – because they are not socially bonded – transform themselves into people who are *able* to do so and who, because they perceive deviant behaviour to hold out the possibility of a net reward, *want* to do so . . .

Attachment refers to a human being's capacity to become affectively involved with another person and hence sensitive to his/her thoughts, feelings and expectations, particularly in regard to their relevance for his/her own behaviour. The proposed relationship of attachment to deviant behaviour is: to the extent that a person is not sensitive to the thoughts, feelings and expectations of conventional others, i.e. not attached, then the person remains free to deviate.

The normal relationship between attachment and freedom to deviate is a negative correlation; that is, as attachments are formed, so the willingness to deviate decreases or becomes situationally restricted, and as these attachments fail to form or are destroyed, so the freedom to deviate remains or is restored.

The second element in social bonding is commitment . . . Stebbins suggests that commitment is 'the awareness of the impossibility of choosing a different social identity or rejecting a particular expectation because of the immanence of penalties involved in making the switch'. In his brilliant essay 'Role Distance', Goffman restricts commitment to

questions of impersonally enforced structural arrangements. An individual becomes committed to something when, because of the fixed and interdependent character of many institutional arrangements, his doing or being this something irrevocably conditions other important possibilities in his life, forcing him to take courses of action, causing other persons to build up their activity on the basis of his continuing in his current undertakings, and rendering him vulnerable to unanticipated consequences of these undertakings. He *thus becomes locked into a position and coerced into living up to the promises and sacrifices built into it.*

Finally, bringing out the biographical development of commitment, Becker suggests that the process of commitment is one in which

the 'normal' person becomes progressively involved in conventional institutions and behaviour ... Several kinds of interests become bound up with carrying out certain lines, as a consequence of actions ... taken in the past ... [He] finds he must adhere to certain lines of behaviour, because many other activities than the one he is immediately engaged in will be adversely affected if he does not. The 'normal person', when he discovers a deviant impulse in himself, is able to check that impulse by thinking of the manifold consequences acting on it would produce for him. He has staked too much on continuing to be normal to allow himself to be swayed by unconventional impulses.

Commitment refers to the *rational* element in the social bond. This concept enables us to make adequate allowance for the fact that most individuals do not persist in lines of activity unless there is something in it for them, even if that something is the negative reward of avoiding severe costs.

The third element in the social bond – beliefs – refers to the capacity to make up one's own mind on the legitimacy of conventional rules, either as a general cluster, or more usually, one at a time. This means that we do not dichotomize human beings into those who accept the legal order and those who do not; instead, we proceed on the basis that the extent to which people believe they should obey the rules of society, or even which rules they should obey, varies, and that the less people believe they should obey the rules, the more likely are they to violate them. Having emphasized the variability in morality, control theorists formulate their propositions in terms of what is made *possible*, rather than what is *required* or *determined*. For example, Hirschi states that 'delinquency is not caused by beliefs that require delinquency, but is rather made possible by the absence of (effective) beliefs that forbid delinquency ... The rejection of conventional values means no more than that individuals retain the option to deviate. They can, in a word, be tempted; whether they will be depends to some extent on the degree to which they are exposed to temptation, but it will also depend upon how *able* they view themselves as being, and how willing they are to experience the perceived net rewards inherent in deviant activities.'...

Control theory's major claim to novelty is that it reconceptualizes the starting point of something which might turn into a deviant career. By stressing the boundlessness of human nature and the necessity for the powerful in an established institutional order to *caress*, *coax* and *convert* newcomers into conformity, control theory reveals that when this objective is not achieved individuals remain at liberty to explore, and that exploration may lead to behaviour labelled deviant by the powerful. Occurrence of special circumstances is not necessary to bring about freedom to deviate; freedom is there all the time as a human possibility. It is lost when human beings surrender themselves to others' reputations and moralities. It is regained, perhaps only momentarily, when they cease to care about others or their own social selves, or find segments of conventional morality distasteful.

67   R. J. Sapsford

The Search for the Criminal Personality

Excerpt from R. J. Sapsford, 'Individual Deviance' in M. Fitzgerald, G. McLennan and J. Pawson (eds.), *Crime and Society*, Routledge & Kegan Paul, 1981, pp. 311–19.

Lombroso is often considered a founding father of criminology because of his rejection of the philosophical and speculative approach to the nature of criminal man and his insistence on empirical evidence. Actually, he was by no means the first to take such a line. Primacy should perhaps be awarded to Franz Joseph Gall some sixty years earlier. Gall's phrenological work, seeking to relate character and abilities to the size and shape of bumps on the skull, is nowadays often written off as the speculations of a crank. However, it was actually a serious scientific attempt to locate centres in the brain which were primarily responsible for various activities; once Gall's presupposition that the structure of the brain would be exactly replicated in the shape of the skull had been discarded, this line of research led to positive results . . .

Gall and Lombroso are but two of a long line of investigators on the trail of the criminal personality, a search which still continues . . . Gall, Lombroso and their successors, take the view that criminals are born, not made, and that criminality is inherited and/or physiologically determined.

The claim that human behaviour can best be understood as the outcome of a process of biological evolution is most strongly expressed in the work of a group of recent writers – among them ethologists and geneticists – who have come collectively to be known as 'sociobiologists'. For example, it is claimed that 'behaviour and social structure, like all other biological phenomena, can be studied as "organs", extensions of the genes that exist because of their superior adaptive value'. Even more dramatic is the way the idea is expressed by Tiger and Fox: 'We have confidently asserted that identifiable propensities for behaviour are in the wiring. Unless we look to divine intervention, these got there by the same route as they got into the wiring of any other animal: by mutation and natural selection' . . .

The evidence tends to be of two kinds: studies demonstrating the influence of inherited traits on behaviour, and ethological field-studies demonstrating how adaptive behaviours become dominant in a species. The sociobiologists tend to specialize more in ethological studies which try to trace the survival function of behaviours and the ways in which they can be transmitted. We all know of examples of selective breeding for traits of behaviour, because we all know that dogs are selectively bred on this basis, but this kind of selectivity is contaminated by the environment, including the actions of the human handler – it is a problem of naturalistic research that it is very difficult to separate out the effects of heredity and early environment. However, controlled studies have been carried out in which the environment is made as similar as possible for different breeds, and human handlers are excluded, and the characteristic behaviours still emerge . . .

More fruitful may be the lines of research which link current human behaviour with that of species which may be considered our evolutionary ancestors, and which try to show the survival-value of given behaviours. In the latter genre we have the development by Hamilton and E. O. Wilson of the notion of 'inclusive fitness' (that a gene's success must be measured in terms or its dominance in a population, not just the survival of particular carriers of it) to explain altruistic behaviour: altruism is a survival characteristic, despite its potential cost to the individual, because it ensures the survival of near relatives, who share a proportion of the benefactor's genes. Such thinking can also be used to explain our inappropriate be-haviours, by showing their former survival potential (remembering that evolution is generally an *extremely* slow process). For example, many of the physiological signs of anger or fear clearly have the function of gearing the body for fight or flight, which would once have been appropriate ways of dealing with the environment, though now outdated in most contexts.

Some present behaviours can be seen in our evolutionary ancestors; for example, smiling occurs among chimpanzees in many of the situations where a human baby will also smile. Criminal behaviour – aggression and acquisitiveness – would be seen by writers of this genre as of obvious survival value in more primitive societies, lingering on but now inappropriate. (Note that we are talking here not of a 'gene for crime', but of the transmission of generalized behavioural tendencies which may sometimes result in crime.)

From the last quarter of the nineteenth century well into the twentieth there has been a succession of studies purporting to show that various dysfunctional traits such as criminality and feeble-mindedness ran as much in 'blood-lines' as do haemophilia, eye-colour and blood-type. The first and most notorious is Richard Dugdale's rather extraordinary book *The Jukes: A Study in Crime, Pauperism, Disease and Heredity*, published in 1877. Visiting New York prisons in an official capacity, Dugdale came across six offenders – their crimes ranged from vagrancy to attempted rape and attempted murder – who were to some degree related by blood ... Dugdale traced in all some twelve hundred ancestors of the Juke family back to their 'founding father', and documented what they considered an untypical and intolerable incidence of crime, pauperism, prostitution and illegitimate birth.

Hutchings and Mednick looked at children (not twins) adopted at birth, and compared them according to the reported criminality of both the adoptive and the biological father. The criminality of the adoptive father seems to make little difference, but children whose biological fathers were criminal were far more likely than others to become criminal themselves ... One should remember that people with some kinds of criminal record are rarely permitted to become adoptive parents. None the less, there seems a strong likelihood that one's genetic inheritance has some effect on one's behaviour.

A definitive answer would be provided if we could identify an actual pattern of genes and show its association with criminal behaviour, but biological science is not yet so far advanced. What we can do, however, is to identify the genetic determinants of sex and thence the genetic consequences of the chromosomes (strings of genes) which determine sex. The normal male has one full-length X sex-chromosome and one shorter Y chromosome, while the normal female has two X chromosomes, and we have long known that certain physical characteristics – tendency to baldness, to colour-blindness and to haemophilia, for example – are carried on the portion of the X chromosome which is not 'masked' by the shorter Y chromosome, so that these conditions are carried dormant by the female but are manifested more frequently (or, in the case of haemophilia, only) in the male. Now most of the population has this system of pairing among sex-chromosomes (XX for females, XY for males), but anomalies occur in which extra chromosomes, either X or Y, are present, and these (comparatively) easily identified anomalies have also been shown to have consequences for physical characteristics and for behaviour. For a while it was thought that the presence of an extra Y chromosome (giving an XYY pattern) might be associated with certain kinds of criminal behaviour, and this illusory hope caused a considerable stir in the criminological world.

Jacobs and her co-workers published a survey of 197 mentally subnormal male patients in the Scottish special hospital of Carstairs who had exhibited dangerous, violent or criminal propensities. Of these 197, twelve exhibited some chromosomal abnormality, and eight (3.5 per cent) had the XYY pattern – the extra Y chromosome. This may fail to catch your interest, but a survey of 1,709 randomly chosen adult males and 266 new-born infants failed to show a single XYY male, so the difference in incidence is actually rather startling. This finding was followed up by researchers all over the Western world – something like 200 papers were published in medical, psychological and criminological journals in the late 1960s and early 1970s – and at first it appeared a real 'find'. Several studies of males in maximum-security establishments seemed to identify the XYY male as prone to mental illness, of lower IQ and achievement, with an anti-social personality, and probably with a history of offences against property, alcoholism and/or covert homosexuality. The syndrome was raised in courts as a medical defence several times in the late 1960s, though never successfully.

However, in later papers things started going wrong. For example, the XYY pattern may be common in maximum-security establishments but it is rare in ordinary prisons and it is clear that most people who have it never finish up in an institution. Disagreements began to emerge on whether this type's proclivity was towards property offences or crimes of violence. An alternative explanation for the higher incidence in security institutions has been offered by Fox: their greater height and size increases the chance of them being labelled as dangerous by psychiatrists and the courts (though an association with criminality still remains after height is controlled).

By now this discovery, which looked so promising in its early years, has more or less lost its interest for criminologists as the contradictions have mounted up.

Deviance in Soviet Society

Excerpts from Walter D. O'Connor, *Deviance in Soviet Society*, Columbia University Press, 1972, pp. 1, 10–11, 256–63.

All social systems have rules: the small system of the family as well as the large nation-state, the fraternal lodge as well as the military unit. And in all these systems, there occur violations of the rules. This is a no less universal characteristic. As a large and complex social system, the Soviet Union is not immune . . .

What then is the impact of Marxist-Leninist ideology on Soviet theorizing about deviance? Marxism-Leninism in its 'official' Soviet version *is* an orthodoxy, with elements impinging directly on issues in the social sciences. Indeed, its supporters offer it as a 'science of society', as the only truly 'scientific' one. Two elements of its model of man are of particular importance here: first, the claim that man is more-or-less 'perfectible' in his earthly existence, and second, that he is basically a social being. These views imply that deviance is not a necessary or eternal phenomenon and that, as a social being, man's tendencies toward deviance are *socially* induced: the conditions of his social existence determine his behaviour, for good or ill, and modification of those conditions will in time change his behaviour.

The two elements need not be indissolubly linked. To those who might believe in perfectibility but who see man himself as less social and his behaviour primarily as a product of individual, organic properties, a commitment to reaching that state of perfection might mean genetic or psychiatric manipulation. To those who discount perfectibility but who do see man as a creature social in essence, there are no easy answers to the problems engendered by the imperfections of both man and the society that shapes him. The latter position might be said to characterize with rough accuracy the presuppositions of many Western theorists of deviance.

But when the beliefs converge, as they do in the Soviet model of a social and perfectible man, they would seem to close off certain channels of inquiry on the one hand, and on the other open up the prospect of an 'optimum' resolution of the problem of deviance through the manipulation of man's social environment . . .

It does seem arguable that there is dissensus between state and public at certain points where the seriousness of a particular variety of deviant behaviour is at issue. This should not be surprising, for, accustomed as Soviet citizens may be to the leading roles of state and party in determining which behaviours are good and which bad, a large sector of their private lives and opinions has remained unpenetrated by official thought over the last fifty years. In principle, and in outward expression, many would agree that the government should offer 'moral leadership', that one's private behaviour is not only one's own concern. But in practice, things are not so simple. As one criminologist notes, the view that *only* the behaviourally deviant are infected by survivals is an erroneous one – many citizens harbour them as attitudes, whether they are 'acted out' or not. The Soviet population, no less than the American, is a reservoir of subterranean values in conflict with, but just as much a part of the popular consciousness as, the approved or official values. They, too affect the attitudes and behaviour of the Soviet citizen.

On the whole, deviance probably is not as salient an issue to the public as it is to the state. The public is not told *how much* deviance there is and is not subjected to American-style alarmist accounts of the spread of criminality. Even were this not the case, the situation might show little change. There are more pressing problems in the daily life of the Soviet citizen than the persistence of deviance. Housing, a varied diet, the availability of consumer goods, and a host of private matters are much more central among his concerns. The state, with control as one of its main functions, is necessarily concerned with deviance; but the citizen, be he deviant or not, is more likely to be concerned with avoiding some of the more onerous manifestations of that control. The state's concern with punishing the more petty forms of deviance may strike him as misplaced.

Can the evidence of dissensus between state and public, as it shows itself in both attitudes and behaviour, and of the differing salience of deviance for the two be placed within the context of differentiation along a 'modern–traditional' continuum . . . Are we dealing here with a modern state imposing demands and priorities on a public with strong traces of traditionalism? Were somewhat different terminology employed in posing these questions, Soviet criminologists might answer them with a cautious 'yes': for who is the bearer of survivals but an incompletely modernized individual, not yet fully accommodated to the realities of socialism? . . .

Much has changed in the post-Stalin era. But the major institutional outlines of the Soviet polity and economy remain those which developed after 1928, and the legacy of coercive modernization is a large element in contemporary Soviet life. If one examines the forms that crime, delinquency, and alcohol problems assume, one can see the legacy reflected there as well. It would be disingenuous to ignore the impact of low living standards, crowded housing, and the pressures of an urban environment on the drinking behaviour of working-class males. To attribute all of this to a traditional drinking culture is not enough: alcohol is a widely employed escape mechanism and many Soviet workers have as much, probably more, to escape from in their contemporary lives as do their counterparts in other societies.

The homicides and physical assaults that frequently take place in crowded communal apartments must be traced at least partly to the tensions generated by a lack of living space, the friction generated by close quarters which some persons certainly find unbearable. And the housing problem, a constant condition of Soviet life for so many years, is far from being solved.

Property offences, which make up such a large proportion of all juvenile and adult crime, cannot be wholly attributed to Soviet 'poverty'. Such crimes exist in affluent societies as well, and they are not always perpetrated by the poor. Yet elements of coercive modernization's legacy also enter here. The petty thefts, the minor swindlings of adults and juveniles both, frequently involve consumer goods in short supply or priced beyond purchase ability. The fact that the modest luxuries of radios, tape recorders, and other items are frequent targets of juvenile thieves points to a general desire to upgrade one's level of enjoyment, to have things that make life 'better'. The taxi driver, the factory worker, the sales person who adds something to his income by illegal means refer in justification sometimes to the bare need to 'get by', sometimes to the desire to get something a little beyond the bare minimum in a society where scarcity and depressed living standards are still part of everyday life and traceable at least in part to the form modernization took in the USSR.

The fact that Soviet modernization was of a socialist variety cannot be blamed, in itself, for these problems. Presumably socialist modernization need not always be as rapid, intense, and coercive as it was in the USSR. But it would not do to ignore one of the apparent consequences of contemporary socialist ownership. Soviet citizens, as others elsewhere, probably find it easier to victimize large, amorphous, impersonal organizations through theft than to steal from each other. This applies no less to the managers and accountants who embezzle from their own organizations than it does to the factory worker who filches cigarettes or galoshes. Socialism is well established, but 'socialist attitudes' towards property are not. Soviet citizens will generally express pride that theirs is a socialist rather than capitalist country, but the tangible rewards of socialism, in terms of better living and equality, have not been sufficient to convince them that in defrauding the state they are robbing themselves. Though they might not verbalize it thus, for many persons, that which belongs to all belongs to no one – and taking it oneself is no great matter.

The gap between official norms and the public's attitudes and behaviour is wide at some points, narrower at others. Attributing some of this to survivals, to the lag of consciousness, as Soviet writers do, is not necessarily incorrect. The traditional and the modern confront each other at many points in Soviet life. But to ignore or minimize basic problems characteristic of contemporary Soviet life which owe their existence to the character of the USSR's modernizing experience, as well as to the ravages of World War Two (a national trauma which cannot be ignored), is to miss another point. There are elements in that life, beyond 'infected' environments, that encourage and provoke deviance. Some the USSR shares with other urban, industrial societies; socialism does not confer immunity. Other elements are more specifically Soviet. But all are real: and the degree to which Soviet theory comes to grips with them may, in the future, be one measure of the amount of that critical self-analysis which is a necessary component of any large-scale change in the USSR.

Crime and Underdevelopment

Excerpts from Colin Sumner, 'Crime, Justice and Underdevelopment' in Colin Sumner (ed.), *Crime, Justice and Underdevelopment*, Heinemann, 1982, pp. 1–5.

We should not be surprised that Western criminological theory is virtually silent on crime in the underdeveloped countries. After all, it does not even take much account of crime in nineteenth-century Europe. It has never been much concerned to locate crime and justice within the broader patterns of social development: even the sociology of crime and justice has tended to be ahistorical and non-developmental. Hence its regular exportation to the poor countries has not helped, and has probably hindered, the growth of a distinctive Third World criminology which links crime and justice in the 'Third World' to the processes and effects of underdevelopment.

That Western criminology has neglected underdevelopment is well illustrated by the fact that the work of its outstanding internationalist, Manuel Lopez-Rey, has hardly affected the debates in criminological theory at all. After a lifetime's work on the subject, spanning sixty countries, his conclusions in a recent book should have been the centre of much attention, especially in the era of radical criminology. However, his experience and reflections led him to conclude that crime is a 'socio-political' concept rather than a universal type of behaviour, that criminological theory says little about the bulk of crime and overemphasizes the extent of juvenile delinquency, and that criminology has now served its historical role because it cannot fulfil the task of solving the 'socio-political' problem of crime. The latter problem, he argues, will not be resolved by offender rehabilitation or social defence but by social justice. Without necessarily agreeing precisely with his formulations, we can easily see why orthodox criminologists are not going to tear down their own edifice and start talking about social justice, the crimes of the multinationals, the corruption amongst post-colonial state officials, the crimes of the colonial state, the exercise of arbitrary power in the militaristic puppet dictatorships of capital, and breaches of international law by aggressive imperialist states. Such phenomena are readily observed, but they must remain beyond the pale for orthodox criminology. After all, if everyone commits crime what is left of the concept of *the criminal personality*? If what counts as crime is much dependent on the political power to criminalize and the financial power to bribe the police what is left of the concepts of *crime* and *criminal behaviour*? What relevance for scientific work could the officials' criminal statistics have? How could one take a sample of prisoners as a sample of criminals? Abandon such concepts, such statistics and such sampling procedures and you abandon criminology as a scientific enterprise. Start to examine the use of criminal law and of crime by the colonialists and you are returned to the criminal economic system underpinning your own state. 'Mass murders, massacres, genocide and general brutality and terrorism against civilians by those in power may be due to the fact that power is in the hands of vandals, hooligans, nitwits and anomic delinquents' . . .

When we reverse the traditional criminological equations and apply them to the powerful, we realize that they were never more than moral/ideological propositions founded on insulting moral categories. Of course, they do not become any more scientific for being reversed, or any more insightful. But, when expelled in anger from the pen of a Ugandan criminologist such as Mushanga, these reverse axioms demonstrate the importance and implications for criminological theory of studying crime and justice in the underdeveloped countries. The categorical and assumptive structure of orthodox criminology could not stand the strain imposed upon it when asked to answer the questions which flow from such study, questions such as the following: Why are the world's prisons full of poor people and political oppositionists? Why is torture a feature of police interrogation in nearly every country in the world? How is it that the rich and powerful throughout the world almost always avoid prosecution and full punishment for their crimes and sometimes even become represented in the world's press as progressive forces (for example the Shah of Iran)? How come that if capitalist development is a force for modernization and civilization, which a 'backward' people 'choose', it has to be imposed upon them by military coercion, criminal law and official crime? . . .

I do not see development in the poor countries as a replay of Western development, as a delayed natural evolution, and therefore I am not just interested in it as a comparative area study. The development of capitalism in the West, in the form of imperialist monopoly capitalism, has meant the underdevelopment of countries and regions exploited by it. In underdeveloped or peripheral capitalist countries and regions, some social forms and processes are different to those in the advanced sectors. This is especially true when the country or region penetrated by capital contained large areas with only pre-feudal forms of social organization, for example, social groups based on nomadic, communal-peasant or household production ... It is the peculiar social relationships between the penetration of advanced capital and the indigenous social structure, and their effects, that destroy the validity of the 'delayed replay' approach. Of course, some processes are similar to those in Western history, for example, the expropriation of the peasantry and extensive urban migration. But the differences are vital – the lack of internal capital, the capital intensiveness of industry, the preservation of backward rural sectors, minimal urban employment chances, and military government.

Clearly, for me, underdevelopment is a distinct process within international capitalist society. It thus involves unique forms of crime and justice, whilst providing some very interesting parallels.

Second-Rate Theories for the Second Sex

Excerpts from Anne Campbell, *Girl Delinquents*, Blackwell, 1981, pp. 36–7, 190–96.

Many writers have had a faulty conception of the phenomena that they were trying to explain. Practically all took it as axiomatic that, as a sex, women were less criminal than men, and that when they did commit crimes, the offences were of a different kind from those of males. This was perhaps one reason why such a very different theoretical position was adopted in relation to females. It is also true that until relatively recently the differences between the behaviour of the sexes was ascribed largely to genetic or biological causes. These were held to determine the types of differential socialization that boys and girls received. Because by nature certain differences existed between the capabilities and interests of boys and girls, it was thought, these should be channelled and developed by different education and training. This assumption of fundamental, 'inherent' differences was reflected in the separate theoretical positions adopted for men and women.

Explanations of female criminality have been based on the view that criminal women are merely reacting like automata to forces beyond their control. The conception of mankind as a subject shifting like a billiard ball in response to different forces that strike him has been the foundation of all positivistic psychology. However, when sociologists finally broke away from this view by suggesting that internal psychological representations might be as important as their external *reality*, and even that man was an active agent with plans and goals, this revision did not extend to females. They continued to be characterized as passive, vacuous, waiting for their parents or their sexuality to push them into delinquency . . .

Borstal girls, like schoolgirls, often fought in the street (28 per cent), but they were much more likely to fight in pubs (23 per cent) and in private houses (30 per cent). The fact that such a high proportion of the fights described happened in houses may account for the much higher levels of physical damage inflicted. As well as cuts and bruises, 32 per cent said that they had broken the bones of their opponent. While this may be no more than 'bullshit', it may also reflect the fact that there were no outsiders to intervene in these private disputes, as well as the absence of limiting rules. As with the schoolgirls, most of the girls had been with friends at the time of the fights. The Borstal girls were much more likely to take on more than one person (52 per cent) and were less likely to have other people fighting on their side (48 per cent). Borstal girls fought predominantly other females, but a higher proportion (27 per cent) had fought with men. Once again, this indicates a higher level of domestic violence and a greater chance of severe injury. The provocative remarks before the fight were very largely direct abuse ('Fuck off!') or insults to the girl's sexual reputation ('Slag!', 'Tart!'). These two categories accounted for 58 per cent of all verbal provocations. In the Borstal groups there was a more distinct tendency to strike the first blow (68 per cent). One of the most striking observations was the extent to which the girls admitted to fear of losing or of being hurt. In many cases this led to an over-reaction, to initiating violence in an attempt to stun the prospective opponent before damage could be sustained by the girl herself:

– If someone else has got a weapon, the other person is bound to pick that up just to show they're not frightened.

– She started picking a fight and it went on for about six weeks, and I was trying to avoid it as much as I could, you know what I mean? 'Cos she might be dead rough like. I was keeping out of her way, like.

– I fight dirty. If they fight dirty with me, I can fight dirtier with them.

Given the free-for-all nature of the fights that the girls described, this degree of fear is hardly surprising. Biting, weapon use and unannounced attacks from behind are all described by the girls as fairly common. Another common theme that emerged was that at a certain point of pain or anger during the fight all control is lost, and the girls' main aim *at that moment* is to 'kill'.

AC When you're fighting do you feel in control?

– If I fight for no particular reason, I know every move I make. But if I'm fighting and there's a real good reason for it then I really lose control and really go mad.

– I don't really lose my temper until she hurts me, but when she's hurt me, then I go mad. I don't even see her. I just grab and everything that I've got she gets.

AC Do you think girls should find their own way of fighting, or should they try and fight like blokes?

– Everything goes blank. You don't know what you're doing.

– You just see red, and you think, 'Kill'. Well, I do anyway. I always go into a fight thinking, 'Kill him', 'cos if I go in thinking, 'Give them a good going over, give them a slap', I know I'm going to get beat.

There are some implicit understandings about the basis of a fight. Girls were indignant about being attacked from behind or when they were off-guard. There was some indication that if weapons were introduced, they should not be used until both girls were armed. It was also understood that all those involved would conspire to keep it a secret from any official authority . . .

– I never go for the throat. I always just start a fight punching in the face, giving them a good crack in the face.

– My brothers, if ever they had fights, it was always punch-ups till about four or five years ago. He (one of my brothers) came in the house one night, big scar on his face, he'd been to hospital, blood all over him. He'd got a glass in his face and ever since then my brother has never had a punch-up. If ever a fight starts in a pub, and I've been in once when he's done it, he glasses them straight away. Ever since then, he's just glassed them. Doesn't give a damn.

– When I was younger, I used to poke forks in people's eyes.

– I still prefer paint brushes, because one time this girl stuck one in my eye and it really hurt. Ever since then, when I was at school I used to do it to them. If someone annoyed me, I used to go straight for their eyes because I knew it would hurt them.

Among Borstal girls 'hardness' seems to be closely associated with vicious attacks, ungoverned by any limiting rules. Expressions of hate and the desire to kill were frequent. None of the girls boasted about damage that they had sustained, though many offered exaggerated accounts of the damage they themselves had inflicted. Rules were considered 'soft'. Most fights were about maintaining or establishing reputations or were connected with very intense emotional involvements. Fear of hurt or loss of reputation were common, and girls were often surprised at their own success in 'bluffing' hardness or beating opponents.

The extent of unconstrained aggression within the girls' families was remarkable, and ... most girls had been systematically encouraged to fight by their parents. In the subcultures from which these girls come fighting seems to have shed its ritual component. Interpersonal violence emerges as a vicious expression of hatred and resentment and is bound up more with establishing and maintaining a tough reputation than with settling disputes. Violence serves less a social function than a personal one; it enhances a feeling of self-worth at the expense of often considerable injury to others. While on one hand deploring it, the girls see no way of managing without it among the people they know.

Michael Levi

White-Collar Crime and the Criminal Process

Excerpt from Michael Levi, *Regulating Fraud*, Tavistock, 1987, pp. xviii–xix, 14–17.

Wheeler, Weisburd, and Bode state that 'white-collar crimes are economic offences committed through the use of some combination of fraud, deception, or collusion'. Such crimes come in many forms: they include acts as diverse as the setting up of businesses to obtain large quantities of goods on credit without intending to pay for them; the use of mail-order businesses to obtain money for goods that one does not intend to supply; the pocketing by brokers or other trustees of funds that they have promised to invest; the diversion of funds to one's own account by means of computers; the illegal use of private inside knowledge to make a profit on share-dealing; and the non-declaration of taxable commercial sales to the tax authorities.

There is a growing tendency among 'white-collar crime' academics to differentiate between crimes *by* business and crimes *against* business; the former are labelled 'corporate crime'; the latter 'white-collar crime'. But useful though this distinction is, it may overstate implicitly the homogeneity of 'crimes *against* business'. Even if one excludes from consideration many forms of business 'malpractice' that are either not criminal at all or whose criminality is ambiguous, to write about 'commercial fraud' is to write about a number of very different sorts of activities; there are frauds by businesspeople against each other; businesspeople against investors – who by volume of securities traded are predominantly institutions or professionals – as well as against small investors, consumers, and tax authorities (who may be regarded as 'corporate crime' rather than 'white-collar crime' victims); and by directors and employees against their companies. Nor is the social-class composition of 'white-collar criminals' simple: they include members of 'the upperworld' and 'the underworld', and comparatively junior employees. Even upmarket-sounding crimes, like insider dealing – where shares are bought or sold unlawfully on the basis of confidential inside information – may be committed by the company chairman or the company typist.

Very few British sociologists or psychologists have displayed much empirical interest in commercial crime. Instead, those – in Europe and Australasia, but less so in North America – who write about law-making and law violation within the upperworld tend to have a legal background and will seek publication in socio-legal journals . . . In the United States, particularly, there is a burgeoning interest in the area of 'regulation' among administrative lawyers and socio-legal scholars, but this too seems often to by-pass criminology and find its place in the specialized 'regulation' journals such as *Law and Policy* and *Negotiation Journal*, plus the less conservative University Law Reviews . . . [where] American criminology seems to have overcome its label of being oriented towards petty juvenile crime.

The official picture of crime and offenders that is generated by criminal statistics shows that crime is primarily an activity conducted by working-class juveniles against motor vehicles, households, and shops. In England and Wales in 1985, fraud and forgery constituted only 3.7 per cent of notifiable offences, 5.7 per cent of convictions for indictable offences, and 1.3 per cent of all convictions (including summary and triable-either-way offences). Those imprisoned for fraud and forgery comprised only 11.8 per cent of those who received unsuspended or partially suspended sentences for indictable offences (9.3 per cent if we include suspended sentences). Most of these offences are relatively minor value cheque frauds rather than major crimes requiring intensive investigative effort and vast trial costs. During the 1980s, expenditure on the criminal justice system in the United Kingdom has boomed, from about £2 billion in 1979–80 to about £4 billion in 1985–6. The police, the courts, the probation service, and the prison service have been expanded to cope with the rise in 'criminal business' (but not of business crime!). There are no detailed sub-totals for particular forms of crime, but very little of this extra expenditure has been devoted to dealing with fraud or business regulatory offences, which comprise a tiny proportion of convicted offenders and criminal justice resources. Pending the estab-lishment of the Serious Fraud Office . . . the most expensive parts of the system are the Fraud Investigation Group – a task force which deals with the most complex frauds – which cost £1.5 million annually, and the Metropolitan Police Company Fraud Department, which cost under £5 million annually. (As a point of comparison, in 1984–5, gross expenditure on the Metropolitan Police totalled £866 million, though there are no separate figures for the CID.)

The political agenda within which fraud may be viewed has changed dramatically, at least during the mid 1980s, in the light of political scandal surrounding Johnson Matthey Bankers, Lloyd's, and insider dealing, but there is nothing unique to fraud about the fact that crime policies are influenced by political pressures. Despite the change of political attitude, the priority that fraud receives is indicated by the fact that in 1985, out of 120,116 police officers in England and Wales, only 588 were allocated to Fraud Squads (though this excludes the fact that many CID officers spend some of their time dealing with relatively minor frauds on division).

Street crime and household crime have understandably dominated criminological as well as political debate, and even on the political left, policy arguments have concentrated on these types of crime rather than on business crime, which has been disregarded as being irrelevant to the alleged drift into a 'law and order society'. However, commercial crime remains interesting not only because of its 'objective' social and economic significance but also precisely because of the ambiguity in whether or not it is or should be part of 'the crime problem'. Particularly in the realm of investor protection, there is continuing debate about whether commercial malpractice is a proper subject for public law – the police and the courts – or whether it should be left to be dealt with principally by private law – civil redress for those wronged – or by 'self-regulatory' bodies of businesspeople and professionals with the unusual constitutional status of being licensed by the state to police crime . . .

Sutherland argues that white-collar crime is organized crime. Nevertheless, as noted and as has become conventional wisdom in criminological circles, the control mechanisms for corporate and for organized crime are different (1) in terms of the social standing of the suspects and (2) in terms of the comparative immunity of 'white-collar crimes' both from police surveillance and from the 'normal' stimulus-response mechanism of crime-prosecution which – corruption apart – we observe in the handling of street crime and organized crime. However, one important change in this demarcation, which has not yet been appreciated sufficiently in Britain, is that the growing involvement of 'professional' and 'organized' criminals in sophisticated fraud, and the increasing use of financial institutions to launder vast quantities of money from fraud (as well as from so-called 'victimless' crimes such as narcotics, gambling, pornography, and prostitution), is bringing official attitudes to regulating 'the upperworld' closer to those of regulating 'the underworld'. This American trend has spread to Britain in the mid-1980s, and has been given impetus by the ease with which those who melted down and resold the £25.5 million gold bullion stolen in the Brinks-Mat robbery – the largest ever robbery in Britain – were able to take from their accounts millions of pounds in notes from over the counter without any questions being asked by the bankers. When the local branch of Barclays ran out of £50 notes, the Bank of England rushed some more to them, again without query. The demands for American-style currency deposit reporting requirements upon banks are reinforced by the siphoning of funds overseas through British banks, allegedly to finance drug deals as a highly profitable form of re-investment. After all, despite falls in the inflation rate during 1985 and 1986, the rational criminal capitalist still needs to make his money work for him!

The strategic role of financial institutions in facilitating international terrorism and the drugs trade has brought in its wake a level of law enforcement interest in commerce that is beginning to prise open banking secrecy and increasingly will bring commercial fraud under police surveillance. This, combined with other social changes discussed in later chapters, means that *some* of the activities of commercial elites are now liable to greater official and social scrutiny than they have been hitherto, particularly in the United States. This observation about upperworld vulnerability to law enforcement does not apply to areas of corporate criminality such as health and safety at work offences, whose investigation has been hived off to non-police regulatory agencies. Moreover, there are powerful counter-pressures from financial institutions and other interested parties (such as arms dealers) who are concerned about the intrusions of government into 'private' commercial transactions and about the implications of this for their profits. (The concern about the profits is left implicit or is made altruistic by talking about 'the damage to the balance of payments'.) But gangster involvement in money-laundering, in the illegal dumping of toxic waste, and in financial fraud is slowly altering the focus of policing, widening the aperture of its lens so that it brings into view at least those parts of the upperworld which intersect with the activities of organized crime groups. In Britain ... in 1986, despite a gradual growth in Fraud Squad manpower, very few state policing resources were devoted to disciplining the upperworld, but developments in the organization of crime (including, but not restricted to, fraud) will make such an extension of policing seem necessary.

Part Twelve
Theoretical Schools

The first three Readings in this section are taken from the writings of three major nineteenth-century thinkers – Karl Marx, Max Weber and Émile Durkheim – who are generally considered to be the great Founding Fathers of sociological theorizing and whose thought is still an essential starting-point for those who strive to develop sociological theory today.

Reading 72, taken from Marx and Engels' *Communist Manifesto*, begins with a sweeping and polemical sketch of the historical conditions which, in their view, have given rise to modern capitalist society and to its distinctive pattern of class conflict. The *Communist Manifesto* was written, however, not just as an exercise in sociological theorizing, but in order to call the working class to revolutionary action and, eventually, to the overthrow of the entire capitalist system.

The relationship of this piece of pamphleteering, written relatively early in their lives, to the great mass of other writing they produced over subsequent decades, is a complex question, and in recent years the debates about 'what Marx really meant' and about the extent to which there is any coherence and continuity as between Marx's early writings and his later work have continued to generate fierce and often complex discussions. No single extract from the huge and complex body of the writings of Marx and Engels – which runs into scores of volumes – can therefore possibly be said to be representative of Marx's essential views, but this one does contain some of the key ideas.

Even in the compressed analysis of the *Manifesto*, their approach is a historical one. The condition of any human society at any point in time can only be understood in terms of its development out of previous society, and primarily through the analysis of class relations, that is, the positions that people hold in the process of economic activity. The basic opposition is between the owners of the means of production and those who work with the means of production, but do not own them – and therefore do not own the product either.

Though classes, in this model, clearly have an economic base, they are also many-sided social groups. Marx never spelled out his concept of social class fully (dying, dramatically, at the point where he was about to do so), so this, too, remains a subject of continuing controversy. But he clearly saw the contrast between the owners of the means of production and those who performed productive labour as involving far more than purely economic differences: the entire way of life of each class differed, too. Classes, then, were social as well as economic groups. But since class relations involve the domination of one class over another, the relationship between them is necessarily also a political one. The dominant class, moreover, exercises its control over the entire society, not only in political terms, but also in terms of the ideas which become dominant in that society.

Though Marx and Engels also studied pre-capitalist societies, they mainly concentrated on the emergence and maturation of the capitalist system, which was then transforming the entire world. Despite its success, this development nevertheless seemed to them to augur also the beginning of the end of class society altogether, for modern capitalism was bringing into existence the means of its own destruction: the new, majority and heavily concentrated working class.

Max Weber is best known for his study of *The Protestant Ethic and the Spirit of Capitalism*, in which he also focused on the emergence of capitalism. But he paid much more attention to the beliefs, motivations and values which had been crucial in generating the entrepreneurial spirit and capitalist attitudes towards work. Protestant doctrines about salvation, he argued, not just technological innovation or work-related organization, were therefore an essential component in any analysis of the rise of capitalism. Unintentionally (for their focus was primarily religious), Protestant beliefs had initially provided the motivation for the kind of unremittingly acquisitive, relentlessly disciplined work which eventually became dominant in Western capitalist societies. Reading 73 is a later statement on the issue, in which kinds of economic ethic other than the Protestant are set against their historical background. It is also a more complex statement than that outlined in *The Protestant Ethic*, which emphasized religion as against other social and economic conditions. Yet religion remains crucial in Weber's argument, especially when he tackles the key question as to why capitalism had developed *in the West* and not elsewhere in the world. To answer that, he found it necessary to look at even wider historical changes than those involved in the rise of capitalism, for many of the key ideas in Protestantism which had important consequences for economic activity, he insisted, had been inherited from a much more ancient religion, Judaism.

In the work of Marx and Weber, the examination of historical processes is central in a way which it is not for the authors of the remaining Readings. Concerned as they were with the origins of modern capitalism, Marx and Weber considered it essential to study its emergence from prior historical forms. To their still very numerous contemporary admirers, subsequent theorists such as Durkheim, Parsons, Blumer, Garfinkel and others seem, in contrast, to be lacking in an awareness of history. Their approach, indeed, is concerned with issues other than those of historical development: they are trying to develop *analytical* approaches which will be valid for the study of *any* kind of social phenomenon (and not just large-scale social organization). Whether these kinds of approach need complementing by adding a historical dimension is a matter of continuing fierce debate. Parsons' theories, in particular, are often denounced as intrinsically 'ahistoric', static, and so on, even though, in his later writings, he was able to use his basic categories – particularly his conception of the tensions within and between social, cultural and personality systems mentioned below, and the tensions that exist at different levels of each kind of all systems – to analyse the rise and fall of the great historic civilizations.

But it is Émile Durkheim (Reading 74) who is usually credited with introducing the functionalist perspective into sociology by seeking to identify the sources of social cohesion: the forces that keep a given society together as a unit. One of his more striking arguments is that crime is not only a normal, but an ineliminable, element in any society, since the very idea of society involves a separation of inside from outside, and this is partly done through social rules, from laws to unwritten moral codes. Those who keep to the rules distance themselves from those who break them, and criminals are therefore treated as 'outsiders' to society, thereby playing a crucial symbolic role in defining the boundaries of the community. Crime, then, may be harmful in some ways both to society and to particular individual victims, but in other ways is beneficial, for it provokes in us reactions of outrage and the desire to punish those who do not conform to the rules, and thereby reinforces the social rules that are crucial in maintaining social cohesion. Our sense of what we have in common, and of the line which separates us from those we condemn as criminals, is thus sharpened by virtue of the performance of criminal acts.

Many are alienated from Talcott Parsons' work (Reading 75) because of his somewhat turgid writing style and because of the unrelenting abstractness of his argument. Even this short extract, in which he sketches out his conception of the structural and dynamic aspects of 'structural functional' analysis and identifies the four 'functional imperatives' which he considers to be the minimal requirements for any working social order, is not easy to read. Parsons was engaged in a particularly ambitious project: no less than the construction of a 'general theory of action' which would bring together all the main social sciences, not just sociology. Hence his analysis of social system organization and its internal requirements is always only one part of the story, for he is also always concerned with the ways in which social systems have to fit with other systems which constitute their environment, in particular the cultural systems and the personality systems into which members of any given society are socialized.

Marx, Weber, Durkheim and Parsons are all concerned primarily with what is often called the 'structural' level of sociological analysis, which means, effectively, the analysis of society as a whole. Ultimately, though, Weber insists, there are only individuals: 'society' does not do anything; people do. In their work, Blumer and Garfinkel (Readings 76 and 77 respectively) pay little attention to society as a whole. They take as their starting-point, rather, Weber's insistence that society consists only of individuals. Though there are important differences between these more recent theorists, they are usually lumped together as 'interactionists' because they appear to analyse social life only as interaction between individuals.

The passage from Blumer (Reading 76) certainly seems to confirm this, for the focus is very much upon the activities of individuals. But he would argue that though theorists such as Durkheim and Parsons purport to be talking about 'society as a whole' or 'the social system', we have to first take a step backwards, and ask whether the use of such abstractions is justified or illuminating. What we really need, Blumer argues, is a quite different kind of theoretical approach to the study of the nature of social life: one which starts by looking at the ways in which individuals act towards each other, establish social relations, and so build up complex social organization.

Symbolic interactionism, of which Blumer was a leading protagonist, and ethnomethodology, whose name was coined and whose essentials were devised by Harold Garfinkel (Reading 77), have both attracted a great deal of attention in recent years because they have developed an alternative to the whole approach both of classical sociology and of contemporary sociologists who take their lead from theorists such as Marx or the functionalists. These modern critics also challenge the claim of those they criticize that the way *they* go about their work is the only truly 'scientific' approach to the study of social life.

Ethnomethodology drew much of its inspiration from the earlier work of Alfred Schutz, as Garfinkel acknowledges in the second half of Reading 77. Though this somewhat difficult Reading can only give a slight indication of the distance that separates ethnomethodology from theories like those of Marx or Parsons, it does show how Schutz and Garfinkel, instead of claiming to be studying society as a whole – as if it were something examined from the outside – advocate the practice of beginning any investigation of social life by examining, from within as it were, how we encounter 'society' in our everyday experience as ordinary members of it. The way we experience our society is as the familiar, everyday site of our activities, a place which we are confident we know and that, by and large, we know in much the same way as do other inhabitants of it. We presuppose a 'common-sense' understanding and organize our conduct towards others by taking it for granted that they will see and understand things as we do. It is the purpose of ethnomethodology to examine the role that 'common sense' has in the production of day-to-day conduct, a project which many sociologists find not only far removed from their concerns but wrong-headed. By now, the plural nature of contemporary sociological theory should be very obvious.

72 Karl Marx and Friedrich Engels

Bourgeois and Proletarians

Excerpts from Karl Marx and Friedrich Engels, *Manifesto of the Communist Party*, Progress Publishers, Moscow, n.d., pp. 39–57. (First published 1848.)

The history of all hitherto existing societies is the history of class struggles.

Freeman and slave, patrician and plebeian, lord and serf, guild-master and journeyman, in a word, oppressor and oppressed, stood in constant opposition to one another, carried on an uninterrupted, now hidden, now open fight, a fight that each time ended, either in a revolutionary re-constitution of society at large, or in the common ruin of the contending classes . . .

Our epoch, the epoch of the bourgeoisie, possesses, however, this distinctive feature: it has simplified the class antagonisms. Society as a whole is more and more splitting up into two great hostile camps, into two great classes directly facing each other: Bourgeoisie and Proletariat.

From the serfs of the Middle Ages sprang the chartered burghers of the earliest towns. From these burgesses the first elements of the bourgeoisie were developed.

The discovery of America, the rounding of the Cape, opened up fresh ground for the rising bourgeoisie. The East-Indian and Chinese markets, the colonization of America, trade with the colonies, the increase in the means of exchange and in commodities generally, gave to commerce, to navigation, to industry, an impulse never before known, and thereby, to the revolutionary element in the tottering feudal society, a rapid development.

The feudal system of industry, under which industrial production was monopolized by closed guilds, now no longer sufficed for the growing wants of the new markets. The manufacturing system took its place. The guildmasters were pushed on one side by the manufacturing middle class; division of labour between the different corporate guilds vanished in the face of division of labour in each single work-shop.

Meantime the markets kept ever growing, the demand ever rising. Even manufacture no longer sufficed. Thereupon, steam and machinery revolutionized industrial production. The place of manufacture was taken by the giant, Modern Industry, the place of the industrial middle class, by industrial millionaires, the leaders of whole industrial armies, the modern bourgeois.

Modern Industry has established the world market, for which the discovery of America paved the way. This market has given an immense development to commerce, to navigation, to communication by land. This development has, in its turn, reacted on the extension of industry; and in proportion as industry, commerce, navigation, railways extended, in the same proportion the bourgeoisie developed, increased its capital, and pushed into the background every class handed down from the Middle Ages . . .

Each step in the development of the bourgeoisie was accompanied by a corresponding political advance of that class . . .

The bourgeoisie has at last, since the establishment of Modern Industry and of the world market, conquered for itself, in the modern representative State, exclusive political sway. The executive of the modern State is but a committee for managing the common affairs of the whole bourgeoisie.

The bourgeoisie, historically, has played a most revolutionary part.

The bourgeoisie, wherever it has got the upper hand, has put an end to all feudal, patriarchal, idyllic relations. It has pitilessly torn asunder the motley feudal ties that bound man to his 'natural superiors', and has left remaining no other nexus between man and man than naked self-interest, than callous 'cash payment' . . .

The bourgeoisie has stripped of its halo every occupation hitherto honoured and looked up to with reverent awe. It has converted the physician, the lawyer, the priest, the poet, the man of science, into its paid wage-labourers.

The bourgeoisie has torn away from the family its sentimental veil, and has reduced the family relation to a mere money relation . . .

It has been the first to show what man's activity can bring about. It has accomplished wonders far surpassing Egyptian pyramids,

Roman aqueducts, and Gothic cathedrals; it has conducted expeditions that put in the shade all former Exoduses of nations and crusades.

The bourgeoisie cannot exist without constantly revolutionizing the instruments of production, and thereby the relations of production, and with them the whole relations of society. Conservation of the old modes of production in unaltered form, was, on the contrary, the first condition of existence for all earlier industrial classes. Constant revolutionizing of production, uninterrupted disturbance of all social conditions, everlasting uncertainty and agitation distinguish and bourgeois epoch from all earlier ones. All fixed, fast-frozen relations, with their train of ancient and venerable prejudices and opinions, are swept away, all new-formed ones become antiquated before they can ossify. All that is solid melts into air, all that is holy is profaned, and man is at last compelled to face with sober senses, his real conditions of life, and his relations with his kind.

The need of a constantly expanding market for its products chases the bourgeoisie over the whole surface of the globe ... The bourgeoisie, by the rapid improvement of all instruments of production, by the immensely facilitated means of communication, draws all, even the most barbarian, nations into civilization. The cheap prices of its commodities are the heavy artillery with which it batters down all Chinese walls, with which it forces the barbarians' intensely obstinate hatred of foreigners to capitulate. It compels all nations, on pain of extinction, to adopt the bourgeois mode of production; it compels them to introduce what it calls civilization into their midst, i.e., to become bourgeois themselves. In one word, it creates a world after its own image.

The bourgeoisie has subjected the country to the rule of the towns. It has created enormous cities, has greatly increased the urban population as compared with the rural, and has thus rescued a considerable part of the population from the idiocy of rural life ...

We see then: the means of production and of exchange, on whose foundation the bourgeoisie built itself up, were generated in feudal society. At a certain stage in the development of these means of production and of exchange, the conditions under which feudal society produced and exchanged, the feudal organization of agriculture and manufacturing industry, in one word, the feudal relations of property became no longer compatible with the already developed productive forces; they became so many fetters. They had to be burst asunder; they were burst asunder.

Into their place stepped free competition, accompanied by a social and political constitution adapted to it, and by the economical and political sway of the bourgeois class . . .

The weapons with which the bourgeoisie felled feudalism to the ground now turned against the bourgeoisie itself.

But not only has the bourgeoisie forged the weapons that bring death to itself; it has also called into existence the men who are to wield those weapons – the modern working class – the proletarians.

In proportion as the bourgeoisie, i.e., capital, is developed, in the same proportion is the proletariat, the modern working class, developed – a class of labourers, who live only so long as they find work, and who find work only so long as their labour increases capital. These labourers, who must sell themselves piecemeal, are a commodity, like every other article of commerce, and are consequently exposed to all the vicissitudes of competition, to all the fluctuations of the market.

Owing to the extensive use of machinery and to division of labour, the work of the proletarians has lost all individual character, and, consequently, all charm for the workman. He becomes an appendage of the machine, and it is only the most simple, most monotonous, and most easily acquired knack, that is required of him. Hence, the cost of production of a workman is restricted, almost entirely, to the means of subsistence that he requires for his maintenance, and for the propagation of his race. But the price of a commodity, and therefore also of labour, is equal to its cost of production. In proportion, therefore, as the repulsiveness of the work increases, the wage decreases. Nay more, in proportion as the use of machinery and division of labour increases, in the same proportion the burden of toil also increases, whether by prolongation of the working hours, by increase of the work exacted in a given time or by increased speed of the machinery, etc . . .

The proletariat goes through various stages of development. With its birth begins its struggle with the bourgeoisie. At first the contest is carried on by individual labourers, then by the workpeople of a factory, then by the operatives of one trade, in one locality, against the individual bourgeois who directly exploits them. They direct their attacks not against the bourgeois conditions of production, but against the instruments of production themselves; they destroy imported wares that compete with their labour, they smash to pieces machinery, they set factories ablaze, they seek to restore by force the vanished status of the workman of the Middle Ages.

At this stage the labourers still form an incoherent mass scattered over the whole country, and broken up by their mutual competition. If anywhere they unite to form more compact bodies, this is not yet the consequence of their own active union, but of the union of the bourgeoisie, which class, in order to attain its own political ends, is compelled to set the whole proletariat in motion, and is moreover yet, for a time, able to do so. At this stage, therefore, the proletarians do not fight their enemies, but the enemies of their enemies, the remnants of absolute monarchy, the landowners, the non-industrial bourgeois, the petty bourgeoisie. Thus the whole historical movement is concentrated in the hands of the bourgeoisie; every victory so obtained is a victory for the bourgeoisie.

But with the development of industry the proletariat not only increases in number; it becomes concentrated in greater masses, its strength grows, and it feels that strength more. The various interests and conditions of life within the ranks of the proletariat are more and more equalized, in proportion as machinery obliterates all distinctions of labour, and nearly everywhere reduces wages to the same low level. The growing competition among the bourgeois, and the resulting commercial crises, make the wages of the workers ever more fluctuating. The unceasing improvement of machinery, ever more rapidly developing, makes their livelihood more and more precarious; the collisions between individual workmen and individual bourgeois take more and more the character of collisions between two classes. Thereupon the workers begin to form combinations (Trades' Unions) against the bourgeois; they club together in order to keep up the rate of wages; they found permanent associations in order to make provision beforehand for these occasional revolts. Here and there the contest breaks out into riots.

Now and then the workers are victorious, but only for a time. The real fruit of their battles lies, not in the immediate result, but in the ever-expanding union of the workers. This union is helped on by the improved means of communication that are created by modern industry and that place the workers of different localities in contact with one another. It was just this contact that was needed to centralize the numerous local struggles, all of the same character, into one national struggle between classes. But every class struggle is a political struggle . . .

This organization of the proletarians into a class, and consequently into a political party, is continually being upset again by the competition between the workers themselves. But it ever rises up again, stronger, firmer, mightier. It compels legislative recognition of particular interests of the workers, by taking advantage of the divisions among the bourgeoisie itself. Thus the ten-hours' bill in England was carried . . .

The bourgeoisie finds itself involved in constant battle. At first with the aristocracy; later on, with those portions of the bourgeoisie itself, whose interests have become antagonistic to the progress of industry; at all times, with the bourgeoisie of foreign countries. In all these battles it sees itself compelled to appeal to the proletariat, to ask for its help, and thus to drag it into the political arena. The bourgeoisie itself, therefore, supplies the proletariat with its own elements of political and general education, in other words, it furnishes the proletariat with weapons for fighting the bourgeoisie.

Further, as we have already seen, entire sections of the ruling classes are, by the advance of industry, precipitated into the proletariat, or are at least threatened in their conditions of existence. These also supply the proletariat with fresh elements of enlightenment and progress.

Finally, in times when the class struggle nears the decisive hour, the process of dissolution going on within the ruling class, in fact within the whole range of old society, assumes such a violent, glaring character, that a small section of the ruling class cuts itself adrift, and joins the revolutionary class, the class that holds the future in its hands. Just as, therefore, at an earlier period, a section of the nobility went over to the bourgeoisie, so now a portion of the bourgeoisie goes over to the proletariat, and in particular, a portion of the bourgeois ideologists, who have raised themselves to the level of comprehending theoretically the historical movement as a whole.

Of all the classes that 'stand face to face with the bourgeoisie today, the proletariat alone is a really revolutionary class. The other classes decay and finally disappear in the face of modern industry; the proletariat is its special and essential product . . .

73   Max Weber

The Evolution of the Capitalist Spirit

Excerpts from Max Weber, *General Economic History* (trans. Frank H. Knight), Allen and Unwin, 1923, pp. 355–61, 364–8.

Traditional obstructions are not overcome by the economic impulse alone. The notion that our rationalistic and capitalistic age is characterized by a stronger economic interest than other periods is childish; the moving spirits of modern capitalism are not possessed of a stronger economic impulse than, for example, an oriental trader ... If the economic impulse in itself is universal, it is an interesting question as to the relations under which it becomes rationalized and rationally tempered in such fashion as to produce rational institutions of the character of capitalistic enterprise.

Originally, two opposite attitudes toward the pursuit of gain exist in combination. Internally, there is attachment to tradition and to the pietistic relations of fellow members of tribe, clan, and house-community, with the exclusion of the unrestricted quest of gain within the circle of those bound together by religious ties; externally, there is absolutely unrestricted play of the gain spirit in economic relations, every foreigner being originally an enemy in relation to whom no ethical restrictions apply; that is, the ethics of internal and external relations are categorically distinct. The course of development involves on the one hand the bringing in of calculation into the traditional brotherhood, displacing the old religious relationship. As soon as accountability is established within the family community, and economic relations are no longer strictly communistic, there is an end of the naïve piety and its repression of the economic impulse. This side of the development is especially characteristic in the West. At the same time there is a tempering of the unrestricted quest of gain with the adoption of the economic principle into the internal economy. The result is a regulated economic life with the economic impulse functioning within bounds ...

The germs of modern capitalism must be sought in a region where officially a theory was dominant which was distinct from that of the East and of classical antiquity and in principle strongly hostile to capitalism. The *ethos* of the classical economic morality is summed up in the old judgement passed on the merchant . . .: *homo mercator vix aut numquam potest Deo placere*; he may conduct himself without sin but cannot be pleasing to God. This proposition was valid down to the 15th century, and the first attempt to modify it slowly matured in Florence under pressure of the shift in economic relations.

The typical antipathy of Catholic ethics, and following that the Lutheran, to every capitalist tendency, rests essentially on the repugnance of the impersonality of relations within a capitalist economy. It is this fact of impersonal relations which places certain human affairs outside the church and its influence, and prevents the latter from penetrating them and transforming them along ethical lines. The relations between master and slave could be subjected to immediate ethical regulation; but the relations between the mortgage creditor and the property which was pledged for the debt, or between an endorser and the bill of exchange, would at least be exceedingly difficult if not impossible to moralize. The final consequence of the resulting position assumed by the Church was that medieval economic ethics excluded higgling, overpricing and free competition, and were based on the principle of just price and the assurance to everyone of a chance to live.

For the breaking up of this circle of ideas the Jews cannot be made responsible as Sombart does. The position of the Jews during the Middle Ages may be compared sociologically with that of an Indian caste in a world otherwise free from castes; they were an outcast people. However, there is the distinction that according to the promise of the Indian religion the caste system is valid for eternity. The individual may in the course of time reach heaven through a course of reincarnations, the time depending upon his deserts; but this is possible only within the caste system. The caste organization is eternal, and one who attempted to leave it would be accursed and condemned to pass in hell into the bowels of a dog. The Jewish promise, on the contrary, points toward a reversal of caste relations in the future world as compared with this. In the present world the Jews are stamped as an outcast people, either as punishment for the sins of their fathers, as Deutero-Isaiah holds, or for the salvation of the world, which is the presupposition of the mission of Jesus of Nazareth; from this position they are to be released by a social revolution. In the Middle Ages the Jews were a guest-people standing outside of political society; they could not be received into any town citizenship group because they could not participate in the communion of the Lord's Supper ... [and enter] into *commercium* and *connubium* with the Christians ...

Ritualistic considerations were responsible for the concentration of Jewish economic life in monetary dealings. Jewish piety set a premium on the knowledge of the law and continuous study was very much easier to combine with exchange dealings than with other occupations. In addition, the prohibition against usury on the part of the Church condemned exchange dealings, yet the trade was indispensable and the Jews were not subject to the ecclesiastical law.

Finally, Judaism had maintained the originally universal dualism of internal and external moral attitudes, under which it was permissible to accept interest from foreigners who did not belong to the brotherhood or established association. Out of this dualism followed the sanctioning of other irrational economic affairs, especially tax farming and political financing of all sorts. In the course of the centuries the Jews acquired a special skill in these matters which made them useful and in demand. But all this was pariah capitalism, not rational capitalism such as originated in the West. In consequence, hardly a Jew is found among the creators of the modern economic situation, the large entrepreneurs; this type was Christian and only conceivable in the field of Christianity. The Jewish manufacturer, on the contrary is a modern phenomenon ... [Yet] since Judaism made Christianity possible and gave it the character of a religion essentially free from magic, it rendered an important service from the point of view of economic history ... If one wishes to study at all the influence of a religion on life one must distinguish between its official teachings and this sort of actual procedure upon which in reality, perhaps against its own will, its places a premium, in this world or the next.

It is also necessary to distinguish between the virtuoso religion of adepts and the religion of the masses. Virtuoso religion is significant for everyday life only as a pattern; its claims are of the highest, but they fail to determine everyday ethics. The relation between the two is different in different religions. In Catholicism . . . the really complete Christian is the monk; but his mode of life is not required of everyone, although some of his virtues in a qualified form are held up as ideals . . . The most worthy individuals in the religious sense withdrew from the world and established a separate community.

Christianity was not alone in this phenomenon, which rather recurs frequently in the history of religions, as is shown by the powerful influence of asceticism, which signifies the carrying out of a definite, methodical conduct of life . . . An analogous phenomenon is present in the Middle Ages in the West. In that epoch the monk is the first human being who lives rationally, who works methodically and by rational means toward a goal, namely the future life. Only for him did the clock strike, only for him were the hours of the day divided — for prayer. The economic life of the monastic communities was also rational. The monks in part furnished the officialdom for the early Middle Ages; the power of the doges of Venice collapsed when the investiture struggle deprived them of the possibility of employing churchmen for oversea enterprises.

But the rational mode of life remained restricted to the monastic circles . . . For the men of the Middle Ages the possibility of unburdening themselves through the channel of the confessional, when they had rendered themselves liable to punishment, meant a release from the consciousness of sin which the teachings of the church had called into being. The unity and strength of the methodical conduct of life were thus in fact broken up . . .

The Reformation made a decisive break with this system . . . The Lutheran Reformation meant the disappearance of the dualistic ethics . . . The other-worldly asceticism came to an end. The stern religious characters who had previously gone into monasteries had now to practise their religion in the life of the world. For such an asceticism within the world the ascetic dogmas of Protestantism created an adequate ethics. Celibacy was not required, marriage being viewed simply as an institution for the rational bringing up of children. Poverty was not required, but the pursuit of riches must not lead one astray into reckless enjoyment . . .

It is true that the acquisition of wealth, attributed to piety, led to a dilemma, in all respects similar to that into which the medieval monasteries constantly fell; the religious guild led to wealth, wealth to fall from grace, and this again to the necessity of re-constitution.

Calvinism sought to avoid this difficulty through the idea that man was only an administrator of what God had given him; it condemned enjoyment yet permitted no flight from the world but rather regarded working together, with its rational discipline, as the religious task of the individual. Out of this system of thought came our word 'calling', which is known only to the languages influenced by the Protestant translations of the Bible. It expresses the value placed upon rational activity carried on according to the rational capitalistic principle, as the fulfilment of a God-given task . . .

This development of the concept of the calling quickly gave to the modern entrepreneur a fabulously clear conscience – and also industrious workers; he gave to his employees as the wages of their ascetic devotion to the calling and of cooperation in his ruthless exploitation of them through capitalism the prospect of eternal salvation, which in an age when ecclesiastical discipline took control of the whole of life to an extent inconceivable to us now, represented a reality quite different from any it has today.

74 Émile Durkheim

The Normality of Crime

Excerpts from Émile Durkheim, *The Rules of Sociological Method* (trans. D. W. Halls), Macmillan, 1982, pp. 97–104. (First published in 1895.)

If there is a fact whose pathological nature appears indisputable, it is crime. All criminologists agree on this score. Although they explain this pathology differently, they none the less unanimously acknowledge it. However, the problem needs to be treated less summarily . . .

Crime is not only observed in most societies of a particular species, but in all societies of all types. There is not one in which criminality does not exist, although it changes in form and the actions which are termed criminal are not everywhere the same. Yet everywhere and always there have been men who have conducted themselves in such a way as to bring down punishment upon their heads. If at least, as societies pass from lower to higher types, the crime rate (the relationship between the annual crime figures and population figures) tended to fall, we might believe that, although still remaining a normal phenomenon, crime tended to lose that character of normality. Yet there is no single ground for believing such a regression to be real. Many facts would rather seem to point to the existence of a movement in the opposite direction. From the beginning of the century statistics provide us with a means of following the progression of criminality. It has everywhere increased, and in France the increase is of the order of 300 per cent. Thus there is no phenomenon which represents more incontrovertibly all the symptoms of normality, since it appears to be closely bound up with the conditions of all collective life. To make crime a social illness would be to concede that sickness is not something accidental, but on the contrary derives in certain cases from the fundamental consitution of the living creature. This would be to erase any distinction between the physiological and the pathological. It can certainly happen that crime itself has normal forms; this is what happens, for instance, when it reaches an excessively high level. There is no doubt that this excessiveness is pathological in nature . . .

We are faced with a conclusion which is apparently somewhat paradoxical. Let us make no mistake: to classify crime among the phenomena of normal sociology is not merely to declare that it is an inevitable though regrettable phenomenon arising from the incorrigible wickedness of men; it is to assert that it is a factor in public health, an integrative element in any healthy society. At first sight this result is so surprising that it disconcerted even ourselves for a long time. However, once that first impression of surprise has been overcome it is not difficult to discover reasons to explain this normality and at the same time to confirm it.

In the first place, crime is normal because it is completely impossible for any society entirely free of it to exist.

Crime, as we have shown elsewhere, consists of an action which offends certain collective feelings which are especially strong and clear-cut. In any society, for actions regarded as criminal to cease, the feelings that they offend would need to be found in each individual consciousness without exception and in the degree of strength requisite to counteract the opposing feelings. Even supposing that this condition could effectively be fulfilled, crime would not thereby disappear; it would merely change in form, for the very cause which made the well-springs of criminality to dry up would immediately open up new ones.

Indeed, for the collective feelings, which the penal law of a people at a particular moment in its history protects, to penetrate individual consciousnesses that had hitherto remained closed to them, or to assume greater authority – whereas previously they had not possessed enough – they would have to acquire an intensity greater than they had had up to then. The community as a whole must feel them more keenly, for they cannot draw from any other source the additional force which enables them to bear down upon individuals who formerly were the most refractory. For murderers to disappear, the horror of bloodshed must increase in those strata of society from which murderers are recruited; but for this to happen the abhorrence must increase throughout society. Moreover, the very absence of crime would contribute directly to bringing about that result, for a sentiment appears much more respectable when it is always and uniformly respected. But we overlook the fact that these strong states of the common consciousness cannot be reinforced in this way without the weaker states, the violation of which previously gave rise to mere breaches of convention, being reinforced at the same time, for the weaker states are no more than the extension and attenuated form of the stronger ones. Thus, for example, theft and mere misappropriation of property offend the same altruistic sentiment, the respect for other people's possessions. However, this sentiment is offended less strongly by the latter action than the former. Moreover, since the average consciousness does not have sufficient intensity of feeling to feel strongly about the lesser of these two offences, the latter is the object of greater tolerance. This is why the misappropriator is merely censured, while the thief is punished. But if this sentiment grows stronger, to such a degree that it extinguishes in the consciousness the tendency to theft that men possess, they will become more sensitive to these minor offences, which up to then had had only a marginal effect upon them. They will react with greater intensity against these lesser faults, which will become the object of severer condemnation, so that, from the mere moral errors that they were, some will pass into the category of crimes. For example, dishonest contracts or those fulfilled dishonestly, which only incur public censure or civil redress, will become crimes. Imagine a community of saints in an exemplary and perfect monastery. In it crime as such will be unknown, but faults that appear venial to the ordinary person will arouse the same scandal as does normal crime in ordinary consciences. If therefore that community has the power to judge and punish, it will term such acts criminal and deal with them as such. It is for the same reason that the completely honourable man judges his slightest moral failings with a severity that the mass of people reserves for acts that are truly criminal. In former times acts of violence against the person were more frequent than they are today because respect for individual dignity was weaker. As it has increased, such crimes have become less frequent, but many acts which offended against that sentiment have been incorporated into the penal code, which did not previously include them.

In order to exhaust all the logically possible hypotheses, it will perhaps be asked why this unanimity should not cover all collective sentiments without exception, and why even the weakest sentiments should not evoke sufficient power to forestall any dissentient voice.

The moral conscience of society would be found in its entirety in every individual, endowed with sufficient force to prevent the commission of any act offending against it, whether purely conventional failings or crimes. But such universal and absolute uniformity is utterly impossible, for the immediate physical environment in which each one of us is placed, our hereditary antecedents, the social influences upon which we depend, vary from one individual to another and consequently cause a diversity of consciences. It is impossible for everyone to be alike in this matter, by virtue of the fact that we each have our own organic constitution and occupy different areas in space. This is why, even among lower peoples where individual originality is very little developed, such originality does however exist. Thus, since there cannot be a society in which individuals do not diverge to some extent from the collective type, it is also inevitable that among these deviations some assume a criminal character. What confers upon them this character is not the intrinsic importance of the acts but the importance which the common consciousness ascribes to them. Thus if the latter is stronger and possesses sufficient authority to make these divergences very weak in absolute terms, it will also be more sensitive and exacting. By reacting against the slightest deviations with an energy which it elsewhere employs against those that are more weighty, it endues them with the same gravity and will brand them as criminal.

Thus crime is necessary. It is linked to the basic conditions of social life, but on this very account is useful, for the conditions to which it is bound are themselves indispensable to the normal evolution of morality and law.

Indeed today we can no longer dispute the fact that not only do law and morality vary from one social type to another, but they even change within the same type if the conditions of collective existence are modified. Yet for these transformations to be made possible, the collective sentiments at the basis of morality should not prove unyielding to change, and consequently should be only moderately intense. If they were too strong, they would no longer be malleable. Any arrangement is indeed an obstacle to a new arrangement; this is even more the case the more deep-seated the original arrangement. The more strongly a structure is articulated, the more it resists modification; this is as true for functional as for anatomical patterns. If there were no crimes, this condition would not be fulfilled, for such a hypothesis presumes that collective sentiments would have attained a degree of intensity unparalleled in history. Nothing is good indefinitely and without limits. The authority which the moral consciousness enjoys must not be excessive, for otherwise no one would dare to attack it and it would petrify too easily into an immutable form. For it to evolve, individual originality must be allowed to manifest itself. But so that the originality of the idealist who dreams of transcending his era may display itself, that of the criminal, which falls short of the age, must also be possible. One does not go without the other.

Nor is this all. Beyond this indirect utility, crime itself may play a useful part in this evolution. Not only does it imply that the way to necessary changes remains open, but in certain cases it also directly prepares for these changes. Where crime exists, collective sentiments are not only in the state of plasticity necessary to assume a new form, but sometimes it even contributes to determining beforehand the shape they will take on. Indeed, how often is it only an anticipation of the morality to come, a progression towards what will be! According to Athenian laws, Socrates was a criminal and his condemnation was entirely just. However, his crime – his independence of thought – was useful not only for humanity but for his country. It served to prepare a way for a new morality and a new faith, which the Athenians then needed because the traditions by which they had hitherto lived no longer corresponded to the conditions of their existence. Socrates' case is not an isolated one, for it recurs periodically in history. The freedom of thought that we at present enjoy could never have been asserted if the rules that forbade it had not been violated before they were solemnly abrogated. However, at the time the violation was a crime, since it was an offence against sentiments still keenly felt in the average consciousness. Yet this crime was useful since it was the prelude to changes which were daily becoming more necessary. Liberal philosophy has had as its precursors heretics of all kinds whom the secular arm rightly punished through the Middle Ages and has continued to do so almost up to the present day.

From this viewpoint the fundamental facts of criminology appear to us in an entirely new light. Contrary to current ideas, the criminal no longer appears as an utterly unsociable creature, a sort of parasitic element, a foreign, unassimilable body introduced into the bosom of society. He plays a normal role in social life. For its part, crime must no longer be conceived of as an evil which cannot be circumscribed closely enough. Far from there being cause for congratulation when it drops too noticeably below the normal level, this apparent progress assuredly coincides with and is linked to some social disturbance. Thus the number of crimes of assault never falls so low as it does in times of scarcity. Consequently, at the same time, and as a reaction, the theory of punishment is revised, or rather should be revised. If in fact crime is a sickness, punishment is the cure for it and cannot be conceived of otherwise; thus all the discussion aroused revolves round knowing what punishment should be to fulfil its role as a remedy. But if crime is in no way pathological, the object of punishment cannot be to cure it and its true function must be sought elsewhere.

75   Talcott Parsons

The Four Functional Imperatives of the Social System

Excerpts from Talcott Parsons, 'An Outline of the Social System', in T. Parsons, E. Shils, K. Naegele and J. Pitts (eds.), *Theories of Society*, Free Press, Glencoe, Illinois, 1961, pp. 36–40.

Structural and Functional Modes of Analysis

Besides identifying a system in terms of its patterns and boundaries, a social system can and should be analysed in terms of three logically independent – i.e, cross-cutting – but also interdependent, bases or axes of variability, or as they may be called, bases of selective abstraction.

The first of these is best defined in relation to the distinction between 'structural' and 'functional' references for analysis . . . The concept of structure focuses on those elements of the patterning of the system which may be regarded as independent of the lower-amplitude and shorter time-range fluctuations in the relation of the system to its external situation. It thus designates the features of the system which can, in certain strategic respects, be treated as constants over certain ranges of variation in the behaviour of other significant elements of the theoretical problem . . .

The functional reference, on the other hand, diverges from the structural in the 'dynamic' direction. Its primary theoretical significance is integrative; functional considerations relate to the problem of *mediation* between two fundamental sets of exigencies: those imposed by the relative constancy or 'givenness' of a structure, and those imposed by the givenness of the environing situation external to the system . . . One should remember that the immediately environing systems of a social system are not those of the physical environment. They are, rather, the other primary subsystems of the general system of action – i.e., the personalities of its individual members, the behaviourally organized aspects of the organisms underlying those personalities, and the relevant cultural systems in so far as they are not fully institutionalized in the social system but involve components other than 'normative patterns of culture' that are institutionalized.

'Dynamic' Modes of Analysis

... A fundamental distinction must be made between two orders of 'dynamic' problems relative to a given system. The first of these concerns the processes which go on under the assumption that the structural patterns of institutionalized culture are given, i.e., are assumed to remain constant. This is the area of problems of *equilibrium* as that concept has been used by Pareto, Henderson, and others, and of homeostasis as used by Cannon ...

The concept of equilibrium is a fundamental reference point for analysing the processes by which a system either comes to terms with the exigencies imposed by a *changing* environment, without essential change in its own structure, or fails to come to terms and undergoes other processes, such as structural change, dissolution as a boundary-maintaining system (analogous to biological death for the organism), or the consolidation of some impairment leading to the establishment of secondary structures of a 'pathological' character ...

The second set of dynamic problems concerns processes involving change in the structure of the system itself. This involves, above all, problems of interchange with the cultural system, however much these may in turn depend upon the internal state of the social system and its relations to other environing systems. Leaving distinctions within the category of internal adjustive processes aside for the moment, one can say that, with respect to its external interchanges, problems of equilibrium for the social system involve primarily its relations to its individual members as personalities and organisms, and, through these, to the physical environment. Problems of structural change, on the other hand, primarily involve its relations to the cultural systems affecting its patterns of institutionalized normative culture ...

Structural differentiation involves genuine *reorganization* of the system and, therefore, fundamental structural change of various subsystems and their relations to each other ...

The Hierarchy of Relations of Control

The third of the three essential axes of theoretical analysis may be defined as concerning a hierarchy of relations of control ... First, the situation in which any given individual acts is, far more than any other set of factors, composed of *other* individuals, not discretely but in ordered sets of relationship to the individual in point. Hence, as the source of his principal facilities of action and of his principal rewards and deprivations, the concrete social system exercises a powerful control over the action of any concrete, adult individual. However, the *patterning* of the motivational system in terms of which he faces this situation also depends upon the social system, because his own personality *structure* has been shaped through the internalization of systems of social objects and of the patterns of institutionalized culture ...

Control Relations within the Social System

... It is possible to reduce the essential functional imperatives of any system of action, and hence of any social system, to four, which I have called pattern-maintenance, integration, goal-attainment, and adaptation ...

The Function of Pattern-Maintenance

The function of pattern-maintenance refers to the imperative of maintaining the stability of the patterns of institutionalized culture defining the structure of the system ... From the point of view of the individual participant in a social system, this may be called his motivational *commitment* to act in accordance with certain normative patterns; this, as we shall see, involves their 'internalization' in the structure of his personality.

Accordingly, the focus of pattern-maintenance lies in the structural category of *values*, which will be discussed presently. In this connection, the essential function is maintenance, at the cultural level, of the stability of institutionalized values through the processes which articulate values with the belief system, namely, religious beliefs, ideology, and the like. Values, of course, are subject to change, but whether the empirical tendency be toward stability or not, the potentialities of disruption from this source are very great, and it is essential to look for mechanisms that tend to protect such order – even if it is orderliness in the process of change.

The second aspect of this control function concerns the motivational commitment of the individual – elsewhere called 'tension-management'. A very central problem is that of the mechanisms of socialization of the individual, i.e., of the processes by which the values of the society are internalized in his personality. But even when values have become internalized, the commitments involved are subject to different kinds of strain . . .

Pattern-maintenance in this sense plays a part in the theory of social systems, as of other systems of action, comparable to that of the concept of inertia in mechanics . . . Properly conceived and used, it does not imply the empirical predominance of stability over change. However . . . social systems show a *tendency* to maintain their structural patterns . . .

The Function of Goal-Attainment

. . . The functions of goal-attainment and adaptation concern the structures, mechanisms, and processes involved in this relation.

We have compared pattern-maintenance with inertia as used in the theory of mechanics. Goal-attainment then becomes a 'problem' in so far as there arises some discrepancy between the inertial tendencies of the system and its 'needs' resulting from interchange with the situation. Such needs necessarily arise because the internal system and the environing ones cannot be expected to follow immediately the changing patterns of process. A goal is therefore defined in terms of equilibrium . . . Goal-attainment or goal-orientation is thus, by contrast with pattern-maintenance, essentially tied to a specific situation.

[Since a] social system [normally has] to protect its integrity . . . the several goals must be arranged in some scale of relative urgency, a scale sufficiently flexible to allow for variations in the situation. For any complex system, therefore, it is necessary to speak of a system of goals rather than of a single unitary goal, a system, however, which must have some balance between integration as a system and flexible adjustment to changing pressures . . .

Goal-orientation . . . concerns, therefore, not commitment to the values of the society, but motivation to contribute what is necessary for the functioning of the system; these 'contributions' vary according to particular exigencies . . .

The Function of Adaptation

The second consequence of plurality of goals ... concerns the difference between the functions of goal-attainment and adaptation ... With a plurality of goals, however, the problem of 'cost' arises. That is, the same scarce facilities will have *alternative* uses within the system of goals, and hence their use for one purpose means sacrificing the gains that would have been derived from their use for another ... For the system, this means a maximum of generalized disposability in the processes of allocation between alternative uses. Within the complex type of social system, this disposability of facilities crystallizes about the institutionalization of money and markets. More generally, at the macroscopic social-system level, the function of goal-attainment is the focus of the political organization of societies, while that of adaptation is the focus of economic organization ... The market system is thus a primary focus of the society's organization for adaptation ...

The Function of Integration

The last of the four functional imperatives of a system of action – in our case, a social system – is that of integration. In the control hierarchy, this stands between the functions of pattern-maintenance and goal-attainment ... The functional problem of integration concerns the mutual adjustments of these 'units' or sub-systems from the point of view of their 'contributions' to the effective functioning of the system as a whole ...

In a highly differentiated society, the primary focus of the integrative function is found in its system of legal norms and the agencies associated with its management, notably the courts and the legal profession. Legal norms at this level, rather than that of a supreme constitution, govern the *allocation* of rights and obligations, of facilities and rewards, between different units of the complex system; such norms facilitate internal adjustments compatible with the stability of the value system or its orderly change, as well as with adaptation to the shifting demands of the external situation. The institutionalization of money and power are primarily integrative phenomena, like other mechanisms of social control in the narrower sense.

Society as Symbolic Interaction

Excerpts from Herbert Blumer, 'Society as Symbolic Interaction', in Herbert Blumer, *Symbolic Interactionism*, Prentice-Hall, Englewood Cliffs, New Jersey, 1969, pp. 83–9.

Sociological thought rarely recognizes or treats human societies as composed of individuals who have selves. Instead, they assume human beings to be merely organisms with some kind of organization, responding to forces which play upon them. Generally, although not exclusively, these forces are lodged in the make-up of the society, as in the case of 'social system', 'social structure', 'culture', 'status position', 'social role', 'custom', 'institution', 'collective representation', 'social situation', 'social norm', and 'values'. The assumption is that the behaviour of people as members *of a society* is an expression of the play on them of these kinds of factors or forces. This, of course, is the logical position which is necessarily taken when the scholar explains their behaviour or phases of their behaviour in terms of one or another of such social factors. The individuals who compose a human society are treated as the media through which such factors operate, and the social action of such individuals is regarded as an expression of such factors. This approach or point of view denies, or at least ignores, that human beings have selves – that they act by making indications to themselves. Incidentally, the 'self' is not brought into the picture by introducing such items as organic drives, motives, attitudes, feelings, internalized social factors, or psychological components. Such psychological factors have the same status as the social factors mentioned: they are regarded as factors which play on the individual to produce his action. They do not constitute the process of self-indication. The process of self-indication stands over against them, just as it stands over against the social factors which play on the human being. Practically all sociological conceptions of human society fail to recognize that the individuals who compose it have selves in the sense spoken of.

Correspondingly, such sociological conceptions do not regard the social actions of individuals in human society as being constructed by them through a process of interpretation. Instead, action is treated as a product of factors which play on and through individuals. The social behaviour of people is not seen as built up by them through an interpretation of objects, situations, or the actions of others. If a place is given to 'interpretation', the interpretation is regarded as merely an expression of other factors (such as motives) which precede the act, and accordingly disappears as a factor in its own right. Hence, the social action of people is treated as an outward flow or expression of forces playing on them rather than as acts which are built up by people through their interpretation of the situations in which they are placed.

These remarks suggest another significant line of difference between general sociological views and the position of symbolic interaction. These two sets of views differ in where they lodge social action. Under the perspective of symbolic interaction, social action is lodged in acting individuals who fit their respective lines of action to one another through a process of interpretation; group action is the collective action of such individuals. As opposed to this view, sociological conceptions generally lodge social action in the action of society or in some unit of society. Examples of this are legion. Let me cite a few. Some conceptions, in treating societies or human groups as 'social systems', regard group action as an expression of a system, either in a state of balance or seeking to achieve balance. Or group action is conceived as an expression of the 'functions' of a society or of a group. Or group action is regarded as the outward expression of elements lodged in society or the group, such as cultural demands, societal purposes, social values, or institutional stresses. These typical conceptions ignore or blot out a view of group life or of group action as consisting of the collective or concerted actions of individuals seeking to meet their life situations. If recognized at all, the efforts of people to develop collective acts to meet their situations are subsumed under the play of underlying or transcending forces which are lodged in society or its parts. The individuals composing the society or the group become 'carriers', or media for the expression of such forces;

and the interpretative behaviour by means of which people form their actions is merely a coerced link in the play of such forces.

The indication of the foregoing lines of variance should help to put the position of symbolic interaction in better perspective. In the remaining discussion I wish to sketch somewhat more fully how human society appears in terms of symbolic interaction and to point out some methodological implications.

Human society is to be seen as consisting of acting people, and the life of the society is to be seen as consisting of their actions. The acting units may be separate individuals, collectivities whose members are acting together on a common quest, or organizations acting on behalf of a constituency. Respective examples are individual purchasers in a market, a play group or missionary band, and a business corporation or a national professional association. There is no empirically observable activity in a human society that does not spring from some acting unit . . .

Corresponding respect must be shown to the conditions under which such units act. One primary condition is that action takes place in and with regard to a situation. Whatever be the acting unit – an individual, a family, a school, a church, a business firm, a labour union, a legislature, and so on – any particular action is formed in the light of the situation in which it takes place. This leads to the recognition of a second major condition, namely, that the action is formed or constructed by interpreting the situation. The acting unit necessarily has to identify the things which it has to take into account – tasks, opportunities, obstacles, means, demands, discomforts, dangers, and the like; it has to assess them in some fashion and it has to make decisions on the basis of the assessment. Such interpretative behaviour may take place in the individual guiding his own action, in a collectivity of individuals acting in concert, or in 'agents' acting on behalf of a group or organization. Group life consists of acting units developing acts to meet the situations in which they are placed.

Usually, most of the situations encountered by people in a given society are defined or 'structured' by them in the same way. Through previous interaction they develop and acquire common understandings or definitions of how to act in this or that situation. These common definitions enable people to act alike. The common repetitive behaviour of people in such situations should not mislead the student into believing that no process of interpretation is in play;

on the contrary, even though fixed, the actions of the participating
people are constructed by them through a process of interpretation.
Since ready-made and commonly accepted definitions are at hand,
little strain is placed on people in guiding and organizing their acts.
However, many other situations may not be defined in a single way
by the participating people. In this event, their lines of action do not
fit together readily and collective action is blocked. Interpretations
have to be developed and effective accommodation of the participants
to one another has to be worked out. In the case of such 'undefined'
situations, it is necessary to trace and study the emerging process of
definition which is brought into play.

In so far as sociologists or students of human society are concerned
with the behaviour of acting units, the position of symbolic interaction requires the student to catch the process of interpretation
through which they construct their actions. This process is not to be
caught merely by turning to conditions which are antecedent to the
process. Such antecedent conditions are helpful in understanding the
process in so far as they enter into it, but as mentioned previously
they do not constitute the process. Nor can one catch the process
merely by inferring its nature from the overt action which is its
product. To catch the process, the student must take the role of the
acting unit whose behaviour he is studying . . .

By and large, of course, sociologists do not study human society in
terms of its acting units. Instead, they are disposed to view human
society in terms of structure or organization and to treat social action
as an expression of such structure or organization. Thus, reliance is
placed on such structural categories as social system, culture, norms,
values, social stratification, status positions, social roles and institutional organization. These are used both to analyse human society
and to account for social action within it. Other major interests of
sociological scholars centre around this focal theme of organization.
One line of interest is to view organization in terms of the functions
it is supposed to perform. Another line of interest is to study societal
organization as a system seeking equilibrium; here the scholar endeavours to detect mechanisms which are indigenous to the system.
Another line of interest is to identify forces which play upon organization to bring about changes in it; here the scholar endeavours,
especially through comparative study, to isolate a relation between
causative factors and structural results.

These respective concerns with organization on the one hand and with acting units on the other hand set the essential difference between conventional views of human society and the view of it implied in symbolic interaction. The latter view recognizes the presence of organization to human society and respects its importance. However, it sees and treats organization differently. The difference is along two major lines. First, from the standpoint of symbolic interaction the organization of a human society is the framework inside of which social action takes place and is not the determinant of that action. Second, such organization and changes in it are the product of the activity of acting units and not of 'forces' which leave such acting units out of account. Each of these two major lines of difference should be explained briefly in order to obtain a better understanding of how human society appears in terms of symbolic interaction.

From the standpoint of symbolic interaction, social organization is a framework inside of which acting units develop their actions. Structural features, such as 'culture', 'social systems', 'social stratification', or 'social roles', set conditions for their action but do not determine their action. People – that is, acting units – do not act toward culture, social structure or the like; they act toward situations. Social organization enters into action only to the extent to which it shapes situations in which people act, and to the extent to which it supplies fixed sets of symbols which people use in interpreting their situations . . .

The conventional procedure of sociologists is (a) to identify human society (or some part of it) in terms of an established or organized form, (b) to identify some factor or condition of change playing upon the human society or the given part of it, and (c) to identify the new form assumed by the society following upon the play of the factor of change. Such observations permit the student to couch propositions to the effect that a given factor of change playing upon a given organized form results in a given new organized form . . . My concern here is not with the validity of such propositions but with the methodological position which they presuppose. Essentially, such propositions either ignore the role of the interpretative behaviour of acting units in the given instance of change, or else regard the interpretative behaviour as coerced by the factor of change. I wish to point out that any line of social change, since it involves change in human action, is necessarily mediated by interpretation on the part of the people caught up in the change – the change appears in the form of new situations in which people have to construct new forms of action. Also, in line with what has been said previously, interpretations of new situations are not predetermined by conditions antecedent to the situations but depend on what is taken into account and assessed in the actual situations in which behaviour is formed. Variations in interpretation may readily occur as different acting units cut out different objects in the situation, or give different weight to the objects which they note, or piece objects together in different patterns . . .

Students of human society will have to face the question of whether their preoccupation with categories of structure and organization can be squared with the interpretative process by means of which human beings, individually and collectively, act in human society. It is the discrepancy between the two which plagues such students in their efforts to attain scientific propositions of the sort achieved in the physical and biological sciences. It is this discrepancy, further, which is chiefly responsible for their difficulty in fitting hypothetical propositions to new arrays of empirical data. Efforts are made, of course, to overcome these shortcomings by devising new structural categories, by formulating new structural hypotheses, by developing more refined techniques of research, and even by formulating new methodological schemes of a structural character. These efforts continue to ignore or to explain away the interpretative process by which people act, individually and collectively, in society. The question remains whether human society or social action can be successfully analysed by schemes which refuse to recognize human beings as they are, namely, as persons constructing individual and collective action through an interpretation of the situations which confront them.

77 Harold Garfinkel

Common-Sense Knowledge of Social Structures

Excerpts from Harold Garfinkel, 'Common-Sense Knowledge of Social Structures', in C. Gordon and K. Gergen (eds.), *The Self in Social Interaction*, Wiley, New York, 1968, pp. 71-4.

Sociologically speaking, 'common culture' refers to the socially sanctioned grounds of inference and action that people use in their everyday affairs and which they assume that other members of the group use in the same way. Socially-sanctioned-facts-of-life-in-society-that-any-bona-fide-member-of-the-society-knows depict such matters as conduct of family life; market organization; distributions of honour, competence, responsibility, goodwill, income, and motives among persons; frequency, causes of, and remedies for trouble; and the presence of good and evil purposes behind the apparent workings of things. Such socially sanctioned facts of social life consist of descriptions of the society from the point of view of the collectivity member's interests in the management of his practical affairs. For the moment, call such knowledge of the organization and operations of the society 'common-sense knowledge of social structures'.

The discovery of common culture consists of the discovery *from within the society* by social scientists of the existence of common-sense knowledge of social structures, and the treatment by social scientists of this knowledge, and of the procedures for its assembly, test, management, transmission, etc., by members of the society as objects of mere theoretical sociological interest.

This paper is concerned with common-sense knowledge of social structures as an object of theoretical sociological interest. Its subject matter is the descriptions of a society which its members, sociologists included, as a condition of their rights to manage and communicate decisions of meaning, fact, method, and causal texture without interference, use and treat as known in common with others, and with others take for granted . . .

A common-sense description is defined by the feature 'known in common with any bona fide member of the collectivity' which is attached to all the propositions which compose it. The late Alfred Schutz, in his work on the constitutive phenomenology of situations of everyday life, analysed the compound character of the feature 'known in common' into its constituent meanings. *Whatever a proposition specifically proposes* – whether it proposes something about the motives of persons, their histories, the distribution of income in the population, the conditions of advancement on the job, kinship obligations, the organization of an industry, the layout of a city, what ghosts do when night falls, the thoughts that God thinks – *if for the user the proposition has the following additional features, it is called a common-sense proposition.*

1. The sense assigned to the description is, from the member's point of view, an assignment that he is required to make; he requires the other person to make the same assignment of sense; and just as he requires the same assignment to hold for the other person, he assumes that the other person requires the same of him.

2. From the user's point of view, a relationship of undoubted correspondence is the sanctioned relationship between the-depicted-appearance-of-the-intended-object and the-intended-object-that-appears-in-this-depicted-fashion.

3. From the user's point of view, the matter that is known, in the manner that it is known, can actually and potentially affect the knower's actions and circumstances, and can be affected by his actions and circumstances.

4. From the user's point of view, the meanings of the descriptions are the products of a standardized process of naming, reification, and idealization of the user's stream of experiences, i.e., the products of the same language.

5. From the user's point of view, the present sense of whatever the description describes is a sense intended on previous occasions that can be intended again in an identical way on an indefinite number of future occasions.

6. From the user's point of view, the intended sense is retained as the temporally identical sense throughout the stream of experience.

7. From the user's point of view, the description has as its contents

of interpretation: (a) a commonly entertained scheme of communication consisting of a standardized system of signals and coding rules, and (b) 'What Anyone Knows', i.e., a pre-established corpus of socially warranted descriptions.

8. From the user's point of view, the actual sense that the description has for him is the potential sense that it would have for the other person were they to exchange their positions.

9. From the user's point of view, to each description there corresponds its meanings that originate in the user's and in the other person's particular biography. From the user's point of view, such meanings are irrelevant for the purposes at hand of either: for the user, both he and the other person have selected and interpreted the actual and potential sense of the proposition in an empirically identical manner that is sufficient for their practical purposes.

10. From the user's point of view there is a characteristic disparity between the publicly acknowledged sense and the personal, withheld sense of the description, and this private sense is held in reserve. From the user's point of view, the description means for the user and the other person more than the user can say.

11. From the user's point of view, alterations of this characteristic disparity remain within the user's autonomous control.

These features have the following properties that make them particularly interesting to the sociological researcher:

1. From the standpoint of the collectivity member, these features are 'scenic' features of his behavioural environment of objects. By 'scenic' I mean that if, for example, we say with respect to the expected correspondence of appearance and object that the member doubts the correspondence, we must assign to the correspondence its feature of a doubted one. Another example: If we say that the member expects that what is known can affect and be affected by his actions, we must assign to what is known, as an object in the member's behavioural environment, its integral feature that it can potentially affect and be affected by his actions. To each of the expectancies that comprise what Schutz called the 'attitude of daily life' there is the corresponding expected feature of the object.

2. These constitutive features are 'seen but unnoticed'. If the

researcher questions the member about them, the member is able to tell the researcher about them only by transforming the descriptions known from the perspective and in the manner of his practical ongoing treatment of them into an object of theoretical reflection. Otherwise the member 'tells the researcher about them by the conditions under which severe' incongruity can be induced. A reflective concern for their problematic character, as well as an interest in them as objects of theoretical contemplation, characteristically occurs as an abiding preoccupation in the experiences of cultural 'strangers'.

3. They are used by the collectivity member as a scheme of interpretation in terms of which he decides the correspondence between actual appearances and the objects intended through their successive actual appearances.

4. These expected features are invariant to the contents of actual descriptions to which they may be attached.

5. The sense of described social structures as unified ensembles of possible appearances is supplied by their constituent feature, 'known in common'.

6. The withdrawal of this feature by alter from ego's descriptions modifies the logical mode of ego's description for alter in a radical way by transforming fact into fiction, conjecture, personal opinion, and the like. In so far as alter, while retaining this feature for his own accounts, withdraws the feature from ego's descriptions, he removes the enforceable character of ego's claim to competence.

7. Modifications of these constituent meanings of 'known in common' transform environments of intended objects to produce the descriptions of social structures of games, of scientific sociological theorizing, of art, of high ceremony, of the theatre play, of official histories, of dreaming, and the like. Dramatic modifications occur in brain injuries, mental deficiency, acute sensory deprivation, hallucinatory drug states. Such modifications are accompanied by corresponding modifications of the social structures produced by actions directed to cultural environments altered in this fashion.

Contrary to prevailing opinion, the common-sense character of knowledge of social structures does not consist in the ironic comparison of such knowledge with 'scientific descriptions'. Instead, it consists entirely and exclusively in the possibility that (a) the sensible character of what these descriptions describe about the society, and/ or (b) their warranted character as grounds for further inference and action, is decided and guaranteed by enforcement of the attitude of daily life as ethical and moral maxims of conduct in theorizing and inquiry. We must suppose that the attitude of daily life operates in the sociological inquiries not only of the members of a society but of professional sociologists as well. Just as sociological inquiries are not confined to professional sociologists, neither is the attitude of daily life confined to 'the man in the street'.

The foregoing properties may be summarized by saying the propositions of the common-sense corpus do not have a sense that is independent of the socially structured occasions on which they are used.

Further properties of the set of such propositions may be mentioned briefly.

(a) The propositions that comprise common-sense accounts typically are unwritten, uncodified, and are passed on from one person to a successor through a system of apprenticeship in their use. (b) Various social-psychological researches have demonstrated the sense of a proposition to be a function of the place of the proposition in a serial order; of the expressive character of the terms that comprise it; of the socially acknowledged importance of the events that are depicted; of the relevance to the need dispositions of the user, of what is being referred to – to mention a few. (c) Their sense is structurally equivocal, being dependent upon the developing course of the occasions of their use. Like a conversation, their sense is built up step by step over the actual course of references to them. (d) As of any present state of affairs, the sense of what a proposition now proposes includes the anticipated, though sketchily known, future further references that will have accrued to it. Its present sense for a user is informed by the user's willingness to continue in the progressive realization of its sense by further elaboration and transformation. This feature is commonly referred to as the 'spirit' of the proposition.

Conclusion

All scientific disciplines have their great prevailing problems to which the methods of the particular discipline represent solutions. In sociology, in the social sciences generally, as well as in the inquiries of everyday life, a prominent problem is that of achieving a unified conception of events that have as their specific formal property that their present character will have been decided by a future possible outcome. Motivated actions, for example, have precisely this troublesome property: It is a matter of great theoretical and methodological import that Max Weber should have defined sociology as the study of human activities in so far as they are governed in their course by the subjective meanings attached to them. In this programmatic statement, Weber provided for this troublesome feature as an essential property of sociology's fundamental occurrences.

The documentary method consists essentially in the retrospective-prospective reading of a present occurrence so as to maintain the constancy of the object as a sensible thing through temporal and circumstantial alternations in its actual appearances. Thereby it shows its particular usefulness as a method that is capable of handling events having this particular time structure. The documentary method occurs as a feature of situations of incomplete information in which effective actions nevertheless must be taken, matters of fact decided, and interpretations made. The method would seem to be an intimate part of a social process wherein a body of knowledge must be assembled and made available for legitimate use despite the fact that the situations it purports to describe (1) are, in the calculable sense of the term, unknown; (2) are in their actual and intended logical structures essentially vague; and (3) are modified, elaborated, extended, if not indeed created, by the fact and manner of being addressed.

Acknowledgements

The publishers gratefully acknowledge permission to reprint copyright material in this book.

Reading 1   Oxford University Press, Inc.
Reading 2   R. A. Nisbet
Reading 3   Tom Bottomore
Reading 4   The Free Press, a Division of Macmillan, Inc.
Reading 5   Tavistock/Ellis Horwood
Reading 6   Doubleday, a Division of Bantam, Doubleday, Dell Publishing Group, Inc. and Penguin Books Ltd
Reading 7   Longman Resources Unit, York
Reading 8   Unwin Hyman Ltd
Reading 9   Schocken Books, a Division of Random House, Inc.
Reading 10 Norwegian University Press
Reading 11 Holt, Rinehart & Winston, Orlando
Reading 12 Wadsworth Publishing Company, Inc.
Reading 13 Cambridge University Press
Reading 14 Monthly Review Foundation
Reading 15 The Merlin Press Ltd
Reading 16 Verso (New Left Books)
Reading 17 The Open University
Reading 18 Routledge, a Division of Routledge, Chapman & Hall Ltd
Reading 19 New Statesman & Society
Reading 20 Basil Blackwell
Reading 21 Routledge
Reading 22 Collins Publishers and the Office of Population Censuses & Surveys
Reading 23 Cynthia Cockburn
Reading 24 Basil Blackwell
Reading 25 C. M. Posner

Reading 26   Oxford University Press
Reading 27   Routledge
Reading 28   Croom Helm, a Division of Routledge, Chapman & Hall Ltd
Reading 29   Sage Publications and Editions de Minuit
Reading 30   Cambridge University Press
Reading 32   Tavistock Publications, a Division of Routledge, Chapman & Hall Ltd
Reading 33   Tavistock Publications
Reading 34   Tavistock Publications and HMSO
Reading 35   Collier Macmillan
Reading 37   Croom Helm
Reading 38   Unwin Hyman Ltd
Reading 39   Routledge and Wadsworth Publishing Company, Inc.
Reading 40   The University of Chicago Press
Reading 41   The Free Press
Reading 42   G. D. Suttles and The University of Chicago Press
Reading 43   Pluto Press
Reading 44   Isabel Emmett, Manchester University Press and the Institute of Social & Economic Research, Memorial University of Newfoundland
Reading 45   Unwin Hyman Ltd
Reading 46   Basil Blackwell
Reading 47   Monthly Review Foundation
Reading 48   Unwin Hyman Ltd
Reading 49   Tavistock Publications
Reading 50   David Silverman
Reading 51   Doubleday and Penguin Books Ltd
Reading 52   Open University Press
Reading 53   Cambridge University Press
Reading 54   The University of California Press
Reading 55   Routledge
Reading 56   Cambridge University Press
Reading 57   Cambridge University Press
Reading 59   Oxford University Press, Inc.
Reading 60   Grafton Books, a Division of the Collins Publishing Group
Reading 61   Oxford University Press, Inc.
Reading 62   Unwin Hyman Ltd
Reading 63   Unwin Hyman Ltd
Reading 64   Basil Blackwell
Reading 65   John Wiley & Sons, Inc.
Reading 66   Holt, Rinehart & Winston, Orlando
Reading 67   The Open University

Reading 68   Columbia University Press
Reading 69   Colin Sumner
Reading 70   Basil Blackwell
Reading 71   Tavistock Publications
Reading 73   Unwin Hyman Ltd
Reading 74   The Free Press and Macmillan, London and Basingstoke
Reading 75   The Free Press
Reading 76   Prentice Hall, Inc., Englewood Cliffs, New Jersey
Reading 77   John Wiley & Sons, Inc.

The publishers have been unable to trace the copyright holder of Reading 31, and they would be interested to hear from any copyright holders not here fully acknowledged.

Index

Discover more about our forthcoming books through Penguin's FREE newspaper...

Penguin Quarterly

It's packed with:

- exciting features
- author interviews
- previews & reviews
- books from your favourite films & TV series
- exclusive competitions & much, much more...

Write off for your free copy today to:
Dept JC
Penguin Books Ltd
FREEPOST
West Drayton
Middlesex
UB7 0BR
NO STAMP REQUIRED

READ MORE IN PENGUIN

In every corner of the world, on every subject under the sun, Penguin represents quality and variety – the very best in publishing today.

For complete information about books available from Penguin – including Puffins, Penguin Classics and Arkana – and how to order them, write to us at the appropriate address below. Please note that for copyright reasons the selection of books varies from country to country.

In the United Kingdom: Please write to *Dept. JC, Penguin Books Ltd, FREEPOST, West Drayton, Middlesex UB7 OBR*

If you have any difficulty in obtaining a title, please send your order with the correct money, plus ten per cent for postage and packaging, to *PO Box No. 11, West Drayton, Middlesex UB7 OBR*

In the United States: Please write to *Penguin USA Inc., 375 Hudson Street, New York, NY 10014*

In Canada: Please write to *Penguin Books Canada Ltd, 10 Alcorn Avenue, Suite 300, Toronto, Ontario M4V 3B2*

In Australia: Please write to *Penguin Books Australia Ltd, 487 Maroondah Highway, Ringwood, Victoria 3134*

In New Zealand: Please write to *Penguin Books (NZ) Ltd,182–190 Wairau Road, Private Bag, Takapuna, Auckland 9*

In India: Please write to *Penguin Books India Pvt Ltd, 706 Eros Apartments, 56 Nehru Place, New Delhi 110 019*

In the Netherlands: Please write to *Penguin Books Netherlands B.V., Keizersgracht 231 NL–1016 DV Amsterdam*

In Germany: Please write to *Penguin Books Deutschland GmbH, Friedrichstrasse 10–12, W–6000 Frankfurt/Main 1*

In Spain: Please write to *Penguin Books S. A., C. San Bernardo 117–6° E–28015 Madrid*

In Italy: Please write to *Penguin Italia s.r.l., Via Felice Casati 20, I–20124 Milano*

In France: Please write to *Penguin France S. A., 17 rue Lejeune, F–31000 Toulouse*

In Japan: Please write to *Penguin Books Japan, Ishikiribashi Building, 2–5–4, Suido, Bunkyo-ku, Tokyo 112*

In Greece: Please write to *Penguin Hellas Ltd, Dimocritou 3, GR–106 71 Athens*

In South Africa: Please write to *Longman Penguin Southern Africa (Pty) Ltd, Private Bag X08, Bertsham 2013*

READ MORE IN PENGUIN

PSYCHOLOGY

Introduction to Jung's Psychology Frieda Fordham

'She has delivered a fair and simple account of the main aspects of my psychological work. I am indebted to her for this admirable piece of work' – C. G. Jung in the *Foreword*

Child Care and the Growth of Love John Bowlby

His classic 'summary of evidence of the effects upon children of lack of personal attention ... it presents to administrators, social workers, teachers and doctors a reminder of the significance of the family' – *The Times*

Recollections and Reflections Bruno Bettelheim

'A powerful thread runs through Bettelheim's message: his profound belief in the dignity of man, and the importance of seeing and judging other people from their own point of view' – William Harston in the *Independent*. 'These memoirs of a wise old child, candid, evocative, heart-warming, suggest there is hope yet for humanity' – Ray Porter in the *Evening Standard*

Sanity, Madness and the Family R. D. Laing and A. Esterson

Schizophrenia: fact or fiction? Certainly not fact, according to the authors of this controversial book. Suggesting that some forms of madness may be largely social creations, *Sanity, Madness and the Family* demands to be taken very seriously indeed.

I Am Right You Are Wrong Edward de Bono

In this book Dr Edward de Bono puts forward a direct challenge to what he calls the rock logic of Western thinking. Drawing on our understanding of the brain as a self-organizing information system, Dr de Bono shows that perception is the key to more constructive thinking and the serious creativity of design.

READ MORE IN PENGUIN

PSYCHOLOGY

Psychoanalysis and Feminism   Juliet Mitchell

'Juliet Mitchell has risked accusations of apostasy from her fellow feminists. Her book not only challenges orthodox feminism, however; it defies the conventions of social thought in the English-speaking countries ... a brave and important book' – *New York Review of Books*

The Divided Self   R. D. Laing

'A study that makes all other works I have read on schizophrenia seem fragmentary ... The author brings, through his vision and perception, that particular touch of genius which causes one to say "Yes, I have always known that, why have I never thought of it before?"' – *Journal of Analytical Psychology*

Po: Beyond Yes and No   Edward de Bono

No is the basic tool of the logic system. *Yes* is the basic tool of the belief system. Edward de Bono offers *Po* as a device for changing our ways of thinking: a method for approaching problems in a new and more creative way.

The Informed Heart   Bruno Bettelheim

Bettelheim draws on his experience in concentration camps to illuminate the dangers inherent in all mass societies in this profound and moving masterpiece.

The Care of the Self   Michel Foucault
The History of Sexuality Vol 3

Foucault examines the transformation of sexual discourse from the Hellenistic to the Roman world in an inquiry which 'bristles with provocative insights into the tangled liaison of sex and self' – *The Times Higher Education Supplement*

Mothering Psychoanalysis   Janet Sayers

'An important book ... records the immense contribution to psychoanalysis made by its founding mothers' – Julia Neuberger in the *Sunday Times*

READ MORE IN PENGUIN

POLITICS AND SOCIAL SCIENCES

Conservatism Ted Honderich

'It offers a powerful critique of the major beliefs of modern conservatism, and shows how much a rigorous philosopher can contribute to understanding the fashionable but deeply ruinous absurdities of his times' – *New Statesman & Society*

Karl Marx: Selected Writings in Sociology and Social Philosophy Bottomore and Rubel (eds.)

'It makes available, in coherent form and lucid English, some of Marx's most important ideas. As an introduction to Marx's thought, it has very few rivals indeed' – *British Journal of Sociology*

Post-War Britain A Political History Alan Sked and Chris Cook

Major political figures from Attlee to Thatcher, the aims and achievements of governments and the changing fortunes of Britain in the period since 1945 are thoroughly scrutinized in this stimulating history.

Inside the Third World Paul Harrison

This comprehensive book brings home a wealth of facts and analysis on the often tragic realities of life for the poor people and communities of Asia, Africa and Latin America.

Medicine, Patients and the Law Margaret Brazier

'An absorbing book which, in addition to being accessible to the general reader, should prove illuminating for practitioners – both medical and legal – and an ideal accompaniment to student courses on law and medicine' – *New Law Journal*

Bread and Circuses Paul Veyne

'Warming oneself at the fire of M. Veyne's intelligence is such a joy that any irritation at one's prejudice and ignorance being revealed and exposed vanishes with his winning ways ... *Bread and Circuses* is M. Veyne's way of explaining the philosophy of the Roman Empire, which was the most successful form of government known to mankind' – *Literary Review*

READ MORE IN PENGUIN

POLITICS AND SOCIAL SCIENCES

National Identity Anthony D. Smith

In this stimulating new book, Anthony D. Smith asks why the first modern nation states developed in the West. He considers how ethnic origins, religion, language and shared symbols can provide a sense of nation and illuminates his argument with a wealth of detailed examples.

The Feminine Mystique Betty Friedan

'A brilliantly researched, passionately argued book – a time-bomb flung into the Mom-and-Apple-Pie image ... Out of the debris of that shattered ideal, the Women's Liberation Movement was born' – Ann Leslie

Peacemaking Among Primates Frans de Waal

'A vitally fresh analysis of the biology of aggression which deserves the serious attention of all those concerned with the nature of conflict, whether in humans or non-human animals ... De Waal delivers forcibly and clearly his interpretation of the significance of his findings ... Lucidly written' – *The Times Higher Educational Supplement*

Political Ideas David Thomson (ed.)

From Machiavelli to Marx – a stimulating and informative introduction to the last 500 years of European political thinkers and political thought.

The Raw and the Cooked Claude Lévi-Strauss

Deliberately, brilliantly and inimitably challenging, Lévi-Strauss's seminal work of structural anthropology cuts wide and deep into the mind of mankind, as he finds in the myths of the South American Indians a comprehensible psychological pattern.

The Social Construction of Reality
Peter Berger and Thomas Luckmann

The Social Construction of Reality is concerned with the sociology of 'everything that passes for knowledge in society', and particularly with that 'common-sense knowledge' that constitutes the reality of everyday life for the ordinary member of society.